GROUNDWORK
FOR COLLEGE
READING
WITH PHONICS

Fourth Edition

GROUNDWORK FOR COLLEGE READING

WITH PHONICS

Fourth Edition

Bill Broderick
CERRITOS COLLEGE

John Langan
ATLANTIC CAPE COMMUNITY COLLEGE

Books in the Townsend Press Reading Series:

Groundwork for College Reading
Groundwork for College Reading with Phonics
Ten Steps to Building College Reading Skills
Ten Steps to Improving College Reading Skills
Ten Steps to Advancing College Reading Skills
Ten Steps to Advanced Reading

Books in the Townsend Press Vocabulary Series:

Vocabulary Basics
Groundwork for a Better Vocabulary
Building Vocabulary Skills
Building Vocabulary Skills, Short Version
Improving Vocabulary Skills
Improving Vocabulary Skills, Short Version
Advancing Vocabulary Skills
Advancing Vocabulary Skills, Short Version
Advanced Word Power

Supplements Available for Most Books:

Instructor's Edition
Instructor's Manual and Test Bank
Online Exercises

Copyright © 2008 by Townsend Press, Inc.
Printed in the United States of America
9 8 7 6 5 4 3 2

ISBN-13 (Student Edition): 978-1-59194-086-9
ISBN-10 (Student Edition): 1-59194-086-9
ISBN-13 (Instructor's Edition): 978-1-59194-088-3
ISBN-10 (Instructor's Edition): 1-59194-088-5

**For book orders and requests for desk copies or supplements,
contact us in any of the following ways:**

By telephone: 1-800-772-6410
By fax: 1-800-225-8894
By e-mail: cs@townsendpress.com
Through our website: www.townsendpress.com

Contents

Preface: To the Instructor   vii

How to Become a Better Reader and Thinker   1

PART I
Phonics and Word Parts   7

1 **Consonants**   **9**
   Reading: The Struggle Continues   *Juan Angel*   29
   Mastery Tests   35

2 **Vowels**   **47**
   Reading: A Lesson in Love   *Casey Hawley*   64
   Mastery Tests   69

3 **Syllables**   **81**
   Reading: Friendship and Living Longer   *Vicky Chan*   94
   Mastery Tests   99

4 **Word Parts**   **111**
   Reading: From Horror to Hope   *Phany Sarann*   122
   Mastery Tests   129

PART II
Ten Steps to College Reading   141

1 **Getting Started**   **143**
   Reading: A Parent Gets a Reading Lesson   *Lucia Herndon*   155
   Mastery Tests   161

2 **Dictionary Use**   **173**
   Reading: Discovering Words   *Malcolm X*   191
   Mastery Tests   197

3 **Vocabulary in Context**   **209**
   Reading: One Less Sucker Lives   *Jeanne R. Smith*   225
   Mastery Tests   231

4 **Main Ideas**   **243**
   Reading: Classroom Notetaking   *Robin White*   258
   Mastery Tests   263

5 **Supporting Details**   **275**
Reading: Winning the Job Interview Game   *Marcia Prentergast*   291
Mastery Tests   297

6 **Finding Main Ideas**   **309**
Reading: Learning Survival Skills   *Jean Coleman*   319
Mastery Tests   327

7 **Signal Words I**   **339**
Reading: Migrant Child to College Woman   *Maria Cardenas*   350
Mastery Tests   361

8 **Signal Words II**   **373**
Reading: Life Over Death   *Bill Broderick*   386
Mastery Tests   393

9 **Inferences**   **405**
Reading: Dare to Think Big   *Dr. Ben Carson*   419
Mastery Tests   425

10 **The Basics of Argument**   **437**
Reading: Why We Shop   *Anita Rab*   450
Mastery Tests   455

PART III
Five Reading Selections   **467**

1 Learning to Read: The Marvel Kretzmann Story   *Mary Sherry*   469

2 The Fist, the Clay, and the Rock   *Donald Holland*   483

3 Joe Davis   *Beth Johnson*   491

4 Rosa: A Success Story   *Edward Patrick*   503

5 The Lady, or the Tiger?   *Frank R. Stockton*   513

PART IV
Combined-Skills Tests   **523**

APPENDIXES

Pronunciation Guide   551

Writing Assignments   553

Limited Answer Key   568

Acknowledgments   576

Index   577

Reading Performance Chart   *Inside back cover*

Preface:
To the Instructor

We all know that many students entering college today do not have the reading and thinking skills needed to do effective work in their courses. For any one of a number of reasons, their background in reading is limited. At the same time, their concerns and interests are those of other college students. These students need to develop their reading skills through the use of adult-level materials.

Groundwork for College Reading with Phonics, Fourth Edition, is designed to develop effective reading and clear thinking. To do so, the book is divided into four parts, each described below.

Part I presents a series of essential word skills:

- Consonants: The rules governing consonants, including single consonants, blends, digraphs, and silent letter combinations
- Vowels: The rules governing long and short vowels
- Syllables: Principles of breaking words into syllables
- Word parts: Common prefixes, suffixes, and roots

Part II begins with a chapter on basic matters: having the right attitude, learning key study skills, and developing a reading habit. The nine chapters that follow present a sequence of skills that college students need to master:

- Knowing how to use the dictionary
- Understanding vocabulary in context
- Recognizing main ideas
- Identifying supporting details
- Locating main ideas in different parts of a passage
- Understanding relationships that involve addition and time
- Understanding relationships that involve examples, contrast, and cause and effect
- Making inferences
- Evaluating arguments

Each chapter in Parts I and II features clear explanations and illustrations of the material or skill in question, followed by a series of practices. Each chapter ends with three review tests, with the third test in each case being a reading selection.

Following each chapter in Parts I and II are six mastery tests. As much as possible, the tests progress in difficulty, giving students the added practice and challenge they may need to learn a skill.

Part III consists of five additional readings that will help improve both reading and thinking skills. Each reading is followed by a series of *Vocabulary Questions* and *Reading Comprehension Questions* that ask students to apply the skills presented in Part II. In addition, an *Outlining, Mapping, or Summarizing* activity after each reading helps students think carefully about the basic content and organization of the selection. *Discussion Questions* then provide instructors one more opportunity to engage students in various reading and thinking skills and to deepen their understanding of a selection.

Part IV consists of twelve combined-skills tests. The tests provide a review of the comprehension skills in Part II and help prepare students for the standardized reading exam that is often a requirement at the end of a semester.

Finally, the **Appendixes** include writing assignments for each of the four reading selections in Part I, the ten reading selections in Part II, and the five reading selections in Part III. These assignments will help students understand that reading, writing, and thinking are closely connected skills.

Important Features of the Book

- **Focus on the basics.** The book seeks to explain, in an extremely clear, step-by-step way, the essential elements of each skill. Many examples are provided to ensure that students understand each point. In general, the focus is on teaching the skills—not just on explaining them and not just on testing them.

- **Frequent practice and feedback.** In the belief that progress is made largely through abundant practice and careful feedback, this book includes numerous activities. Students can get immediate feedback on the practice exercises in Parts I and II by turning to the limited answer key at the back of the book. The answers to the review and mastery tests in Parts I and II, the reading questions in Part III, and the combined-skills tests in Part IV are in the *Instructor's Manual.*

    The limited answer key increases the active role that students take in their own learning. Also, they are likely to use the answer key in an honest and positive way if they know that they may be tested on the many activities and selections for which answers are not provided. (Answers not in the book can be easily copied from the *Instructor's Edition* or the *Instructor's Manual* and passed out at the teacher's discretion.)

- **High interest level.**   Dull and unvaried readings and exercises work against learning. Students need to experience genuine interest and enjoyment in what they read. Teachers as well should be able to take pleasure in the selections, for their own good feeling about them can carry over favorably into class work. The readings in the book, then, have been chosen not only for the appropriateness of their reading level but also for their compelling content. They should appeal to a wide range of students— developmental students, students for whom English is a second language, and Adult Basic Education students. They also take into account the diverse backgrounds of such students.

- **Ease of use.**   The logical sequence in each chapter—from explanation to example to practice to review tests to mastery tests—helps make the skills easy to teach. The book's organization into distinct parts also makes for ease of use. Within a single class, for instance, instructors can work on a particular skill in Part I or II, review another skill with a mastery test, and provide variety by having students read one of the selections in Part III. The limited answer key at the back of the book also makes for versatility: it means that an instructor can assign parts of each chapter for self-teaching. Finally, the mastery tests—each on its own tear-out page—and the combined-skills tests make it a simple matter for a teacher to test and evaluate student progress.

- **Integration of skills.**   Students do more than learn the skills individually in Parts I and II. They also learn to apply the skills together through the reading selections in Parts I, II, and III and through the combined-skills tests in Part IV. They become effective readers and thinkers by means of a good deal of practice in applying a combination of skills.

- **Online exercises.**   As they complete each skills chapter, students are invited to go online to the Townsend Press website to work on two additional practice exercises that reinforce what has been taught in the chapter.

- **Thinking activities.**   Thinking activities—in the form of outlining, mapping, and summarizing—are a distinctive feature of the book. In addition, three discussion questions at the end of each reading selection encourage student reflection, as do the writing activities that are provided for each selection.

- **Supplementary materials.** The three helpful supplements listed below are available at no charge to instructors who have adopted the text. The two print supplements can be obtained quickly by calling Townsend Press (1-800-772-6410), by sending a fax on school letterhead to 1-800-225-8894, or by e-mailing Customer Service at **cs@townsendpress.com**.

  1 An *Instructor's Edition*—chances are that you are holding it in your hand—is identical to the student book except that it also provides hints for teachers (see the front of the book), answers to all the practices and tests, and comments on most answers. *No other book on the market has such detailed and helpful annotations.*

  2 A combined *Instructor's Manual and Test Bank* includes suggestions for teaching the course, a model syllabus, and readability levels for the text and the reading selections. The test bank contains **four** additional mastery tests for the skills chapters in Part I and Part II—all on letter-sized sheets so they can be copied easily for use with students.

  3 *Online exercises* provide two additional mastery tests for most of the skills in Parts I and II of the book. The exercises contain a number of user-and instructor-friendly features: brief explanations of answers, a sound option, frequent mention of the user's first name, a running score, and a record-keeping score file.

- **One of a sequence of books in the TP reading series.** *Groundwork for College Reading* and *Groundwork for College Reading with Phonics* are the basic texts in the series. They are suitable for ESL students and basic adult learners.

  Ten Steps to Building College Reading Skills is often the choice for a first college reading course.

  Ten Steps to Improving College Reading Skills is an intermediate text appropriate for the core developmental reading course offered at most colleges.

  Ten Steps to Advancing College Reading Skills is a higher-level developmental text than the *Improving* book. It can be used as the core text for a more advanced class, as a sequel to the intermediate book, or as a second-semester alternative to it.

  Finally, *Ten Steps to Advanced Reading* is the most advanced text in the series. It can also be used as a sequel (or a second-semester alternative) to either the *Improving* or the *Advancing* text.

  A companion set of vocabulary books, listed on the copyright page, has been designed to go with the TP reading books. Recommended to accompany this book is *Groundwork for a Better Vocabulary*.

  Together, the books and their full range of supplements form a sequence that should be ideal for any college reading program.

To summarize, *Groundwork for College Reading with Phonics, Fourth Edition,* provides a sequence of key skills to help developmental college students become independent readers and thinkers. Through an appealing collection of readings and a carefully designed series of activities and tests, students receive extensive guided practice in the skills. The result is an integrated approach to learning that will, by the end of a course, produce better readers and stronger thinkers.

Changes in the Fourth Edition

- **Major chapter additions.** Three chapters newly added to the book are "Getting Started," "Inferences," and "The Basics of Argument." To make room for the new chapters, there are five fewer readings in what is now Part III of the book. Instructors should note that another version of this book is now available: *Groundwork for College Reading* does not cover phonics and word parts but contains a full set of ten readings in Part II.

- **Fresh materials.** Almost three-quarters of the practice materials in the book are new, along with seven new readings. All the chapters in Parts I and II now begin with a preview titled "This Chapter in a Nutshell." Chapters that have undergone considerable revision include "Dictionary Use," "Main Ideas," and the two chapters on relationships, now titled "Signal Words I" and "Signal Words II."

- **Greater visual appeal.** The fourth edition uses illustrations, cartoons, book covers, and photographs to provide practice in or reinforcement of comprehension skills. The materials are not just visual window dressing; they serve a meaningful pedagogical purpose. In addition, more color, as well as boxes, rules, and screens, is used to highlight material. The book is more visually friendly without becoming visually cluttered.

- **Alternate editions.** Instructors now have two choices available: editions of the book with or without phonics, depending on the backgrounds and needs of the students in their classes. In contrast to *Groundwork for College Reading with Phonics*, *Groundwork for College Reading* has one additional reading but does not include the four chapters on phonics and word parts.

Acknowledgments

Bill Broderick and I worked together on the first two editions of this book; in the third edition, most of the changes were his own. Now, seven years later, and after Bill's untimely passing, I have thoroughly revised the book. However, Bill's name remains on the cover as a tribute to this dedicated and caring teacher whose respect for life was evident not only in his commitment to students, but also in his advocacy for the humane treatment of animals.

For this revision, I am grateful for helpful suggestions provided by the following reviewers: Shirley Carpenter, Richard J. Daley College; Herbert Chambers, Rowan-Cabarrus Community College; Susan Clark, Metropolitan Community College—Longview; Marcella Farina, University of Central Florida; Bonnie Helberg, Cerritos College; Teresa Ward, Butte College; Karma Williams, Atlanta Technical College; Sherry Wilson, Crowder College; and Barbara Yanofsky, Three Rivers Community College.

At Townsend Press, I thank Bill Blauvelt, Denton Cairnes, Beth Johnson, Paul Langan, Ruth A. Rouff, and Barbara Solot for help they provided along the way. I owe special thanks to my long-time colleague Janet Goldstein for her superb design, editing, and organizational skills. When Janet comes to the plate, she hits home runs. Her talents have also made possible the creation of the *Instructor's Edition,* complete with answers and marginal comments, that accompanies the book.

It is always a special pleasure to work with people who aspire toward excellence. With help from my colleagues in the teaching profession and at Townsend Press, I have been able to create a much better book than I could have managed on my own.

John Langan

How to Become a Better Reader and Thinker

The chances are that you are not as good a reader as you should be to do well in college. If so, it's not surprising. You live in a culture where people watch an average of *over seven hours of television every day!* All that passive viewing does not allow much time for reading. Reading is a skill that must be actively practiced. The simple fact is that people who do not read very often are not likely to be strong readers.

• How much television do you watch on an average day?_____ hours

Another reason for not reading much is that you may have a lot of responsibilities. You may be going to school and working at the same time. You may have a lot of family duties as well. If you have free time, you may feel too tired to read. It might seem easier to turn on the TV than to pick up a book.

• Do you do any regular reading—for example, a daily newspaper or a weekly magazine? _____

• When are you most likely to do your reading? _____

A third reason for not reading is that reading may not have been a pleasant experience in school. You may not have been good at reading, or you may not have enjoyed what you were given to read. As a result, you may have concluded that reading in general is not for you.

• Do you think that school made you dislike reading, rather than enjoy it?

_____

If you feel you need to improve your reading, *Groundwork for College Reading with Phonics,* Fourth Edition, should help you a lot. The book will help you build a solid foundation in the most important skills you need to become a better reader. To find out just how this book can help, read the next several pages and do the brief activities as well. The activities are easily completed and will give you a quick, helpful overview of the book.

HOW THE BOOK IS ORGANIZED

The book is organized into four main parts:

Part I: Phonics and Word Parts (pages 7–140)

- Look at the table of contents starting on page v. How many chapters in Part I deal with phonics? _____ How many deal with word parts? _____

Part II: Ten Steps to College Reading (pages 141–466)

The ten steps to college reading are listed in the table of contents starting on page v. Turn to that page to fill in the steps missing below:

1 Getting Started

2 _____

3 Vocabulary in Context

4 _____

5 Supporting Details

6 Finding Main Ideas

7 Signal Words I

8 _____

9 Inferences

10 _____

Each chapter in Parts I and II is developed in the same way.

First of all, clear explanations and examples help you *understand* the chapter. Practices then give you the "hands-on" experience needed to *learn* the content of the chapter.

- How many practices are there in the third chapter, "Vocabulary in Context" (pages 209–230)? _____

Closing each chapter are three review tests. The first one reviews the information presented in the chapter.

- On which page is Review Test 1 for "Vocabulary in Context"? _____

The second review test consists of activities that help you practice the skill presented in the chapter.

- On which pages is Review Test 2 for "Vocabulary in Context"? _____

The third review test centers on a reading selection that both gets you reading and gives you practice in the skill you learned in the chapter.

- What is the title of the reading selection in the "Vocabulary in Context" chapter? _____

Following each chapter are six mastery tests that gradually increase in difficulty.

- On what pages are the mastery tests for the "Vocabulary in Context" chapter? _____

The tests are on tear-out pages that can be easily removed and handed in to your instructor. So that you can track your progress, there is a score box at the top of the first page of each test. Your score can also be entered into the "Reading Performance Chart" on the inside back cover of the book.

Part III: Five Reading Selections (pages 467–522)

The five reading selections that make up Part III are followed by activities that give you practice in all of the skills studied in Part II. Each reading begins in the same way. Look, for example, at "Rosa: A Success Story," which starts on page 503. What are the headings of the two sections that come before the reading itself?

- _____

- _____

Note that the vocabulary words in "Words to Watch" are followed by the numbers of the paragraphs in which the words appear. Look at the first page of "Rosa: A Success Story" and explain how each vocabulary word is marked in the reading itself.

- _____

Activities Following Each Reading Selection

After each selection, there are four kinds of activities to improve the reading and thinking skills you learned in Part II of the book.

1   The first activity consists of **vocabulary questions**—questions involving vocabulary in context as well as "Words to Watch."

   • Look at the vocabulary questions for "Rosa: A Success Story" on pages 506–508. The first five questions deal with understanding vocabulary in context. How many questions then help you learn words taken from "Words to Watch"? _____

2   The second activity consists of ten **reading comprehension questions**— questions involving vocabulary in context, main ideas, supporting details, signal words, inferences, and argument.

   • Look at the questions for "Rosa: A Success Story" on pages 508–510. Note that the questions are labeled so you know which skill you are practicing in each case. How many questions deal with the central point and main ideas? _____

3   The third activity involves **outlining, mapping,** or **summarizing**. Each of these activities will sharpen your ability to get to the heart of a selection and to think logically and clearly about what you read.

   • What kind of activity is provided for "Rosa: A Success Story" on page 510–511? _____

   • What kind of activity is provided for "The Fist, the Clay, and the Rock" on page 489? _____

   • What kind of activity is provided for "The Lady, or the Tiger?" on pages 520–521? _____

   Note that a **map**, or diagram, is a visual way of organizing material. Like an outline, it shows at a glance the main parts of a selection.

4   The fourth activity consists of **discussion questions**. These questions provide a chance for you to deepen your understanding of each selection.

   • How many discussion questions are there for "Rosa: A Success Story" (page 511)—and for every other reading? _____

Part IV: Combined-Skills Tests (pages 523–549)

This part of the book provides a series of combined-skills tests that help you practice a number of the skills in the book.

- How many "Combined-Skills Tests" are there on pages 523–549? _____

These tests are made up of short passages that closely resemble the ones typically found in standardized tests.

Appendixes (pages 551–575)

The first section in the "Appendixes" is a pronunciation guide. It tells you how to use the information provided for pronouncing the vocabulary words in this book.

The second section is "Writing Assignments." Reading and writing are closely connected skills, and writing practice will improve your ability to read closely and think carefully.

- How many assignments are offered for each reading? _____

Also included in the appendixes is a limited answer key.

HELPFUL FEATURES OF THE BOOK

1 The book centers on *what you really need to know* to become a better reader and thinker. It presents key comprehension skills and explains the most important points about each one.

2 The book gives you *lots of practice*. We seldom learn a skill only by hearing or reading about it; we make it part of us by repeated practice. There are, then, many activities in the text. They are not "busywork" but carefully designed materials that should help you truly learn each skill.

Notice that after you learn each skill in Parts I and II, you go on to the next step: review tests and mastery tests that ask you to apply the skill. And as you move from one skill to the next, you continue to practice and reinforce the ones already learned.

3 The selections throughout the book are *lively and appealing*. Dull and unvaried readings work against learning, so subjects have been carefully chosen for their high interest level. All the selections here are good examples of how what we read can capture our attention. For example, start reading "A Lesson in Love" (page 64) or the account, with photographs, of a former drug dealer who turned his life around (page 491) or the timeless short story "The Lady, or the Tiger?" (page 513)—and try to *stop* reading.

HOW TO USE THE BOOK

1   A good way to proceed is to read—and reread—the explanations and examples in a chapter in Part I or Part II until you feel you understand the ideas presented. Then carefully work through the practices. As you finish each one, check your answers with the "Limited Answer Key" that starts on page 568.

 For your own sake, *don't just copy in the answers without trying to do the practices!* The only way to learn a skill is to practice it first and then use the answer key to give yourself feedback. Also, take whatever time is needed to figure out just why you got some answers wrong. By using the answer key to help teach yourself the skills, you will prepare yourself for the review and mastery tests at the end of each chapter as well as the other reading tests in the book. Your instructor can supply you with answers to those tests.

 If you have trouble catching on to a particular skill, stick with it. In time, you will learn each skill.

2   Read the selections first with the intent of simply enjoying them. There will be time afterward for rereading each selection and using it to develop your comprehension skills.

3   Keep track of your progress. Fill in the charts at the end of each chapter in Parts I and II and each reading selection in Part III. And in the "Reading Performance Chart" on the inside back cover, enter your scores for the review tests and mastery tests as well as the reading selections. These scores can give you a good view of your overall performance as you work through the book.

 In summary, *Groundwork for College Reading with Phonics, Fourth Edition*, has been designed to interest and benefit you as much as possible. Its format is straightforward, its explanations are clear, its readings are appealing, and its many practices will help you learn through doing. *It is a book that has been created to reward effort*, and if you provide that effort, you will make yourself a better reader and a stronger thinker. I wish you success.

John Langan

Part I

PHONICS AND WORD PARTS

1

Phonics I: Consonants

THIS CHAPTER IN A NUTSHELL

- Twenty-one of the twenty-six letters of the English alphabet are consonants.
  - Fifteen consonants have only one sound when they appear by themselves: **b, f, h, j, k, l, m, n, p, r, t, v, w, y,** and **z**.
  - Six consonants have more than one sound: **c, g, d, q, s,** and **x**.
- There are three types of consonant combinations:
  - **Consonant blends** are combinations that blend the sounds of single consonants, such as **sc**ore, **spl**ash, **br**oke, and li**ft**.
  - **Consonant digraphs** are pairs that combine to make a new sound: **ph**one, **th**eir, **ch**ip.
  - **Silent consonants** are not pronounced in certain combinations: com**b**, **w**rite, **k**now.

What do you do when you are reading and come across a word you can't pronounce? Do you ignore the word, hoping it isn't important? Do you ask someone how the word is pronounced? What you should do is look at the word, break it into syllables, sound out each syllable, and put the word back together again. To put it another way, you should use a very helpful method known as phonics.

Phonics tells you how to break a word into parts called syllables and how to pronounce each syllable. It is true that English letters don't always sound the way you expect them to. But phonics can help you figure out the sounds of most words. And when phonics isn't enough, you can use a dictionary (see pages 173–196).

This chapter explains the pronunciation of consonants. Chapter 2 will cover the most important points about vowels. Chapter 3 will show you how to break words into syllables. Finally, Chapter 4 will help you learn common word parts (prefixes, roots, and suffixes) that are building blocks in many words. What you learn in each of these chapters will help you in the ones that follow. In these first four chapters, the keys to improvement are practice and patience. By working carefully on each activity, you will sharpen your ability to pronounce words.

But you'll also need to practice using phonics in everyday reading. You'll find it helpful to read the selections that end each chapter in Part II as well as the selections in Part III of this book. And you should also get into the habit of reading, every day, something that interests you—in magazines, newspapers, and books. Slowly but surely, you will improve your reading.

CONSONANTS

Twenty-one of the twenty-six letters in the English alphabet are **consonants**. (The others are vowels, which will be discussed in Chapter 2.) The consonants are shown in the box below.

Consonants

b	c	d	f	g	h	j
k	l	m	n	p	q	r
s	t	v	w	x	y	z

The sounds of consonants are made when the tongue, lips, or teeth block the air that comes out of your mouth as you speak. In this chapter, you'll learn about the most common sounds of consonants. These three areas will be covered:
- Single Consonants with Only One Sound
- Single Consonants with More Than One Sound
- Three Types of Consonant Combinations

SINGLE CONSONANTS WITH ONLY ONE SOUND

The fifteen consonants listed below generally have only one sound. Each letter is followed by three examples. See if you can add a fourth example of the sound, using the space provided. The first one is done for you.

b   bed   able   crab   _____*best*_____

f	fan	gift	grief	_____
h	hog	behave	reheat	_____
j	jab	jaw	banjo	_____
k	kiss	bakery	peek	_____
l	lump	delay	heel	_____
m	mud	dime	ram	_____
n	neck	unit	lemon	_____
p	pat	open	creep	_____
r	rub	carol	dear	_____
t	tub	note	heat	_____
v	vine	river	hive	_____
w	web	award	sewer	_____
y	yell	yawn	mayor	_____
z	zoom	crazy	quiz	_____

SINGLE CONSONANTS WITH MORE THAN ONE SOUND

The following consonants have more than one sound:

c	g	d	q	s	x

Common sounds for each of these letters are explained below.

1 Sounds of c

When **c** is followed by **e**, **i**, or **y**, it usually has the sound of **s** as in *salt*. This is called the **soft sound** of **c**.

Below are five words with the soft sound of **c**. See if you can add a sixth word with the soft sound of **c** in the space provided.

cell	city	cereal
bicycle	circus	_____

Whenever **c** is not followed by **e, i,** or **y,** it sounds like **k.** This is known as the **hard sound** of **c.** Below are five words with the hard sound of **c.** See if you can add a sixth word with the hard sound of **c** in the space provided.

can   cub   actor

bicycle   circus   _____

➤ Practice 1

Use a check mark to show whether the boldfaced **c** in each word has the soft sound (like the sound of **s** in *cell*) or the hard sound (like the sound of **k** in *can*). The first two are done for you as examples.

	Soft sound of **c** (sounds like **s**)	Hard sound of **c** (sounds like **k**)
1. ice	✓	
2. care		✓
3. circle		
4. custom		
5. peace		
6. postcard		
7. decide		
8. record		
9. panic		
10. decent		

2 Sounds of g

The consonant **g** has two common sounds. These sounds follow the same principle as **c.** When **g** is followed by **e, i** or **y,** it often has the sound of the letter **j.** This is the **soft sound** of **g.** Below are five words with the soft sound of **g.** See if you can add a sixth word with the soft sound of **g** in the space provided.

germ   gin   gym

angel   magic   _____

(There are some common exceptions to this rule, including such words as *get, girl,* and *gift.*)

When **g** is not followed by **e, i** or **y**, it usually has its **hard sound**, as in *gum* and *leg*. Below are five words with the hard sound of **g**. See if you can add a sixth word with the hard sound of **g** in the space provided.

game   goal   guess

ago   pig   _____

> ## ➤ Practice 2

Use a check mark to show whether the boldfaced **g** in each word has the soft sound (like the **g** in *germ*) or the hard sound (like the **g** in *game*). The first two are done for you as examples.

	Soft sound of **g** (as in *germ*)	Hard sound of **g** (as in *game*)
1. gentle	✓	
2. guest		✓
3. rage		
4. green		
5. pigeon		
6. fog		
7. frigid		
8. gesture		
9. legal		
10. fragment		

3 Sounds of d

The consonant **d** usually sounds like the **d** in *dot*. Here are some words with the usual sound of **d**:

date   si**d**e   blee**d**

At times **d** sounds like **j**. Here are some words in which **d** sounds like **j**:

e**d**ucate   sche**d**ule   sol**d**ier

There is no sure guideline for knowing when **d** sounds like **j**. But once in a while, you will find that giving a **d** the sound of **j** will be the key to recognizing a word.

4   Sounds of *q (qu)*

The consonant **q**, in English, is always followed by **u**. **Qu** is always followed by a vowel and usually sounds like **kw**. Here are some words in which **qu** sounds like **kw**:

queen   **qu**ilt   re**qu**ire

Sometimes **qu** sounds like **k**. Here are some words in which **qu** sounds like **k**:

anti**que**   pla**que**   mos**qu**ito

Qu will usually sound like **k** when a word ends in **que** or in a word that comes to us directly from a foreign language, such as *mosquito* (from Spanish) or *quiche* (from French).

5   Sounds of *s*

The consonant **s** usually sounds like the **s** in *salt.* Here are some other words in which **s** has its usual sound:

soup   unsafe   bus

Sometimes **s** sounds like **z**, as in the word *those.* The **z** sound is common in two situations: 1) when **s** comes between two vowels (as in *rose*), and 2) at the end of a word that shows possession or ownership (such as *his*). Here are some other words in which **s** sounds like **z**:

nose   reason   hers

6   Sounds of *x*

The consonant **x** usually sounds like **ks**. Here are some words in which **x** sounds like **ks**:

fox   next   Mexico

When the combination **ex** is followed by a vowel, then **x** usually sounds like **gz**. Here are some words in which **x** sounds like **gz**:

exact   exam   exist

Finally, when **x** begins a word (which is rare), it has the sound of **z**, as in the word *Xerox.*

THREE TYPES OF CONSONANT COMBINATIONS

A **consonant combination** is two or more consonants that work together. There are three kinds of consonant combinations:

- **Consonant blends**: Combinations that blend the sounds of single consonants.

  Examples: **sp**it   **f**e**lt**   **scr**een

- **Consonant digraph**s: Consonant pairs that combine to make a new sound.

  Examples: rou**gh**   wi**sh**   **th**in

- **Silent consonants**: Consonants that are silent in certain combinations.

  Examples: lam**b**   si**ck**   **w**rong

Each type of consonant combination is explained on the following pages.

Consonant Blends

Consonant blends are two or more neighboring consonants that keep their own sounds but are spoken together. The sounds blend with each other, or run together. For example, the letters **sm** are a consonant blend. To pronounce this blend, just pronounce the **s** and then glide into the sound of the **m**. This is the sound you say at the beginning of the word *smile*.

Below are some words that begin with consonant blends. Read the words to yourself, and notice that you can hear the sound of each of the boldfaced consonants.

     bread   **fl**y   **st**eam

Consonant blends also occur in the middle and at the end of words. Read the following words to yourself, and notice that you can hear the sound of each boldfaced consonant.

     mon**st**er   pi**nk**   soun**d**

Here are four major types of consonant blends:

1. Blends that begin with **s**
2. Blends that end in **l**
3. Blends that end in **r**
4. Other blends in the middle or at the end of a word

Each type of consonant blend is listed and illustrated on the following pages. Read the words given as examples, and note the sounds of their consonant blends.

1   Blends that begin with *s*

sc-	scr-	sk-	sl-	sm-
sn-	sp-	spl-	spr-	squ-
st-	str-	sw-		

The consonant blends in the box above are found at the beginning and in the middle of words. In addition, three of them are also found at the end of words: **-sk**, **-sp**, and **-st**.

Below, two words illustrate each type of blend that begins with *s*. In the space provided, add a third example of each blend.

sc	**sc**ore	**sc**ab	_____
scr	**scr**ap	**scr**eam	_____
sk	**sk**ate	a**sk**	_____
sl	**sl**am	a**sl**eep	_____
sm	**sm**all	**sm**og	_____
sn	**sn**ore	un**sn**ap	_____
sp	**sp**ank	wa**sp**	_____
spl	**spl**ash	**spl**it	_____
spr	**spr**out	re**spr**ay	_____
squ	**squ**eak	**squ**are	_____
st	**st**eel	be**st**	_____
str	**str**eet	in**str**uct	_____
sw	**sw**ear	**sw**eet	_____

➤ *Practice 3*

A. Find the five words below that have a consonant blend beginning with **s**. Remember that this blend may occur anywhere in a word. Write the words in the blank spaces.

slip	crisp	mask	pints	seat
sew	side	some	squeal	west

_____   _____   _____

_____   _____

B. Find the five words below that have a consonant blend beginning with **s**, and write them in the blank spaces.

Reverend Billy Graham speaks of a time early in his career when he arrived in a small town to preach a sermon. Wanting to mail a letter, he asked a young boy where the post office was. When the boy told him, Rev. Graham thanked him and said, "If you'll come to the church this evening, you can hear me tell everyone how to get to Heaven."

"I don't think I'll be there," the boy said. "You don't even know what street the post office is on."

_____   _____   _____

_____   _____

2   Blends that end in *l*

bl-	cl-	fl-	gl-	pl-

These consonant blends may be at the beginning or in the middle of a word. Examples are **bless** and *apply*.

Below, two words illustrate each type of blend ending in **l**. In the space provided, add a third example of each blend.

bl	**bl**ess	un**bl**ock	_____
cl	**cl**am	de**cl**ine	_____
fl	**fl**ag	re**fl**ect	_____
gl	**gl**ad	ea**gl**e	_____
pl	**pl**ay	ap**pl**y	_____

➤ *Practice 4*

A. Find the five words below that have a consonant blend ending with **l**. Remember that this blend may occur at the beginning or in the middle of a word. Write the words in the blank spaces.

blank	boil	class	deal	glass
imply	inflame	lame	lick	lug

_____   _____   _____

_____   _____

B. Read the paragraph below, and find the five words that have a consonant blend ending with **l**. Write them in the blank spaces.

Recently, a woman in Florida was shopping on eBay, the popular computer auction site. When she left the room, her son Jack began to play with the keyboard. He hit the "buy it now" button and purchased a pink Cadillac for $17,000. Luckily, the seller had plenty of sympathy when he learned that Jack was only 3. He did not blame the boy or his parents. He was glad to put the Cadillac back on the market.

_____   _____   _____

_____   _____

3   Blends that end in *r*

br-	cr-	dr-	fr-	gr-
pr-	tr-			

These consonant blends may be at the beginning or in the middle of a word. Examples are *brain* and *contract*.

Below, two words illustrate each type of blend ending in **r**. In the space provided, add a third example of each blend.

br	**bro**ke	em**bra**ce	_____
cr	**cri**me	in**cre**ase	_____
dr	**dre**am	ad**dre**ss	_____
fr	**fr**ee	a**fr**aid	_____
gr	**gr**eed	tele**gr**am	_____
pr	**pr**ay	ex**pr**ess	_____
tr	**tr**ain	con**tr**act	_____

➤ *Practice 5*

A. Find the five words below that have a consonant blend ending with **r**. Remember that this blend may occur at the beginning or middle of a word. Write the words in the blank spaces at the top of the next page.

across	entrance	frog	jawbreaker	liar
rage	revert	rope	target	trade

_____   _____   _____

_____   _____

B. Read the paragraph below and find the five words that have a consonant blend ending in **r.** Write them in the blank spaces.

If you are looking at a used car, make sure to give it more than a simple visual inspection. Most used cars look good just sitting on a lot or in a driveway. Take the car out on the road. This will help you to see if the important parts of the car are in good shape. For instance, you'll be able to see if the steering system is on-center. You'll be able to tell if the brakes grab or if they are loose. You'll find out how the transmission is acting. And pushing down on the gas pedal will help you see if there are any problems in picking up speed. A road test is a must if you want to make sure you are buying the right used car.

_____   _____   _____

_____   _____

4 Other blends in the middle or at the end of a word

-ft	-ld	-lt	-mp	-nd
-nk	-nt			

These consonant blends may be at the end of a word, as in _lift,_ or at the end of a syllable within the word, as in _wanted._

Below, two words illustrate each type of blend at the end of a syllable or word. In the space provided, add a third example of each blend.

ft	li**ft**	so**ft**ly	_____
ld	chi**ld**	go**ld**en	_____
lt	be**lt**	me**lt**down	_____
mp	la**mp**	du**mp**ster	_____
nd	ha**nd**	wi**nd**shield	_____
nk	i**nk**	ba**nk**book	_____
nt	fro**nt**	pai**nt**ing	_____

➤ *Practice 6*

A. Find the five words below that have a consonant blend at the end of a syllable or at the end of a word. Write the words in the blank spaces.

bumper	glad	handcuff	mild	prod
punt	sank	sweep	very	wire

_____   _____   _____

_____   _____

B. Complete the passage by filling in each blank with the word that contains a consonant blend at the end of a syllable or at the end of the word.

Rico and Maria were having a *(tough, difficult)* _____ time deciding how to spend the holiday weekend. Rico suggested that they *(camp, hike)* _____ in a nearby state park, where he could go fishing. Maria wanted to visit her parents in *(New Jersey, Rhode Island)* _____. They could take care of the *(children, kids)* _____, while she and Rico could relax and *(find, buy)* _____ bargains in the factory outlets. Since they couldn't agree, they finally decided to stay home and *(begin, start)* _____ fixing up the house.

Consonant Digraphs

You have just learned that in consonant blends, each consonant is pronounced. In the blend **nt**, for example, two sounds are heard. However, there are some pairs of consonants with only one sound. And that sound is very different from the sound of either of the two letters. A pair of consonants with only one sound is called a **digraph**.

Three types of digraphs are explained below:

1 Digraphs that sound like **f**: **gh** and **ph**
2 Digraphs with new sounds of their own: **sh** and **th**
3 A digraph with three sounds: **ch**

1   Digraphs that sound like *f*: *gh* and *ph*

The digraphs **gh** and **ph** do not sound like either of the letters they contain. Instead, they each have the sound of a single consonant: **f**.

Following are examples of words in which **gh** sounds like **f**. Note that this digraph appears at the end of a syllable or word.

laughing   enough   tough

Following are examples of words in which **ph** sounds like **f**. Note that this digraph may appear at the beginning, in the middle, and at the end of words.

phone   dol**ph**in   gra**ph**

2   Digraphs with new sounds of their own: *sh* and *th*

The digraphs **sh** and **th** do not sound like any single letter. Instead, they have sounds of their own.

Below are some words that include the digraph **sh**. Pronounce the words to yourself, and note that **sh** is not a blended sound of **s** plus the sound of **h**. It is a completely different sound.

show   wa**sh**er   fi**sh**

The digraph **th** has two sounds of its own that are similar to each other. Say the following two groups of words out loud (not in a whisper), and you will hear the slight difference in the two **th** sounds. If you pronounce these words correctly, you will feel a slight vibration of your tongue as you say the words with the "voiced **th** sound." There is no vibration when you say the words with an "unvoiced **th** sound." Instead, you should feel a rush of air between your teeth when you complete the unvoiced **th**.

Voiced **th** sound	Unvoiced **th** sound
their	**th**ird
they	**th**in
there	**th**ank
ba**th**e	ba**th**

3   A digraph with three sounds: *ch*

The digraph **ch** has three different sounds. The most common is the sound that you hear in the word *check*. Here are some other words in which **ch** has that sound. As you pronounce each word, note that the sound of **ch** is hard and short.

chip   **ch**ief   ran**ch**

Ch can also sound like another digraph: **sh**. Here are some words in which **ch** sounds like **sh**:

chef   **ch**ute   Mi**ch**elle

These two sounds, **ch** and **sh**, are very different from each other. If you have trouble hearing the difference between them, think of the **ch** as being a short, forceful sound, such as the one you might make if you are sneezing: "Ah-**ch**oo!"

The **sh** is a much more gentle sound, like the sound you would make if you were trying to quiet a young child: "**Shhhh.**"

Finally, **ch** can also have the same sound as a single consonant: **k**. Here are some words in which **ch** sounds like **k**:

chorus	**ch**emist	**ch**aracter
Christian	**ch**rome	**ch**ronic

Notice that all the words in the second line above begin with **chr**. Whenever **ch** is followed by **r**, **ch** will sound like **k**.

➤ Practice 7

Complete each sentence by filling in the blank with the word that has a consonant digraph.

1. Professor Tate stopped lecturing when a bug flew into her *(eye, nose, mouth)* _____.

2. The *(Chinese, Swedes, Indians)* _____ once trained lions to help them hunt large animals.

3. If you cut off a piece of a *(starfish, lizard, spider)* _____, the piece will grow into a new animal.

4. Kim's new job didn't leave her much time to *(exercise, shop, travel)* _____.

5. The catchy *(words, phrase, tune)* _____ from the ad he heard on the radio stayed with Nate all day.

6. Bianca forgot to take the car out of gear, and it kept going until it *(hit, crashed, bumped)* _____ against the garage wall.

7. Scientists have developed dairy products that are low in *(fat, calories, cholesterol)* _____.

8. The excuse that Mike missed his date with Sarah because he was studying sounded *(phony, made-up, false)* _____ to her.

9. One of the largest cities in the United States is *(New York, Chicago, San Francisco)* _____.

10. If you have a *(bad, hard, rough)* _____ day at work, it may help to come home and take a hot bath.

Silent Consonants

See if you can pronounce these two common words:

knee   comb

If you pronounced them correctly, you did not hear all of the consonants. In the first word, the **k** is silent. In the second word, the **b** is silent.

In certain letter combinations, one consonant is pronounced and one is silent. Below are some common consonant combinations where you will find one letter pronounced and one letter silent. Examples of each combination are also included. Say the words to yourself so you can hear that one letter is silent.

mb	**b** is silent after **m**:		
	bo**mb**	li**mb**	cli**mb**
ck	**c** is silent before **k**:		
	de**ck**	sti**ck**	pa**ck**er
gn	**g** is silent before **n**:		
	gnaw	**gn**at	si**gn**
wh	**h** is often silent after **w** when **wh** begins a word:		
	white	**wh**isper	**wh**ip
who	**w** is often silent when a word begins with **who**:		
	who	whose	whole
kn	**k** is silent before **n**:		
	know	**kn**ife	**kn**ick-**kn**ack
wr	**w** is silent before **r**:		
	wreck	**wr**ite	un**wr**ap

When two of the same consonant are next to each other, one of them is silent:

bell   add   narrow   fuss

Note: Some speakers pronounce **wh** with a different sound in words beginning with **wha**, **whe**, or **whi**. The sound they make is an unvoiced digraph: **hw**. For example, they would pronounce these pairs of words differently:

weather, **wh**ether   **W**ales, **wh**ales   wear, **wh**ere   wine, **wh**ine

Ask your instructor which pronunciation is standard for your part of the country.

➤ *Practice 8*

Complete each sentence by filling in the word that has a silent consonant.

1. To *(know, believe, think)* _____ that something is true, scientists need to see proof.

2. When Dominic woke up, he was so hungry that he ate an entire box of *(Cheerios, Rice Krispies, Cocoa Puffs)* _____.

3. If you visit a petting zoo, be careful that a baby *(goat, pony, lamb)* _____ does not nibble too hard on your fingers.

4. A key to making good bread is knowing how to *(bake, prepare, knead)* _____ it.

5. When Alex called the office to find out where his *(bonus, order, check)* _____ was, he was told, "It's in the mail."

6. Many types of birds enjoy leftover bread *(crumbs, pieces, bits)* _____ that people throw their way.

7. Canada is a beautiful country, but its short summers are *(hot, humid, muggy)* _____ and full of insects.

8. Merchandise that is sold at *(discount, retail, wholesale)* _____ prices often attracts people looking for the best bargain.

9. Maurice was glad to get the greeting card until he read its *(contents, poem, message)* _____: "Roses are red, violets are blue; because of you, I caught the flu."

10. Lewis Carroll, author of *Alice's Adventures in Wonderland*, liked to *(eat, write, sleep)* _____ standing up.

An Important Final Note

You have learned a lot of guidelines in this chapter, and more are coming in the chapters that follow. You may wonder if it is possible to remember them all. If so, it may interest you to know that skillful readers don't think about guidelines as they read. In fact, most don't remember what the guidelines are.

This doesn't mean that guidelines are not helpful at first. You will make better progress if you review the principles and words in this chapter and the next three chapters often. Even when your instructor is finished with these chapters, review the words in them until these words are easy for you to read. When you can read the words, you will be able to read many others that are like them. And once you know how to pronounce the words with ease, you won't need to think about the guidelines.

If you feel your progress is too slow, get help from your school's learning resource center or a tutor. But if you have done the work in this chapter carefully, you are probably reading better already. Progress happens slowly, and you are usually not aware of it. One way to keep track of your progress is to read a paragraph or two into a tape recorder. Then play the tape back to yourself at the end of this course to see how much you have improved.

Finally, don't forget the one activity that builds good readers best—reading. Read not only school material but as much nonschool material as you can—in newspapers, magazines, and books. Read something every day that especially interests you, even if it's only for a few minutes on the bus, during a coffee break, or before you go to sleep. If you do, you will find before long that you can read faster and understand better what you are reading.

CHAPTER REVIEW

In this chapter, you learned the following:

- Fifteen consonants have *only one sound* when they stand alone:
  b, f, h, j, k, l, m, n, p, r, t, v, w, y, and **z.**

- Six consonants have *more than one sound:* **c, g, d, q, s,** and **x.**

c	certain, curtain	**q**	queen, antique
g	wage, wag	**s**	soup, nose
d	date, educate	**x**	fox, exact, Xerox

- There are three types of consonant combinations:

  — **Consonant blends** are combinations that blend the sounds of single consonants, such as the following:

  Blends beginning with s:
  score, scrap, skate, slam, small, snore, spank, splash, sprout, squeak, steel, street, swear

  Blends ending with l:
  bless, clam, flag, glad, play

  Blends ending with r:
  broke, crime, dream, free, greed, pray, train

  Blends at the end of a syllable or word:
  lift, child, belt, dumpster, windbag, bankbook, wanting

  — **Consonant digraphs** are pairs of consonants that combine to make a new sound, such as the following:

  Digraphs that sound like f:
  gh laughing   **ph** phone

  Digraphs with sounds of their own:
  sh fish   **th** *(voiced)* their   **th** *(unvoiced)* third

  A digraph with three sounds—ch:
  chip   chef   chorus

  — **Silent consonants** are consonants that are not pronounced in certain combinations, including the following:

mb comb	gn gnaw	who whose	wr write
ck deck	wh white	kn: know	

  Two consonants together: bell, narrow, fuss

On the Web: If you are using this book in class, you can visit our website for additional practice with consonant sounds. Go to **www.townsendpress.com** and click on "Online Exercises."

➤ Review Test 1

To review what you have learned in this chapter, answer each of the following questions. Write the letter of the correct answer in the space provided.

_____ 1. Most of the letters in the English alphabet are
    A. vowels.
    B. consonants.
    C. blends.

_____ 2. Most of the consonants in the English alphabet
    A. have only one sound.
    B. have more than one sound.
    C. are silent.

_____ 3. All of the following letter combinations—**sc, sk, st, pl, bl, br, dr, nd,** and **nt**—
    A. contain a silent consonant.
    B. are examples of consonant blends.
    C. are examples of consonant digraphs.

_____ 4. A consonant digraph is a consonant combination that
    A. blends together.
    B. makes a new sound.
    C. always sounds the same.

➤ **Review Test 2**

A. Find the five words that have the *hard* sound of **c** (as in *can*) or of **g** (as in *game*). Write them in the blank spaces.

cent	come	curse	cut	gun
hug	huge	twice	mercy	page

1. _____

2. _____

3. _____

4. _____

5. _____

B. Find and write down the five words that contain consonant blends.

bribe	found	heater	motion	repair
smile	stain	unplug	visit	voice

6. _____

7. _____

8. _____

9. _____

10. _____

C. Complete each sentence by filling in the word that has a consonant digraph.

11. *(Ketchup, milk)* _____ was once sold as a medicine.

12. *(Elephants, Ants)* _____ need only two hours of sleep a day.

13. A *(blinking, flashing)* _____ light makes a good fire alarm for the deaf.

14. The best way to avoid getting a bad *(cold, cough)* _____ is to wash your hands a lot during the day.

15. "When in doubt," said Mark Twain, "tell the *(truth, facts)* _____."

D. Find and write down the five words with silent consonants.

alert	bitten	blend	bounce	cheese
reign	slug	truck	whole	wrong

16. _____

17. _____

18. _____

19. _____

20. _____

➤ *Review Test 3*

Here is a chance to apply your understanding of consonant sounds to a full-length reading. This selection is about the struggles in one man's life, from childhood to adulthood. Juan Angel takes on the challenges he faces, one by one. Think about what keeps him going as you read "The Struggle Continues." Then answer the phonics questions that follow.

Words to Watch

Following are some words in the reading that do not have strong context support. Each word is followed by the number of the paragraph in which it appears and its meaning there. These words are indicated in the reading by a small circle (°).

curiosity (5) desire to know something
GED (10) general equivalency diploma (equal to a high-school diploma)
flexible (10) able to be adjusted and changed

THE STRUGGLE CONTINUES

Juan Angel

1 My name is Juan Angel. I am thirty years old, and I was born in Mexico.

2 As a child, I was alone for most of the time. My father was an alcoholic, and he left my family and me when I was three years old. My mother had to struggle to survive by working from place to place in Mexico. Her effort to support me was not enough because of low salaries, so she left to work in the United States.

3 I lived with some of my relatives in a little village in Mexico and worked from dawn to sunset and ate sometimes once a day. I felt I would die of starvation and hard work. My relatives spent the money that my mother sent me. They claimed that I was just a child and didn't need it. As a child, I was not able to resist. After five years of being mistreated by my relatives, I went to live with my grandmother, who lived in another village.

4 When I moved into my grandmother's house, I started a new life. By then, I was eight years old. I felt proud of myself for the first time because I had made my first big decision in life.

5 My grandmother had some pigs, so I had to feed them. One day I was feeding them close to a water stream when I saw two boys passing by. They carried some books with them. I saw them every day walking down a grassy road while I fed those pigs. My curiosity° grew, and one day I stopped them on their way back home. I asked

them what they were doing, and they told me that they were attending school. I wanted to know if they knew how to read, and they started reading and writing to show me. I simply couldn't believe it. When they left, I scratched my head and nodded for a moment, looking toward the sky. I said, "Going to school! That's the next step I have to work on." After I finished feeding those pigs, I went home. While I was walking home, I thought about how I would get my grandmother to allow me to go to school. I knew it was going to be hard to do. There were around twenty boys in the village, and only the two I met were going to school.

6   My grandmother wanted me to stay with the pigs. So for two years I stayed with her before taking my next step. I then left my grandmother and found a place to sleep in the town where the school was. The two boys I knew took me to the school, and I told my story to the principal. His name was Juan, also. He told me that my age (ten years old) made me too old to come to the school. But then he spoke with his teachers, and they all agreed to let me enter. They knew my desire to learn was great.

7   A week later my grandmother found me. I cried while I explained to her why I had left home. She hugged me very hard, and then she went to talk to the principal and give her approval. I then returned to live with her and walked the two miles back and forth to school every day. I had to feed the pigs early in the morning before I went to school and after I came home from school. I also chopped wood for cooking and did other chores as well. I was a responsible man in charge of a household. My grandmother and I lived happily for six years while I was in primary school.

8   After I finished my first six years in school, I had to make another tough decision. The secondary school I wished to attend was in another town about three hours away by bus. I hated to leave my grandmother, but I wanted to stay in school. I visited her weekends when I had enough money to do so. By the start of my second year in the school, I began to worry about her health and the bad chest pains she felt in her heart.

9   One day a friend of mine came looking for me at the school. He told me that my grandmother was very sick. I at once returned to see her. She was

lying down with a blanket on the floor. When she saw me, she hugged me very hard. Then she began to ask how my school was. I could hardly answer her because tears ran down my cheeks as never before. She asked me not to cry, but I couldn't stop. She told me to continue in school, and I promised her I would. A few minutes later, she died in my arms. I felt that everything was torn apart inside me. I thought that I could never overcome the painful experience of losing my grandmother.

10   My mother, who was here in the United States, got there in time for the funeral. She asked me to go back with her, but I refused her offer. So she returned to the United States, and I stayed in Mexico for another four years of school. She continued asking me to join her. Finally, I moved to the United States. I took English classes at night and worked days. My English teacher told me about a Hispanic program where I could get my GED° diploma. There was no stopping me: I finished the program and earned my GED. Soon after, I started working on a farm, growing alfalfa. I worked three years, and then I quit to find a more flexible° job so I could attend college.

11   Now I'm working in a feed department on a swing shift, and I'm a student at Blue Mountain Community College in the mornings. I have dealt with many obstacles in my life since childhood, and I have overcome them. It has not been easy, but I believe in success through education. Even though I know the struggle is not over yet, I will keep a hopeful smile toward the future.

On his job at the alfalfa farm, Juan Angel spent part of his time repairing harvest equipment.

Phonics Questions

Use phonics clues you learned from this chapter to answer the following questions. In the space provided, write the letter of your choice for each question.

_____ 1. Which word from the sentence below has a consonant digraph?
  A. *thirty*
  B. *old*
  C. *Mexico*

  "I am thirty years old, and I was born in Mexico." (Paragraph 1)

_____ 2. The word *alcoholic*, used in the sentence below, contains
  A. two soft **c** sounds.
  B. a hard **c** sound and a soft **c** sound.
  C. two hard **c** sounds.

  "My father was an alcoholic, and he left my family and me when I was three years old." (Paragraph 2)

_____ 3. The word *grew*, used in the sentence below, contains
  A. a soft **g** sound.
  B. a hard **g** sound.

  "My curiosity grew, and one day I stopped them on their way back home." (Paragraph 5)

_____ 4. The word *spent,* used in the sentence below, contains
  A. two consonant blends.
  B. two consonant digraphs.
  C. one consonant blend and one consonant digraph.

  "My relatives spent the money that my mother sent me." (Paragraph 3)

_____ 5. Which word from the sentence below has an **s** that sounds like **z**?
  A. *grandmother's*
  B. *house*
  C. *started*

  "When I moved into my grandmother's house, I started a new life." (Paragraph 4)

_____ 6. Which words from the sentence below have consonant blends?
  A. *big* and *decision*
  B. *time* and *because*
  C. *felt* and *proud*

  "I felt proud of myself for the first time because I had made my first big decision in life." (Paragraph 4)

_____ 7. Which word from the sentence below has a silent letter combination?
   A. *they*
   B. *writing*
   C. *show*

   "I wanted to know if they knew how to read, and they started reading and writing to show me." (Paragraph 5)

_____ 8. The word *chores*, used in the sentence below, contains a
   A. consonant blend.
   B. consonant digraph.
   C. silent letter combination.

   "I also chopped wood for cooking and did other chores as well." (Paragraph 7)

_____ 9. Which word from the sentence below has a soft **c** sound?
   A. *could*
   B. *overcome*
   C. *experience*

   "I thought that I could never overcome the painful experience of losing my grandmother." (Paragraph 9)

_____ 10. The word *who*, used in the sentence below, contains a
   A. silent consonant.
   B. consonant blend.
   C. consonant digraph.

   "My mother, who was here in the United States, got there in time for the funeral." (Paragraph 10)

Discussion Questions

1. Why do you think Juan's grandmother changed her mind about his going to school?

2. When Juan's grandmother died, Juan's mother asked him to move to the United States with her, but Juan refused her offer. What reasons might he have had for refusing her?

3. Based on the reading, what do you think are Juan's strongest personal qualities? Tell what parts of the story reveal each quality you mention.

Note: Writing assignments for this selection appear on page 555.

With Juan and his wife, Hilda, are their children
(left to right), Vianey, Danny, and Juan, Jr.

Check Your Performance   PHONICS I: CONSONANTS

Activity	Number Right	Points	Score
Review Test 1 (4 items)	_____	× 5 =	_____
Review Test 2 (20 items)	_____	× 2 =	_____
Review Test 3 (10 items)	_____	× 4 =	_____
		TOTAL SCORE =	_____%

Enter your total score into the **Reading Performance Chart: Review Tests** on the inside back cover.

CONSONANTS: Mastery Test 1

A. Use a check mark (✓) to show whether the boldfaced letter in each word has the soft sound of **c** or **g** (as in *cell* or *germ)* or the hard sound of **c** or **g** (as in *can* or *game).*

	Soft sound	*Hard sound*
1. **c**oat	_____	_____
2. re**c**ent	_____	_____
3. **g**ain	_____	_____
4. pa**g**e	_____	_____
5. **c**igar	_____	_____

B. Fill in each blank with the word that contains a consonant blend.

Some very (6. *unusual, strange)* _____ messages have been (7. *found, seen)* _____ on gravestones. For example, the gravestone of one (8. *teacher, professor)* _____ reads: "School is out. Teacher has gone home." Written on another (9. *grave, tomb)* _____ is this message: "I told you I was sick!" One that is especially (10. *brief, odd)* _____ is "That is all."

C. Find the five words that contain a consonant digraph, and write them in the blank spaces. (A reminder: a digraph is a pair of consonants with one sound that differs from the sound of either of the letters.)

depart	enough	grain	Joseph	kitten
pamphlet	rose	she	think	toy

11. _____   14. _____

12 _____   15. _____

13. _____

(Continues on next page)

D. Complete each sentence by filling in the word that has at least one silent consonant.

16. (*Knitting, Painting*) _____ can be a relaxing activity.

17. Leaving your homework where the dog can get at it would be a (*stupid, dumb*) _____ mistake.

18. By the time you finish playing a tough set of tennis, you may be soaked with sweat. Even your (*wristband, headband*) _____ may be all wet.

19. Being (*lost, stuck*) _____ in traffic is not an acceptable excuse for missing a final exam.

20. The chief of a Midwestern Native American tribe was buried (*sitting, lying*) _____ on his favorite horse.

CONSONANTS: Mastery Test 2

A. Complete each sentence by filling in the word that has the *hard* sound of **c** (as in *can*) or of **g** (as in *game*).

1. Most people should include high fiber such as *(celery, cabbage)* _____ in their diet.

2. In one unusual hairstyle, the hair stands up straight and the ends are tinted *(gold, orange)* _____.

3. Many *(castles, palaces)* _____ have secret rooms and passageways.

4. Raleigh is the capital of *(North Carolina, Georgia)* _____.

5. Many *(geniuses, great people)* _____ did poorly in school, including Thomas Edison and Albert Einstein.

B. Find the five words that contain one or more consonant blends, and write them in the blank spaces.

| comet | glad | grin | parade | pathway |
| prank | redwood | silly | skill | slim |

6. _____   9. _____

7. _____   10. _____

8. _____

C. Find the five words below that have a consonant digraph (a pair of consonants with one sound that differs from the sound of either of the letters). Write the words in the blank spaces.

Phil had planned for this day for two years. He had worked evenings and summers, saving all he could. Finally, he had enough money to buy the car he had dreamed of. He walked into a local showroom, pointed to a red Corvette, and wrote a check for a down payment.

11. _____   14. _____

12 _____   15. _____

13. _____

(Continues on next page)

D. (16–25.) Circle the ten words in the box that contain a silent consonant. The words are either straight across or straight down. Here are the words you are looking for:

comb	duck	knock	knot	numb
sign	tack	wrap	wreck	write

w	r	a	p	x	s	i	g	n
z	f	w	f	l	g	o	f	h
c	h	r	t	a	c	k	p	z
o	u	i	m	s	t	p	q	f
m	c	t	s	w	r	e	c	k
b	n	e	h	o	t	z	o	n
q	u	e	d	u	c	k	o	o
z	m	t	h	e	i	u	m	c
o	b	k	k	n	o	t	t	k

CONSONANTS: Mastery Test 3

A. Use a check mark (✓) to show whether the boldfaced letter in each word has the soft sound of **c** or **g** (as in *cell* or *germ)* or the hard sound of **c** or **g** (as in *can* or *game).*

	Soft sound	*Hard sound*
1. sa**g**a	_____	_____
2. **c**eiling	_____	_____
3. **g**inger	_____	_____
4. lettu**c**e	_____	_____
5. re**c**ord	_____	_____

B. Fill in each blank space with the word that contains a consonant blend.

Have you been to the zoo lately? If your answer is "no," you are in for a (6. *surprise, shock)* _____ on your next visit. Zoos are changing. They were first (7. *created, used)* _____ to show off rare animals, which were housed in (8. *tiny, small)* _____ cages. Now, zoos (9. *raise, breed)* _____ animals that are in danger of disappearing. Also, the animals are now housed in spaces that are larger and more like the (10. *lands, areas)* _____ they come from.

C. Find the five words that have a silent consonant, and write them in the blank spaces.

chewing	expect	knob	limb	manhunt
memory	perform	pudding	sack	wrist

11. _____   14. _____

12 _____   15. _____

13. _____

(Continues on next page)

D. (16–25.) Circle the ten words in the box that contain a consonant digraph (a pair of consonants with one sound that differs from the sound of either of the letters). The words are either straight across or straight down. Here are the words you are looking for:

ashore	bath	death	dish	gopher
photo	show	them	tough	with

a	b	a	t	h	q	u	u	w
w	r	x	h	n	u	s	d	t
i	f	d	e	a	t	h	c	o
t	p	u	m	c	r	o	f	u
h	h	n	f	o	b	w	r	g
g	o	p	h	e	r	z	y	h
l	t	m	g	p	c	w	z	m
g	o	t	a	s	h	o	r	e
d	i	s	h	u	i	n	g	b

CONSONANTS: Mastery Test 4

A. Find the five words that contain a *soft* **c** (as in *cell)* or a *soft* **g** (as in *germ),* and write them in the blank spaces.

A recent concert held to benefit earthquake victims made many people angry. First, the price of admission was too high. Next, it seemed like ages before each band set up and was ready to perform. Finally, the seats were so far away from the stage that people could barely see the performers.

1. _____   4. _____

2. _____   5. _____

3. _____

B. (6–15.) Circle the ten words in the box that contain a consonant blend. The words are either straight across or straight down. Here are the words you are looking for:

blush	brief	faint	hunt	round
skate	sneeze	special	stamp	trip

h	o	h	z	s	t	a	m	p
u	f	t	x	n	w	h	y	s
n	b	r	i	e	f	n	k	f
t	h	i	s	e	v	n	t	a
i	o	p	b	z	x	s	l	i
s	k	a	t	e	f	r	q	n
k	a	t	r	o	u	n	d	t
b	l	u	s	h	i	h	e	r
r	u	s	p	e	c	i	a	l

(Continues on next page)

C. Find the five words that have a consonant digraph (a pair of consonants with one sound that differs from the sound of either of the letters). Write the five words in the blank spaces.

bullfrog	cartoon	cheap	desk	eagle
flush	phase	rough	thousand	violet

16. _____   19. _____

17 _____   20. _____

18. _____

D. Fill in each blank with the word that contains at least one silent consonant.

Have you ever tried to (21. *compose, write*) _____ an essay, only to stare at a blank sheet of paper because no ideas come to your mind? This happens to everyone, even (22. *well-known, famous*) _____ authors. Some say it is helpful to get away from the project for a while and do something (23. *entirely, wholly*) _____ different. Others say that this approach is (24. *wrong, poor*) _____. They prefer to jot down anything on paper. They feel that (25. *with luck, in time*) _____, jotting down ideas will help them to gather their thoughts and get on with the writing.

CONSONANTS: Mastery Test 5

A. Complete each sentence by filling in the word which has the *soft* sound of **c** (as in *cell*) or of **g** (as in *germ*).

1. Just when I thought I had finally won a game of Blackjack, my sister tossed out a(n) *(jack, ace)* _____ and yelled, "That makes 21!"

2. It is generally better to be *(courteous, civil)* _____ than hostile to people you dislike.

3. Most schools require teachers to know basic life-saving *(procedures, techniques)* _____, such as CPR and the Heimlich maneuver.

4. Too much rain can make a mess of a yard's *(vegetation, garden)* _____.

5. Martina was proud when she was named the outstanding *(principal, educator)* _____ of her district.

B. Complete each sentence by filling in the word that has a consonant blend.

6. President Teddy Roosevelt once said, "Speak *(softly, now)* _____ and carry a big stick."

7. In ancient Egypt, cats were so *(respected, admired)* _____ that anyone killing a cat could be punished by death.

8. Whenever my father said, "This is going to hurt me more than you," I knew I was about to be *(punished, spanked)* _____.

9. A hurricane can be so *(powerful, strong)* _____ that it can knock over trees as if they were toothpicks.

10. If you *(run, bump)* _____ into another car, it is a good idea to check for damage.

(Continues on next page)

C. Complete each sentence by filling in the word that has a consonant digraph.

11. Some *(fish, birds)* _____ can be frozen alive and then brought back to life by being defrosted.

12. A research paper can look more impressive if you insert a *(diagram, graph)* _____ into the text.

13. If you are not satisfied with your meal at a restaurant, ask your waiter or waitress to send it back to the *(chef, cook)* _____.

14. When she heard her class *(giggle, laugh)* _____, Professor McNee realized that she was lecturing on the wrong subject.

15. I *(thought, believed)* _____ that ice-skating would be easy—until I tried it.

D. Complete each sentence by filling in the word that has at least one silent consonant.

16. Even experienced skaters sometimes *(fall, trip)* _____ unexpectedly.

17. A dog is considered a *(dumb, friendly)* _____ animal because it cannot speak.

18. A loud *(knocking, pounding)* _____ on the door woke me from a sound sleep.

19. Once I catch a cold, I am likely to begin *(coughing, running a fever)* _____.

20. I cut my *(thumb, finger)* _____ because I rushed when I was chopping the onion.

CONSONANTS: Mastery Test 6

A. Read the passage below and fill in each blank with the word that has a *hard* **c** or **g** sound.

Various professional sports are competing for the attention of the American (1. *audience, public*) _____. Baseball and football are still the two most popular sports. However, increasing media coverage has opened the door for other sports. For example, basketball has won over (2. *countless, large*) _____ numbers of fans. Hockey, the national sport of (3. *Iceland, Canada*) _____, has (4. *advanced, gained*) _____ in popularity as well. And on the horizon is the world's most popular sport— (5. *auto races, soccer*) _____.

B. Read the passage below and fill in each blank with a word that has a consonant blend.

In 1965, a seventeen-year-old named (6. *Fred, Guido*) _____ DeLuca borrowed $1,000 from a (7. *bank, relative*) _____ and used it to (8. *start, open*) _____ a (9. *sandwich, doughnut*) _____ shop in Bridgeport, Connecticut. Within a year, he had opened two others. By 1973, there were sixteen shops. Five years later, DeLuca had (10. *ninety, one hundred*) _____ shops operating. You probably recognize the name of these shops: Subway.

(Continues on next page)

45

C. Read the passage below and fill in each blank with the word that has at least one consonant digraph.

It is not uncommon for college students to want to help people become successful. Yet there are differing opinions on the best way to (11. *accomplish, attain*) _____ this end. Some students choose education as their major, believing that this career choice will give them the (12. *chance, opportunity*) _____ to help people to gain (13. *enough, sufficient*) _____ knowledge to reach their own goals. Other students turn to business as the major most suited to helping others. This (14. *view, philosophy*) _____ says that the best way to help people is to first become (15. *prosperous, rich*) _____ and then use part of your fortune to help them start their own businesses. What do you think?

D. Read the passage below and fill in each blank with the word that has a silent consonant.

Would you want to be a celebrity? Think carefully before you say "yes." Being rich and well- (16. *known, liked*) _____ would certainly have its good parts, but the bad parts are pretty (17. *unpleasant, horrible*) _____. Celebrities lose any chance of living a private life. Whether they're (18. *shopping, looking*) _____ for clothes, going on a date, or taking their children to school, they are being chased by photographers. And those photographers don't want just any shot. They want the most embarrassing, unflattering, or (19. *scandalous, shocking*) _____ picture possible. If they can catch the celebrity having an argument, or looking ugly, or crying, they can sell that photograph for a (20. *whole lot, great deal*) _____ of money.

2

Phonics II:
Vowels

THIS CHAPTER IN A NUTSHELL

● You will learn about the most common sounds of vowels. Following are the areas that will be covered:

— Short vowel sounds
— Long vowel sounds
— Other vowel sounds

Copyright 1997 by Randy Glasbergen.

TEST FRIDAY!

GLASBERGEN

"Class, I've got a lot of material to cover,
so to save time, I won't be using vowels today.
Nw lt's bgn. Pls trn t pg 122."

As the cartoon suggests, without vowels, words would be impossible to pronounce.

The sounds of vowels are made with an open mouth, unblocked by teeth, tongue, or lips. Here are the five letters that are **vowels** in the English language:

a   e   i   o   u

In addition, **y** is sometimes a vowel.

In this chapter, you'll learn about the most common sounds of vowels. Following are the areas that will be covered:

- Short Vowel Sounds
- Long Vowel Sounds
- Other Vowel Sounds

SHORT VOWEL SOUNDS

The list below shows how the short vowel sounds are pronounced. Note that a common symbol for the short sound of a vowel is a cup-shaped curve over the vowel. This symbol is used in many dictionaries to show that a vowel has a short sound.

ă   sounds like the **a** in *pat*.
ĕ   sounds like the **e** in *pet*.
ĭ   sounds like the **i** in *pit*.
ŏ   sounds like the **o** in *pot*.
ŭ   sounds like the **u** in *cut*.

Remembering these words will help you keep each short vowel sound in mind.

➤ *Practice 1*

A. Practice with the Short *a* Sound

Say each word below to yourself. Write an **a** with a cup symbol (ă) beside each word that contains a short **a** sound, like the **a** in *pat*. Put an **X** beside words that do not have the short **a** sound. The first two are done for you as examples.

1. crack	ă		6. tame	_____
2. stay	X		7. jam	_____
3. land	_____		8. pain	_____
4. tap	_____		9. bank	_____
5. face	_____		10. ache	_____

B. Practice with the Short *e* Sound

Say each word below to yourself. Write an **e** with a cup symbol (ĕ) beside each word that contains a short **e** sound, like the e in *pet.* Put an **X** beside words that do not have the short **e** sound. The first two are done for you as examples.

1.	bent	ĕ	6.	less	_____
2.	feed	X	7.	sea	_____
3.	cream	_____	8.	speed	_____
4.	get	_____	9.	end	_____
5.	here	_____	10.	fresh	_____

C. Practice with the Short *i* Sound

Say each word below to yourself. Write an **i** with a cup symbol (ĭ) beside each word that contains a short **i** sound, like the **i** in *pit.* Put an **X** beside words that do not have the short **i** sound. The first two are done for you as examples.

1.	will	ĭ	6.	file	_____
2.	spike	X	7.	hint	_____
3.	slim	_____	8.	ride	_____
4.	lime	_____	9.	pin	_____
5.	disk	_____	10.	mice	_____

D. Practice with the Short *o* Sound

Say each word below to yourself. Write an **o** with a cup symbol (ŏ) beside each word that contains a short **o** sound, like the o in *pot.* Put an **X** beside words that do not have the short **o** sound. The first two are done for you as examples.

1.	coat	X	6.	block	_____
2.	stop	ŏ	7.	load	_____
3.	cone	_____	8.	rock	_____
4.	soak	_____	9.	grow	_____
5.	fox	_____	10.	bond	_____

E. Practice with the Short *u* Sound

Say each word below to yourself. Write a **u** with a cup symbol (**ŭ**) beside each word that contains a short **u** sound, like the **u** in *cut*. Put an **X** beside words that do not have the short **u** sound. The first two are done for you as examples.

1.	bulb	ŭ	6.	bump	_____
2.	fuse	X	7.	sure	_____
3.	bum	_____	8.	blue	_____
4.	tune	_____	9.	uncle	_____
5.	hug	_____	10.	cute	_____

Rule for Short Vowel Sounds

Compare the sounds of the words in columns 1 and 2 below. Which column lists words with the short sound of the vowels?

	Column 1	Column 2
a	hat	hate
e	pet	Pete
i	fill	file
o	rob	robe
u	cut	cute

Column 1 lists words with the short vowel sound. Notice that there is only one vowel in each word in the first column and that each vowel is followed by one or more consonants. That is the pattern of the **rule for short vowel sounds**:

> **When a word or syllable has only one vowel and that vowel is followed by one or more consonants, the vowel is usually short.**

A **syllable** is a word or part of a word having one vowel sound. The word *hatbox,* for instance, has two syllables: hat-box. Each syllable has one vowel, and each vowel is followed by one consonant. This tells you that the vowel in each part of *hatbox* is short. You will learn more about syllables in Chapter 3.

☑ *Check Your Understanding*

Below are two examples of this rule for each of the vowels, **a**, **e**, **i**, **o**, and **u**. See if you can add a third example in each space provided.

Short-vowel rule with **a**:   ham   back   _____

Short-vowel rule with **e**:   end   let   _____

Short-vowel rule with **i**:   sit   bill   _____

Short-vowel rule with **o**:   hop   lot   _____

Short-vowel rule with **u**:   dull   sun   _____

➤ *Practice 2*

Complete each sentence below by filling in the word that contains a short vowel sound. The short vowel may be **a**, **e**, **i**, **o**, or **u**.

1. When you're driving, the last thing you want is for the engine to *(die, stop)* _____.

2. The floodwaters came up to the *(back, rear)* _____ of our house.

3. An old saying says, "A crying baby is a *(fine, hungry)* _____ baby."

4. It is not healthy to eat too much *(meat, fat)* _____.

5. The first *(real, rubber)* _____ tires were invented long before automobiles—they were used on bicycles.

6. Gambling has been legal for a long time in the state of *(Nevada, Maine)* _____.

7. Margarine and *(oil, butter)* _____ contain the same amount of fat.

8. Even a person with a great personality can wake up in a *(bad, mean)* _____ mood.

9. Many bald men *(believe, think)* _____ that a hat makes a good fashion statement.

10. The *(frame, body)* _____ of a blue whale contains so much blubber that the whale can go for months without eating.

LONG VOWEL SOUNDS

The list below shows how the long vowel sounds are pronounced. Read them to yourself, and you'll see that **each vowel sounds like the letter's name**.

Notice that the symbol for the long sound is a straight line over the letter.

ā   sounds like the **a** in *pay.*
ē   sounds like the **e** in *bee.*
ī   sounds like the **i** in *pie.*
ō   sounds like the **o** in *toe.*
ū   sounds like the **u** in *fuse.*

Note: Some dictionaries show the long **u** sound as **yo͞o** rather than **ū**. But for the activities here, you can simply use **ū**.

➤ *Practice 3*

A. Practice with the Long *a* Sound

Say each word below to yourself. Write an **a** with a line on top of it (**ā**) beside each word that contains a long **a** sound, like the **a** in *pay.* Put an **X** beside words that do not have the long **a** sound. The first two are done for you as examples.

1. rake   ___ā___   6. pain   _____
2. stack   ___X___   7. ram   _____
3. plant   _____   8. span   _____
4. tape   _____   9. sad   _____
5. race   _____   10. stay   _____

B. Practice with the Long *e* Sound

Say each word below to yourself. Write an **e** with a line on top of it (**ē**) beside each word that contains a long **e** sound, like the **e** in *bee.* Put an **X** beside words that do not have the long **e** sound. The first two are done for you as examples.

1. beam   ___ē___   6. meat   _____
2. fed   ___X___   7. spend   _____
3. feed   _____   8. street   _____
4. wet   _____   9. bent   _____
5. her   _____   10. free   _____

C. Practice with the Long *i* Sound

Say each word below to yourself. Write an **i** with a line on top of it (ī) beside each word that contains a long **i** sound, like the **i** in *pie*. Put an **X** beside words that do not have the long **i** sound. The first two are done for you as examples.

1. wine   ī
2. sip   X
3. crime   _____
4. list   _____
5. die   _____

6. fist   _____
7. mint   _____
8. bride   _____
9. pink   _____
10. mile   _____

D. Practice with the Long *o* Sound

Say each word below to yourself. Write an **o** with a line on top of it (ō) beside each word that contains a long **o** sound, like the **o** in *toe*. Put an **X** beside words that do not have the long **o** sound. The first two are done for you as examples.

1. code   ō
2. stoop   X
3. bone   _____
4. float   _____
5. box   _____

6. flock   _____
7. loan   _____
8. lock   _____
9. blow   _____
10. strong   _____

E. Practice with the Long *u* Sound

Say each word below to yourself. Write a **u** with a line on top of it (ū) beside each word that contains a long **u** sound, like the **u** in *fuse*. Put an **X** beside words that do not have the long **u** sound. The first two are done for you as examples.

1. flub   X
2. use   ū
3. runt   _____
4. huge   _____
5. cure   _____

6. thump   _____
7. mute   _____
8. blunt   _____
9. cube   _____
10. cut   _____

Rules for Long Vowel Sounds

Rule 1: Silent e

Compare the sounds of the words in column 1 and column 2. Which column lists words with a long vowel sound?

	Column 1	Column 2
a	hat	hate
e	pet	Pete
i	fill	file
o	rob	robe
u	cut	cute

The second column lists words with a long vowel sound. The **e** that ends each word makes the first vowel long, and the final **e** itself is not pronounced. That is the pattern of the **silent-*e* rule**:

> **When a word or syllable ends in a vowel-consonant-e, the vowel before the consonant is long and the final e is silent.**

☑ Check Your Understanding

Below are two examples of this rule for each of the vowels **a, e, i, o,** and **u.** See if you can add a third example in each space provided.

Silent-**e** rule with **a:**   name   flake   _____

Silent-**e** rule with **e:**   scene   here   _____

Silent-**e** rule with **i:**   ride   mine   _____

Silent-**e** rule with **o:**   hope   nose   _____

Silent-**e** rule with **u:**   cube   refuse   _____

➤ Practice 4

Complete each sentence by filling in the word that has at least one syllable which follows the silent-**e** rule.

1. The forest fire burned many (*oak, elm, pine*) _____ and maple trees.

2. When we first meet someone, we decide whether he or she is a person we can (*trust, like, enjoy*) _____.

3. When you go to class, make sure you have your *(notebook, textbook, pen)*
_____ with you.

4. It's *(dangerous, risky, unsafe)* _____ to fall asleep on top of an electric blanket.

5. Is climbing a tall mountain a *(brave, fearless, bold)* _____ adventure or a foolish one?

Rule 2: Two Vowels Together

Each word below has two vowels together that produce a long vowel sound. Pronounce each word, and then read the explanation that follows.

seed	plea	play
see	hail	tie
please	road	toe

The words above follow the **rule for two vowels together**:

When two of certain vowels are together, the first vowel is long and the second is silent.

☑ Check Your Understanding

Below are vowel combinations that usually follow this rule. Two examples are provided for each. Add a third example in the space provided.

ai	aid	aim	_____
ay	pay	stay	_____

Note: In the **-ay** combination, **y** is a vowel. (See page 57.)

ea	eat	cream	_____
ee	knee	feet	_____
ie	lie	tied	_____
oa	oat	toad	_____
oe	hoe	goes	_____

➤ *Practice 5*

Complete each sentence by filling in the word that follows the two-vowels-together rule.

1. You must be patient if you want to *(train, ride, own)* _____
   a horse.

2. In 1896, the first modern Olympics were held in *(Italy, Greece, France)*

   _____.

3. The entire life span of some insects can last all of a *(minute, day, month)*

   _____.

4. Before taking a shower, make sure you have enough *(time, soap, hot water)*

   _____.

5. Some people like individual sports such as tennis, while others prefer

   (team, group, joint) _____ sports like softball.

Rule 3: Final Single Vowel

In each example below, a single vowel ends a word or syllable. Pronounce each word, and listen to the sound of each boldfaced vowel.

me	she	hi
notice	music	basic

The words above follow the **rule for a final single vowel**:

A single vowel at the end of a word or syllable (other than silent e) usually has a long sound.

➤ *Practice 6*

In each item, three words are underlined. In the space provided, write the one underlined word that is an example of the final single vowel rule.

1. Gold was one of the first precious <u>metals</u> discovered by <u>people</u>. It is <u>also</u>
   one of the rarest metals. _____

2. Scientists have learned that the web of a <u>spider</u> can be <u>three</u> times stronger
   than iron of the same <u>thickness</u>. _____

3. On the average, Americans today sleep <u>over</u> an hour <u>less</u> than Americans of fifty <u>years</u> ago. _____

4. A computer <u>crash</u> can <u>erase</u> valuable information, which <u>may</u> then be lost forever. _____

5. In a <u>famous</u> magic trick, the magician <u>escapes</u> from a locked cell by using a key <u>hidden</u> on his body. _____

OTHER VOWEL SOUNDS

The Vowel y

When **y** starts a word (as in *yell*), it is considered a consonant. Otherwise, **y** is a vowel and usually has one of the following three vowel sounds:

- In the middle of a word or syllable, **y** usually sounds like short **i**, as in *myth, gym,* and *syllable.*
- At the end of a one-syllable word, **y** sounds like long **i**, as in *my, sty,* and *fry.*
- At the end of a word with more than one syllable, **y** sounds like long **e**, as in *many, baby,* and *city.* Sometimes Y will sound like long **i**, as in *deny, July,* and *reply.*

(Remember that **y** is also considered a vowel when it follows the letter **a**. The combination **ay**, as in *play* and *stay,* follows the rule for two vowels together: the **a** is long and the **y** is silent.)

➤ Practice 7

In the space provided, show whether the **y** in each word sounds like a consonant (**y**), short **i** (ĭ), long **i** (ī), or long **e** (ē). The first three are done for you.

1. stingy	ē		6. lynch	_____
2. hymn	ĭ		7. yellow	_____
3. yes	y		8. marry	_____
4. sadly	_____		9. youth	_____
5. by	_____		10. cyst	_____

Sounds of Vowels Followed by *r*

When **r** follows a vowel, it changes the sound of the vowel. A vowel that comes just before an **r** is usually neither long nor short, but in between. To see how this works, say the words below to yourself. Notice how the sound of the vowel—and the shape of your mouth—change a bit when the vowel is followed by **r**.

Long vowels	Short vowels	Vowels followed by **r**
cane	can	car
heat	help	her
site	sit	sir
code	cod	cord
fuel	fun	fur

➤ Practice 8

Identify each boldfaced vowel with one of the following:

- the symbol for a long vowel sound (¯)
- the symbol for a short vowel sound (˘)
- an **r** if the vowel sound is changed by an **r**

The first three have been done for you.

1. g**a**s	˘a		6. f**i**rm	_____
2. h**a**rd	r		7. kn**ee**	_____
3. p**a**ge	¯a		8. r**u**n	_____
4. s**ai**nt	_____		9. sp**o**rt	_____
5. t**e**rm	_____		10. tr**i**ck	_____

Long and Short *oo*

When two **o**'s appear together, they are pronounced in one of two ways. One pronunciation is called the **long double o sound**, as in *boot.* Here are some other words with the long sound of **oo**:

sp**oo**n   r**oo**m   f**oo**d

The other pronunciation is called the **short double o sound**, as in *foot.* Here are some other words with the short sound of **oo**:

st**oo**d   g**oo**d   c**oo**k

➤ *Practice 9*

In the space provided, show whether each **oo** vowel sound is long ($\overline{oo}$) or short ($\breve{oo}$). The first two are done for you as examples.

1. choose   __$\overline{oo}$__   6 soot   _____

2. shook   __$\breve{oo}$__   7. wool   _____

3. loose   _____   8. proof   _____

4. brook   _____   9. zoo   _____

5. cartoon   _____   10. crook   _____

CHAPTER REVIEW

In this chapter, you learned the following:

- **Short vowels** are shown in some dictionaries by a cup-shaped symbol over the vowel: ă, ĕ, ĭ, ŏ, ŭ.

  Rule for short vowel sounds: When a word or syllable has only one vowel and that vowel is followed by one or more consonants, the vowel is usually short: *pat, pet, pit, pot, cut.*

- **Long vowels** have the sound of their own name and are shown in some dictionaries by a line over the vowel: ā, ē, ī, ō, ū.

  Here are the rules for long vowels:

  — *The silent-***e** *rule:* When a word or syllable ends with vowel-consonant-**e**, the vowel before the consonant is long and the final **e** is silent: *hate, Pete, bite, robe, cute.*

  — *The two-vowels-together rule:* When two of certain vowels are together, the first vowel is long and the second is silent: *aim, pay, eat, knee, lie, oat, hoe.*

  — *The final single vowel rule:* A single vowel at the end of a word or syllable (other than silent **e**) usually has a long sound: *me, hi, notice, music.*

  (Continues on next page)

- **Y is a vowel** when it does not begin a word.

  Here are the rules for the sounds of the vowel **y**:

  — *Short-**i** sound:* In the middle of a word or syllable, **y** usually sounds like short **i**: *myth*.

  — *Long-**i** sound:* At the end of a one-syllable word, **y** sounds like long **i**: *my*.

  — *Long-**e** sound:* At the end of a word with more than one syllable, **y** usually sounds like long **e**: *many*. Sometimes **y** sounds like long **i**: *deny*.

- **The sound of a vowel followed by r** is usually neither long nor short, but in between: *car.*

- The **long double o sound** is the vowel sound in *boot.* The **short double o sound** is the vowel sound in *foot.*

 On the Web: If you are using this book in class, you can visit our website for additional practice with vowel sounds. Go to **www.townsendpress.com** and click on "Online Exercises."

➤ *Review Test 1*

To review what you have learned in this chapter, answer each of the following questions. Write the letter of the correct answer in the space provided.

_____ 1. A word or syllable usually has a short vowel sound when
   A. a consonant is followed by a single vowel.
   B. a single vowel is followed by one or more consonants.
   C. a vowel is followed by a consonant and then the letter **e**.

_____ 2. TRUE OR FALSE? The silent-**e** rule states that when a word or syllable ends in vowel-consonant-**e**, the first vowel is long and the **e** ending the word is silent.

_____ 3. The two-vowels-together rule states that when two of certain vowels are together in a word,
   A. the first is long and the second is short.
   B. both vowels are long.
   C. the first is long and the second is silent.

_____ 4. When **y** is in the middle of a word,
   A. it is a consonant.
   B. it usually sounds like short **i**.
   C. it usually sounds like short **e**.

➤ *Review Test 2*

A. For each item below, write a word with the vowel sound shown. Choose from the words in the box; use each word once.

| cram | dress | dust | file | green |
| home | mix | nod | place | used |

1. Short **a** sound: _____

2. Long **a** sound: _____

3. Short **e** sound: _____

4. Long **e** sound: _____

5. Short **i** sound: _____

6. Long **i** sound: _____

7. Short **o** sound: _____

8. Long **o** sound: _____

9. Short **u** sound: _____

10. Long **u** sound: _____

B. Here are the rules for long vowel sounds:

Silent **e:** When a word or syllable ends in a vowel-consonant-**e**, the vowel before the consonant is long and the final **e** is silent.

Two vowels together: When two of certain vowels are together, the first vowel is long and the second is silent.

Final single vowel: A single vowel at the end of a word or syllable (other than a silent **e**) usually has a long sound.

Beside each word, write the name of the rule that applies: Silent **e**, Two Vowels Together, or Final Single Vowel. In the second space, write a short explanation of the rule. Note the example.

Example:

toast   *Two Vowels Together*   *The **o** is long, and the **a** is silent.*

11. face   _____   _____

12. go   _____   _____

13. road   _____   _____

14. steal   _____   _____

15. plane   _____   _____

C. Here are the rules for **y** as a vowel:

Sounds of y

> *Short-***i** *sound:* In the middle of a word or syllable, **y** usually sounds like short **i**.
>
> *Long-***i** *sound:* At the end of a one-syllable word, **y** sounds like long **i**.
>
> *Long-***e** *sound:* At the end of a word with more than one syllable, **y** usually sounds like long **e**.

Beside each word, identify the **y** sound by writing in one of the following:

    ĭ (short **i**)   ī (long **i**)   ē (long **e**).

In the second space, write a short explanation of the rule that applies. Note the example.

Example:

    ready   __ē__   *At end of word with more than one syllable*

16. sky   _____   _____

17. party   _____   _____

18. system   _____   _____

19. hurry   _____   _____

20. dry   _____   _____

➤ Review Test 3

Here is a chance to apply your understanding of vowel and consonant sounds to a full-length reading. Can you imagine a more terrifying experience than being on a plane that appears destined to crash? What if you were traveling with your young child? Which emotion would take over—love or terror? This selection is a true story about such an event. After you read the selection, answer the phonics questions that follow.

Words to Watch

Following are some words in the reading that do not have strong context support. Each word is followed by the number of the paragraph in which it appears and its meaning there. These words are indicated in the reading by a small circle (°).

apparent (3): obvious
streamed (6): flowed
clenching (6): closing tightly
chaos (8): complete disorder and confusion
grief (8): deep sorrow
compelled (9): forced

A LESSON IN LOVE

Casey Hawley

1 I learned a lesson about terror, and about love that is stronger than terror. I learned it on a flight I took six years ago, and only now can I speak of it without tears filling my eyes.

2 When our flight left the Orlando airport that Friday, I settled back, I intended to do some light reading on the brief flight.

3 But I put down my magazine when it became apparent° that this was not going to be a calm flight. Our plane began bumping up and down and from side to side. Soon the plane began

dipping wildly, one wing or the other turning downward. Passengers, bags, and coffee cups lurched and banged around the little cabin. Then we heard our pilot over the loudspeaker.

"We are having some difficulties," 4 he announced. "At this time, we appear to have no nose-wheel steering. We will be returning to the Orlando airport at this time. We are not sure our landing gear will lock, so the flight attendants will prepare you for a bumpy landing. Also, if you look out the windows, you will see that we are dumping fuel from our fuel tanks. We want to have as little on board as possible in the event of a rough touchdown."

5   In other words, we were about to crash.

6   I watched as the fuel, hundreds of gallons of it, streamed° past my window out of the plane's tanks. Then, moving my attention away from that spilling fuel, I looked at my fellow travelers. I was stunned by what I saw. Some of their faces were actually gray with terror. Some people cried and screamed. A few of the men gripped their armrests tightly, clenching° their teeth, and their jaws were tightly closed. No one faces death without fear, I thought. I wondered if there was anyone whose inner strength would provide peace and calm at such a moment. I saw no such person.

7   I didn't see anyone, but then I heard a quiet, calm voice. A couple of rows to my left, a woman was speaking in a normal, conversational tone. There was no tension in her lovely, warm voice.

8   Then I saw the mother who was talking, in the midst of all the chaos°, to her child. The woman was looking full into the face of her daughter, who seemed about four and was sitting in her lap. The child listened closely, sensing the importance of her mother's words. The two seemed untouched by the sounds of grief° and fear all around. It was as if a circle had been drawn around the two of them. Panic and grief could not cross the line.

9   I tried hard to hear what this mother was saying to her child. I felt compelled° to hear. Finally, I made out what this soft, sweet voice was saying.

Over and over again, the mother said, "I love you so much. Do you know for sure that I love you more than anything?"

"Yes, Mommy," the little girl said.   10

"And remember, no matter what   11 happens, that I love you always. And that you are a good girl. Sometimes things happen that are not your fault. You are still a good girl, and my love will always be with you."

And with that, the mother strapped   12 the seat belt over both of them. She then wrapped her body over the little girl's and prepared to crash.

For whatever reason, our landing   13 gear held, and our landing was not the tragedy we feared it would be. It was over in seconds. We filed out of the plane, grateful to have escaped injury or death.

But I took something away from   14 the plane that day. I knew that none of the other people on that plane, myself included, could have done what that mother did. Was she born with a far greater share of courage than the rest of us? I doubt it. I think what I saw that day was evidence that a parent's love for a child is an amazing source of strength. While facing her own death, this mother was able to reach deep into herself. She reached far past the fear she must have felt. Calmly and surely, she spent what could have been her last seconds on Earth promising her little girl that she would always be safe in her mother's love.

For those few minutes, I was in the   15 presence of a love that is truly stronger than the fear of death: the love of a parent for a child.

Phonics Questions

Use phonics clues you learned from this and the previous chapter to answer the following questions. In the space provided, write the letter of your choice for each question.

_____ 1. In the word *six*, used in the sentence below, the **x** sounds like
   A. **ks.**
   B. **gz.**
   C. **z.**

   "I learned it on a flight I took six years ago. . . . " (Paragraph 1)

_____ 2. In the word *years*, used in the sentence below, the **y** is a
   A. consonant.
   B. vowel.

   "I learned it on a flight I took six years ago. . . . " (Paragraph 1)

_____ 3. Which word from the sentence below has a **y** that sounds like long **e**?
   A. *only*
   B. *my*
   C. *eyes*

   "I learned it on a flight I took six years ago, and only now can I speak of it without tears filling my eyes." (Paragraph 1)

_____ 4. Which word from the sentence below has a silent consonant and a consonant blend?
   A. *magazine*
   B. *became*
   C. *apparent*

   "But I put down my magazine when it became apparent that this was not going to be a calm flight." (Paragraph 3)

_____ 5. In the word *plane*, used in the sentence below,
   A. the vowels have their short vowel sounds.
   B. the **a** is long and the **e** is short.
   C. the **a** is long and the **e** is silent.

   "Soon the plane began dipping wildly, one wing or the other turning downward." (Paragraph 3)

_____ 6. The word *crash*, used in the sentence below, has
   A. two consonant blends.
   B. two consonant digraphs.
   C. a consonant blend and a consonant digraph.

   "In other words, we were about to crash." (Paragraph 5)

_____ 7. In the word *clenching*, used in the sentence below,
   A. the first **c** is hard, and the second is soft.
   B. the first **c** is soft, and the second is hard.
   C. the first **c** is hard, and the second is part of a consonant digraph.

   "A few of the men gripped their armrests tightly, clenching their teeth, and their jaws were tightly closed." (Paragraph 6)

_____ 8. The **s** in the word *mother's*, used in the sentence below,
   A. has its usual sound, as in *salt.*
   B. sounds like **z**.

   "The child listened closely, sensing the importance of her mother's words." (Paragraph 8)

_____ 9. In the word *reach*, used in the sentence below, the vowel sound follows which rule?
   A. The silent-**e** rule
   B. The two-vowels-together rule
   C. The sounds of vowels followed by an **r**

   "While facing her own death, this mother was able to reach deep into herself." (Paragraph 14)

_____ 10. Which word from the sentence below follows the Silent-**e** Rule?
   A. *she*
   B. *her*
   C. *safe*

   "Calmly and surely, she spent what could have been her last seconds on Earth promising her little girl that she would always be safe in her mother's love." (Paragraph 14)

Discussion Questions

1. The author states that she learned of a "love that is stronger than terror." Do you think love is always stronger than terror? Or was the event the author describes just an unusual incident?

2. The pilot of the aircraft tells the passengers exactly what is happening, saying, for example, "we are not sure our landing gear will lock" and "we are dumping fuel from our fuel tanks. We want to have as little on board as possible in the event of a rough touchdown." Should the pilot have been so open with his passengers, who were then struck with fear, or should he have said nothing and concentrated on flying the plane? Why?

3. In your opinion, what is the strongest love that exists? The love of a parent for a child? What about love for a parent? Or for a spouse? Is all love the same?

Note: Writing assignments for this selection appear on page 556.

Check Your Performance   **PHONICS II: VOWELS**

Activity	Number Right	Points	Score
Review Test 1 (4 items)	_____	× 5 =	_____
Review Test 2 (20 items)	_____	× 2 =	_____
Review Test 3 (10 items)	_____	× 4 =	_____
	TOTAL SCORE	=	_____ %

Enter your total score into the **Reading Performance Chart: Review Tests** on the inside back cover.

VOWELS: Mastery Test 1

A. For each item below, write a word with the vowel sound shown. Choose from the words in the box; use each word once.

cute	grant	not	rope	skip
slide	stage	stun	tent	three

1. Short **a** sound: _____

2. Long **a** sound: _____

3. Short **e** sound: _____

4. Long **e** sound: _____

5. Short **i** sound: _____

6. Long **i** sound: _____

7. Short **o** sound: _____

8. Long **o** sound: _____

9. Short **u** sound: _____

10. Long **u** sound: _____

B. Here are the rules for long vowel sounds:

Silent **e:** When a word or syllable ends with vowel-consonant-**e**, the vowel before the consonant is long and the final **e** is silent.

Two vowels together: When two of certain vowels are together, the first vowel is long and the second is silent.

Final single vowel: A single vowel at the end of a word or syllable (other than a silent **e**) usually has a long sound.

Beside each word, write the name of the rule that applies: Silent **e**, Two Vowels Together, or Final Single Vowel. In the second space, write a short explanation of the rule. Note the example.

Example

boat	*Two Vowels Together*	*The **o** is long, and the **a** is silent.*
11. hope	_____	_____
12. she	_____	_____
13. neat	_____	_____
14. cane	_____	_____
15. goal	_____	_____

(Continues on next page)

C. Here are the rules for **y** as a vowel:

Sounds of y

> *Short-***i** *sound:* In the middle of a word or syllable, **y** usually sounds like short **i**.
>
> *Long-***i** *sound:* At the end of a one-syllable word, **y** sounds like long **i**.
>
> *Long-***e** *sound:* At the end of a word with more than one syllable, **y** usually sounds like long **e**.

Beside each word, identify the **y** sound by writing in one of the following:

    ĭ (short **i**)   ī (long **i**)   ē (long **e**).

In the second space, write a short explanation of the rule that applies. Note the example.

Example

    empty   __ē__   _At end of word with more than one syllable_

16. fly   _____   _____

17. happy   _____   _____

18. mystic   _____   _____

19. try   _____   _____

20. worry   _____   _____

VOWELS : Mastery Test 2

A. Beside each word, write its vowel sound.

- If the vowel is short, write ă, ĕ, ĭ, ŏ, or ŭ.
- If the vowel is long, write ā, ē, ī, ō, or ū.
- If the vowel is followed by **r**, write **r**.

1. bleed _____   6 hot _____

2. trick _____   7. stay _____

3. park _____   8. write _____

4. check _____   9. cute _____

5. stump _____   10. fork _____

B. Complete each sentence by filling in the word with a **short** vowel sound. Remember that a vowel followed by **r** is neither long nor short.

11. When a dog relaxes, usually its tail wags and its ears *(drape, droop, drop)*

_____ .

12. Many students find that a term paper takes as many as *(four, five, ten)*

_____ hours longer than they expected.

13. The fifty-year-old maple tree in the back yard is full of *(sap, leaves, life)*

_____ .

14. On weekends, some people unwind by taking a long *(drive, run, hike)*

_____ in the country.

15. A glass window pane and a(n) *(oak, steel, brick)* _____ wall are made with the same main ingredient: sand.

(Continues on next page)

C. Here are the rules for long vowel sounds:

> *Silent* **e:** When a word or syllable ends with vowel-consonant-**e**, the vowel before the consonant is long and the final **e** is silent.
>
> *Two vowels together:* When two of certain vowels are together, the first vowel is long and the second is silent.
>
> *Final single vowel:* A single vowel at the end of a word or syllable (other than a silent **e**) usually has a long sound.

Use the rules to help you write the words below in the right spaces.

hi	snake	soap
treat	wrote	

	Silent-e rule	*Two-vowels-together rule*	*Final vowel rule*
16.	_____	18. _____	20. _____
17.	_____	19. _____	

D. Use a check (✓) to indicate whether the **oo** in each word is long or short.

	Long **oo**	*Short* **oo**
21. room	_____	_____
22. crook	_____	_____
23. noon	_____	_____
24. stood	_____	_____
25. proof	_____	_____

VOWELS : Mastery Test 3

A. Circle each word in the box that contains a *short* vowel sound. The words appear either straight across or straight down. Then write each word under the correct heading.

Here are the words to look for:

add	bench	chin	flat	nun
plod	quilt	clock	smell	stuff

s	t	u	f	f	t	f	l	y
m	e	a	d	l	y	k	n	o
e	a	p	o	a	d	d	u	u
l	k	l	w	t	o	w	n	r
l	o	o	n	s	d	u	s	b
o	a	d	c	l	o	c	k	e
c	a	s	e	e	o	z	i	n
n	o	c	h	i	n	i	k	c
q	u	i	l	t	b	e	e	h

Short a	*Short e*	*Short i*	*Short o*	*Short u*
1._____	3._____	5._____	7._____	9._____
2._____	4._____	6._____	8._____	10._____

B. Complete each sentence below by filling in the word that has a *long* vowel sound. (Remember that a vowel followed by **r** is neither long nor short.)

11. The tune-up on my car at Harry's Rapid Service Shop was *(fast, quick, speedy)* _____ but poorly done.

12. After being out in the cold, *(Jill, Jake, Jack)* _____ looked forward to a hot cup of cocoa.

(Continues on next page)

13. After a rain, children like to *(push, float, sink)* _____ paper boats in sidewalk puddles.

14. A college assignment that at first seems *(easy, dumb, effortless)* _____ can in fact be very challenging and useful.

15. If you *(put, install, place)* _____ a special radio signal in your car, the police can trace the car if it's stolen.

C. Use a check (✓) to indicate whether the **y** in each word sounds like ĭ, ī, or ē.

	Short i	*Long i*	*Long e*
16. holy	_____	_____	_____
17. spy	_____	_____	_____
18. symbol	_____	_____	_____
19. funny	_____	_____	_____
20. cry	_____	_____	_____

D. Find the five words with **oo** in the paragraph below. Write the words in the blank spaces at the left, and use a check (✓) to show whether each **oo** has a long or short sound.

If you are looking for a new apartment, remember that each place has drawbacks as well as pluses. For instance, the apartment may be in a great location or have a terrific view. But you must pay attention to details. Make sure that the bed you have will fit in the bedroom. Is the bath area large enough, or is it so small that you will have trouble finding space for toothpaste and shampoo? And make sure that you won't need to buy a set of tools to repair the place.

	Long **oo**	*Short* **oo**
21. _____	_____	_____
22. _____	_____	_____
23. _____	_____	_____
24. _____	_____	_____
25. _____	_____	_____

VOWELS : Mastery Test 4

A. Circle each word in the box that contains a ***long*** vowel sound. The words appear either straight across or straight down. Then write each word under the correct heading.

Here are the words to look for:

boat	cheese	claim	cute	glide
stain	sweet	toast	use	wise

s	s	w	e	e	t	g	w	c
s	f	e	w	k	r	l	i	h
t	o	n	v	y	w	i	s	e
a	p	t	c	a	n	d	k	e
i	b	p	l	q	n	e	v	s
n	o	n	a	n	u	s	e	e
q	a	c	i	l	i	t	x	n
r	t	o	m	o	c	u	t	e
y	d	t	o	a	s	t	o	n

Long a	*Long e*	*Long i*	*Long o*	*Long u*
1._____	3._____	5._____	7._____	9._____
2._____	4._____	6._____	8._____	10._____

B. Complete each sentence below by filling in the word that has a ***short*** vowel sound. (Remember that a vowel followed by **r** is neither long nor short.)

11. If you water your plants too much or too little, they are likely to *(die, wilt, droop)* _____.

12. Enrique was not looking forward to spending two weeks with his aunt in *(New York, Montana, Ohio)* _____.

(Continues on next page)

13. Heart disease accounts for one *(half, third, fourth)* _____ of all American deaths each year.

14. I turned to tell my *(wife, date, sister)* _____ that I thought the play was boring, but she was already asleep.

15. Children learning to tell directions on a map sometimes use the rhyme, "If you want to go *(north, west, east)* _____, left is best."

C. Here are the rules for long vowel sounds:

> *Silent* **e:** When a word or syllable ends with vowel-consonant-**e**, the vowel before the consonant is long and the final **e** is silent.
>
> *Two vowels together:* When two of certain vowels are together, the first vowel is long and the second is silent.
>
> *Final single vowel:* A single vowel at the end of a word or syllable (other than a silent **e**) usually has a long sound.

Beside each word, write the name of the rule that applies: Silent **e**, Two Vowels Together, or Final Single Vowel.

16. beef   _____   21. grime   _____

17. shape   _____   22. we   _____

18. no   _____   23. slope   _____

19. bail   _____   24. train   _____

20. cream   _____   25. loaf   _____

VOWELS : Mastery Test 5

A. Complete each sentence by writing in the word with a **short** vowel sound. Remember that a vowel followed by **r** is neither long nor short.

1. Sharri's *(apple, peach, lime)* _____ tree bore so much fruit that she gave much of it away.

2. The newspaper carried a story about a 90-year-old woman who still *(swims, bikes, skates)* _____ every day.

3. Amad keeps a spare key *(below, near, under)* _____ a big rock by his back door.

4. A triathlon consists of three *(parts, events, sports)* _____: a swim, a bike ride, and a run.

5. Despite the best efforts of firefighters, the fire continued to *(burn, expand, blaze)* _____.

B. Complete each sentence by writing in the word that has a **long** vowel sound. Remember that a vowel followed by **r** is neither long nor short.

Then, using the rules for long vowel sounds below, write the letter of the rule the word follows: Silent e, Two Vowels Together, or Final Single Vowel.

Here are the rules for long vowel sounds:

Silent **e:** When a word or syllable ends with vowel-consonant-**e**, the vowel before the consonant is long and the final **e** is silent.

Two vowels together: When two of certain vowels are together, the first vowel is long and the second is silent.

Final single vowel: A single vowel at the end of a word or syllable (other than a silent **e**) usually has a long sound.

6. Although gorillas look as if they could kill anything they touch, they are usually very *(calm, gentle, peaceful)* _____ creatures.

_____ 7. The word you chose follows this rule:
   A. Silent **e**   B. Two Vowels Together   C. Final Single Vowel

(Continues on next page)

8. The way Mimi remembers a phone number is to repeat it *(six, nine, ten)* _____ times.

_____ 9. The word you chose follows this rule:
A. Silent **e**   B. Two Vowels Together   C. Final Single Vowel

10. When it started raining hard, Teresa began to *(race, dash, run)* _____ across the parking lot to her car.

_____11. The word you chose follows this rule:
A. Silent **e**   B. Two Vowels Together   C. Final Single Vowel

12. Scientists continue to *(goad, prod, urge)* _____ us to eat breakfast, as it is considered the most important meal of the day.

_____13. The word you chose follows this rule:
A. Silent **e**   B. Two Vowels Together   C. Final Single Vowel

14. A man at the toy store was showing how to use a new *(ball, yo-yo, truck)* _____.

_____15. The word you chose follows this rule:
A. Silent **e**   B. Two Vowels Together   C. Final Single Vowel

C. Complete the following sentence by filling in the word that has a **y** which sounds like a short **i**.

16. Many scientists believe that tales of the hairy humanlike creature called Bigfoot are just *(myths, fantasy, yarns)* _____.

D. Complete each sentence with the word that has a **y** which sounds like a long **i**.

17. Willy's *(tricky, sly, sneaky)* _____ ways got him into trouble with his family and friends.

18. The weather report called for continued *(cloudy, dry, foggy)* _____ conditions.

E. Complete each sentence with the word that has a **y** which sounds like a long **e**.

19. When Juan asked for the keys to the car, his father answered, "*(Yes, Maybe, Surely)* _____."

20. Ever since my little brother got a toy drum, he wants to *(carry, play, try)* _____ it all day long.

VOWELS : Mastery Test 6

A. Fill in each blank with the word that has a *short* vowel sound.

Most owls nest in trees and come out at night to (1. *eat, fly, hunt*) _____. An exception is the burrowing owl. This (2. *little, tiny, wee*) _____ owl is only about (3. *six, eight, nine*) _____ inches high. As its name suggests, it nests underground. This owl hunts during the day and can be seen sitting on fence posts near its (4. *home, mate, nest*) _____. Once common throughout the Southwest, the burrowing owl is in danger of extinction, mostly because of (5. *huge, large, vast*) _____ development projects.

B. In the following paragraph, ten words are boldfaced. Each word fits under one of the headings below. Write the words in the appropriate spaces.

Where would **we** be without the **fish** in the sea? Half of the world's population depends on fish as its **main** source of food. **Yet** there are danger signs that the oceans are being overfished. Four of the richest fishing areas of the **world** include the west **coast** of Australia, the **west** coast of South America, the Mediterranean Sea, and the **east** coast of Asia. In the past **five** years, the fish catch in each of **these** areas has declined significantly.

Silent-e rule	*Two-vowels-together rule*	*Final vowel rule*
6. _____	8. _____	11. _____
7. _____	9. _____	
	10. _____	

Short vowel rule	*Vowel followed by* **r**
12. _____	15. _____
13. _____	
14. _____	

(Continues on next page)

C. Find the five words with **oo** in the paragraph below. Write the words in the blank spaces on the left, and use a check (✓) to show whether each **oo** has a long or short sound.

      The hot summer day was too much for Sal. Rather than stay around the house and watch TV all day, he thought it might be nice to take the family on a picnic. "We'll pick up some food on the way and go to the park," he said. "Maybe I'll do some fishing." Sal's wife, Diana, loved the idea. The last thing they wanted to do was cook in a hot kitchen. And the kids liked the idea as well. At the park, Sal Jr. got into a touch football game. Daughter Darlene sat beneath a large oak tree, reading a mystery novel. And Sal—well, he fell asleep in the sun before he even baited his hook.

		Long **oo**	*Short* **oo**
16.	_____	_____	_____
17.	_____	_____	_____
18.	_____	_____	_____
19.	_____	_____	_____
20.	_____	_____	_____

3

Phonics III: Syllables

THIS CHAPTER IN A NUTSHELL

- This chapter reminds you what a syllable is.
- It then provides five rules that help you break words into syllables:
    1 Divide between two consonants.
    2 Divide before a single consonant.
    3 Divide before a consonant + **le**.
    4 Divide after prefixes and before suffixes.
    5 Divide between the words in a compound word.

To pronounce long words that are unfamiliar to you, you should first separate them into parts called *syllables*. Five rules in this chapter will help you divide words into syllables. You can then focus on pronouncing each syllable and go on to read the entire word.

SYLLABLES

A **syllable** is a word or part of a word that has only one vowel sound. This vowel sound is spoken together with any consonant sounds in the syllable.

For example, the word *rip* has just one vowel sound, so it has only one syllable. The sounds of **r**, short **i**, and **p** are all spoken together. The word *fast* also has only one vowel sound. The sounds of **f**, short **a**, and the consonant blend **st** are all spoken together.

A word with more than one syllable is pronounced in parts. For example, *sunscreen* is pronounced in two parts, each with its own vowel sound: *sun* and *screen*. The vowel sound in the first syllable is short **u**, so the sounds of **s**, short

u, and **n** are all spoken together. The second syllable starts with the consonant blend **scr**, then has a long **e** vowel sound, then the single consonant **n**. By separating a word into its syllables, you can use phonics rules to pronounce each syllable correctly. Then you can put the syllables together for the right pronunciation of the word.

Some one-, two-, and three-syllable words are listed below. Say each word to yourself. Notice the single vowel sound in each syllable. Also note any consonant sounds that are spoken with the vowel.

One-syllable words	Two-syllable words	Three-syllable words
go	kindness	happily
I	golden	Superman
fun	moral	upbringing
stand	confess	president
Fred	happy	syllable

Now, in the blank spaces below, write each of the following words under the correct heading:

brother	clock	dishonest
grandparent	lunch	market

One-syllable words	Two-syllable words	Three-syllable words
_____	_____	_____
_____	_____	_____

You should have added *clock* and *lunch* to the one-syllable list, *brother* and *market* to the two-syllable list, and *grandparent* and *dishonest* to the three-syllable list.

Words with More Than One Vowel in a Syllable

In the lists above, each syllable contains just one vowel with one vowel sound. However, some words and syllables have *two* vowels but only *one* vowel sound. They include the following:

1 Words with a silent final e

Here are some words in which the final **e** is silent.

Eve	rose	same	tune	write

Each word has two vowels but only one vowel sound. In each case, the final **e** is silent. Since each word has only one vowel *sound,* each is a one-syllable word.

(As you learned in Chapter 2, when a word ends with vowel-consonant-e, the vowel before the consonant is long and the final **e** is silent.)

2 Words with two vowels together in which one vowel is silent

Here are some examples of words with this pattern:

pair	play	heat	breed	pie
soap	toe			

Each word has two vowels together but only one vowel sound. In each case, the second vowel is silent. Since each word has only one vowel *sound,* each is a one-syllable word. (As you learned in Chapter 2, when two of certain vowels are together, the first one is long, and the second is silent.)

➤ *Practice 1*

Fill in the blank spaces below. Note the examples.

	Number of vowels	Number of vowel sounds	Number of syllables
Examples:			
silent	2	2	2
ride	2	1	1
1. boat			
2. doe			
3. cane			
4. heel			
5. among			
6. chair			
7. however			
8. least			
9. freezing			
10. amuse			

FIVE RULES FOR DIVIDING WORDS INTO SYLLABLES

You have learned that each syllable has one vowel sound. That knowledge and the following rules will help you divide words into syllables. There are exceptions, but the rules can be followed much of the time.

Dividing between Two Consonants

Rule 1: **When two consonants come between two vowels, divide between the consonants.**

This rule is also known as the VC/CV (vowel-consonant/consonant-vowel) pattern. Here are examples of words divided according to rule 1:

donkey: don-key   happen: hap-pen   silver: sil-ver

To break each word into syllables, divide between the consonants: between **n** and **k** in *donkey,* between **p** and **p** in *happen,* and between **l** and **v** in *silver.*

☑ *Check Your Understanding*

According to the VC/CV rule, where would you divide the following words? Draw a line between the syllables.

hostage   import   tunnel

The correct divisions for these words are *hos-tage, im-port,* and *tun-nel.*

Pronunciation tip: A vowel before two consonants usually has a short sound. For example, the **o** in *hostage,* the **i** in *import,* and the **u** in *tunnel* each have a short sound. (As you learned in Chapter 2, when a word or syllable has one vowel followed by one or more consonants, the vowel is usually short.)

➤ *Practice 2*

Break the following words into syllables by dividing between two consonants (VC/CV). Note the example.

Example: arrest   _____*ar-rest*_____

1. candy   _____

2. napkin   _____

3. harbor   _____

4. trumpet   _____

5. muffin   _____

Dividing between Three Consonants

At times a word will have three consonants in a row, as in these examples:

applaud   monster   surprise

In such cases, you usually divide between the first consonant and the second two, as shown below:

ap-plaud   mon-ster   sur-prise

The second and third consonants form a **consonant blend**—two or more consonants that keep their sounds but are spoken together.

➤ *Practice 3*

Break each of the following words into syllables by dividing between a consonant and a consonant blend. Note the example.

Example: displace   _____*dis-place*_____

1. central   _____

2. address   _____

3. complete   _____

4. attract   _____

5. obscure   _____

Dividing before a Single Consonant

> *Rule 2:* **When a single consonant comes between two vowel sounds, divide before the consonant.**

This rule is also known as the V/CV (vowel/consonant-vowel) pattern. Here are examples of words that are divided according to rule 2:

      even: e-ven   minus: mi-nus   pony: po-ny

To break each word into syllables, divide before the single consonant: between the **e** and **v** in *even*, between the **i** and **n** in *minus*, and between the **o** and **n** in *pony*.

☑ Check Your Understanding

According to the V/CV rule, where would you divide the following words? Draw a line between the syllables.

      baby   female   moment

The correct divisions for these words are *ba-by, fe-male,* and *mo-ment.*

Pronunciation tip: A vowel before a single consonant division often has a long sound. For example, the **a** in *baby,* the first **e** in *female,* and the **o** in *moment* all have long sounds. (As you learned in Chapter 2, when a single vowel other than silent **e** ends a word or syllable, the vowel is usually long.)

➤ Practice 4

Break each of the following words into syllables by dividing before the single consonant (V/CV). Note the example.

    Example: cater   *ca-ter*_____

    1. bonus   _____

    2. item   _____

    3. final   _____

    4. major   _____

    5. unit   _____

Dividing before a Consonant + *le*

> **Rule 3: If a word ends in a consonant followed by *le*, the consonant and *le* form the last syllable.**

The words below are divided according to this rule.

handle: han-dle   cable: ca-ble   simple: sim-ple

According to the consonant + **le** rule, where would you divide the following words? Draw a line between the syllables.

ankle   circle   middle

The correct divisions for these words are *an-kle, cir-cle*, and *mid-dle.*

➤ Practice 5

Break the following words into syllables by dividing before the consonant + **le**. Note the example.

Example: table   _____ *ta-ble* _____

1. idle   _____

2. ripple   _____

3. purple   _____

4. title   _____

5. gargle   _____

Dividing after Prefixes and before Suffixes

> **Rule 4: Prefixes and suffixes are usually separate syllables.**

Prefixes are word parts that are added to the beginnings of words. Here are some common prefixes:

ad-	com-	con-	de-	dis-	ex-
in-	non-	pre-	re-	sub-	un-

Suffixes are word parts that are added to the ends of words. Here are some common suffixes:

-able	-en	-er	-ful	-ing	-ist
-less	-ly	-ment	-ness	-sion	-tion

Below are examples of words divided according to rule 4.

prefix: pre-fix   unfair: un-fair   player: play-er   statement: state-ment

The divisions above are made after the prefixes (*pre-* and *un-*) and before the suffixes (*-er* and *-ment*).

According to the rule for prefixes and suffixes, where would you divide the following words? Draw a line between the syllables.

holding   compete   cheapen   racist

The correct divisions for these words are *hold-ing, com-pete, cheap-en,* and *rac-ist.*

➤ Practice 6

Break the following words into syllables by dividing after a prefix or before a suffix. Note the example.

Example: preview   *pre-view*

1. mission   _____

2. advice   _____

3. unbend   _____

4. playful   _____

5. export   _____

6. nation   _____

7. mindless   _____

8. consist   _____

9. react   _____

10. disease   _____

The Suffix -*ed*

The suffix -*ed* is a separate syllable only when it follows **d** or **t**, as in the following examples.

ended: end-ed   molded: mold-ed   dented: dent-ed   quilted: quilt-ed

Otherwise, -*ed* is not a separate syllable. It is the end of a syllable.

played: played   happened: hap-pened   wondered: won-dered

In *played,* -*ed* does not follow **d** or **t**, so it is not a separate syllable; *played* is a one-syllable word. In *happened* and *wondered,* -*ed* also does not follow a **d** or **t**. So in each of those words, it is the end of a syllable, not a separate syllable.

➤ *Practice 7*

Indicate with a check (✓) whether the -*ed* in each word is a separate syllable or not. Note the example.

	Separate syllable	*Not a separate syllable*
Example: pleased	_____	___✓___

(In *pleased,* -*ed* does not follow **d** or **t**, so it is not a separate syllable.)

	Separate syllable	*Not a separate syllable*
1. parted	_____	_____
2. boxed	_____	_____
3. lived	_____	_____
4. minded	_____	_____
5. rested	_____	_____

Dividing between the Words in a Compound Word

> *Rule 5:* Compound words are always divided between the words they contain.

A **compound word** is a combination of two words. When compound words are broken into syllables, they are always divided between the words they contain. Here are examples:

bloodstream: blood-stream   goldfish: gold-fish   ringside: ring-side

According to the rule for compound words, where would you divide the following words? Draw a line between the syllables.

breakfast   railroad   redhead

The correct divisions for these words are *break-fast, rail-road,* and *red-head.*

➤ Practice 8

Break the following words into syllables by dividing between the words they contain. Note the example.

Example: southeast   _____*south-east*_____

1. notebook   _____

2. raincoat   _____

3. popcorn   _____

4. workshop   _____

5. seashell   _____

A Final Note

Although there are exceptions to the rules in this chapter, the rules will usually help you divide a word into syllables. Then, to sound out each syllable, you can apply the phonics principles you learned in Chapters 1 and 2.

If you are in doubt about how to pronounce a word, you can turn to the dictionary. In Part II, Chapter 2, "Dictionary Use," you will learn how to use dictionary symbols to pronounce words.

CHAPTER REVIEW

In this chapter, you learned the following:

- A **syllable** is a word or part of a word that has only one vowel sound. So to figure out the number of syllables in a word, count the number of vowel *sounds*. Some vowels are silent, including the following:
  — Silent **e**: ros**e**

  — The second letter of certain vowel pairs: p**ai**r, pl**ay,** h**ea**t, br**ee**d, p**ie**, s**oa**p, t**oe**

- Five rules can help you divide words into syllables:
  — *Rule 1 (VC/CV):* When two consonants come between two vowels, divide between the consonants: sil-**v**er.

    If a word has three consonants in a row, divide between the first consonant and the consonant blend: mo**n-st**er.

  — *Rule 2 (V/CV):* When a single consonant comes between two vowel sounds, divide before the consonant: po-**ny**.

  — *Rule 3:* If a word ends in a consonant followed by **le**, the consonant and **le** form the last syllable: han-**dle**.

  — *Rule 4:* Prefixes and suffixes are usually separate syllables: **un**-fair, play-**er**.

  — *Rule 5:* Compound words are always divided between the words they contain: **gold-fish**.

On the Web: If you are using this book in class, you can visit our website for additional practice with dividing words into syllables. Go to **www.townsendpress.com** and click on "Online Exercises."

➤ Review Test 1

To review what you have learned in this chapter, answer each of the following questions. Write the letter of the correct answer in the space provided.

_____ 1. TRUE OR FALSE? A syllable is a word or part of a word that contains only one vowel sound.

_____ 2. When two consonants come between two vowels, divide
A. before the two consonants.
B. between the two consonants.
C. after the two consonants.

_____ 3. When a single consonant comes between two vowel sounds,
A. divide before the consonant.
B. divide after the consonant.
C. both vowel sounds will usually be long.

_____ 4. TRUE OR FALSE? Prefixes and suffixes are usually separate syllables.

➤ Review Test 2

A. Using the rules shown in the box, divide the following words into syllables. For each word, also write the number of the rule that applies. The first one has been done for you.

> **Rule 1. Divide between two consonants.**
> **Rule 2. Divide before a single consonant.**

	Syllable division	Rule numbers
1. pencil	*pen-cil*	*1*
2. system		
3. focus		
4. comment		
5. music		
6. silent		
7. lecture		

8. important _____ _____ _____

9. privacy _____ _____ _____

10. attorney _____ _____ _____

B. Using the rules shown in the box, divide the words below into syllables. For each word, also write the number of the rule that applies. The first one has been done for you.

> **Rule 3. Divide before a consonant followed by *le*.**
> **Rule 4. Divide after prefixes and before suffixes.**
> **Rule 5. Divide between the words in a compound word.**

	Syllable division	*Rule numbers*	
11. footstep	*foot-step*	5	
12. payment	_____	_____	
13. sample	_____	_____	
14. sailboat	_____	_____	
15. trouble	_____	_____	
16. joyful	_____	_____	
17. bottle	_____	_____	
18. replacement	_____	_____	_____
19. nonsmoker	_____	_____	_____
20. disable	_____	_____	_____

➤ *Review Test 3*

Here is a chance to apply your understanding of syllables to a full-length reading. This selection explains that other people can help keep us healthy. How do we know this is true? Vicky Chan offers some interesting evidence. After reading this selection, answer the questions that follow about syllables and other phonics topics.

Words to Watch

Following are some words in the reading that do not have strong context support. Each word is followed by the number of the paragraph in which it appears and its meaning there. These words are indicated in the reading by a small circle (°).

> *subjects* (2): people being studied in an experiment
> *tend* (5): are likely
> *responsive* (5): reacting easily
> *abrupt* (9): sudden

FRIENDSHIP AND LIVING LONGER

Vicky Chan

1   Do you want to be healthier and live longer? Spend time with your friends. That is the advice given by several medical studies. These surveys show that people with strong social ties—to friends, family, and loved ones, even to pets—live longer and enjoy better health than lonely people.

2   One study in California, for example, followed 7,000 people over a period of nine years. The subjects° were asked to describe their social ties. Some said that they were isolated from others. These subjects had death rates two or three times higher than people with families and friends.

3   The stronger the social ties to others, the study found, the lower the death rate. This pattern held true for men and women, young and old, rich and poor. The race of the subject did not change the result. It also applied to people with different lifestyles. Cigarette smokers who had friends lived longer than friendless smokers. Joggers involved with other people lived longer than joggers who lived isolated lives.

4   Another study supports this result. The University of Michigan looked at 2,754 adults in a town in Michigan. The researchers carefully measured their

subjects' health at the beginning of the study. The lonely, isolated people started out as healthy as the others. But over ten years, they were two to four times as likely to die.

5   Other findings also show the health value of personal ties. Married men and women tend° to live longer than single, divorced, or widowed people of the same age. In nursing homes, patients became more aware and responsive° when they played with cats and dogs. Pet owners are more likely to survive heart attacks than people without pets.

6   Another kind of proof that social ties support good health comes from Japan. Most Japanese people live lives in cities as crowded, noisy, and polluted as ours. Such a way of life seems unhealthy. Yet the Japanese are among the healthiest and longest-lived people in the world. One reason may be their diet. Another reason, though, is their way of life. Japanese° have strong ties to family and coworkers. These ties are rarely broken. For example, companies tend to move coworkers as a group, rather than one at a time. Thus the work groups remain the same.

7   Studies of Japanese-Americans support the importance of the role of Japanese social life in good health. Japanese-Americans who live in strongly Japanese neighborhoods and have mainly Japanese friends tend to live longer than those who do not. Both groups eat mostly American-style food, and many in both groups smoke and drink. Thus it appears to be the strong social ties of Japanese communities that keep their members healthy.

8   Why is it more healthy to have friends and loved ones? We don't know, exactly. But there are probably several reasons. In part, people with strong social ties may simply have more to live for. They have loved ones or family who share their lives. They have friends who call them and ask them how they're doing. They have get-togethers to look forward to.

9   Social contacts also protect us from the shocks of life. At some point, each of us moves, changes a job, or loses a loved one. Such abrupt° changes tend to cause increases in the rates of many diseases. These include heart disease, cancer, strokes, and mental illnesses. Accidents are also more likely to happen to people whose lives have suddenly changed. Friends, loved ones, even a loyal dog can help us to get through the otherwise very rough changes that we must deal with in life.

10   Finally, friends and loved ones can affect our health in still another way. If we are smokers, they may help us to quit. If we overeat, they may urge us to cut back. They can remind us to go for medical checkups. And if we have fears or sadnesses deep inside us, friends can help us face and overcome them. By caring for us, in other words, friends and family help us to care for ourselves.

11   Close human ties make life not only fuller, but also longer. Caring for others, and being cared for by them, is a more healthy way to live.

Phonics Questions

Use phonics clues you learned from chapters 1–3 to answer the following questions. In the space provided, write the letter of your choice for each question.

_____ 1. The word *change*, used in the sentence below, contains a
    A. soft **c** sound.
    B. hard **c** sound.
    C. consonant digraph.

      "The race of the subject did not change the result." (Paragraph 3)

_____ 2. The word *another*, used in the sentence below, contains
    A. a consonant digraph.
    B. a consonant blend.
    C. both a digraph and a blend.

      "Another study supports this result." (Paragraph 4)

_____ 3. The word *years*, used in the sentence below, contains a
    A. short vowel sound.
    B. long vowel sound.

      "But over ten years, they were two to four times as likely to die." (Paragraph 4)

_____ 4. The word *remain,* used in the sentence below, contains
    A. two short vowel sounds.
    B. two long vowel sounds.
    C. one short vowel sound and one long vowel sound.

      "Thus the work groups remain the same." (Paragraph 6)

_____ 5. The *y* in the word *why*, used in the sentence below, sounds like a
    A. short **i**.
    B. long **i**.
    C. long **e**.

      "Why is it more healthy to have friends and loved ones?" (Paragraph 8)

_____ 6. The word *polluted*, used in the sentence below, contains
   A. one syllable.
   B. two syllables.
   C. three syllables.

   "Most Japanese people live lives in cities as crowded, noisy, and polluted as ours." (Paragraph 6)

_____ 7. The word *forward*, used in the sentence below, is broken into syllables as follows:
   A. forw-ard.
   B. for-ward.
   C. fo-rw-ard.

   "They have get-togethers to look forward to." (Paragraph 8)

_____ 8. The word *protect*, used in the sentence below, is broken into syllables as follows:
   A. pro-tect.
   B. prot-ect.
   C. pro-te-ct.

   "Social contacts also protect us from the shocks of life." (Paragraph 9)

_____ 9. The word *suddenly*, used in the sentence below, is broken into syllables as follows:
   A. sudden-ly.
   B. sudd-en-ly.
   C. sud-den-ly.

   "Accidents are also more likely to happen to people whose lives have suddenly changed." (Paragraph 9)

_____ 10. The word *overcome*, used in the sentence below, is broken in syllables as follows:
   A. ov-er-come.
   B. o-ver-come.
   C. over-come.

   "And if we have fears or sadnesses bottled up inside us, friends can help us face and overcome them." (Paragraph 10)

Discussion Questions

1. Do you agree that "social contacts . . . protect us from the shocks of life"? If so, what do you think are some of the ways these contacts keep us from feeling pain? Give an example.

2. Why do you think playing with cats and dogs helps people in nursing homes? Is there something the animals do for patients that doctors and nurses cannot?

3. How can people who have trouble making friends cope with crisis? In what ways could they form social ties?

Note: Writing assignments for this selection appear on page 556–557.

Check Your Performance   **PHONICS III: SYLLABLES**

Activity	Number Right	Points	Score
Review Test 1 (4 items)	_____	× 5 =	_____
Review Test 2 (20 items)	_____	× 2 =	_____
Review Test 3 (10 items)	_____	× 4 =	_____
	TOTAL SCORE	=	_____ %

Enter your total score into the **Reading Performance Chart: Review Tests** on the inside back cover.

SYLLABLES: Mastery Test 1

A. Using the rules shown in the box, divide the following words into syllables. For each word, also write the number of the rule that applies. Note the example.

> **Rule 1. Divide between two consonants.**
> **Rule 2. Divide before a single consonant.**

	Syllable division	Rule number
Example: divide	di-vide	2
1. forward		
2. occur		
3. motive		
4. welcome		
5. unite		
6. soda		

B. Using the rules shown in the box, divide the words below into syllables. For each word, also write the number of the rule that applies. Note the example.

> **Rule 3. Divide before a consonant followed by *le*.**
> **Rule 4. Divide after prefixes and before suffixes.**
> **Rule 5. Divide between the words in a compound word.**

	Syllable division	Rule number
Example: moonlight	moon-light	5
7. cripple		
8. gladly		
9. hallway		
10. distrust		
11. puzzle		
12. cloudburst		
13. goodness		

(Continues on next page)

C. Complete each sentence by underlining the compound word. Then, in the space provided, divide the compound word into syllables.

14. Kenny's first stop in registering for classes was _____ the school (*fieldhouse, library, gymnasium*).

15. Studies show that single men are more likely _____ than married men to have an emotional (*disorder, breakdown, collapse*).

16. Jogging is considered good exercise, but _____ running on the (*grass, pavement, sidewalk*) can be hard on the feet.

17. A tidal wave begins with a (*landslide,* _____ *movement, shaking*) on the ocean floor.

D. Three words below have a prefix or suffix. In the spaces provided, write those words, dividing them into syllables.

| badly | delayed | kneepad |
| movement | statue | pilot |

18. _____   19. _____   20. _____

SYLLABLES: Mastery Test 2

A. Using the rules shown in the box, divide the following words into syllables. For each syllable break, write the number of the rule that applies. Note the example.

> **Rule 1. Divide between two consonants.**
> **Rule 2. Divide before a single consonant.**

	Syllable division	Rule numbers	
Example: abandon	a-ban-don	2	1
1. entertain	_____	_____	_____
2. diplomat	_____	_____	_____
3. absolute	_____	_____	_____
4. hibernate	_____	_____	_____
5. alcohol	_____	_____	_____
6. terminal	_____	_____	_____

B. Using the rules shown in the box, divide the following words into syllables. For each syllable break, write the number of the rule that applies. Note the example.

> **Rule 3. Divide before a consonant followed by *le*.**
> **Rule 4. Divide after prefixes and before suffixes.**
> **Rule 5. Divide between the words in a compound word.**

	Syllable division	Rule numbers	
Example: subtitle	sub-ti-tle	4	3
7. unfriendly	_____	_____	_____
8. outfielder	_____	_____	_____
9. previewing	_____	_____	_____
10. rattlesnake	_____	_____	_____
11. newlywed	_____	_____	_____
12. grandmother	_____	_____	_____
13. puzzlement	_____	_____	_____

(Continues on next page)

C. Complete each sentence by underlining the word with a prefix, a suffix, or both. Then, in the space provided, divide the underlined word into syllables.

14. I saw enough of the (*preview, plotline, story*) _____
to know that I didn't want to see the movie.

15. The letter had been (*proofread, refolded, torn*) _____
and put back into the envelope.

16. Dr. Nomo is a (*splendid, skillful, well-known*) _____
surgeon.

17. When we pay for college (*credit,* _____
instruction, coursework), we appreciate
high school's cost-free education.

D. Three words below are compound words. In the spaces provided, write those words, dividing them into syllables.

| daybreak | hundred | magnet |
| pasture | pathway | schoolroom |

18. _____   19. _____   20. _____

SYLLABLES: Mastery Test 3

A. Using the rules shown in the box, divide the following words into syllables. Then write the numbers of the two rules that apply. For each word, first use any of rules 3–5 that apply before using rule 1 or rule 2.

> **Rule 1. Divide between two consonants.**
> **Rule 2. Divide before a single consonant.**
> **Rule 3. Divide before a consonant followed by _le_.**
> **Rule 4. Divide after prefixes and before suffixes.**
> **Rule 5. Divide between the words in a compound word.**

	Syllable division	*Rule numbers*	
1. tomato	_____	_____	_____
2. incubate	_____	_____	_____
3. disconnect	_____	_____	_____
4. sincerely	_____	_____	_____
5. researcher	_____	_____	_____
6. anklebone	_____	_____	_____
7. solution	_____	_____	_____
8. belonging	_____	_____	_____
9. housekeeping	_____	_____	_____
10. photograph	_____	_____	_____

B. Complete each sentence by underlining the compound word. Then, in the space provided, divide the word into syllables.

11. When I'm hungry, I know I can find a snack   _____
    in the (*cupboard, refrigerator, pantry*).

12. The three-hundred-pound football player   _____
    had an unusual hobby for a professional
    athlete: (*needlepoint, sewing, checkers*).

(Continues on next page)

13. People in southern California fear the (*earthquakes,* _____
    tornadoes, temperatures) that are common in the area.

14. Though she was an excellent athlete, Cindy was   _____
    a(n) (*commonplace, ordinary, terrible*) student.

15. One of the most dangerous jobs is that of a (*soldier,* _____
    firefighter, skier).

C. Each word below has three syllables. Using the rules you have learned in this
chapter, write the letter of the correct way to divide each word into syllables.

Note: For each word, first use any of rules 3–5 that apply before using rule 1 or
rule 2.

_____16. unable
      A. un-a-ble   B. un-ab-le   C. u-na-ble

_____17. equipment
      A. equ-ip-ment   B. e-qui-pment   C. e-quip-ment

_____18. conviction
      A. con-vic-tion   B. conv-ict-ion   C. con-vi-ction

_____19. candlelight
      A. cand-le-light   B. can-dle-light   C. cand-lel-ight

_____20. remorseful
      A. rem-orse-ful   B. re-morse-ful   C. re-mor-seful

SYLLABLES: Mastery Test 4

A. Using the rules shown in the box, divide the following words into syllables. Then write the numbers of the two rules that apply. For each word, first use any of rules 3–5 that apply before using rule 1 or rule 2.

> **Rule 1. Divide between two consonants.**
> **Rule 2. Divide before a single consonant.**
> **Rule 3. Divide before a consonant followed by _le_.**
> **Rule 4. Divide after prefixes and before suffixes.**
> **Rule 5. Divide between the words in a compound word.**

	Syllable division	Rule numbers
1. outstanding	_____	_____ _____
2. rearrange	_____	_____ _____
3. settlement	_____	_____ _____
4. incorrect	_____	_____ _____
5. following	_____	_____ _____
6. glassmaker	_____	_____ _____
7. electron	_____	_____ _____
8. expensive	_____	_____ _____
9. handlebar	_____	_____ _____
10. pillowcase	_____	_____ _____

B. Underline the five words that end in **-le**. Then in the spaces below, divide those words into syllables.

> See if you can solve this riddle. In a terrible car accident, a father is killed and his young son seriously hurt. The boy is rushed to the hospital, where the surgeon on duty takes one look at the horrible sight and says, "I'm unable to operate on this boy. He's my son." How is this possible? The answer, of course, is this: The surgeon is the boy's mother.

11. _____   14. _____

12. _____   15. _____

13. _____   (Continues on next page)

C. Complete each sentence by underlining the word that has *both* a prefix and a suffix. Then, in the space provided, divide the word into syllables.

Note: For each word, first use rules 3–5 before applying rule 1 or rule 2.

16. After (*adjusting, changing, following*) your diet and workout schedule, you are likely to feel and look much healthier.

_____

17. As a student, try to believe in yourself. For instance, do not have a (*disbelieving, doubtful, questioning*) look on your face if your professor tells you that you have earned an A for your project.

_____

18. Raoul is a (*mechanic, designer, principal*).

_____

19. One characteristic of a good dog is its (*devotion, attachment, loyalty*) to its master.

_____

20. Experts say that most car accidents are (*awful, dangerous, preventable*).

_____

D. Each word below has either three or four syllables. Using the rules you have learned in this chapter, circle the letter of the correct way to divide each word into syllables.

Note: For each word, first use rules 3–5 before applying rule 1 or rule 2.

_____21. determined
    A. de-ter-min-ed   B. de-ter-mined   C. det-erm-in-ed

_____22. nondrinker
    A. non-drin-ker   B. nond-rin-ker   C. non-drink-er

_____23. subtraction
    A. subt-rac-tion   B. sub-tract-ion   C. sub-trac-tion

_____24. prepayment
    A. pre-pay-ment   B. prep-ay-ment   C. pre-paym-ent

_____25. favorable
    A. fav-or-ab-le   B. fa-vor-a-ble   C. fa-vor-ab-le

SYLLABLES: Mastery Test 5

A. Each word below has three syllables. Using the rules shown in the box, divide each word into syllables. Then write the number of the rule that applies to each division.

Note: For each word, first use any of rules 3–5 that apply before applying rule 1 or rule 2.

> **Rule 1. Divide between two consonants.**
> **Rule 2. Divide before a single consonant.**
> **Rule 3. Divide before a consonant followed by *le*.**
> **Rule 4. Divide after prefixes and before suffixes.**
> **Rule 5. Divide between the words in a compound word.**

	Syllable division	*Rule numbers*	
1. nonrural	_____	_____	_____
2. cheeseburger	_____	_____	_____
3. unlawful	_____	_____	_____
4. sunbonnet	_____	_____	_____
5. mountaintop	_____	_____	_____
6. flamethrower	_____	_____	_____
7. motorbike	_____	_____	_____
8. belittle	_____	_____	_____
9. opening	_____	_____	_____
10. chairperson	_____	_____	_____

(Continues on next page)

B. Complete the passage by filling in each blank with the word that has *both* a prefix and a suffix. Then, in the spaces provided below, divide the words you chose into syllables, using Rule 4.

Marta Beckett was a dancer living in New York City. In 1962, she and her husband were driving through a tiny town in Death Valley, California. Quite (11. *unexpectedly, annoyingly, surprisingly*) _____, their car broke down. There Marta (12. *found, discovered, observed*) _____ an abandoned theater. She rented the building for $45 a year and has been performing a solo show there ever since. The small town is a(n) (13. *unpromising, questionable, imperfect*) _____ place to have a theater. Sometimes, if the tourists come, she has an audience of hundreds. Sometimes there are only a handful of people watching. Sometimes there is nobody at all. But Marta never feels alone. On the walls surrounding her, she has painted an audience of smiling faces. It is (14. *unbelievable, amazing, wonderful*) _____ that Marta, now in her 80s, continues to dance for whoever cares to come. Many younger womener would find her life (15. *exhausting, tiring, fatiguing*) _____, but Marta Beckett is doing what she loves.

11. _____   14. _____

12. _____   15. _____

13. _____

C. Five words below have three syllables. In the space provided, write each word, dividing it into syllables.

Note: For each word, first use any of rules 3–5 that apply before applying rule 1 or rule 2.

If you work at a computer all day and complain of neck aches and backaches, a new exercise may help you. To relieve tension, you should do the following. First, put your arms flat on the desk. Next, rest your head on your arms. Then straighten the curve in your lower back. Stay in place for twenty seconds. Finally, lift your head. You should feel an improvement right away. Repeat this routine as needed.

16. _____   19. _____

17. _____   20. _____

18. _____

SYLLABLES: Mastery Test 6

A. Each word below has three syllables. Using the rules shown in the box, divide each word into syllables. Then write the number of the rule that applies to each division.

Note: For each word, first use any of rules 3–5 that apply before applying rule 1 or rule 2.

> **Rule 1. Divide between two consonants.**
> **Rule 2. Divide before a single consonant.**
> **Rule 3. Divide before a consonant followed by *le*.**
> **Rule 4. Divide after prefixes and before suffixes.**
> **Rule 5. Divide between the words in a compound word.**

	Syllable division	*Rule numbers*
1. principal	_____	_____ _____
2. external	_____	_____ _____
3. Eskimo	_____	_____ _____
4. revolver	_____	_____ _____
5. cannibal	_____	_____ _____
6. marketplace	_____	_____ _____
7. conviction	_____	_____ _____
8. reprimand	_____	_____ _____
9. vacancy	_____	_____ _____
10. cardholder	_____	_____ _____

(Continues on next page)

B. Complete the passage by filling in each blank with the word that has *both* a prefix and a suffix. Then, in the spaces provided below, divide the words you chose into syllables, using Rule 4.

> When people vacation, one of the most popular destinations is the island chain of Hawaii. The warm sun and gentle trade winds can melt away one's stress. Some people swear the islands are the perfect (11. *medicine, prescription, choice*) _____ for an ideal vacation. But where do the residents of Hawaii go for a (12. *relaxing, special, pleasant*) _____ time? There are several places Hawaiians go to get away from it all. One of their favored destinations may seem (13. *questionable, unlikely, strange*) _____—Las Vegas, Nevada, which has a dry, dusty climate, (14. *totally, completely, altogether*) _____ different from Hawaii's moist tropical environment. Yet many Hawaiians enjoy activities in Las Vegas, such as shows and gambling. However, the Hawaiians' favorite vacation spot is one familiar to most Americans: Disneyland.

11. _____   13. _____

12. _____   14. _____

C. Six words below have three syllables. In the space provided, write each word, dividing it into syllables.

Note: For each word, first use any of rules 3–5 that apply before applying rule 1 or rule 2.

> A revealing survey about patients' feelings toward their doctors was recently released. The results may seem surprising. Only 31 percent of patients felt that their doctors spent enough time with them. Also, 42 percent thought that their physicians were not clear when explaining their health problems. A full 63 percent felt that doctors make too much money. And 69 percent said that they had started to lose confidence in doctors.

15. _____   18. _____

16. _____   19. _____

17. _____   20. _____

4

Phonics IV: Word Parts

THIS CHAPTER IN A NUTSHELL

- This chapter will help you learn 30 common word parts that are used in many words.

- Prefixes appear at the beginning of words; roots appear anywhere in a word; and suffixes appear at the end of words.

Learning common word parts will help your pronunciation, spelling, and vocabulary. You will be able to pronounce and spell more words because you will recognize common parts used in those words. And because word parts have meanings, knowing them can help you figure out the meaning of a word you don't know.

There are three types of word parts:

1 Prefixes
2 Suffixes
3 Roots

This chapter will help you learn ten of each, thirty common word parts in all.

PREFIXES

A **prefix** is a word part that is added to the beginning of a word. When a prefix is added to a word, it changes the word's meaning. For example, the prefix *un* means "not." So when *un* is added to the word *known*, a word with the opposite meaning is formed: *unknown*.

Another prefix is *mis*, which can mean "badly." When *mis* is added to *fortune,* the resulting word is *misfortune*, which means "bad fortune." So you can see that knowing the meaning of a prefix can help you figure out the meaning of the word it is in.

Below are ten common prefixes and their meanings. Alternative forms of some prefixes are shown in parentheses. The practice that follows will help you learn these prefixes.

Prefix	Examples
ex—out, from	exit
in (**im**)—within, into; not	inside, improbable
pre—before	prepare
post—after	postgraduate
sub—below, under	submarine
super—over, above, beyond	superior
mis—badly; wrong	mislead, misunderstand
mono—one	monotony
un—not	unwanted
re—again, back	rewrite, respond

➤ Practice 1

Carefully read the meanings of each pair of prefixes. Then, in each sentence, complete the partial word (in *italics*) with the prefix that fits. Write the full word in the space provided. The first one is done for you.

    1 ex—out, from   **Example:** exit
    2 in (**im**)—within, into; not   **Examples:** inside; improbable

A. The girls at first decided to (. . . *clude*) _____*exclude*_____ Ginger from their party because they knew she would want to watch television all night.

B. The girls then voted to (. . . *clude*) _____ Ginger when she said she would bring the popcorn and chips.

C. If your driver's license has (. . . *pired*) _____, you'd better not drive until you get it renewed.

D. At the bank, many people don't want to wait for a human teller, so instead they use an (. . . *personal*) _____ bank machine.

3 pre—before   ***Example:*** prepare
4 post—after   ***Example:*** postgraduate

   A. Because lightning (. . . *cedes*) _____ thunder by several seconds, we see the flash before we hear the boom.

   B. At the end of her letter, my daughter wrote a sweet (. . . *script*) _____: "P. S. I love and admire you."

   C. The football field was flooded after the storm, so the school had to (. . . *pone*) _____ the season's first game.

   D. Many people skip over the (. . . *face*) _____ of a book and begin reading at the first chapter.

5 sub—below, under   ***Example:*** submarine
6 super—over, above, beyond   ***Example:*** superior

   A. The best thing about the (. . . *way*) _____ is that it's so fast that you don't have to stay on it long.

   B. That movie had one ghost too many; I got bored by all the (. . . *natural*) _____ events.

   C. The carpenter explained that he would have to install a (. . . *floor*) _____ before putting down the linoleum.

   D. Carla is a born (. . . *visor*) _____: she loves to watch over other people's work.

7 mis—badly; wrong   ***Examples:*** mislead; misunderstand
8 mono—one   ***Example:*** monotony

   A. Scott is so afraid of making a (. . . *take*) _____ that he never raises his hand in class.

   B. My history instructor always reads his lectures in a (. . . *tone*) _____; this single tone of voice shows that he is as bored with his lectures as his students are.

   C. (. . . *gamy*) _____ is not limited to humans. Some animals also have only one mate throughout their lives.

   D. That dog is going to (. . . *behave*) _____ unless you take him for a walk right now.

9 un—not   **Example:** unwanted
10 re—again, back   **Examples:** rewrite, respond

A. "Never (. . . *peat*) _____ yourself," my English teacher said. "Never, never, never."

B. As (. . . *likely*) _____ as it may seem, the male seahorse gives birth, carrying the eggs inside him until after they hatch.

C. After working a double shift at the hospital, Ramon was (. . . *able*) _____ to keep his eyes open during psychology class.

D. Because our electric blender makes so much noise, I've lent it to a neighbor in the hope that she'll never (. . . *turn*) _____ it.

SUFFIXES

A **suffix** is a word part that is added to the end of a word. Like prefixes, suffixes can change the meanings of words. For instance, by adding the suffix *less* (which means "without") to the word *life*, we get a word with the opposite meaning: *lifeless*.

Also, a suffix can change a word's part of speech. The suffix *ly*, for instance, can change the adjective *sad* to the adverb *sadly*.

Below are ten common suffixes and their meanings. Alternative forms of some suffixes are shown in parentheses. The practice that follows will help you learn these suffixes.

Suffix	Examples
able (**ible**)—able to be	enjoyable, edible
ion (**tion**)—state of being; act of	limitation, celebration
er (**or**)—a person who does something	dancer, mayor
ist—a person skilled at something	artist, therapist
ful—full of	joyful, suspenseful
less—without	homeless
ism—a practice; a belief or set of principles	terrorism, communism
ment—state of being	engagement
ish—similar to	foolish
ly—in a certain way; at a certain time	loudly, hourly

➤ *Practice 2*

Carefully read the meanings of each pair of suffixes. Then, in each sentence, complete the partial word (in *italics*) with the suffix that fits. Write the full word in the space provided.

11 able (ible)—able to be   ***Examples:*** enjoyable, edible
12 ion (tion)—state of being; act of   ***Examples:*** limitation, celebration

   A. If a task seems too large to handle, try to break it down into *(manage . . .)*

       _____ parts.

   B. The hunter did such a good *(imitat . . .)* _____ of a
      deer's love-call that another hunter nearly shot him.

   C. My daughter finds it *(comfort . . .)* _____ to read with
      her head hanging over the side of the bed and her book on the floor.

   D. Barb saw her high-school boyfriend at her class *(reun . . .)*

       _____, and now they are dating again.

13 er (or)—a person who does something   ***Examples:*** dancer, mayor
14 ist—a person skilled at something   ***Examples:*** artist, therapist

   A. As a *(visit . . .)* _____ to the rocket base, I had to pass
      through three security checks before seeing my first rocket.

   B. A research *(scient . . .)* _____ lives for the day he or
      she discovers something that will benefit humanity.

   C. The *(wait . . .)* _____ at Ella's Country Diner was so
      rude that I complained to the owners.

   D. Elton John is not only an outstanding showman; he is also a talented

      (pian . . .) _____.

15 ful—full of   ***Examples:*** joyful, suspenseful
16 less—without   ***Example:*** homeless

   A. On Thanksgiving everyone feels *(thank . . .)* _____ —
      except the turkey.

   B. Francisco and Susana are both so unpleasant that the world would be

      (grate . . .) _____ if they married each other.

   C. Before he smashed up his car, Jose was a *(care . . .)* _____

      driver. Since then, he drives more cautiously than anyone else I know.

   D. When I had the flu, I felt *(help . . .)* _____ —I had
      trouble moving, thinking, and breathing.

17 ism—a practice; a belief or set of principles   ***Examples:*** terrorism, communism

18 ment—state of being   ***Example:*** engagement

   A. Mr. Bell practices *(Catholic . . .)* _____, and his wife practices Judaism.

   B. After thirty years of *(imprison . . .)* _____, Eli was not sure if he could live in the real world.

   C. There was a lot of *(excite . . .)* _____ at work today—two people angrily told the boss they were quitting.

   D. Our neighborhood group helps the police deal with the problems of theft and *(vandal . . .)* _____.

19 ish—similar to   ***Example:*** foolish

20 ly—in a certain way; at a certain time   ***Examples:*** loudly, hourly

   A. Harry's *(child . . .)* _____ behavior at the party was more like that of a three-year-old than a thirty-year-old.

   B. Sharks are attracted by soft music such as waltzes, but they leave *(immediate . . .)* _____ if they hear rock music.

   C. Actor Brad Pitt's success is due in part to his *(boy . . .)* _____ smile.

   D. Phone companies look forward to Mother's Day even more *(eager . . .)* _____ than mothers do; it's the day on which the most long-distance phone calls are made.

ROOTS

A **root** is a word's basic part and carries its fundamental meaning. Sometimes two roots combine to form a word. The word *telegraph*, for example, is made up of two roots: *tele* (which means "from a distance") and *graph* (which means "write").

Prefixes and suffixes also combine with roots to make words. For instance, the prefix *pre* (meaning "before") and the root *dict* (meaning "say") form the word *predict*. And the root *aud* (meaning "hear") and the suffix *ible* (meaning "able to be") form *audible*, which means "able to be heard."

On the next page are ten common roots and their meanings. Alternative forms of some roots are shown in parentheses. The practice that follows will help you learn these roots.

Root	Examples
bene (bon)—good, well	benediction, bonus
port—carry	transport
bio—life	biology
ven (vent)—come	revenue, invent
man (manu)—hand	manage, manufacture
ped (pod)—foot	pedestal, tripod
auto—self	automatic
tele—far, over a distance	telescope
spect—look	inspect
aud (audi, audit)—hear	audience, auditorium

➤ *Practice 3*

Carefully read the meanings of each pair of roots. Then, in each sentence, complete the partial word (in *italics*) with the root that fits. Write the full word in the space provided.

21 **bene (bon)**—good, well   *Examples:* benediction, bonus
22 **port**—carry   *Example:* transport

A. I bought a (. . . *able*) _____ CD player that I can carry to the beach.

B. Jogging is supposed to be good for the body, but I don't see what's

(. . . *ficial*) _____ about blisters and muscle cramps.

C. The mass murderer was known to his neighbors as a very gentle,

(. . . *volent*) _____ man who fed leftover pizza to squirrels.

D. My duffel bag was so heavy that I asked a (. . . *er*) _____ to carry it to the airport ticket line.

23 **bio**—life   *Example:* biology
24 **ven (vent)**—come   *Examples:* revenue, invent

   A. (. . . *feedback*) _____ is a method that teaches people to control some body functions, including blood pressure.

   B. A successful *(con . . . tion)* _____ will have people come together to share their ideas.

   C. For our Fourth of July parade, people of all ages line up together on the main *(a . . . ue)* _____.

   D. Reading his (. . . *graphy*) _____, the actor remarked, "Well, I never realized I had such an exciting life."

25 **man (manu)**—hand   *Examples:* manage, manufacture
26 **ped (pod)**—foot   *Examples:* pedestal, tripod

   A. The giant organ had so many switches and keys that it required great skill to (. . . *ipulate*) _____ them all.

   B. Some (. . . *dlers*) _____ used to go from town to town on foot to sell their products.

   C. Jeri enjoys having attractive nails, so she has a (. . . *icure*) _____ twice a month.

   D. Too many drivers forget that (. . . *estrians*) _____ have the right of way in a crosswalk.

27 **auto**—self   *Example:* automatic
28 **tele**—far, over a distance   *Example:* telescope

   A. Modern technology has produced a (. . . *vision*) _____ so small that it's part of a wristwatch.

   B. It was Karl Benz of Germany, not Henry Ford, who invented the (. . . *mobile*) _____; Ford invented the assembly line.

   C. In his (. . . *biography*) _____, *Why Me?* Sammy Davis, Jr., wrote about how he had to fight racism in the early stages of his career.

   D. When my parents blamed me for our unusually high (. . . *phone*) _____ bill, I said, "Can I help it if I have so many friends?"

29 spect—look   *Example:* inspect
30 audi (audit)—hear   *Examples:* audience, auditorium

    A. In addition to books, many libraries lend various types of (. . . *o-visual*)

      _____ materials, such as language tapes and videocassettes.

    B. So many singers wanted a role in the Broadway musical that over three

      hundred showed up for the (. . . *tion*) _____.

    C. The game lasted so long that most (. . . *ators*) _____
      went home; only a few dozen people stayed to see the end.

    D. Benjamin Franklin invented the first (. . . *acles*) _____
      with two-part lenses, for seeing both near and far.

CHAPTER REVIEW

In this chapter, you learned the following:

- Learning common word parts will help your pronunciation, spelling, and vocabulary.

- There are three types of word parts:

    — Prefixes appear at the beginning of a word: ***unknown, misfortune***

    — Suffixes appear at the end of a word: *lifeless, sadly*

    — Roots can appear anywhere in a word: ***predict, audible, revenue***

On the Web: If you are using this book in class, you can visit our website for additional practice with word parts. Go to **www.townsendpress.com** and click on "Online Exercises."

➤ Review Test 1

To review what you have learned in this chapter, answer each of the following questions. Write the letter of the correct answer in the space provided.

_____ 1. The prefix *un* (as in *unlucky*) means
     A. below.
     B. not.
     C. back.

_____ 2. When a prefix is added to a word, it changes the word's
     A. ending.
     B. meaning.
     C. part of speech.

_____ 3. A suffix can change
     A. a word's part of speech.
     B. a word's meaning.
     C. both of the above.

_____ 4. The basic meaning of a word is carried in its
     A. prefix.
     B. suffix.
     C. root.

➤ Review Test 2

Use the word parts in the box to complete the words in the following sentences. Use each word part only once.

bio — life	**ment** — state of being
ex — out, from	**pre** — before
ible — able to be	**spect** — look
in — within, into	**sub** — below, under
ism — a belief or practice	**tele** — far, over a distance

1. A fortuneteller (. . . *dicted*) _____ that I'd soon suffer a financial loss; then he charged me fifty dollars.

2. There are many foods I find it hard to resist, (. . . *cluding*)

    _____ American cheese, chocolate candy, vanilla ice cream, and cherry pie.

3. A fourteenth-century book on table manners warns that "one who blows his nose in the tablecloth" lacks *(refine . . .)* _____.

4. Before using dried mushrooms in a recipe, you should (. . . *merge*)

    _____ them in water for a short time.

5. Certain colors that are *(vis . . .)* _____ to bees and butterflies cannot be seen by humans.

6. Martin's continued bad behavior finally got him (. . . *pelled*)

    _____ from school.

7. A nature photographer may invest hundreds of dollars on a (. . . *photo*)

    _____ lens for a camera so that he or she can take pictures of wildlife from a safe distance.

8. For my (. . . *logy*) _____ project, I observed the way mold grows on unwashed dishes.

9. The spiritual practice of *(Hindu . . .)* _____ includes the belief that when someone dies, his or her soul begins a new life.

10. One of nature's most beautiful (. . . *acles*) _____ is thousands of monarch butterflies coming together at their winter home.

➤ Review Test 3

Here is a chance to apply your understanding of word parts to a full-length reading. Phany Sarann was caught in a terrible war in Southeast Asia. Destruction and cruelty were all around her. She knew she needed a way out and believed that education and learning English were her salvation. This is her story, one of courage in the face of severe hardships.

Words to Watch

Following are some words in the reading that do not have strong context support. Each word is followed by the number of the paragraph in which it appears and its meaning there. These words are indicated in the reading by a small circle (°).

communal (4): public
bribe (9): an illegal payoff
evaporated (13): disappeared
relieve (19): make less serious

FROM HORROR TO HOPE

Phany Sarann

1   For the hundredth time, I closed my bedroom door, fell on the bed, and started to sob. Covering my face, I tried to cry silently. I didn't want my aunt and uncle to hear. Once again I asked myself why they were so cruel to me. Didn't they remember that they had invited me to work for them in America in exchange for my college education? My uncle had gone to college in Cambodia. Why didn't he understand that education was so important to me, too? My life had already been too full of challenges. Having gone through so much and come so far, would I be defeated now?

2   When Pol Pot's Khmer Rouge soldiers* took charge of my life and my country in 1975, they forced people like my family, who lived in a city, to move to the countryside. My father understood that we would be gone for a long time. He made sure we took everything possible with us. Somehow, somewhere, he found a tractor and trailer. Since my three sisters and I were little, we rode on the wagon while my older brother and the adults walked behind. The horrible April weather cooked us and turned the dirt roads to dust. We settled first in a remote mountainous region, where we had to carry all our water from a muddy canal about half an hour's walk away. Later the Khmer Rouge moved us to a site along a river. There, at least, we could catch fish to eat. Soon my father was trading smoked fish for oranges, coffee, rice, and medicine.

3   After a year, the local authorities sent an oxcart to move our family again. They said it was because our settlement was too crowded. However, my mom said the real reason was that my dad would not respect their authority. Dad hated having the uneducated local people control everything. They controlled the crops we grew, the chickens we raised, the people we talked to, the places we could and could not go, and even the family's children.

4   After we were moved, we were all together for a few months. Then the Khmer Rouge began to separate our family. My brother and oldest sister were sent to a labor camp to dig canals

---

*The murderous dictator Pol Pot and his military group, the Khmer Rouge, ruled the country of Cambodia for four years and were responsible for the deaths of over one million people.

by hand. My father was sent away for months to cut wood for the communal° kitchens. While I missed him, I was too hungry to feel much of anything but emptiness. My mother had to work in the rice fields all day, but thankfully she could come home at night. There were no schools and no hospitals. Many people died of starvation, disease, and exhaustion. Even tiny children worked: as soon they were big enough to walk, they joined us in the rice fields. Day after day we walked behind the rice cutters, collecting the stems that they had missed. All our dreams were about finding food. The rice we harvested was hidden away or exported while we were given only one cup of watery grain a day. To survive, we ate whatever we could find: rats, crickets, caterpillars, snakes, frogs, and boiled banana tree bark. Our only hope was that some day our country would be rescued from the Khmer Rouge.

5   The horror grew worse when my father was accused of stealing one of our own chickens. My parents heard that my father would soon be "taken," which we knew meant executed, so he decided to escape. On the day he ran away, my sister and I met him on our way back from the fields. "Look after yourselves and tell your mother that I am leaving," he said. "I do not know when I will see you again."

6   In March of 1979, government troops came to set us free. It took us two days to walk from the village back to town. Since I did not have shoes, I tried to make some from layers of leaves. When they fell apart, I cried and limped along on blistered feet. At first, we thought our nightmare was over because there were no more killings and nobody was forcing us to work. But we were starving. My mother exchanged her diamond ring for rice to feed our hungry family. After the rice was gone, we began a series of moves, trying to find a place where life would be better. But there was no peace, because the Khmer Rouge and the new government troops were at war. Finally we arrived again in our old home.

7   All this time we kept hoping to see my father's face again. But in late 1981 we all wept to learn of his death. He had been shot by the Khmer Rouge as he swam across a river to escape them. There would be no more support from the man who was the most important part of our family. My mother was very sad. Still, she struggled hard to bring up four daughters by herself.

8   That same year, we three younger girls began school. My sisters eventually quit in favor of going to work, but I felt that getting an education was the most important goal in my life. Struggling through high school was especially difficult because my family did not understand why I was doing it. Cambodians believed that education was important only for boys. Daughters were not encouraged to go to school. Many times when I came home from school, exhausted from studying, my mom would complain. "What makes you tired?" she would ask. "You just go there, sit and listen, but do nothing! But I have to carry heavy loads and move all the time!" My mother also kept reminding me that she could not support me past high school. How could I continue my

education? Then, after I graduated from high school in 1989 and my mother offered to buy me a small stall at the local market, I had an idea. I told her, "I will not sell things at the market, but if I do all the housework and all the cooking for the whole family, can I keep on studying? If I study English now, I can find a good job to support myself later." While she did not give me an answer, she did not make me go to the market either.

9   Even without my mother's support, I kept trying to get into college. However, I soon found how corrupt the educational system was. If I didn't have the money to pay a bribe°, I would not be admitted even though my test scores were good. I sadly gave up the thought of college, but I started studying English in a private class. I would wake up every morning at 4:30 and ride my bicycle through the cold, dark streets to my class. I never wanted to get out of bed and go out into the cold. I was also scared people might hurt me and take my bike. But I went anyway. Soon, I found four Cambodians who wanted to speak English, so I began teaching them what I was learning. Life was full of challenges, but I was learning English and earning money too.

10   I realized how much more I had to learn when I took a job working for the United States Agency for International Development (USAID). After each staff meeting, I left the room with an aching head and an unsure feeling about what I was supposed to do. Having to make presentations in English was like a nightmare for me. Writing reports in English was the worst of all. The simplest report took me hours and hours because I spent so much time checking words in a dictionary.

11   After a year my uncle, who had immigrated to Houston, Texas, asked me to come to work in his doughnut shop. In exchange, he promised to pay for my education in America. In great excitement, I quit my good job at USAID, said farewell to my family and friends, and came to Texas. This seemed like a dream come true—not only would I receive a good education, but I would meet many new people and have wonderful new experiences.

12   But the reality of my life in America was nothing like my dreams. Before school began, I worked hard seven days a week. When the school term started, I worked every weekend. I arranged hot doughnuts on the shelves, filled napkin boxes, made coffee, cleared tables, and sold doughnuts. Many times each day I washed all the trays we used for displaying and serving doughnuts. The hot water burned my hands, but my uncle and aunt refused to let me wear gloves, for fear they would slow me down.

13   Instead of treating me like a member of their family, my uncle and aunt regarded me with great suspicion. Because they were afraid I would steal money from the registers, they gave me working clothes with no pockets. Regularly, they searched my room, went through my belongings, and even opened and read my mail. Even my little bit of free time was not my own. I was allowed to go only to classes. When I asked to go to the Buddhist temple to honor my father on Cambodian New Year's Day and the

Day of the Dead, the answer was "No." My dreams of making new friends evaporated°, too. My uncle and aunt did not allow me to say anything but "Hi" or "Good morning" to people who came in the doughnut shop. I felt I was living in a prison with no walls.

14   Once the shop was closed, the work continued. My uncle and aunt expected me to keep house for their family. I had to prepare their main meal every day and clean up after it. Three times a week, I mopped the floors and scrubbed the fixtures. I also swept and dusted all through the house once a week. How could they have forgotten to tell me that they also expected me to do all of this? But I swallowed my anger and kept quiet.

15   After ten months of this life, my uncle announced that he could not pay for my tuition anymore and that I had to go back to Cambodia. The excuse was a lie; I knew his business was making money. This sad experience with my aunt and uncle taught me not to trust people just because they are relatives.

16   While I felt angry, used, and scared, I also felt the freedom of the decision before me. Would I let my uncle force me to return to Cambodia? I decided the answer was no. I left my uncle's house and moved in with Nancy Dean, my former English teacher. Hearing of my plight, my former boss at USAID offered me a plane ticket to Michigan, where I could live with her parents and continue my education.

17   How excited I was to travel to Michigan, and how nervous—I had never met the people I was going to live with. However, the minute I got off the plane and met Gale and Roberta Lott, I knew a new life was about to begin. Gale and Roberta treat me as one of their children. The special attention they give me makes me feel complete for the first time in my life. Good things have continued to happen since I enrolled at Lansing Community College. I like all my classes, people are very friendly, and I have found a part-time job in the Student and Academic Support office.

18   My past has been full of challenges; some of these I could control, and some I could not. Learning to deal with challenges has made me a stronger person with the confidence to realize my dreams. I plan to transfer to a university and graduate with a bachelor of arts degree and then return to my homeland. I hope that a degree from an American university will help me move into a leadership role in Cambodia. Since education for women is still not valued there, my next challenge will be to make my culture understand that educating women will make my country a better place for everyone.

Update

19   Phany graduated from Lansing Community College and then went on to earn a B.A. degree in international relations at Michigan State University. She has recently returned to her homeland, and her plan is to find a job working with the government and international non-profit organizations to relieve° poverty in Cambodia.

Word Parts Questions

Use the word part clues you learned in this chapter to answer the following questions. In the space provided, write the letter of your choice for each question.

_____ 1. In the sentence below, the word *uneducated* means
    A. able to be educated.
    B. well educated.
    C. not educated.

    "Dad hated having the uneducated local people control everything." (Paragraph 3)

_____ 2. In the sentence below, the word *starvation* means
    A. before being starved.
    B. without being starved.
    C. the state of being starved.

    "Many people died of starvation, disease, and exhaustion." (Paragraph 4)

_____ 3. In the sentence below, the word *cutters* means
    A. people who are full of cutting.
    B. people who cut.
    C. people who do not cut.

    "Day after day we walked behind the rice cutters, collecting the stems that they had missed." (Paragraph 4)

_____ 4. In the sentence below, the word *exported* means
    A. taken above.
    B. correctly taken.
    C. taken out to another place.

    "The rice we harvested was hidden away or exported while we were given only one cup of watery grain a day." (Paragraph 4)

_____ 5. In the sentences below, the word *eventually* means
    A. at a time that came later.
    B. at a great distance.
    C. in a skilled way.

    "That same year, we three younger girls began school. My sisters eventually quit in favor of going to work . . . ." (Paragraph 8)

_____ 6. In the sentence below, the words *reminding me* mean
   A. telling me again.
   B. telling me inside.
   C. telling me over a distance.

   "My mother also kept reminding me that she could not support me past high school." (Paragraph 8)

_____ 7. In the sentence below, the word *sadly* means
   A. without being sad.
   B. done in a sad way.
   C. before being sad.

   "I sadly gave up the thought of college, but I started studying English in a private class." (Paragraph 9)

_____ 8. In the sentence below, the word *unsure* means
   A. very sure.
   B. not sure.
   C. sure ahead of time.

   "I left the room with an aching head and an unsure feeling about what I was supposed to do." (Paragraph 10)

_____ 9. In the sentence below, the words *immigrated to* mean
   A. moved into.
   B. moved out of.
   C. moved because of beliefs.

   "After a year my uncle, who had immigrated to Houston, Texas, asked me to come to work in his doughnut shop." (Paragraph 11)

_____ 10. In the sentence below, the word *regularly* means
   A. like regular people.
   B. according to regulations.
   C. in a regular way.

   "Regularly, they searched my room, went through my belongings, and even opened and read my mail." (Paragraph 13)

Discussion Questions

1. Was Phany's mother right in not supporting Phany's desire to continue her education by going to college? What was her mother's point of view? What was Phany's point of view? Why do you think their views were so different?

2. What were the reasons Phany's uncle first wanted her to come to the United States? Why do you think he changed his mind and wanted to send her back to Cambodia?

3. Phany's job at her uncle's doughnut shop turned out to be a nightmare. What is the worst job you have ever had? What made it so terrible? Describe one or two incidents that show just how awful the job was.

Note: Writing assignments for this selection appear on pages 557–558.

Check Your Performance   **PHONICS IV: WORD PARTS**

Activity	Number Right	Points	Score
Review Test 1 (4 items)	_____	× 5 =	_____
Review Test 2 (10 items)	_____	× 4 =	_____
Review Test 3 (10 items)	_____	× 4 =	_____
	TOTAL SCORE	=	_____ %

Enter your total score into the **Reading Performance Chart: Review Tests** on the inside back cover.

WORD PARTS: Mastery Test 1

Use the word parts in the box to complete the words in the sentences below. Use each word part only once.

auto — self	**mono** — one
bene — good, well	**ped** — foot
er — a person who does something	**re** — again, back
ex — out, from	**un** — not
ion — act of	**ven** — come

1. A *(research . . .)* _____ found that students tend to learn better when lectures contain some humor.

2. Some lakes and rivers have become so *(. . . clean)* _____ that they have actually caught fire.

3. The company president wrote his *(. . . biography)* _____ and gave it out as a holiday gift to his employees, who would have preferred money to the story of their boss's life.

4. A skirt with an elastic waistband can *(. . . pand)* _____ to fit women of many sizes.

5. Before starting my car in cold weather, I need to pump the gas *(. . . al)* _____ a few times.

6. David Letterman performs alone at the beginning of *The Late Show*, when he gives his *(. . . logue)* _____.

7. Whenever my mother tells me that the *(. . . fits)* _____ will outweigh the drawbacks, I know she's about to ask me to do something unpleasant.

8. Sometimes course *(registrat . . .)* _____ seems to last longer than the courses themselves.

(Continues on next page)

9. To *(. . . fresh)* _____ themselves, some Japanese workers take yawn breaks: They all raise their arms and yawn at the same time—for thirty seconds.

10. Many people attended the spy *(con . . . tion)* _____; however, no one was willing to wear a name-tag.

WORD PARTS: Mastery Test 2

Use the word parts in the box to complete the words in the following passage. Read the passage through one time before trying to complete the words. Use each word part once.

er — a person who does something	**ist** — a person skilled at something
ex — out, from	**ly** — in a certain way
ful — full of	**re** — again
in — within	**spect** — look
ion — state of being	**tele** — far, over a distance

When a murder takes place, how do the police get information about the killer? First, they *(in . . .)* (1) _____ the scene of the crime. Maybe the murderer left some fingerprints on a *(. . . phone)* (2) _____, a doorknob, or a glass. Other clues that point to specific individuals *(. . . clude)* (3) _____ footprints (perhaps showing the pattern of wear in a shoe), hairs, and traces of blood. A close examination of the victim's body can also be very *(use . . .)* (4) _____. A stab wound may be matched to the blade of a particular knife. *(Similar . . .)* (5) _____, *(special . . . s)* (6) _____ can determine from a bullet wound the kind of gun that was used and the distance from which the bullet was fired. And once the bullet is *(. . . tracted)* (7) _____ from the body, it too will show marks that link it to only one gun. Increasingly, the methods for tracking down *(kill . . . s)* (8) _____ provide more than clues; they offer positive *(identificat . . .)* (9) _____.

(Continues on next page)

131

It is hoped that such exact police methods will persuade many would-be criminals to *(. . . consider)* (10) _____ their plans.

WORD PARTS: Mastery Test 3

Use the word parts in the box to complete the words in the sentences below. Use each word part only once.

able — able to be	**mono** — one
audi — hear	**pre** — before
ish — similar to	**sub** — below, under
ly — in a certain way	**super** — over, above, beyond
mis — badly, wrong	**tele** — far, over a distance

1. The *(. . . ence)* _____ starting clapping as soon as the famous actress walked onstage and spoke her first line.

2. When the bus turned on its side, several passengers were *(serious . . .)* _____ injured.

3. Looking through the powerful *(. . . scope)* _____, we could see Saturn's rings.

4. According to a survey, the average person spends about a year of his or her life searching for *(. . . placed)* _____ objects.

5. Because she was *(. . . occupied)* _____ with an earlier assignment, Roz didn't hear the teacher ask her a question.

6. Today, many reporters travel with a small *(port . . .)* _____ computer.

7. The lecturer spoke in such a *(. . . tone)* _____ that he almost put the students to sleep.

8. The scholarship is awarded on the basis of both financial need and *(. . . ior)* _____ grades.

(Continues on next page)

9. The car was so *(. . . standard)* _____ that within months the fuel pump needed replacing and the bumper fell off.

10. Whenever I catch my *(devil . . .)* _____ son snatching a piece of candy, he says, "I was taking it for you, Mommy."

WORD PARTS: Mastery Test 4

Use the word parts in the box to complete the words in the following passage. Read the passage through one time before trying to complete the words. Use each word part once.

aud — hear	**man** — hand
ex — out, from	**ment** — state of being
ful — full of	**pre** — before
in — within	**re** — again, back
ly — in a certain way	**spect** — look

Last night in a dream, an angel came to me and asked, "Would you like to see hell?" After *(. . . paring)* (1) _____ myself to see a terrible *(. . . acle)* (2) _____, I went with the angel. Suddenly we stood *(. . . side)* (3) _____ a large room draped with blue velvet. In the middle of this *(beauti . . .)* (4) _____ room was a huge golden pot filled with sweet-smelling food. Many people sat around the pot. Each held a spoon of silver. The spoons' handles were so long that the people could reach the pot and scoop out food. They couldn't, however, *(. . . age)* (5) _____ to bring the food to their mouths. The only *(. . . ible)* (6) _____ sounds were moans of pain. I realized that everyone was starving.

"Now would you like to see heaven?" asked the angel. I *(eager . . .)* (7) _____ agreed. To my *(amaze . . .)* (8) _____, the next room I saw looked just like the first—with the same golden pot

(Continues on next page)

135

and the same silver spoons. However, here everyone appeared to be (*. . . tremely*) (9) _____ happy. The people were talking and laughing and looked well-fed.

Puzzled, I said, "In the other room there was only misery. Here there is only joy. How can this be?" With a wise smile, the angel (*. . . plied*) (10) _____, "Here they feed each other."

WORD PARTS: Mastery Test 5

A. Use the word parts in the box to complete the words in the sentences below. Use each word part only once.

bio — life	**less** — without
ism — a belief or practice	**port** — carry
ist — a person skilled at something	

1. The stock-market crash of 1929 left many people *(penni . . .)* _____—they had no money at all.

2. Mark Twain was a riverboat captain and a gold miner before he went on to become one of America's most famous *(humor . . . s)* _____.

3. One type of *(vegetarian . . .)* _____ excludes all dairy products and eggs.

4. To know about chemical reactions in the body, doctors must study *(. . . chemistry)* _____.

5. The richly dressed movie star entered the hotel lobby, followed by a *(. . . er)* _____ carrying her four large suitcases.

(Continues on next page)

B. (6–10.) Use the word parts in the box to complete the words in the following passage. Read the passage through one time before trying to complete the words. Use each word part once.

er — a person who does something	**sub** — below, under
ful — full of	**un** — not
spect — look	

According to the American Kennel Club, the Labrador retriever is the nation's most popular breed. What does this mean if you want a Lab puppy? Be very *(care . . .)* (6) _____ before you buy. When a breed is known to be number one, a flood of people look for puppies. *(. . . fortunately)* (7) _____, this usually attracts the dishonest type of *(breed . . .)* (8) _____ who raises *(. . . standard)* (9) _____ puppies just for the profit. These dogs have few of the qualities that made the breed popular. The best advice is to buy a puppy from a reputable source, and always *(in . . .)* (10) _____ the puppy first.

WORD PARTS: Mastery Test 6

A. Use the word parts in the box to complete the words in the sentences below. Use each word part only once.

ible — able to be	**tele** — far, over a distance
pod — foot	**un** — not
pre — before	

1. The kitten at the animal shelter looked so *(. . . loved)* _____ that I just had to adopt her.

2. The woman's feet hurt, so she went to the *(. . . iatrist)* _____ to have her corns removed.

3. The lawyer urged the jury not to *(. . . judge)* _____ the defendant, but to wait for all the facts before making up their minds.

4. The acrobat is so *(flex . . .)* _____ that he can wrap his legs around his head.

5. The Learning Center contains a *(. . . conference)* _____ room where staff members can talk on a special TV to people on other campuses.

(Continues on next page)

B. (6–10.) Use the word parts in the box to complete the words in the following passage. Read the passage through one time before trying to complete the words. Use each word part once.

ful — full of	**post** — after
less — without	**re** — again, back
ly — in a certain way	

High-school reunions provide an opportunity to *(. . . acquaint)* (6) _____ yourself with former classmates. However, some people are a little nervous when attending a reunion. So here are some tips for a *(success . . .)* (7) _____ experience. First, pamper yourself; make yourself look your best. Second, wear something that makes a statement. Buy a stunning *(strap . . .)* (8) _____ dress or a sharp silk suit. Next, try to be outgoing. Keep in mind that you are a worthwhile person, and speak to other people *(confident . . .)* (9) _____. But even if you have had a fantastic life, don't act superior. Take the time to find out what your classmates have done in their *(. . .-high-school)* (10) _____ years. Finally, go with the attitude that you are going to have a good time. That is the main reason for attending reunions.

Part II

TEN STEPS TO COLLEGE READING

1

Getting Started

THIS CHAPTER IN A NUTSHELL

- You must truly want to succeed in college and be willing to work at it.
- You must go to class, take notes, and make good use of your time.
- You must develop the reading habit.

© 1998 Randy Glasbergen. www.glasbergen.com

GLASBERGEN

"It's not enough to be in her class.
She actually expects you to *learn* something."

Hello, and welcome to the book. The chapters that follow will help you learn important reading skills. This first chapter is going to cover three other keys to success. I'll discuss your attitude about the course in which you are using this book, basic study skills, and your reading habits.

YOUR ATTITUDE ABOUT THIS COURSE

The course in which you are using this book can help you become a better reader and writer. It can also help you get off to a strong start in college. But as the above cartoon suggests, it's not enough to just *be* in this course, or to just be in college. Instead, you must have the attitude that you are going to work hard and learn as much as you can.

You need to believe in the saying, "No pain, no gain." You must be ready to work hard in this course to improve your language skills. The heart of the matter is not the speed at which you will learn. The heart of the matter is your determination that "I *will* learn."

Discovering the Need to Work

I have seen a number of students over the years who have acted more like zombies in class than like live people. Such students are their own worst enemies. It's clear they regard themselves as unlikely to succeed in school. They walk into the classroom carrying defeat on their shoulders the way other students carry textbooks under their arms.

I'd look at them slouching in their seats and staring into space and think, "What terrible things have gone on in their lives that they've quit already? They have so little faith in their ability to learn that they're not even trying." Such students often suddenly disappear one day. Sadly, no one pays much attention because they had already disappeared in spirit long before.

When I have seen such students with defeat in their eyes, I have wanted to shake them by the shoulders and say, "You are not dead. Be proud and pleased that you have brought yourself this far. Don't give up now." Such people should not let self-doubt stop them from trying. They should roll up their sleeves and get to work. They should decide to try to learn.

What I have seen happen is that a spark will catch fire. Students will discover the meaning that school can have in their lives.

Here is one student's account of such a discovery:

> My present feeling about college is that it will improve my life. My first attitude was that I didn't need it. I had been bored by high school where it seemed we spent grades 9 to 12 just reviewing everything we had learned up through grade 8.
>
> When I entered college in January, I thought it was fun but that's all. I met a lot of people and walked around with college textbooks in my hand, playing the game of being a college student. Some weeks I went to class, and other weeks I didn't go at all and went off on trips instead. I didn't do much studying. I really wasn't into it but was just going along with the ball game. Sometimes kids would be going to an early class when I would be be getting home from an all-night party.
>
> Then two things happened. My sociology class was taught by a really cool person who would ask us a lot of questions, and they began getting to me. I started asking myself questions and looking at myself and thinking,

"What's goin' on with me? What do I want and what am I doing?" Also I discovered I could write. I wrote a paragraph about my messy brother that was read in class and everyone roared. Now I'm really putting time into my writing and my other courses as well.

Just the other day my writing teacher asked me, "What is the point at which you changed? Was there a moment of truth when the switch turned to 'On' in your head?" I don't know the exact moment, but it was just there, and now it seems so real I can almost touch it. I know this is my life and I want to be somebody and college is going to help me do it. I'm here to improve myself, and I'm going to give it my best shot.

Evaluating Your Attitude toward School

Take a moment to think about your own attitude toward learning. Put a check (✓) by the item or items that apply to you. (If you agree with some sentences in an item but not others, cross out the ones you do not agree with.)

_____ School has never really turned me on. I feel I can start to study if I need to, but I don't want to. What's wrong with being a bit lazy? Life is supposed to be about enjoying yourself and having some fun. I want to take it easy and have as many good times as I can for now.

_____ I want to do more in school, but I'm afraid of really giving it a good effort. What if I try my best and I still get lousy grades? People will just laugh at me. I don't want to look foolish, so I'm probably just going to drift along and not call any attention to myself.

_____ I'm not ready to learn a lot of stuff that is not going to be of any value to me as far as I can see. Why should I study stuff that has no interest for me?

_____ I'm not an active student who tries my best all the time. But I'm not a zombie either. I do some studying, just not as much as other people would like me to. I should probably do more, and I'm going to work on that and try to do a better job of taking charge of my studies.

_____ I'm on the move, and I have taken charge of my life. There is something inside me that is strong and determined to succeed. I feel in my heart of hearts that nothing is going to stop me. It's my life, and I'm going to work hard and respect myself and gain success and happiness.

If you have a chance, share your answers with other students. Spend some time talking with each other about what your attitude is and how you can improve it.

TWO BASIC STUDY SKILLS

There are two basic study skills that are sure to make you a better student. After teaching first-year college students for many years, I know just how important these skills are.

Skill 1: Go to Class and Take Lots of Notes

More than anything else, here is what you must do to succeed in school:

1 Go to class.

2 Take good notes.

Why You Must Attend Class

The instructor will use class time to present the key ideas of the course. If you are not in class to hear and write down these ideas, you are not going to learn anything. Also, you greatly increase your chances of failing the course!

There are only two alternatives to class attendance. You can read and study the textbook and hope to learn the key ideas of the course from it. But textbook study will take you many hours. Even then, you still won't know which ideas the teacher feels are most important. Those ideas are the ones most likely to appear on exams.

You can also use the notes of another student. However, those notes cannot make up for the experience of actually being in class and hearing the instructor talk about key ideas. At best, the notes of another student can help you fill in any missing information in your own notes.

Why You Must Take Notes

You must write down the material presented in class because forgetting begins almost immediately! Studies have shown that within two weeks you will probably forget a good deal of what you have heard in class.

- In fact, how much class material do you think most people do forget in just two weeks? Check (✓) the answer you think is correct:

    ___ 20 percent is forgotten within two weeks.

    ___ 40 percent is forgotten within two weeks.

    ___ 60 percent is forgotten within two weeks.

    ___ 80 percent is forgotten within two weeks.

Studies have shown that within two weeks most people forget 80% of what they have heard!

- Now see if you can guess how much class material people typically forget within four weeks:

  ___ 85 percent is forgotten within four weeks.

  ___ 90 percent is forgotten within four weeks.

  ___ 95 percent is forgotten within four weeks.

The fact is that within four weeks people typically forget 95% of the information they have heard in class! So the reality of the matter is that, no matter how carefully you listen to a classroom lecture, you forget very quickly—and you forget a great deal. To guard against forgetting, you should write down much of the information presented in class. If you just listen and don't write, you're heading for trouble. The point bears repeating: *you should get a written record of what an instructor presents in class.*

- How many notes do you typically take in class?

  ___ A lot

  ___ Some

  ___ Very few

If you have not checked "A lot," make it your intention to take a lot of notes from now on.

Skill 2: Organize Your Time

Do you consider yourself an organized person or a disorganized one? Check the description below that applies to you:

  ___ *I'm organized.* I get to places on time, I keep up with school work, I'm always ready for tests, and I allow plenty of time for planning and working on papers.

  ___ *I'm somewhere in the middle* between organized and disorganized.

  ___ *I'm disorganized.* I'm often late for appointments or forget them, I miss classes, I work on papers and cram for tests at the last minute.

If you have not checked the first item above, you need to learn more about how to control your time. The skillful use of time will help you enormously in school and in life.

Here are three steps to take to control your time:

1 First, pay close attention to the course outline, or **syllabus**, that your instructors will probably give you during the first week of class. That syllabus will most likely give you the dates of exams and tell you when papers or reports are due.

2 Second, move all those dates onto a **large monthly calendar**—a calendar that has a good-sized block of white space for each date. Hang the calendar in a place where you'll be sure to see it every day—perhaps above your desk or on a bedroom wall.

OCTOBER

Sun	Mon	Tue	Wed	Thurs	Fri	Sat
			1	2	3	4
5	6 *English paper*	7	8	9 *Math test*	10	11
12	13	14	15 *History test*	16	17	18
19	20	21 *Math test*	22	23	24	25
26	27	28	29	30 *Speech report*	31	

3 Third, buy a small notebook and write down every day a **"to do" list** of things that need to get done that day. Decide which items are most important and handle them first. (If you have classes that day, going to those classes will be "A" priority items. Other items may be a "B" or a "C" in importance.) Carry your list with you during the day, referring to it every so often and checking off items as you complete them.

• Look at the "to do" list on the next page. Place an A, B, or C in front of each item, depending on how important you think it is.

To Do — Monday

> 1. *Go to History and English class.*
> 2. *Study for math test tomorrow.*
> 3. *Cash check at bank.*
> 4. *Meet Ben for lunch.*
> 5. *Check e-mail.*
> 6. *Pick up drinks and snacks for later.*

- Answer these questions:

1. Of the three steps for organizing time, which is the most important one for you, and why?

   _____

2. Which step is the second most important for you, and why?

   _____

YOUR READING HABITS

Recently I was at a conference that featured a panel of first-year college students. They were asked, "If you could give just one bit of advice to high-school kids, what would it be?" One student answered, "I can answer that in one word: '**Read**. Read everything you can. The more you read, the better off you're going to be.'" Up and down the panel, heads nodded. No one disagreed with this advice.

All these students agreed because they had learned the truth about reading—that it is at the very heart of education. They had been in college long enough to know that the habit of regular reading is needed for success in school and life. Here are four specific reasons why you should become a regular reader:

1 **Real Pleasure.** Chances are that you have done little reading for pleasure in your life. Perhaps you grew up in a home like mine where a television set was the center of the household. Perhaps you got off to a bad start in reading in school and never seemed to catch up. Or maybe you were eager to learn about reading when you began school but didn't like what you had to read. You may then have decided that reading wasn't for you.

The truth is that reading can open the door to a lifetime of pleasure and adventure. Take the time to walk through that door. You may learn that one of the great experiences of life is the joy of reading for its own sake.

2 **Language Power.** Research has shown beyond any question that regular reading improves your vocabulary, writing, and thinking skills—as well as your reading skills. If you want more language power in your life, reading is the way to get it.

3 **Job Power.** Regular reading will increase your chances for job success. In today's world more than ever before, jobs involve the processing of words and information. Studies have found that the better your command of words, the more success you are likely to have. Nothing will give you a command of words like regular reading.

There are countless stories about people who went on to successful careers after developing the reading habit. One is the story of Ben Carson, who as a boy believed that he was "the dumbest kid" in his fifth-grade class. After he started reading two books a week, at his mother's insistence, his entire world changed. Within two years he had moved to the head of his class, and he was later to become Dr. Benjamin Carson, a world-famous neurosurgeon at Johns Hopkins University Hospital.

4 **Human Power.** Reading enlarges the mind and the heart. It frees us from the narrow limits of our own experience. Knowing how other people view important matters helps us decide what we ourselves think and feel. Reading also helps us connect with others and realize our shared humanity. Someone once wrote, "We read in order to know that we are not alone." We become less isolated as we share the common experiences, emotions, and thoughts that make us human. We grow more sympathetic and understanding because we realize that others are like us.

How to Become a Better Reader

I can make my point here by asking you two questions:

- What is the best way to learn how to become a good cook?

    _____ A. Study cookbooks.

    _____ B. Take a class on how to cook.

    _____ C. Watch films of good cooks.

    _____ D. Help out a good cook.

    _____ E. Practice cooking.

You know the answer. The best way to become a good cook is to practice cooking. We become good at a skill by practicing the skill.

- What, then, is the best way to become a better reader?

Based on question 1, you can probably guess. Write your answer here:

_____

The best way to become a better reader is to do a lot of reading. In this book, you will do a good amount of reading at the same time you learn and practice key reading skills. All the reading and practice are sure to make you a better reader.

At the same time, I strongly recommend that you not limit your reading to what is in this book. I know from my many years of working with students that you should **read even more**. It's like becoming a good cook: the more you cook, the better you become. The more you read, the better you become.

A Question, and a Challenge

- How many books would you guess you have read in your life? _____

I have had many students say they have never read a single book from cover to cover in their lives. At most they read a book or two in school, but their memories of such books are seldom pleasant ones. They often describe that reading as a kind of forced death march—a chapter at a time with lots of worksheets and quizzes. Such experiences are not true reading experiences.

- Are you willing to take on this challenge: To read at least one outside book at the same time you are using this textbook?

    ___ Yes   ___ No   ___ Maybe

If you have answered "Yes," here are some ways to proceed:

- Go to the Townsend Press website at **www.townsendpress.com** and click on "Free from Townsend Press." You'll be able to download one of several free books. For example, one you might like is titled *Reading Changed My Life!*

- Get book suggestions from friends, family, or your instructor. Then visit a bookstore or library to find a book that interests you and read it.

- Take advantage of the special offer on page 159.

CHAPTER REVIEW

In this chapter, you learned the following:

- Your attitude about school is a key to your success. You must be determined to do the hard work needed to do well in your courses.
- If you don't go to class and take notes, you may be wasting your time in college.
- Take control of your time by using a monthly calendar and a "to do" list.
- Regular reading will improve your reading, vocabulary, writing, and thinking skills. If you want more language power in your life, reading is the way to get it.

The next chapter—Chapter 2—will show you how to use a dictionary to help you understand what you read.

➤ *Review Test 1*

To review what you've learned in this chapter, answer the following questions by writing the letter of each correct answer.

_____ 1. To do well in school, you must
   A. have the ability to learn quickly.
   B. be determined to work hard.
   C. have respect for teachers.
   D. seek help from others.

_____ 2. To become a better reader, you must
   A. read more.
   B. study more.
   C. write more.
   D. take a course in reading.

_____ 3. Regular reading can
   A. increase your chances for job success.
   B. give you more language power.
   C. help you grow as a person.
   D. all of the above.

_____ 4. After you make up a "to do" list, you should
   A. hang it on your wall.
   B. mark down dates when papers or reports are due.
   C. decide on which items are most important.
   D. check it at least once a week.

➤ *Review Test 2*

_____ 1. How determined are you to do the **hard work** needed to succeed in school? On the following scale of *Passive* to *Determined*, where would you rate yourself?

Passive   1   2   3   4   5   6   7   8   9   10   **Determined**

Comment here on the rating you have given yourself:

_____

_____

_____

_____ 2. How good a job have you done **managing time** in your life so far? On the following scale, rate your degree of success.

Little or no time control   1   2   3   4   5   6   7   8   9   10   **Strong time control**

Comment here on the rating you have given yourself:

_____

_____

_____

_____ 3. How much of a **reader** have you been in your life so far? On the following scale of _Nonreader_ to _Active reader_, where would you put yourself?

Nonreader   1   2   3   4   5   6   7   8   9   10   **Active reader**

Comment here on the rating you have given yourself:

_____

_____

_____

4. Based on your ratings above, what will be your biggest challenge in school, and why will it be such a challenge?

_____

_____

_____

➤ *Review Test 3*

The selection that follows is about a mother who wants to do as much as she can for her children. But it turns out she is not doing one important thing that she should. Read the selection carefully. Then answer the questions that follow to check your general understanding of the material.

Words to Watch

Below are some words in the reading that do not have strong context support. Each word is followed by the number of the paragraph in which it appears and its meaning there. These words are marked in the reading by a small circle (°).

mollified (7): quieted; calmed
launched (16): started
skepticism (20): doubt

A PARENT GETS A READING LESSON

Lucia Herndon

1   The woman rushed into the school, out of breath. She hurried up to the reading teacher who was seated next to me at a table of books.

2   "What's this I hear about the kids not having reading books?" she demanded of the teacher.

3   It was back-to-school night at a local elementary school, and parents were there for a first chat with their children's teachers. I was there to tell people about an after-school program available at my church, located only a block away.

4   This parent had heard that the school was not making reading books available to students this year, and she was furious.

5   "I want my kids to read!" she said, her voice getting louder. "I tell them all the time they have to read. How can they do that if the school doesn't give them a book?"

6   The reading teacher tried to relieve her fears by telling her that each grade had reading books and showed her examples of the books her children would receive in their class.

7   The woman was somewhat mollified°, but still had a full head of steam. "I tell my kids all the time that they have to read, but they just want to tear the books up," she said. "So I don't let them have books at home. I expect the school to have books for them."

8   She went on to say how hard she works—indeed, she was wearing a uniform that evening, having rushed from work to make it to school; she hadn't a chance to go home to change.

9 "And when I'm not working, I'm home cooking and cleaning, washing their clothes," she said.

10 I had been sitting there quietly while the tirade went on. She hadn't been speaking to me, although it was clear she wanted everyone within earshot to know how hard she was working to provide for her children.

11 Finally I could contain myself no longer.

12 "Do you read to your children?" I asked.

13 She looked at me as if I hadn't just heard her say how hard she worked.

14 "I don't have time to read to them," she said. "I'm working all the time. When I get home, I'm tired. I tell them to go read by themselves."

15 "Well, do you read for your own pleasure?" I asked. "Do your children see you reading a book when you have a spare moment?"

16 She launched° into another explanation about being too busy or tired to do any reading.

17 "So your children think of reading as a chore or punishment," I said quietly. "It's not something they see you do or enjoy."

18 She opened her mouth again, and I waited for what I expected was more elaboration on how hard she worked to provide a home for her children.

19 "You're saying they'll read if they see me read?" she asked. "Yes," I said, a smile on my face. "You've got it! You know kids will do what they see you do. If you take five minutes before bedtime and read to them all, you might find you have as much fun as they do. You're relaxing, but you're working hard for your kids."

20 She nodded her head, although with some skepticism°.

21 "Try it once," I said. "Might be good."

22 So what was I trying to say to this harried mother? First, that everyone can appreciate hard work. But children require other things as well—some of a parent's time and attention and care. That parents can be teachers by modeling the behavior they want their children to adopt as their own. And that parents have such power over their children it can be frightening if used poorly.

23 I don't know if I convinced this mother to try something new.

24 Have I convinced you?

Questions about the Reading

For each question, write the letter of your answer in the space provided.

_____ 1. In the sentence below, the word *tirade* (tī′rād′) probably means
    A. an angry speech.
    B. an apology.
    C. a meeting.
    D. an interview.

       "I had been sitting there quietly while the tirade went on." (Paragraph 10)

_____ 2. In the sentence below, the word *elaboration* (ĭ-lăb′ər-ā′shən) probably means
A. confusion.
B. jokes.
C. difficult questions.
D. added details.

> "She opened her mouth again, and I waited for what I expected was more elaboration on how hard she worked to provide a home for her children." (Paragraph 18)

_____ 3. In the sentences below, the word *harried* (hăr′ēd) probably means
A. mild and pleasant.
B. annoyed and overworked.
C. bright and questioning.
D. passive and lazy.

> "So what was I trying to say to this harried mother? First, that everyone can appreciate hard work. But children require other things as well. . . ." (Paragraph 22)

_____ 4. Which statement best expresses the main idea of the entire selection?
A. Parents who work too hard are cheating their kids.
B. It is the school's responsibility to teach kids to love reading.
C. Reading should not be seen as a chore or a punishment.
D. Parents need to model the behavior that they want for their children.

_____ 5. When the mother arrived at back-to-school night, she
A. was very late.
B. seemed unconcerned.
C. was wearing a uniform.
D. had her children with her.

_____ 6. The author was at back-to-school night because
A. she had a child in the teacher's class.
B. she knew the angry mother would be there and wanted to talk with her.
C. she was a teacher at the school.
D. she wanted to tell parents about an after-school program.

_____ 7. The mother probably
A. thought she was doing everything right for her children.
B. was worried that the teacher didn't like her.
C. had only one child.
D. had loved to read when she was young.

_____ 8. The mother seemed to believe that
- A. reading is a waste of time.
- B. it is the job of the school, not the parents, to encourage reading.
- C. her children were being treated unfairly by their teachers.
- D. it was too late to teach her children to like reading.

_____ 9. The author probably
- A. thought the woman was a terrible mother.
- B. did not believe that the woman worked hard.
- C. had met the mother on other occasions.
- D. believed the woman needed to show, not just say, that reading was important.

_____ 10. The author suggests that the mother
- A. may not change her attitude about reading with her children.
- B. will certainly go home and begin reading to her children.
- C. does not really care if her children read or not.
- D. should quit her job to spend more time with her children.

Discussion Questions

1. Why does the mother say she does not let the children have their own books at home? What effect do you think this decision has had on her children?

2. What are some ways that a parent can encourage a child to love reading?

3. Educating a child is a big responsibility. Who should play a greater role—the school or the parent? Is there anything the parent can do that the school cannot?

Note: Writing assignments for this selection appear on page 558.

Check Your Performance   **GETTING STARTED**

Activity	*Number Right*	*Points*	*Score*
Review Test 1 (4 items)	_____	× 5 =	_____
Review Test 2 (4 items)	_____	× 5 =	_____
Review Test 3 (10 items)	_____	× 6 =	_____
		TOTAL SCORE =	_____%

Enter your total score into the **Reading Performance Chart: Review Tests** on the inside back cover.

A Special Offer

To promote your reading growth, Townsend Press will send you three books at no charge except for postage and handling. Here are the three books:

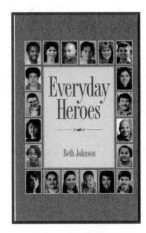

*Great Stories of
Suspense and Adventure*

Ten Real-Life Stories

Everyday Heroes

Use the order form below, enclosing five dollars to cover the cost of shipping and handling. You'll then be sent these three very readable books.

ORDER FORM

YES! Please send me copies of *Great Stories of Suspense and Adventure, Ten Real-Life Stories,* and *Everyday Heroes.* Enclosed is five dollars to cover the shipping and handling of the books.

Please PRINT the following very clearly. It will be your shipping label.

Name _____

Address _____

City _____ *State* _____ *Zip* _____

MAIL TO:

Townsend Press Book Center, 439 Kelley Drive, West Berlin, NJ 08091.

GETTING STARTED: Mastery Test 1 (Your Attitude)

Looking Inside Yourself

1. Here is a list of some of the reasons that students are in college. Check (✓) those that apply to you. Use the space provided to add others that may apply.

    _____ To prepare for a specific career.

    _____ To please my parents.

    _____ To set an example for my children or my brothers or sisters.

    _____ To be with friends who are in college.

    _____ To help me figure out just what I want to do with my life.

    _____ To help me speak English better and adjust to life in America.

    _____ To educate myself.

    _____ To fill in time and have some fun before getting a job.

    _____ To help me get a promotion at work.

    _____ To take advantage of VA benefits or other special funding.

    _____ Other: _____

    _____

    _____ Other: _____

    _____

2. What are some of the personal **strengths** that will help you as a student?

    _____

    _____

    _____

    _____

3. What are some of the personal **challenges** that you must overcome to be a good student?

    _____

    _____

    _____

    _____

(Continues on next page)

4. For many students, a main reason for being in college is to prepare for a career—the specific kind of work they intend to do in life. What is your long-term career goal—or what do you think might be your career goal?

_____

_____

_____

_____

_____

_____

5. There is a familiar saying that the longest journey begins with a single step. To achieve a long-term career goal, you must set and work toward a series of short-term goals. In the space below, list your short-term goals for this semester in college. What specifically do you want to achieve *this semester*?

_____

_____

_____

_____

_____

_____

GETTING STARTED: Mastery Test 2 (Your Attitude)

Escape Habits

Here are some of the habits that people practice to avoid working hard in school. Read about each habit and use a check (✓) to rate yourself.

If you see yourself in any of these situations, you need to know it. Once you are aware of a problem, you can begin to deal with it.

1. **"I Can't Do It."**

Some people will let themselves be discouraged by bad grades. They'll think, "There's no use trying. I'm just not any good at this." But the only way people will really know that they cannot do something is by first trying—giving it their best shot. If you think you "can't do it," the reason may be that you have given up far too soon.

My use of this habit: _____ Often _____ Sometimes _____ Never

2. **"I'm Too Busy."**

Some people make themselves too busy. Perhaps they work more hours on a part-time job than they need to. Perhaps they spend too much time with family or friends. They create excuses for not taking the time to study hard.

My use of this habit: _____ Often _____ Sometimes _____ Never

3. **"I'll Do It Later."**

Everyone tends at times to put things off. But some students time and time again put off what needs to be done so they can watch TV, talk to a friend, take naps, go to the movies, play cards, or do any one of a hundred other things. These students often wind up cramming for tests and writing last-minute papers. Then they seem surprised and angry at their low grades.

My use of this habit: _____ Often _____ Sometimes _____ Never

4. **"I'm Bored with the Subject."**

Students sometimes explain that they are doing poorly in a course because the instructor or the subject matter is boring. But on the whole, courses and instructors balance out: Some are boring; some are exciting; many are in between. If a course is not interesting, students should work even harder so that they can leave the course behind once and for all.

My use of this habit: _____ Often _____ Sometimes _____ Never

(Continues on next page)

5. **"I'm Here, and That's What Counts."**

   Some students spend their first weeks in college lost in a dangerous kind of dream. They feel, "All will be well, for here I am in college. I have a student ID in my pocket, classes to go to, and textbooks under my arm. All this proves I am a college student. I have made it." Such students imagine they will get something for nothing. But such a hope is a false one. Life seldom gives us something for nothing—and school won't either.

   My use of this habit: _____ Often _____ Sometimes _____ Never

6. Of the five habits listed here, which ones (if any) do you think will be the greatest challenge for you? Why?

   _____

   _____

   _____

   _____

   _____

GETTING STARTED: Mastery Test 3 (Study Skills)

A. Making a Daily "To Do" List

A "to do" list is a written list—on paper—of things that need to get done. It is a very powerful tool for organizing one's life and making the best use of one's time. Successful people in all walks of life use the "to do" list. With a pen and a piece of paper, you can have exactly the same tool to organize and manage your life.

Use the space below to make up your own "to do" list for tomorrow. Here are some examples of entries: "Do journal entry for English class"; "Study for math quiz"; "Call Mom"; "Do laundry."

After you list all the items, label them A, B, or C in importance. Making the best use of your time means paying most attention to "A" and "B" items. If need be, "C" items can carry over to another day.

To Do

(Continues on next page)

B. Using a Large Monthly Calendar

You should buy or make a large monthly calendar. Be sure your calendar has a good-sized block of white space for each date. Then write on the calendar the important things you have to do as well as the dates for papers and tests.

Place the calendar in a place where you will see it every day. It allows you, in one quick glance, to get a clear picture of what you need to do during each month of the semester.

Use the calendar below to write in important dates in your life for this month.

Sun	Mon	Tue	Wed	Thurs	Fri	Sat

GETTING STARTED: Mastery Test 4 (Study Skills)

A. To get a better sense of how much time you have each day, fill out the weekly study schedule below and on the next page. Include your meals, travel time, courses, study times, hours of any job, as well as "R&R" (rest, relaxation, time with friends, and the like).

To begin, add the word TRAVEL to the appropriate time blocks. Then add the word MEAL. Then add the names of your COURSES. Then add JOB (if any). Then add STUDY in the blocks where you see time for study and which you intend to use for study. Finally, add R&R (for "rest and relaxation"), as time permits.

Time	Monday	Tuesday	Wednesday	Thursday	Friday	Saturday	Sunday
6–7 am							
7–8 am							
8–9 am							
9–10 am							
10–11 am							
11 am–12 noon							
12–1 pm							
1–2 pm							
2–3 pm							
3–4 pm							
4–5 pm							
5–6 pm							
6–7 pm							
Subtotal Study Hrs							

(Carry these hours forward to the next page)

(Continues on next page)

Time	Monday	Tuesday	Wednesday	Thursday	Friday	Saturday	Sunday
7–8 pm							
8–9 pm							
9–10 pm							
10–11 pm							
11 pm–12 mid							
12–1 am							
1–2 am							
Subtotal from p. 167							
Total Study Hrs							

B. Based on your weekly study schedule, what is the total number of study hours you can schedule each week?

_____

GETTING STARTED: Mastery Test 5 (Reading)

Think about and then write out your answers to the questions that follow.

1. What was the attitude about reading in your home? Was it positive or negative? Explain.

   _____

   _____

   _____

   _____

   _____

   _____

2. How did your family's attitude about reading affect your development as a reader? Did you do a lot of reading—or very little reading?

   _____

   _____

   _____

   _____

   _____

   _____

3. What about your friends and brothers or sisters? Were they readers or nonreaders? How did their attitude affect your attitude toward reading?

   _____

   _____

   _____

   _____

   _____

   _____

(Continues on next page)

4. How much attention was given to reading in the school or schools you went to? Did school help you develop a positive attitude about reading—or a negative one? Explain.

_____

_____

_____

_____

_____

_____

5. TV, movies, music, video games, and the Internet are all distractions in everyday life that keep people from reading. Do such distractions limit your reading? How much?

_____

_____

_____

_____

_____

_____

GETTING STARTED: Mastery Test 6 (Reading)

Here are some ways to become a regular reader. Check (✓) the way or ways that you think would work for you.

____ 1. Create a half hour or hour of reading in your daily schedule. That time might be during your lunch hour, or late afternoon before dinner, or the half hour or so before you turn off your light at night. Find a time that is possible for you, and make reading then a habit.

   • What time would probably best fit your schedule? _____

____ 2. Subscribe to a daily newspaper (or visit it online) and read the sections that interest you. Keep in mind that it is not *what* you read that matters—for example, you should not feel that you must read the editorial section if opinion columns are not your interest. What does matter is *the very fact that you read.* Feel perfectly free to read whatever you like: the sports page, the fashion section, movie reviews, front-page stories—even the comics.

   • What sections are you most likely to read?

   _____

   _____

   _____

____ 3. Subscribe to one or more magazines. Browse in the magazine section of your library or a local bookstore; chances are you'll find some magazines that interest you. You may want to consider a weekly news magazine, such as *Newsweek;* a weekly general-interest magazine such as *People;* or any number of special-interest monthly magazines such as *Glamour*, *Sports Illustrated*, *Essence*, or *Health.*

   You'll find subscription cards within most magazines. Also, on many college bulletin boards you'll see display cards offering a wide variety of magazines at discount rates for students.

   • Do you already subscribe to any magazine(s)? Which one(s)?

   _____

   _____

(Continues on next page)

___ 4. Read aloud to children in your family, whether younger brothers or sisters or sons or daughters or nephews or nieces. Alternatively, have a family reading time when you and the children take turns reading.

• Do you already read aloud to any young person in your family?

_____

___ 5. Read books on your own. This is the most important step on the road to becoming a regular reader. Reading is most enjoyable when you get drawn into the special world created by a book. You can travel in that world for hours, unmindful of everyday concerns. Too many people are addicted to smoking or drugs or television; you should try, instead, to get hooked on books.

What should you read? Select anything that interests you. That might be comic books, fantasies or science fiction, horror and mystery stories, romances, adventure or sports stories, biographies and autobiographies, or how-to books. To select a book, browse in a bookstore, library, or reading center. Find something you like and begin reading. If you stick to it and become a regular reader, you may find that you have done nothing less than change your life.

• Look at the list of Townsend Library books by going to **www.townsendpress.com**. What are the titles of several books you might like to read on your own?

_____

_____

_____

_____

_____

2

Dictionary Use

THIS CHAPTER IN A NUTSHELL

- You should own both a paperback and a hardbound dictionary.
- You can use a computer to visit online dictionaries.
- Use spelling hints to help you look up in the dictionary a word you cannot spell.
- A dictionary entry will tell you how a word is spelled and pronounced and give you the various meanings of the word. It will also provide other helpful information about words.

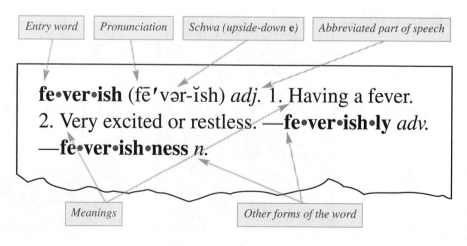

| Entry word | Pronunciation | Schwa (upside-down e) | Abbreviated part of speech |

fe•ver•ish (fē′vər-ĭsh) *adj.* 1. Having a fever.
2. Very excited or restless. —**fe•ver•ish•ly** *adv.*
—**fe•ver•ish•ness** *n.*

| Meanings | Other forms of the word |

The dictionary is a valuable tool. To help you make use of it, this chapter explains in a clear and detailed way what you need to know about dictionaries and the information they provide.

OWNING YOUR OWN DICTIONARIES

You can benefit greatly by owning two dictionaries. The first one you should own is a paperback dictionary you can carry with you. Any of the following would be an excellent choice:

The American Heritage Dictionary, Paperback Edition
The Random House Dictionary, Paperback Edition
The Merriam-Webster Dictionary, Paperback Edition

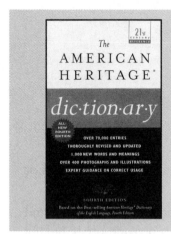 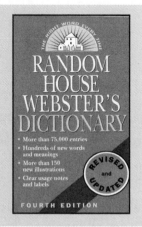 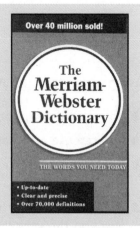

The second dictionary you should own is a desk-sized, hardcover edition which should be kept in the room where you study. All the above dictionaries come in hardbound versions:

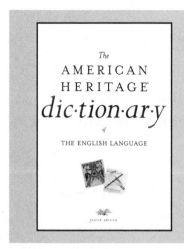 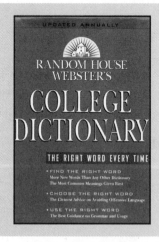 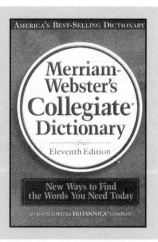

These hardcover dictionaries contain a good deal more information than the paperback editions. For instance, a desk-sized dictionary defines far more words than a paperback dictionary. And there are more definitions for each word, as well. They are worth the extra cost.

If you can, invest in a new dictionary so you will have up-to-date information on old and new words. A dictionary is easily among the best investments for learning that you will ever make.

ONLINE DICTIONARY

If you have a computer and it is connected to the Internet, you may find it easy to check words online. Here is a dictionary site you can go to:

www.merriam-webster.com

If you go online to this site and type in the word *confront*, this is the page you may see:

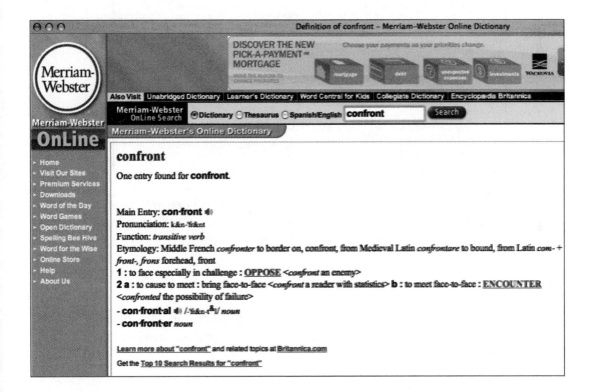

Notice the speaker icon next to the word *confront*. **If you click on this icon, the word will be pronounced for you.**

This site will also give you information on *synonyms* (words with similar meanings to the word you have looked up) and *antonyms* (words with opposite meanings to the word you have looked up). Synonyms and antonyms are explained further on pages 187 and 213–217.

FINDING WORDS IN THE DICTIONARY

Using Guidewords to Find a Word

One way to find a given word in a dictionary is to use **guidewords**—the pair of words at the very top of each dictionary page. Shown below are the top and bottom parts of a page in one paperback dictionary.

---

155   **cluster • cobra**

²**cluster** *vb* : to grow or gather in a cluster
¹**clutch** \\ˈkləch\ *vb* : to grasp with or as if with the hand
²**clutch** *n* **1** : the claws or a hand in the act of grasping; *also* : CONTROL, POWER **2** : a device for gripping an object **3** : a coupling used to connect and disconnect a driving and a driven part of a mechanism; *also* : a lever or pedal operating such a coupling **4** : a crucial situation

nous coal and used in dyes and drugs
co–an·chor \\ˈkō-ˈaŋ-kər\ *n* : a newscaster who shares the duties of head broadcaster
coarse \\ˈkōrs\ *adj* **coars·er; coars·est 1** : of ordinary or inferior quality **2** : composed of large parts or particles ⟨∼ sand⟩ **3** : CRUDE ⟨∼ manners⟩ **4** : ROUGH, HARSH — **coarse·ly** *adv* — **coarse·ness** *n*
coars·en \\ˈkōrs-ᵊn\ *vb* : to make or become coarse

---

coal gas *n* : gas from coal; *esp* : gas distilled from bituminous coal and used for heating
co·a·li·tion \\ˌkō-ə-ˈli-shən\ *n* : UNION; *esp* : a temporary union for a common purpose — **co·a·li·tion·ist** *n*
coal oil *n* : KEROSENE
coal tar *n* : tar distilled from bitumi-

hastily
cob·bler \\ˈkä-blər\ *n* **1** : a mender or maker of shoes **2** : a deep-dish fruit pie with a thick crust
cob·ble·stone \\ˈkä-bəl-ˌstōn\ *n* : a naturally rounded stone larger than a pebble and smaller than a boulder
co·bra \\ˈkō-brə\ *n* [Pg *cobra* (de

The first guideword tells what the first word is on that page; the second guideword tells what the last word is on the page. All the word entries on the page fall alphabetically between the two guidewords.

➤ *Practice 1*

Following are five pairs of dictionary guidewords followed by other words. Underline the **three** words in each series that would be found on the page with the guidewords.

1. **camp / candidate**

   camera   campus   canary   cancer   candle

2. **hoax / holiness**

   holdup   history   hollow   holiday   hog

3. **lesson / lever**

length   letter   liberty   lettuce   level

4. **raft / rake**

railroad   radio   raise   raincoat   ranch

5. **shame / shaving**

sharp   shapely   shallow   shampoo   sheep

Finding a Word You Can't Spell

"If I can't spell a word," you might ask, "how can I find it in the dictionary?" The answer is that you have to guess what the letters might be.

Guessing is not too difficult with certain sounds, such as the sounds of *b* and *p*. But other sounds are more difficult to pin down because they can belong to more than one letter. And that's where the guessing comes in. Here are three hints to help in such cases:

Hint 1: If you're not sure about the vowels in a word, you will simply have to experiment. Vowels often sound the same. So try an *i* in place of an *a*, an *i* in place of an *e*, and so on. If, for example, you don't find a word that sounds as if it begins with *pa*, try looking under *pe*, *pi*, *po*, *pu* or *py*.

Hint 2: Following are groups of letters or letter combinations that often sound alike. If your word isn't spelled with one of the letters in a pair or group shown below, it might be spelled with another in the same pair or group. For example, if it isn't spelled with a *k*, it may be spelled with a *c*.

c / k	**c / s**	**f / v / ph**	**g / j**	**qu / kw / k**	**s / c / z**
sch / sc / sk	**sh / ch**	**shun / tion / sion**		**w / wh**	**able / ible**
ai / ay	**al / el / le**	**ancy / ency**	**ate / ite**	**au / aw**	**ea / ee**
er / or	**ie / ei**	**ou / ow**	**oo / u**	**y / i / e**	

Hint 3: Consonants are sometimes doubled in a word. If you can't find your word with a single consonant, try doubling it.

➤ *Practice 2*

For this practice you will need a dictionary. Try using your ear, the hints on the previous page, and guidewords to help you find the correct spelling of the following words. Write each correct spelling in the answer space.

1. revize _____
2. kiddnap _____
3. pleeze _____
4. beleive _____
5. realy _____

6. skoolteecher _____
7. writting _____
8. libary _____
9. definately _____
10. acros _____

LEARNING FROM A DICTIONARY ENTRY

Each word being defined in a dictionary is in **boldface type**. Here is a sample entry:

Sample Dictionary Entry

> **dis•tress** (dĭ-strĕs′) *n.* 1. Extreme anxiety or pain. 2. In need of immediate assistance: *The police helped the motorist in distress.* —*v.* **-tressed, -tress•ing, -tress•es.** To cause anxiety or pain: *I didn't mean to distress you.*

All of the following information may be provided in a dictionary entry:

1 Spelling and Syllables

2 Pronunciation Symbols and Accent Marks

3 Parts of Speech

4 Irregular Forms of Words

5 Definitions (Meanings)

6 Synonyms

The rest of this chapter will look at each kind of information above.

1   Spelling and Syllables

The dictionary first gives the correct spelling and syllable breakdown of a word. Dots separate the words into syllables. Each syllable is a separate sound, and each sound includes a vowel. In the entry shown above, *distress* is divided into two syllables.

How many syllables are in these words?

harsh   **ru•mor**   **ex•cep•tion**   **in•stall•ment**

The dots tell you that *harsh* has one syllable, *rumor* has two syllables, and *exception* and *installment* have three syllables each.

➤ Practice 3

Use your dictionary to separate the following words into syllables. Put large dots between the syllables. Then write the number of syllables in each word.

Example: con•for•mi•ty   ____4____ syllables

1. f r a g m e n t   _____ syllables

2. i n j e c t i o n   _____ syllables

3. c o m p l i c a t e   _____ syllables

4. i n s e n s i t i v e   _____ syllables

5. c o m m u n i c a t i o n   _____ syllables

2   Pronunciation Symbols and Accent Marks

A dictionary entry word is followed by information in parentheses, as in the entry for *distress*:

dis•tress (dĭ-strĕs′)

The information in parentheses shows how to pronounce the word. It includes two kinds of symbols: pronunciation symbols and accent marks. Following are explanations of each.

Pronunciation Symbols

The pronunciation symbols tell the sounds of the consonants and the vowels in a word. The sounds of the consonants are probably familiar to you, but you may find it helpful to review the vowel sounds. Vowels are the letters *a, e, i, o,* and *u.* (Sometimes *y* is also a vowel, as in *myself* and *copy.*) To know how to pronounce the vowel sounds, use the pronunciation key in your dictionary. Here is a sample pronunciation key:

Pronunciation Key

ă hat	ā pay	âr care	ä card	ě ten	ē she	ĭ sit
ī hi	îr here	ŏ lot	ō go	ô all	oi oil	ou out
o͝o look	yo͝o cure	o͞o cool	yo͞o use	ŭ up	ûr fur	th thick
th then	ə ago, item, easily, gallop, circus					

To use the above key, match the symbol (**ă, ā,** and so on) with the letter or letters in **bold print** in the short word that follows the symbol. For instance, **ă** (also called "short *a*") sounds like the *a* in *hat.*

You can pronounce the *i* in *distress* by first finding the matching symbol within the parentheses. Note that the matching symbol for *i* is **ĭ**. Then look for that symbol in the Pronunciation Key. It shows you that the *i* has the sound of *i* in the short word *sit.* You can also use the Pronunciation Key to pronounce the *e* in *distress*. It shows you that the **ě** is pronounced like the *e in ten.*

A long vowel (a vowel with a line over it) has the sound of its own name. Long *a* (**ā**) sounds like the *a* in *pay*; long *e* (**ē**) sounds like the *e* in *she*; and so on.

Finally, note that the last pronunciation symbol in the key looks like an upside-down e: **ə**. This symbol is known as the **schwa**. As you can see by the words that follow it, the schwa has a very short sound that sounds like "uh" (as in *ago, gallop,* and *circus*) or "ih" (as in *item* and *easily*). It usually sounds much like the "uh" a speaker makes when pausing.

➤ *Practice 4*

Refer to the pronunciation key on the facing page to answer the questions about the following ten words. In the space provided, write the letter of each of your answers.

_____ 1. **contest** (kŏn′tĕst′)
The *o* in *contest* is pronounced like the *o* in
A. *lot.*   B. *go.*

_____ 2. **impress** (ĭm-prĕs′)
The *i* in *impress* is pronounced like the *i* in
A. *sit.*   B. *hi.*

_____ 3. **evident** (ĕv′ĭ-dənt)
The first *e* in *evident* is pronounced like the *e* in
A. *ten.*   B. *she.*

_____ 4. **betray** (bĭ-trā′)
The *a* in *betray* is pronounced like the *a* in
A. *hat.*   B. *pay.*

_____ 5. **poker** (pō′kər)
The *o* in *poker* is pronounced like the o in
A. *lot.*   B. *go.*

_____ 6. **humane** (hyo͞o-mān′)
The *u* in *humane* sounds like the *oo* in
A. *look.*   B. *cool.*

_____ 7. **license** (lī′səns)
The *i* in *license* sounds like the *i* in
A. *sit.*   B. *hi.*

_____ 8. **mastery** (măs′tə-rē)
The *a* in *mastery* is pronounced like the *a* in
A. *hat.*   B. *pay.*

_____ 9. **remedy** (rĕm′ĭ-dē)
The *y* in *remedy* is pronounced like the *e* in
A. *ten.*   B. *she.*

_____10. **disappear** (dĭs′ə-pîr′)
The *a* in *disappear* sounds like the
A. *a* in *hat.*   B. schwa in *ago.*

➤ *Practice 5*

Below are pronunciation symbols for five common words. Write in the word in each case and also the number of schwa sounds in each word. The first item has been done for you as an example.

Pronunciation symbols	*Word itself*	*Number of schwas*
1. (ĭn′stənt)	*instant*	1
2. (mĭr′ə-kəl)	_____	_____
3. (ə-fĕns′)	_____	_____
4. (ĭn-tĕl′ə-jənt)	_____	_____
5. (rĭ-lī′ə-bəl)	_____	_____

Accent Marks

Notice the black marks in the pronunciation guide (the information shown in parentheses) for the word *information*. The marks look a little like apostrophes.

in•for•ma•tion (ĭn′fər-mā′shən)

The darker line (′) is a bold accent mark, and it shows which syllable has the strongest stress. That means the third syllable in *information* is pronounced a little louder than the other three. Syllables without an accent mark are unstressed. Some syllables—like the first syllable in *information*—are in between, and they are marked with a lighter accent mark (′).

Say *information* to yourself. Can you hear that the strongest accent is on *ma*, the third syllable? Can you hear that the first syllable, *in*, is also accented, but not as strongly? If not, say the word to yourself again until you hear the differences in accent sounds.

Here are some familiar words with syllable divisions and accent marks shown in parentheses. Use those guides to help you pronounce the words to yourself.

- bat•tle (băt′l)
- dis•gust (dĭs-gŭst′)
- ap•prov•al (ə-prōō′vəl)
- fa•vor•a•ble (fā′vər-ə-bəl)
- ex•am•i•na•tion (ĭg-zăm′ə-nā′shən)

➤ *Practice 6*

Answer the questions following each of the five words below.

1. **mag•net** (măg′nĭt)

   A. How many syllables are in *magnet?* _____

   B. Which syllable is most strongly accented? _____

2. **en•cour•age** (ĕn-kûr′ĭj)

   A. How many syllables are in *encourage?* _____

   B. Which syllable is more strongly accented? _____

3. **grat•i•tude** (grăt′ĭ-tōōd′)

   A. How many syllables are in *gratitude?* _____

   B. Which syllable is most strongly accented? _____

4. **re•li•a•ble** (rĭ-lī′ə-bəl)

   A. How many syllables are in *reliable?* _____

   B. Which syllable is more strongly accented? _____

5. **a•pol•o•gize** (ə-pŏl′ə-jīz′)

   A. How many syllables are in *apologize?* _____

   B. Which syllable is most strongly accented? _____

3 Parts of Speech

Every word in the dictionary is either a noun, a verb, an adjective, or another part of speech. In dictionary entries, the parts of speech are shown by letters in italics. In the entry below for *progress*, for example, the abbreviations *n.* and *v.* tell us that *progress* is both a noun and a verb.

> **prog•ress** (prŏg′rĕs′) *n.* Movement toward a goal; steady advance
> —*v.* (prə-grĕs′). To move along; advance.

When a word is more than one part of speech, the dictionary gives the definitions for each part of speech separately. In the above entry for *progress*, the abbreviation telling us that *progress* is a noun comes right after the pronunciation symbols; the definitions of the noun follow. When the noun meaning ends, the abbreviation *v.* tells us that the verb pronunciation and definitions will follow.

Parts of speech are abbreviated in order to save space. Following are the most common abbreviations for parts of speech:

n. — noun	*v.* — verb
pron. — pronoun	*conj.* — conjunction
adj. — adjective	*prep.* — preposition
adv. — adverb	*interj.* — interjection

Note: Many dictionaries use the abbreviations *tr.* and *intr.* (or *vt* and *vi*) to indicate two types of verbs, not other parts of speech. The abbreviations *tr.* and *vt* stand for a transitive verb (one that has a direct object). The abbreviations *intr.* and *vi* stand for an intransitive verb (one that does not have a direct object).

➤ Practice 7

Use your dictionary to list the parts of speech (*noun, verb, adjective*) for each of the following words. Each word has more than one part of speech.

Parts of speech

1. attack   A. _____   B. _____

2. wonder   A. _____   B. _____

3. pinch   A. _____   B. _____

4. respect   A. _____   B. _____

5. quiet   A. _____   B. _____

4 Irregular Forms of Words

Look at the following two words and the forms that follow them in most dictionaries.

draw (drô) *v.* **drew** (dro͞o), **drawn, draw•ing**

la•zy (lā′zē) *adj.* **la•zi•er, la•zi•est**

When other forms of a word are spelled in an irregular way (differently from the main form of the word), those forms are shown. As you can see in the examples above, those forms are given after the part of speech in an entry. With irregular verbs, the dictionary gives the past tense (*drew*) and the past participle (*drawn*), as well as the present participle (*drawing*). With adjectives, the dictionary gives the comparative (*lazier*) and superlative (*laziest*) forms.

Plural forms of irregular spellings are also included in this spot in an entry. For example, the entry for *city* begins:

cit•y (sĭt′ē) *n., pl.* **cities**

After the part of speech of *city* (*n.* for noun), the entry shows the irregular form of the plural (*pl.*) of *cities*.

Finally, comparative forms of adjectives and adverbs are also given at this point in an entry. Here are two examples:

good (gŏŏd) *adj.* **bet•ter** (bĕt′ər), **best** (bĕst)

high (hī) *adj.* **-er, -est**

➤ *Practice 8*

Use your dictionary to answer the following questions.

1. What is the plural spelling of the noun *party*? _____

2. What are the past tense and past participle forms of the verb *write*?

    _____   _____

3. What is the plural spelling of the noun *life*? _____

4. What are the past tense and past participle forms of the verb *speak*?

    _____   _____

5. What are the comparative forms of the adjective *little*?

    _____

5   Definitions

Words often have more than one meaning. When they do, their **definitions** (meanings) may be numbered in the dictionary. You can tell which definition of a word fits a given sentence by the meaning of the sentence. For example, the following are three of the definitions of the noun form of *judgment* given in most dictionaries.

1. A decision made in a court of law.
2. The ability to think carefully about something.
3. An opinion or conclusion.

Which of these definitions best fits the sentence below?

> The parents showed good judgment in refusing to put a television in their son's room.

The answer is definition 2: The parents thought carefully about whether to give their son a personal television and then decided against it.

➤ *Practice 9*

Below are three words and their dictionary definitions. A sentence using each word is also given. Choose the dictionary meaning that best fits each sentence.

1. **suspect:** **1.** To regard as likely or probable.
   2. To distrust or doubt.
   3. To think of as guilty without proof.

   Which definition of *suspect* fits the sentence below? _____

   I *suspect* the exam is going to be all essay questions.

2. **quick:** **1.** Very fast; rapid.
   2. Thinking or learning fast.

   Which definition of *quick* fits the following sentence? _____

   My boss has a *quick* temper.

3. **instruct:** **1.** To teach a subject or skill.
   2. To give orders to; direct.

   Which definition of *instruct* fits the following sentence? _____

   The doctor *instructed* the nurse to take my blood pressure.

6 Synonyms

A **synonym** is a word whose meaning is similar to that of another word. For instance, two synonyms for the word *help* are *aid* and *assist*.

Dictionary entries sometimes end with synonyms. For example, the word *forgive* in some dictionaries ends with the synonyms *excuse* and *pardon*. A hardbound dictionary in particular will provide synonyms for a word and explain the differences in meaning among the various synonyms.

More information on synonyms as well as **antonyms** (words with opposite meanings) can be found in a **thesaurus** (thĭ-sôr′əs), which is a collection of synonyms and antonyms. If you have access to the Internet, you can find a free thesaurus online by going to

www.merriam-webster.com or **www.thesaurus.com**

Or check on your computer to see if it has a built-in thesaurus. For example, if you use Microsoft Word on a Macintosh computer, just click on "Tools" and then choose "Thesaurus." (If you are using Word for Windows, type F7, or click on "Review" and then "Thesaurus.")

Or you may want to buy a paperback thesaurus, which you can find in almost any bookstore. Here are three good ones:

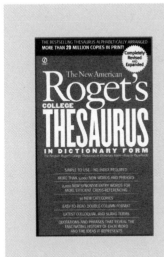  

CHAPTER REVIEW

In this chapter, you learned the following:

* It helps to own two dictionaries. One should be a small paperback you can carry with you. The other should be a large hardbound version for use at home.

* If you have a computer, you can easily find a dictionary online.

* Guidewords and the spelling hints on page 177 will help you find a word in the dictionary.

* A dictionary entry will tell you: 1) how a word is spelled and broken into syllables; 2) how the word is pronounced; 3) the word's part (or parts) of speech; 4) other forms of the word; 5) definitions of the word. Some dictionaries will also list synonyms—words that mean nearly the same as the word.

The next chapter—Chapter 3—will show you how you can use context, rather than a dictionary, to figure out the meaning of a word.

On the Web: If you are using this book in class, you can visit our website for additional practice in using the dictionary. Go to **www.townsendpress.com** and click on "Online Exercises."

➤ *Review Test 1*

To review what you've learned in this chapter, answer each of the following questions by writing the letter of the answer you think is correct.

_____ 1. Use the guidewords at the top of every dictionary page to help you
   A. pronounce a word in a dictionary.
   B. find a word in a dictionary.
   C. define a word in a dictionary.

_____ 2. In a pronunciation key, a dark accent mark shows
   A. which syllable has the strongest stress.
   B. which syllable has the weakest stress.
   C. that the word has only one syllable.

_____ 3. TRUE OR FALSE? A schwa usually sounds like the "uh" a speaker makes when pausing.

_____ 4. Dictionary entries will show you all of the following **except**
   A. how to spell a word.
   B. how to pronounce a word.
   C. the meaning or meanings of a word.
   D. common spelling errors of a word.

➤ *Review Test 2*

A. Below are three pairs of dictionary guidewords followed by a series of other words. In the space provided, write the letter of the **one** word in each series which would be found on the page with the guidewords.

_____ 1. **fountain / fracture**
   A. fragment   B. found   C. fourteen

_____ 2. **midnight / military**
   A. middle   B. million   C. midterm

B. Use your dictionary and the spelling hints on page 177 to find the correct spelling of the following words.

3. busness _____

4. vizitor _____

5. sirprise _____

6. realy _____

C. Use your dictionary to put dots between the syllables in each word. Then write out the word with the correct pronunciation symbols, including the accent mark or marks.

7. m i c r o s c o p e _____

8. p r o n u n c i a t i o n _____

D. Answer the questions about the two words below. The pronunciation key on page 180 will help you answer the questions.

_____ 9. In **ca•ble** (kā′bəl), the *a* is pronounced like the *a* in what common word?

    A. *hat*   B. *pay*   C. *card*

_____ 10. In **hes•i•tate** (hĕz′ĭ-tāt), the *e* is pronounced like the *e* in what common word?

    A. *ten*   B. *she*   C. *item*

➤ *Review Test 3*

Here is a chance to apply your understanding of dictionary use to a full-length reading. This selection is a true story about Malcolm X, an African-American civil rights leader in the 1950s and 1960s. In this excerpt from his autobiography, Malcolm X (with his coauthor, Alex Haley) explains how he used his time in jail to become "truly free." Read the selection and then answer the questions that follow.

Words to Watch

Following are some words in the reading that do not have strong context support. Each word is followed by the number of the paragraph in which it appears and its meaning there. These words are indicated in the reading by a small circle (°).

> *painstaking* (5): very careful
> *ragged* (5): uneven
> *burrowing* (6): digging
> *succeeding* (7): following
> *word-base* (8): vocabulary
> *bunk* (8): bed

DISCOVERING WORDS

Malcolm X with Alex Haley

1 It was because of my letters [which Malcolm X wrote to people outside while he was in jail] that I happened to stumble upon starting to acquire some kind of a homemade education.

2 I became increasingly frustrated at not being able to express what I wanted to convey in letters that I wrote. . . . And every book I picked up had few sentences which didn't contain any- where from one to nearly all the words that might as well have been in Chinese. When I skipped those words, of course, I really ended up with little idea of what the book said. . . .

3 I saw that the best thing I could do was get hold of a dictionary—to study, to learn some words. I requested a dictionary along with some tablets and pencils from the Norfolk Prison Colony school.

4 I spent two days just riffling uncertainly through the dictionary's pages. I'd never realized so many words existed! I didn't know *which* words I needed to learn. Finally, just to start some kind of action, I began copying.

5 In my slow, painstaking°, ragged° handwriting, I copied into my tablet everything printed on that first page,

down to the punctuation marks. I believe it took me a day. Then, aloud, I read back to myself everything I'd written on the tablet. Over and over, aloud, to myself, I read my own handwriting.

6   I woke up the next morning, thinking about those words—immensely proud to realize that not only had I written so much at one time, but I'd written words that I never knew were in the world. Moreover, with a little effort, I also could remember what many of these words meant. I reviewed the words whose meanings I didn't remember. Funny thing, from the dictionary's first page right now, that *aardvark* springs to my mind. The dictionary had a picture of it, a long-tailed, long-eared, burrowing° African mammal, which lives off termites caught by sticking out its tongue as an anteater does for ants.

7   I was so fascinated that I went on—I copied the dictionary's next page. And the same experience came when I studied that. With every succeeding° page, I also learned of people and places and events from history. Actually, the dictionary is like a miniature encyclopedia. Finally, the dictionary's A section had filled a whole tablet—and I went on into the B's. That was the way I started copying what eventually became the entire dictionary. It went a lot faster after so much practice helped me to pick up handwriting speed.

8   I suppose it was inevitable that as my word-base° broadened, I could for the first time pick up a book and read and now begin to understand what the book was saying. Anyone who has read a great deal can imagine the new world that opened. Let me tell you something: From then until I left the prison, in every free moment I had, if I was not reading in the library, I was reading on my bunk°. You couldn't have gotten me out of books with a wedge. Months passed without my even thinking about being imprisoned. In fact, up to then, I never had been so truly free in my life.

Dictionary Questions

Answer the dictionary questions that follow about words in this selection. Use your dictionary when needed.

_____ 1. *Stumble* (in "I happened to stumble upon starting to acquire some kind of a homemade education") would be found on the dictionary page with which guidewords?
A. **strongbox / study**
B. **success / sufficient**
C. **student / style**
D. **stock / store**

_____ 2. Below are dictionary definitions of *stumble*. Choose the meaning that best fits *stumble* in "I happened to stumble upon starting to acquire some kind of a homemade education."
   A. To strike the foot against something
   B. To walk unsteadily
   C. To discover accidentally

_____ 3. Below are dictionary definitions of *acquire*. Choose the meaning that best fits *acquire* in "I happened to stumble upon starting to acquire some kind of a homemade education."
   A. To buy (an object)
   B. To learn or develop (a skill, habit, or quality)
   C. To achieve (a reputation)

_____ 4. Below are dictionary definitions of *convey*. Choose the meaning that best fits *convey* in "I became increasingly frustrated at not being able to express what I wanted to convey in letters that I wrote. . . ."
   A. To carry, bring, or take from one place to another
   B. To communicate
   C. To lead or conduct

5. Malcolm says that "I suppose it was inevitable that as my word-base broadened, I could for the first time pick up a book and read and now begin to understand what the book was saying."

   Use your dictionary to find the definition of *inevitable* and write the meaning here: _____

   _____

6. How many syllables are in *inevitable,* and which syllable is accented?

   _____   _____

7. What part of speech is *inevitable*? _____

8. *Aardvark* was a word on the first page of Malcolm X's dictionary. Select a word on the first page of your dictionary. The word should have two or more syllables.

   Write the word and its definition(s) here: _____

   _____

9. Use your dictionary to write out the word again, this time putting dots between the syllables in the word.

_____

10. Finally, write out the pronunciation of the word (which often appears in parentheses), showing pronunciation symbols and including the accent mark or marks.

_____

Questions about the Reading

For each question, write the letter of your answer in the space provided.

_____ 1. In the sentence below, the word *riffling* (rĭf′lĭng) probably means
   A. flipping.
   B. writing.
   C. destroying.
   D. laughing.

   "I spent two days just riffling uncertainly through the dictionary's pages." (Paragraph 4)

_____ 2. In the sentence below, the word *wedge* (wĕj) probably means
   A. page.
   B. magazine.
   C. tool used to separate objects.
   D. tool used to press objects together.

   "You couldn't have gotten me out of books with a wedge." (Paragraph 8)

_____ 3. Which statement best expresses the main idea of the entire selection?
   A. Increasing his vocabulary opened Malcolm's mind in exciting ways.
   B. When he arrived in prison, Malcolm's vocabulary was poor.
   C. Reading the dictionary is the best way to learn new vocabulary words.
   D. Malcolm used his time in prison constructively.

_____ 4. What seems to be the main idea of paragraph 2?
   A. While in prison, Malcolm liked to write letters.
   B. A lot of the words Malcolm saw in books might as well have been written in Chinese.
   C. When Malcolm came to a word he didn't understand, he skipped it.
   D. Malcolm's poor vocabulary began to frustrate him as he tried to read and write.

_____ 5. Malcolm requested a dictionary so that
   A. he could improve his spelling.
   B. he could learn what an aardvark was.
   C. he could have something to read.
   D. he could learn new words.

_____ 6. Malcolm's work with the dictionary went faster after he
   A. learned to write more quickly.
   B. got an assistant to help him.
   C. got a typewriter.
   D. learned shorthand.

_____ 7. How much of the dictionary did Malcolm eventually copy?
   A. The A's
   B. The A's and B's
   C. A through P
   D. All of it

_____ 8. Malcolm compared the dictionary to
   A. the Bible.
   B. a miniature encyclopedia.
   C. a novel.
   D. a magazine.

_____ 9. Malcolm probably
   A. was very intelligent, but did not have a lot of education.
   B. was a college graduate.
   C. wanted to become a professional writer.
   D. stopped reading much after he was released from prison.

_____10. The selection suggests that
   A. becoming a reader transformed Malcolm's life.
   B. Malcolm was innocent of the crime that had sent him to prison.
   C. Malcolm expected other prisoners to follow his example.
   D. Malcolm hoped to shorten his prison sentence by studying.

Discussion Questions

1. What is your impression of Malcolm X? After reading this short selection, what kind of person do you think he was?

2. At the end of the selection, Malcolm X says that even though he was still in jail, he "never had been so truly free" in his life. What does he mean by that? What is it that makes you feel free?

3. Malcolm X decided to improve his vocabulary in order to express himself better in letters. What was it that made you decide to continue your education? What do you hope to do with the knowledge you are gaining?

Note: Writing assignments for this selection appear on pages 558–559.

Check Your Performance   **DICTIONARY USE**

Activity	Number Right	Points	Score
Review Test 1 (4 items)	_____	× 5 =	_____
Review Test 2 (10 items)	_____	× 2 =	_____
Review Test 3 (20 items)	_____	× 3 =	_____

TOTAL SCORE   =   _____%

Enter your total score into the **Reading Performance Chart: Review Tests** on the inside back cover.

DICTIONARY USE: Mastery Test 1

A. Below are two pairs of dictionary guidewords followed by a series of other words. On the answer line, write the letter of the **one** word in each series which would be found on the page with the guidewords.

_____ 1. **coverage / crab**

     A. court   B. coward   C. cracked

_____ 2. **gate / gear**

     A. general   B. gasoline   C. gather

B. Use your dictionary and the spelling hints on page 177 to find the correct spelling of the following words.

3. bycicle _____

4. takeing _____

5. hury _____

6. beleive _____

C. Use your dictionary to put dots between the syllables in each word. Then write out the word with the correct pronunciation symbols, including the accent marks.

7. c i r c u m s t a n c e _____

8. i n s i g n i f i c a n t _____

(Continues on next page)

D. Use the following pronunciation key to answer the questions below.

Pronunciation Key

ă hat	ā pay	âr care	ä card	ě ten	ē she	ĭ sit
ī hi	îr here	ŏ lot	ō go	ô all	oi oil	ou out
ŏŏ look	yŏŏ cure	ōō cool	yōō use	ŭ up	ûr fur	th thick
th then	ə ago, item, easily, gallop, circus					

9. In *dignity* (dĭg′nĭ-tē), the *y* is pronounced like the *e* in what common word? _____

10. In *dignity* (dĭg′nĭ-tē), the *i*'s are pronounced like the *i* in what common word? _____

DICTIONARY USE: Mastery Test 2

A. Below are two pairs of dictionary guidewords followed by a series of other words. On the answer line, write the letter of the **one** word in each series which would be found on the page with the guidewords.

_____ 1. **prize / process**

       A. private   B. problem   C. professor

_____ 2. **snowy / soccer**

       A. soak   B. social   C. snob

B. Use your dictionary and the spelling hints on page 177 to find the correct spelling of the following words.

    3. lable _____

    4. froun _____

    5. acshun _____

    6. ordurly _____

C. Use your dictionary to put dots between the syllables in each word. Then write out the word with the correct pronunciation symbols, including the accent marks.

    7. e n e r g e t i c _____

    8. d e m o n s t r a t i o n _____

(Continues on next page)

D. Use the following pronunciation key to answer the questions below.

Pronunciation Key

ă hat	ā pay	âr care	ä card	ĕ ten	ē she	ĭ sit
ī hi	îr here	ŏ lot	ō go	ô all	oi oil	ou **out**
ŏŏ look	yŏŏ cure	ōō cool	yōō use	ŭ up	ûr fur	th thick
th then	ə ago, item, easily, gallop, circus					

9. In *firetrap* (fīr′trăp′), the *i* is pronounced like the *i* in what common word?

_____

10. In *firetrap* (fīr′trăp′), the *a* is pronounced like the *a* in what common word?

_____

DICTIONARY USE: Mastery Test 3

A. Below are two pairs of dictionary guidewords followed by a series of other words. On the answer line, write the letter of the **one** word in each series which would be found on the page with the guidewords.

_____ 1. **flavor / flexible**

     A. flesh   B. flatter   C. float

_____ 2. **jeweler / job**

     A. jingle   B. jealous   C. join

B. Use your dictionary and the spelling hints on page 177 to find the correct spelling of the following words.

   3. dicide _____

   4. komplete _____

C. Use your dictionary to put dots between the syllables in each word. Then write out the word with the correct pronunciation symbols, including the accent marks.

   5. f u n d a m e n t a l_____

   6. a p p r o x i m a t e_____

(Continues on next page)

D. Use the pronunciation key to answer the questions that follow.

Pronunciation Key

ă hat	ā pay	âr care	ä card	ĕ ten	ē she	ĭ sit
ī hi	îr here	ŏ lot	ō go	ô all	oi oil	ou out
ŏŏ look	yŏŏ cure	ōō cool	yōō use	ŭ up	ûr fur	th thick
th then	ə ago, item, easily, gallop, circus					

7. In *shallow* (shăl′ō), the *a* is pronounced like the *a* in what common word?

   _____

8. In *shallow* (shăl′ō), the *o* is pronounced like the *o* in what common word?

   _____

9. In *precise* (prĭ-sīs′), the first *e* is pronounced like the *i* in what common word?

   _____

10. In *precise* (prĭ-sīs′), the *i* is pronounced like the *i* in what common word?

   _____

DICTIONARY USE: Mastery Test 4

Answer the following questions about the dictionary entries for *verdict* and *maintain*. Use the pronunciation key below for help as needed.

Pronunciation Key

ă hat	ā pay	âr care	ä card	ĕ ten	ē she	ĭ sit
ī hi	îr here	ŏ lot	ō go	ô all	oi oil	ou out
ŏŏ look	yŏŏ cure	ōō cool	yōō use	ŭ up	ûr fur	th thick
th then	ə ago, item, easily, gallop, circus					

ver•dict (vûr′dĭkt) *n.* **1.** The finding of a jury in a trial. **2.** A judgment, opinion, or conclusion that is expressed about something.

_____ 1. Which syllable in *verdict* is accented?
   A. The first   B. The second

_____ 2. The *e* in *verdict* is pronounced like the
   A. *e* in *ten*.   B. *u* in *fur*.

_____ 3. What part of speech is *verdict*?
   A. Noun   B. Verb   C. Adjective

_____ 4. Which definition of *verdict* best fits the sentence below—1 or 2?

   Tim's verdict on the new video game was that it was well worth the money.

_____ 5. Which definition of *verdict* best fits the sentence below—1 or 2?

   When the guilty verdict was announced, the defendant began to sob.

(Continues on next page)

main•tain (mān-tān′) *v.* **1.** To carry on; continue. **2.** To keep in good repair. **3.** To provide for; support. **4.** To defend against criticism. **5.** To declare to be true. —**main•tain′a•ble** *adj.* —**main′te•nance** *n.*

_____ 6. Both *a*'s in *maintain* sound like the
     A. *a* in *hat.*   B. *a* in *pay.*

_____ 7. How many syllables are in the word *maintainable*?

_____ 8. What part of speech is *maintenance*?
     A. Noun   B. Verb   C. Adjective

_____ 9. Which definition of *maintain* best fits the sentence below—1, 2, 3, 4, or 5?

It can be costly to properly maintain a house.

_____10. Which definition of *maintain* best fits the sentence below—1, 2, 3, 4, or 5?

My grandmother maintains that Ronald Reagan was one of our greatest presidents.

DICTIONARY USE: Mastery Test 5

Answer the following questions about the dictionary entries for *linger* and *solitary*. Use the pronunciation key below for help as needed.

Pronunciation Key

ă hat	ā pay	âr care	ä card	ě ten	ē she	ĭ sit
ī hi	îr here	ŏ lot	ō go	ô all	oi oil	ou out
ŏŏ look	yŏŏ cure	ōō cool	yōō use	ŭ up	ûr fur	th thick
th then	ə ago, item, easily, gallop, circus					

ling•er (lĭng′gər) *v.* **1.** To put off leaving a place because you are reluctant to go. **2.** To remain alive, although very weak, while gradually dying. **3.** To take longer than usual to do something, usually because you are enjoying yourself. **4.** To persist: *an aftertaste that lingers.* —**lin′ger•er** *n.* —**lin′ger•ing•ly** *adv.*

_____ 1. Which syllable in *linger* is accented?
    A. The first   B. The second

_____ 2. The *i* in *linger* is pronounced like the *i* in
    A. *hi.*   B. *sit.*

_____ 3. What part of speech is *lingerer*?
    A. Noun   B. Verb   C. Adjective

_____ 4. Which definition of *linger* best fits the sentence below—1, 2, 3, or 4?

    Joan liked to linger in the garden when the roses were in bloom.

_____ 5. Which definition of *linger* best fits the sentence below—1, 2, 3, or 4?

    It was sad to watch Phil's grandfather linger in the hospital with lung cancer.

(Continues on next page)

sol•i•tar•y (sŏl′ĭ-tĕr′ē) *adj* **1.** Done without the company of other people. **2.** Preferring to be or live alone. **3.** In a remote location; secluded. **4.** Existing as the only one of its kind. —**sol′i•tar′i •ness** *n.*

_____ 6. The *o* in *solitary* sounds like the
      A. *o* in *go*.   B. *o* in *lot*.

_____ 7. How many syllables are in the word *solitary*?

_____ 8. What part of speech is *solitariness*?
      A. Noun   B. Verb   C. Adjective

_____ 9. Which definition of *solitary* best fits the sentence below—1, 2, 3, or 4?
Deep in the woods, we came upon a solitary cabin.

_____10. Which definition of *solitary* best fits the sentence below—1, 2, 3, or 4?
Surfing the Internet is usually a solitary pastime.

DICTIONARY USE: Mastery Test 6

A. Answer the following questions about the dictionary entries for *assert* and *interfere*. Use the pronunciation key below for help as needed.

Pronunciation Key

ă hat	ā pay	âr care	ä card	ĕ ten	ē she	ĭ sit
ī hi	îr here	ŏ lot	ō go	ô all	oi oil	ou out
o͝o look	yo͝o cure	o͞o cool	yo͞o use	ŭ up	ûr fur	th thick
th then	ə ago, item, easily, gallop, circus					

as•sert (ə-sûrt′) *v.* **1.** To state something as being true. **2.** To keep or defend. **3.** To put (oneself) forward boldly or forcefully. —**as•ser′tive** *adj.* —**as•ser′tive•ly** *adv.* —**as•ser′tive•ness** *n.*

_____ 1. Which syllable in *assert* is accented?
     A. The first   B. The second

_____ 2. The *e* in *assert* is pronounced like the
     A. *u* in *up*.   B. *u* in *fur.*

_____ 3. What part of speech is *assertive*?
     A. Noun   B. Verb   C. Adjective

_____ 4. Which definition of *assert* best fits the sentence below—1, 2, or 3?

    When the bully pushed ahead of me in line, I asserted myself by pushing him back.

_____ 5. Which definition of *assert* best fits the sentence below—1, 2, or 3?

    My English teacher likes to assert that everyone should read Shakespeare.

(Continues on next page)

in•ter•fere (ĭn'tər-fîr') *v.* **in•ter•fered, in•ter•fer•ing 1.** To delay, hinder, or obstruct the natural or desired course of something. **2.** To intrude in the affairs of others; meddle. **3.** To cause electronic interference. **4.** To obstruct, block, or hinder illegally an opponent in sport. —**in'ter•fer'ence** *n.* —**in'ter•fer'er** *n.*

_____ 6. The *i* in *interfere* sounds like the *i* in
     A. *hi.*   B. *sit.*

_____ 7. How many syllables are in the word *interfered*?

_____ 8. What part of speech is *interference*?
     A. Noun   B. Verb   C. Adjective

_____ 9. Which definition of *interfere* best fits the sentence below—1, 2, 3, or 4?

     Carol didn't like it when her best friend tried to interfere with her relationship with Kevin.

_____10. Which definition of *interfere* best fits the sentence below—1, 2, 3, or 4?

     An accident at rush hour interfered with the flow of traffic along the expressway.

B. Use your dictionary to find the correct spelling of the following words. (Feel free to use the spelling hints on page 177.)

    11. instructer _____

    12. practis _____

    13. recieve _____

    14. impresion_____

    15. eazy _____

C. Use your dictionary to put dots between the syllables in each word. Then write out the word with the correct pronunciation symbols, including the accent marks.

    16. a b r u p t _____

    17. f a t i g u e _____

    18. e x t r a v a g a n t_____

    19. e s s e n t i a l _____

    20. m i s i n t e r p r e t _____

3

Vocabulary in Context

THIS CHAPTER IN A NUTSHELL

- You don't always have to use a dictionary to learn the meanings of new words in your reading. You can often use context clues to figure out the meaning of a word.
- There are four kinds of context clues:
  — Examples of the new word
  — Synonyms (words that mean the same as the new word)
  — Antonyms (words that mean the opposite of the new word)
  — The rest of the sentence or the passage

Do you know the meaning of the word *consolidate*? Look at the following *Frank and Ernest* cartoon and see if the context helps you choose the correct answer:

Frank and Ernest

FRANK AND ERNEST: © Thaves / Dist. by Newspaper Enterprise Assocation, Inc.

____ *Consolidate* (kən-sŏl′ĭ-dāt′) means

A. separate. B. cancel. C. combine into one.

Frank and Ernest are seeking a large single loan for their financial worries. (Of course, the joke is that all their small debts will now be replaced by "one giant nightmare" of a loan.) The **context**—the words surrounding the unfamiliar word—tells us that *consolidate* means "combine into one." In this chapter, you will learn how to use context to figure out the meanings of words.

UNDERSTANDING VOCABULARY IN CONTEXT

Do you know the meaning of the word *queries*? How about the word *tedious*? Or the word *transmit*?

You may be having trouble coming up with the meanings of these words. However, you will be more likely to know what they mean when you see them in complete sentences. Read each sentence below and see if you can understand the meaning of the word in *italics*. In the space provided, write the letter of the meaning you think is correct. Then read the explanation.

_____ 1. Julia was nervous about answering the detective's *queries*. Why was he asking so many questions, anyway?

Queries (kwîr′ēz) are
A. charges.   B. questions.   C. statements of fact.

_____ 2. Most of my history teacher's lectures were *tedious*, but the one about what really happened on Paul Revere's famous ride was very interesting.

Tedious (tē′dē-əs) means
A. interesting.   B. long.   C. boring.

_____ 3. Mosquitoes *transmit* sleeping sickness through biting.

Transmit (trăns-mĭt′) means
A. spread.   B. enjoy.   C. cure.

Explanation:

In each sentence above, the context provides clues to the word's meaning. You may have guessed from the context that *queries* means "questions," that *tedious* means "boring," and that *transmit* means to "spread."

Using context clues to understand the meaning of unfamiliar words will help you in two ways:

1 It will save you time when reading. You will not have to stop to look up words in the dictionary. (Of course, you won't *always* be able to understand a word from its context, so you should have a dictionary nearby as you read.)

2 It will improve your "working vocabulary"—words you recognize as you read and will eventually be able to use when you speak and write.

TYPES OF CONTEXT CLUES

Here are four common types of context clues:

1 Examples

2 Synonyms

3 Antonyms

4 General Sense of the Sentence or Passage

In the following sections, you will read about and practice each type of clue. The practices will sharpen your skills in using context clues and help you add new words to your vocabulary.

Remember *not* to use a dictionary for these practices. Their purpose is to help you develop the skill of figuring out what words mean *without* using a dictionary. Pronunciations are provided in parentheses for the words, and a guide to pronunciation is on page 551.

1 Examples

An unfamiliar word may appear with examples that reveal what the word means. Look at the cartoon below and see if the examples help you choose the correct meaning of the word *commitment*:

Copyright © Randy Glasbergen.
www.glasbergen.com

"You have a 30-year mortgage, a 5-year car lease, and a lifetime gym membership ... but you're afraid of commitment?"

_____ *Commitment* (kə-mĭt′mənt) means

A. a promise to do something.

B. an opportunity for something.

C. an opinion about something.

The three examples of commitment—a 30-year mortgage, a 5-year car lease, and a lifetime gym membership—help you understand that *commitment* means "a promise to do something."

☑ *Check Your Understanding*

Now read the items that follow. An *italicized* word in each sentence is followed by examples that serve as context clues for that word. These examples, which are **boldfaced**, will help you figure out the meaning of each word. On each line, write the letter of the answer you think is correct.

Note that examples are often introduced with signal words and phrases like *for example, for instance, including,* and *such as.*

_____ 1. *Assets* (ăs′ĕts′) such as **good health**, **a loving family**, and **an enjoyable job** make life rewarding.

 Assets are

 A. things of value.   B. rewards on the job.   C. helpful people.

 Hint: Remember that in the exercises in this chapter, you can insert into each sentence the word you think is the answer. For example, substitute *things of value, rewards on the job,* or *helpful people* into sentence 1 in place of *assets* to see which one fits.

_____ 2. A coyote's *prey* (prā) includes **squirrels**, **rabbits**, and **mice**.

 Prey means

 A. friends.   B. victims.   C. replacement.

_____ 3. The sports car had *defects* (dē′fĕkts′)—for example, **a dented fender** and **torn seats**—but I didn't care. I had wanted a Corvette for years, and I was going to buy it.

 Defects are

 A. faults.   B. out-of-date features.   C. foreign qualities.

Explanation:

1. The correct answer is A. The examples given—good health, a loving family, and a job you enjoy—show that assets are "things of value."

2. The correct answer is B. The examples—squirrels, rabbits, and mice—reveal that prey are "victims."

3. The correct answer is A. The examples—a dented fender and torn seats—show that defects are "faults."

➤ *Practice 1: Examples*

Read each item below and then do two things:
1. Underline the examples that suggest the meaning of the word in *italics*.
2. Write the letter of the word's meaning on the answer line.

_____ 1. We often communicate what we mean by using *gestures* such as the thumbs-up sign, hands on the hips, and a shrug of the shoulders.

Gestures (jĕs′chərs) are
A. motions of the body.　　B. good feelings.　　C. hand signals.

_____ 2. Newspaper reporters have been fired for *fictitious* reporting that included quotations which were never said and events that never occurred.

Fictitious (fĭk-tĭsh′əs) means
A. true-life.　　B. unknown.　　C. not real.

_____ 3. *Obnoxious* behavior in a movie theater—for instance, burping, loud talking, or playing around—is considered childish by most people.

Obnoxious (ŏb-nŏk′shəs) means
A. very unpleasant.　　B. acceptable.　　C. funny.

_____ 4. For better health and a longer life, doctors recommend *wholesome* activities, including exercising daily and eating nutritious foods.

Wholesome (hōl′səm) means
A. boring.　　B. skillful.　　C. healthy.

_____ 5. Examples of *distractions* that always seem to occur during an important test include coughing, sighing, and scraping of chairs.

Distractions (dĭ-străkt′shənz) are things that
A. are friendly.　　B. take away　　C. increase your
　　　　　　　　　　　your attention.　　ability to perform.

2　Synonyms

Context clues are often found in the form of **synonyms**: one or more words that mean the same or almost the same as the unknown word. Look again at the sentences on page 210: "Julia was nervous about answering the detective's *queries*. Why was he asking so many questions, anyway?" Here the synonym "questions" tells you the meaning of *queries*.

Now look at the cartoon below about a boy talking to his mother.

Copyright 2004 by Randy Glasbergen.
www.glasbergen.com

GLASBERGEN

**"Don't humiliate me, Mom.
I feel worthless enough already."**

Notice that the synonym for *humiliate*—expressed in the words of the young man who says "I feel worthless enough already"—helps you understand that *humiliate* (hyōō′mĭl′ē-āt′) means "to make feel ashamed."

☑ *Check Your Understanding*

Each item below contains a word or phrase that is a synonym of the *italicized* word. Underline the synonym in each sentence. Then read the explanation that follows.

1. Hal was a *mediocre* (mē′dē-ō′kər) student. He was an average baseball player, as well.

2. It is hard to believe that my millionaire cousin was once *indigent* (ĭn′dĭ-jənt), so poor that he walked the streets without knowing where his next meal would come from.

3. Most companies have a *regulation* (rĕg′yə-lā′shən) allowing new mothers to take three months off from work. Some firms also have a rule allowing fathers the same time off.

Explanation:

In each sentence, the synonym probably helped you understand the meaning of the word in italics:

1. Someone who is *mediocre* at something is "average."

2. Someone who is *indigent* is "poor."

3. A *regulation* is a "rule."

➤ Practice 2: Synonyms

Each item below includes a synonym of the *italicized* word. Write each synonym in the space provided.

_____ 1. Some people hate to admit an error. My boss, for instance, will never *concede* (kən-sēd′) that he might be wrong.

_____ 2. You may be *reluctant* (rĭ-lŭk′tənt) to give a speech now, but the more speaking practice you get, the less unwilling you will be.

_____ 3. The *absurd* (əb-sûrd′) idea that people from outer space live among us is as ridiculous as the belief that the Earth is flat.

_____ 4. Students are often *apprehensive* (ăp′rĭ-hĕn′sĭv) of final exams, but with the right study skills, they don't have to be fearful.

_____ 5. The belief that you can drink and then drive safely is a *fallacy* (făl′ə-sē); unfortunately, this false idea is held by many people.

3 Antonyms

Antonyms—words and phrases that mean the opposite of a word—are also useful as context clues. For example, *soft* is the opposite of *hard*, and *worried* is the opposite of *relieved*. Antonyms are often signaled by words such as *unlike, but, however, instead of, in contrast,* or *on the other hand.*

Look again at the sentence on page 210: "Most of my history teacher's lectures were *tedious*, but the one about what really happened on Paul Revere's famous ride was very interesting." Here the word *but* helps suggest that *tedious* must be the opposite of *interesting*.

Look also at the cartoon below about a married couple doing household chores:

"Before the kids, we had nothing to do.
Now we're overwhelmed."

Notice that the antonym "nothing to do" helps you figure out that *overwhelmed* (ō'vər-hwĕlmd') must mean "having too much to do."

☑ *Check Your Understanding*

In each of the following sentences, underline the word or phrase that means the opposite of the *italicized* word. Then, on the answer line, write the letter of the meaning of the italicized word. Finally, read the explanation that follows.

_____ 1. The *adverse* weather conditions forced us to stay inside for most of our vacation. The day the weather finally turned nice, we had to leave.

     Adverse (ăd-vûrs') means

     A. nice.   B. bad.   C. summer.

_____ 2. I thought it was difficult to *ascend* the mountain, but I discovered that climbing down it was even worse.

     Ascend (ə-sĕnd')means

     A. climb up.   B. walk around.   C. climb down.

_____ 3. After years of *defying* my parents, I decided life might be better if I tried agreeing with them once in a while.

     Defying (dĭ-fī'yĭng) means

     A. avoiding.   B. obeying.   C. opposing.

Explanation:

1. The correct answer is B. *Adverse* weather conditions are the opposite of "nice" ones—they are bad.

2. The correct answer is A. To *ascend* is the opposite of "climbing down"—when you ascend, you climb up.

3. The right answer is C. *Defying* one's parents is the opposite of "agreeing with them." When you defy people, you oppose what they say.

➤ Practice 3: Antonyms

Each item below includes a word or phrase that is an antonym of the *italicized* word. Underline each of those antonyms. Then, on the line, write the letter of the meaning of the italicized word.

_____ 1. Your science project is much more *elaborate* than mine. In fact, mine looks very simple compared with yours.

Hint: What would be the opposite of *elaborate*?

Elaborate (ĭ-lăb′ər-ĭt) means
A. plain.　　　　B. large.　　　　C. complicated.

_____ 2. Gordon's family worried that he would remain an *obscure* author all his life. However, he believed that someday he would be famous.

Obscure (ŏb-skyŏor′) means
A. unknown.　　　B. well-known.　　　C. good.

_____ 3. The attorney introduced facts she felt were *relevant* to the case. But the judge said the facts were unrelated to the trial.

Relevant (rĕl′ə-vənt) means
A. legal.　　　　B. related.　　　　C. known.

_____ 4. When providing directions, give the steps *in sequence*. If they are out of order, those trying to follow the directions will become confused.

In sequence (sē′kwəns) means
A. all at once.　　B. in order.　　　C. in a confusing way.

_____ 5. The teacher *commended* two students on the outstanding work they were doing. Then he criticized the rest of class for doing so poorly.

Commended (kə-mĕnd′ed) means
A. blamed.　　　　B. graded.　　　　C. praised.

4 General Sense of the Sentence or Passage

Often, the context of a new word contains no examples, synonyms, or antonyms. In such cases, you must do a bit of detective work and try to make a guess based on any clues provided.

Look at the cartoon below about a job interview.

Copyright 2001 by Randy Glasbergen.
www.glasbergen.com

GLASBERGEN

"Allen is an incredible, wonderful, fun, generous, exciting, kind, loving, brilliant, very special human being. This personal reference from your mother is quite impressive."

The glowing reference (from the job applicant's mother!) helps you realize that *impressive* (ĭm-prĕs′ĭv) means "very favorable."

☑ Check Your Understanding

In each sentence below, look for general clues to the meaning of the word in *italics*. Then write the letter of the answer you feel is the meaning of the italicized word.

_____ 1. Elena thought she had *ample* time to review her notes before the afternoon exam. Then she discovered her watch was incorrect—she was actually late for the test!

Ample (ăm′pəl) means
A. no. B. plenty of. C. little.

_____ 2. At the animal shelter, Rita fell in love with a poodle, but Dan couldn't resist a collie. So they felt that there was no *alternative* but to keep both animals.

An *alternative* (âl-tûr′nə-tĭv) is a
A. choice. B. reason. C. mystery.

_____ 3. As a *consequence* of his bad report card, my brother could not watch TV until his grades improved.

A *consequence* (kŏn′sĭ-kwĕns′) is a

A. right.   B. result.   C. chance.

Explanation:

1. The correct answer is B. *Ample* means "plenty of." Rita mistakenly thought she had plenty of time to think about the exam.

2. The right answer is A. An *alternative* is a "choice." Rita and Dan felt they had no choice but to take both dogs home.

3. The correct answer is B. A *consequence* is a "result." The result of the brother's bad report card was not being able to watch TV until his teachers reported that he had improved.

➤ Practice 4: General Sense of the Passage

Figure out the meaning of the word in *italics* by looking for general clues. Then, on the line, write the letter of the meaning you think is correct.

_____ 1. My brother felt it would be *futile* to try to make the basketball team. The other players were all at least eight inches taller than he was.

Futile (fyōot′l) means

A. easy.   B. useless.   C. expensive.

_____ 2. The *impact* of the crash was so great that you couldn't tell the make of either car. Both were totally destroyed.

Impact (ĭm′păkt) means

A. force.   B. time.   C. place.

_____ 3. The young eagle was clearly a *novice* at flying. As he tried to land, he got himself caught in a thornbush.

A *novice* (nŏv′ĭs) is a

A. bird.   B. success.   C. beginner.

_____ 4. At a party given by a company for its clients, employees are expected to *mingle* with the guests to make the guests feel more comfortable.

Mingle (mĭng′gəl) *with* means

A. bother.   B. mix with.   C. sell things to.

_____ 5. Big band music was popular during the 1940s. It then disappeared from the music scene, but has been *revived* in recent years.

Revived (rĭ-vīvd′) means

A. lost.   B. brought back to life.   C. destroyed.

An Important Point about Textbook Definitions

You don't always have to use context clues or the dictionary to find definitions. Very often, textbook authors provide definitions of important terms. They usually follow a definition with one or more examples to to make sure that you understand the word being defined.

Here is a short textbook passage that includes a definition and an example. Note that the term to be defined is set off in **boldface** type, and the definition then follows.

> [1]**Phobias** are fears that are out of proportion to the actual danger in a situation. [2]Some people, for example, have a fear of riding in elevators. [3]But there is almost no chance that a cable could break and that the elevator would suddenly plunge to the ground. [4]Other people may have a phobia about spiders, dogs, driving over a bridge, or being trapped in a confined space. [5]In all such cases, there is an unreasonable desire to avoid the feared activity or object.

Textbook authors, then, often do more than provide context clues: they set off their definitions in *italic* or **boldface** type, as above. When they take the time to define and give examples of a term, you should assume that the material is important enough to learn.

More about textbook definitions and examples appears on pages 374–376 in the "Signal Words II" chapter.

CHAPTER REVIEW

In this chapter, you learned the following:

- To save time when reading, you should try to figure out the meanings of unfamiliar words. You can do so by looking at their *context*—the words surrounding them.

- There are four kinds of context clues: **examples** (marked by words like *for example, for instance, including,* and *such as*); **synonyms** (words that mean the same as unknown words); **antonyms** (words that mean the opposite of unknown words); and **general sense of the sentence** (clues in the sentence or surrounding sentences about what words might mean).

- Textbook authors typically set off important words in *italic* or **boldface** type and define those words for you, often providing examples as well.

The next chapter—Chapter 4—will introduce you to the most important of all comprehension skills, finding the main idea.

 On the Web: If you are using this book in class, you can visit our website for additional practice in understanding vocabulary in context. Go to **www.townsendpress.com** and click on "Online Exercises."

➤ *Review Test 1*

To review what you've learned in this chapter, answer the following questions by writing the letter of each correct answer.

_____ 1. The context of a word is
  A. its meaning.
  B. its opposite.
  C. the words around it.

_____ 2. Which type of context clue often follows signal words like *including, such as,* and *for instance?*
  A. Example
  B. Synonym
  C. Antonym

_____ 3. In the sentence below, which type of context clue is provided for the italicized word?
  A. Example
  B. Synonym
  C. Antonym

   Students often prefer a *lenient* teacher to a strict one, but they may learn more from the strict teacher.

_____ 4. Often, when textbook authors introduce a new word, they provide a definition and help make the meaning of the word clear by including one or more
  A. examples.
  B. synonyms.
  C. antonyms.

➤ Review Test 2

A. Look at the cartoon below and then answer the question that follows.

Copyright 1997 by Randy Glasbergen.
www.glasbergen.com

GLASBERGEN

"Why do I struggle so much and you cope so well?"

_____ 1. Using the context clues in the cartoon, write the letter of the best meaning of *cope* (kōp) in the space provided.

    A. deal effectively   B. fail to relate   C. try harder

B. Using context clues for help, write the letter of the best meaning for each italicized word.

_____ 2. Judges are supposed to be *impartial*, but the judge in the trial didn't seem fair to me.

    Impartial (ĭm-pär′shəl) means

    A. not listening.   B. not honest.   C. not favoring one side or the other.

_____ 3. After standing empty for fifteen years, the old mansion had *deteriorated*. The wood was decaying, the plaster was peeling, and most of the windows had been broken.

    Deteriorate (dĭ-tîr′ē-ə-rāt′) means to

    A. become older.   B. become worse.   C. become empty.

_____ 4. Successful students have learned that if they *adhere to* a schedule, they accomplish more. When they don't stick to a set routine, they get less done.

    Adhere (ăd-hîr′) *to* means

    A. faithfully follow.   B. avoid.   C. buy.

_____ 5. At an accident scene, police must determine whose version of the accident *distorts* the events and whose tells it just as it happened.

Distorts (dĭ-stôrts′) means
A. explains.   B. describes falsely.   C. forgets.

_____ 6. If you are pushed and have your books knocked to the floor, you may find it hard to *refrain* from yelling at the person who caused the accident.

Refrain (rĭ-frān′) means
A. continue.   B. hold back.   C. take.

_____ 7. Olga always comes up with quick *retorts* to people's comments, but I can never think of a clever answer until it's too late.

A _retort_ (rĭ-tôrt′) is a
A. clever reply.   B. dumb remark.   C. kind response.

_____ 8. Experts say exercise makes the appetite *diminish*. So wanting to lose weight provides another good reason to exercise.

Diminish (dĭ-mĭn′ĭsh) means
A. grow larger.   B. get smarter.   C. get smaller.

_____ 9. Antonio made a *pretense* of writing the answers to the essay test, but he was just scribbling. He hadn't studied for the test at all.

Pretense (prē′tĕns′) means
A. intelligent attempt.   B. false show.   C. slow effort.

_____10. Twins separated early in life often lead *parallel* lives. For instance, many study the same subjects, get similar jobs, and marry the same kind of person.

Parallel (păr′ə-lĕl′) means
A. vastly different.   B. matching.   C. boring.

➤ Review Test 3

Here is a chance to apply the skill of understanding vocabulary in context to a full-length reading. If you have ever been cheated by someone, you will probably understand the feelings that motivated the author to write her essay. After reading it, answer the vocabulary and reading questions that follow.

Words to Watch

Below are some words in the reading that do not have strong context support. Each word is followed by the number of the paragraph in which it appears and its meaning there. These words are marked in the reading by a small circle (°).

acute (1): severe, extreme
skeptical (9): doubting
scurried (12): rushed
deceit (21): dishonesty
cynical (24): believing that people are motivated only by selfishness

ONE LESS SUCKER LIVES

Jeanne R. Smith

1 The thing that struck me most about him was his acute° discomfort.

2 He approached the door of the newspaper office timidly, opened it, and stood on the threshold as if uncertain about the kinds of creatures he would face inside.

3 He wore regular work clothes. There was nothing extraordinarily distinguishing about him. He just looked nervous and uncomfortable.

4 He'd never done anything like this in his life, he told me as he timidly neared my desk.

5 He didn't even know how to go about it . . . but if I would just bear with him, maybe he could get his story out.

6 He was just so embarrassed.

7 He was a driver for the Arnold Baking Company, he said. His truck had broken down up the highway, filled with his day's delivery of breadstuffs. He'd gladly give our office staff a few loaves of our favorite bread if only someone could lend him eight dollars to catch a bus back to his company to get a substitute truck.

8 Oh, this was just so embarrassing.

9 Seeing what might have been a slightly skeptical° look on my face, he produced a wad of credit and identification cards. One in particular, an Arnold ID card, had his picture on it. He was who he said he was. And he really did need help.

10 He just sat there looking woebegone while I pondered whether or not to help my fellow man in distress. He seemed overjoyed when I pulled out my wallet, searched for eight bucks, and handed the money to him.

11 He was so grateful. After all, this had been so embarrassing.

12   He scurried° out the door, promising English muffins as a thank-you when he returned before our office closed at five.

13   I never saw him again.

14   In fact, when I called the Arnold Baking Company the next day to inquire about their poor driver with all the truck trouble, I found that they never heard of him.

15   Indeed, someone from Arnold's called back to warn me that this same man had pulled the same scam on someone in Cherry Hill . . . the same story . . . the same ID cards . . . the same eight bucks.

16   Everyone ribbed me about being too trusting. I got kind advice from the local police department when I reported the flim-flam so others could be alerted to the perpetrator's method.

17   But no one taught me as valuable a lesson as the con artist himself. And, thanks to him, someday, some person who is really in need will find a deaf ear when he or she approaches me for help. At least when it comes to money, anyway.

18   That's really very sad.

19   We were brought up to believe in the virtue of helping one's neighbor. One of the greatest commandments given by the Almighty involves the way we should treat each other.

20   Just try it.

21   After the incident, I pondered what it was about the whole thing that really stuck in my craw. Was it the money? Or was it the lie? . . . the deceit°? . . . the con?

22   It really wasn't the money. Had the guy come into the office, poured out his heart about being out of work, with sick kids and nowhere else to turn, I probably would have given him the money to help out. At least before yesterday I might have.

23   It was the lie and the deliberate attempt to cheat me out of money that really angers me.

24   It's probably true that there's a sucker born every minute. But yesterday, one sucker died. And a wiser, more cynical° person emerged.

25   There's the pity of it all.

Vocabulary in Context Questions

For each question, write the letter of your answer in the space provided.

_____ 1. In the sentences below, the word *timidly* (tǐm′ǐd-lē) means
   A. confidently.
   B. shyly.
   C. loudly.
   D. on schedule.

   "He approached the door of the newspaper office timidly, opened it, and stood on the threshold as if uncertain about the kinds of creatures he would face inside. . . . He just looked nervous and uncomfortable." (Paragraphs 2–3)

_____ 2. In the sentence below, the word *wad* (wŏd) means

A. story.
B. large number.
C. lack.
D. photograph.

"Seeing what might have been a slightly skeptical look on my face, he produced a wad of credit and identification cards." (Paragraph 9)

_____ 3. In the sentences below, the word *woebegone* (wō′bĭ-gôn) means

A. pleased.
B. healthy.
C. unhappy.
D. confident.

"Oh, this was just so embarrassing. . . . He just sat there looking woebegone while I pondered whether or not to help my fellow man . . . and seemed overjoyed when I pulled out my wallet." (Paragraphs 8 and 10)

_____ 4. In the sentence below, the word *pondered* (pŏn′dərd) means

A. thought about.
B. remembered.
C. forgot about.
D. knew.

"He just sat there looking woebegone while I pondered whether or not to help my fellow man." (Paragraph 10)

_____ 5. In the sentence below, the word *scam* (skăm) means

A. practical joke.
B. anger.
C. agreement.
D. dishonest scheme.

"Indeed, someone from Arnold's called back to warn me that this same man had pulled the same scam on someone in Cherry Hill . . . the same story . . . the same ID cards . . . the same eight bucks." (Paragraph 15)

_____ 6. In the sentence below, the word *flim-flam* (flĭm′flăm′) means

A. truck trouble.
B. embarrassment.
C. cheating.
D. credit cards.

"I got kind advice from the local police department when I reported the flim-flam so others could be alerted to the perpetrator's method." (Paragraph 16)

_____ 7. In the sentence below, the word *perpetrator* (pŭr′pĭ-trāt′ər) means

A. the one who committed the crime.
B. a beginner.
C. a citizen.
D. a witness.

"I got kind advice from the local police department when I reported the flim-flam so others could be alerted to the perpetrator's method." (Paragraph 16)

_____ 8. In the sentences below, the phrase *stuck in my craw* (krô) means
    A. delighted me.   C. informed me.
    B. destroyed me.   D. troubled me.

"After the incident, I pondered what it was about the whole thing that really stuck in my craw. Was it the money? Or was it the lie?" (Paragraph 21)

_____ 9. In the sentence below, the word *deliberate* (dĭ-lĭb′ər-ĭt) means
    A. easy.   C. planned.
    B. fair.   D. weak.

"It was the lie and the deliberate attempt to cheat me out of money that really angers me." (Paragraph 23)

_____ 10. In the sentences below, the word *emerged* (ĭ-mûrjd′) means
    A. disappeared.   C. died.
    B. took advantage.   D. appeared.

"It's probably true that there's a sucker born every minute. But yesterday, one sucker died. And a wiser, more cynical person emerged." (Paragraph 24)

Questions about the Reading

For each question, write the letter of your answer in the space provided.

_____ 1. A central idea in "One Less Sucker Lives" is that the author
    A. realizes that most people are dishonest.
    B. feels grateful to the con man for teaching her a lesson.
    C. is glad that she reported the con man to the police.
    D. regrets that she has lost her trust in people as a result of being cheated.

_____ 2. The main idea of paragraphs 1–6 is that
    A. the author is not used to being approached by strange–looking men.
    B. there is nothing extraordinarily distinguished about the man.
    C. the author is most impressed by the man's acute discomfort.
    D. the author works in a busy newspaper office.

_____ 3. The main idea of paragraph 9 is that
    A. the man had an Arnold Baking identification card.
    B. the writer was skeptical of the man's story.
    C. the man seemed to really be who he said he was.
    D. the man had credit cards.

_____ 4. The writer worked at
    A. a police station.
    B. a newspaper office.
    C. an office of the Arnold Baking Company.
    D. a truck stop.

_____ 5. In return for her help, the man promised the writer
    A. to pay back her money with interest.
    B. to help someone in need himself someday.
    C. to bring her some English muffins.
    D. to write her a thank-you letter.

_____ 6. The author realizes she has been cheated when
    A. the man does not call her later that day.
    B. she reads a local newspaper story about a con man operating in the area.
    C. she receives a call from the local police department warning her of a scam.
    D. someone from the Arnold Baking Company calls to warn her about the con man.

_____ 7. We can guess that the man
    A. wants others to feel sorry for him.
    B. is genuinely needy.
    C. regrets having to cheat other people.
    D. is not very intelligent.

_____ 8. The man probably
    A. was going from place to place pretending to be someone he wasn't.
    B. was an employee of the Arnold Baking Company.
    C. felt very bad about lying to the writer.
    D. had never cheated anyone out of money before.

_____ 9. We can assume that the writer
    A. is really grateful for what the man taught her.
    B. feels bitter and sad about the lesson she learned.
    C. thinks that the man who asked her for money should be arrested.
    D. wishes she had given the man more money.

_____10. The next time someone tells the writer a hard-luck story, she will most likely
  A. listen sympathetically.
  B. call the police.
  C. not give the person anything.
  D. demand that the person give her eight dollars.

Discussion Questions

1. When people on the street ask you for money, do you ever give them anything? Why or why not? If you sometimes do, how do you decide which person to help?

2. What was the "lesson" the writer learned from the incident? If the incident had happened to you, would you feel you had learned the same lesson? Why or why not?

3. Have you ever had to ask a stranger for help? What were the circumstances? How did the stranger respond?

Note: Writing assignments for this selection appear on page 559.

Check Your Performance   **VOCABULARY IN CONTEXT**

Activity	*Number Right*	*Points*	*Score*
Review Test 1 (4 items)	_____	× 5 =	_____
Review Test 2 (10 items)	_____	× 4 =	_____
Review Test 3 (20 items)	_____	× 2 =	_____
		TOTAL SCORE =	_____%

Enter your total score into the **Reading Performance Chart: Review Tests** on the inside back cover.

VOCABULARY IN CONTEXT: Mastery Test 1

A. For each item below, underline the **examples** that suggest the meaning of the italicized word. Then, on the answer line, write the letter of the meaning of that word.

_____ 1. The students showed all the signs of *apathy*, including scribbling instead of taking notes, constantly looking at the clock, and writing messages to one another.

Apathy (ăp′ə-thē) means
A. lack of interest.   C. curiosity.
B. attention.   D. surprise.

_____ 2. Many healthy elderly people are *vigorous* enough to enjoy such activities as swimming, jogging, and biking.

Vigorous (vĭg′ər-əs) means
A. hard to learn.   C. having energy.
B. childlike.   D. relaxing.

_____ 3. Some little children think they can *respond to* a question on the phone by nodding or shaking their heads.

Respond (rĭ-spŏnd′) *to* means
A. repeat.   C. answer.
B. leave.   D. avoid.

B. Each item below includes a word that is a **synonym** of the italicized word. Write the synonym of the italicized word in the space provided.

_____ 4. It is not *appropriate* (ə-prō′prē-ĭt) to wear cut-off jeans to most job interviews. Nor is it suitable to smoke during an interview.

_____ 5. When people are angry with each other, a *frank* (frăngk) discussion can be helpful. An honest exchange of ideas can lead to an understanding of the other person's point of view.

_____ 6. The *ultimate* (ŭl′tə-mĭt) reward for working hard at school is earning a degree. Similarly, the greatest reward for working hard on the job is a big promotion.

(Continues on next page)

C. Each item below includes a word that is an **antonym** of the italicized word. Underline the antonym of each italicized word. Then, on the answer line, write the letter of the meaning of the italicized word.

_____ 7. College students often complain that a course is either overly *complex* or too simple.

   Complex (kəm-plĕks′) means
   A. interesting.   C. difficult.
   B. dull.   D. crowded.

_____ 8. Although Juan's efforts to get back together with Margarita were truly *earnest*, she thought he was being dishonest.

   Earnest (ûr′nĭst) means
   A. successful.   C. amazing.
   B. pleasing.   D. honest.

D. Use the **general sense of each sentence** to figure out the meaning of each italicized word. Then, on the answer line, write the letter of the meaning of the italicized word.

_____ 9. Some people have a *phobia* about heights. They can't look down from the top of a tall building without feeling as if they are about to fall.

   Phobia (fō′bē-ə) means
   A. humorous situation.   C. pleasant experience.
   B. fear.   D. determination.

_____ 10. Tidal waves sometimes *accelerate* until they reach a speed of 450 miles an hour.

   Accelerate (ăk-sĕl′ə-rāt) means
   A. slow down.   C. bend.
   B. speed up.   D. destroy.

VOCABULARY IN CONTEXT: Mastery Test 2

A. For each item below, underline the **examples** that suggest the meaning of the italicized term. Then, on the answer line, write the letter of the meaning of that word.

_____ 1. *Remote* areas such as the deserts of Arizona and the wilderness of Alaska appeal to people who want to get away for a while.

    Remote (rǐ′mōt) means

    A. populated.   C. wealthy.

    B. fancy.   D. out-of-the-way.

_____ 2. *Traits*—including height, eye color, and hair color—are passed on from generation to generation.

    Traits (trātz) are

    A. features.   C. rights.

    B. materials.   D. suggestions.

_____ 3. *Awkward* movements are common for infants learning to walk. Sometimes they will fall backwards; at other times they will move sideways instead of going forward.

    Awkward (ôk′wərd) means

    A. correct.   C. silly.

    B. clumsy.   D. expected.

B. Each item below includes a word or words that are a **synonym** of the italicized word. Write the synonym of the italicized word in the space provided.

_____ 4. I can't *comprehend* (kŏm′prǐ-hĕnd′) how a computer works, but at least I understand how to use it.

_____ 5. A good prison *reforms* (rē-fôrms′) inmates. If it makes them better people, they are less likely to return to prison.

_____ 6. Travel by jet has *altered* (ôl-tərd) the way people experience the world. For many, the "wide" world has changed into a much smaller place.

(Continues on next page)

C. Each item below includes a word that is an **antonym** of the italicized word. Underline the antonym of each italicized word. Then, on the answer line, write the letter of the meaning of the italicized word.

_____ 7. The idea that certain people can communicate with the dead is an *illusion*. The truth is that people who claim to be speaking with the dead are making up the "messages" as they go along.

   Illusion (ĭ-lōō′zhən) means
   A. stupidity.   C. fun.
   B. false idea.   D. example.

_____ 8. It is important to keep *alert* in class. If you are sleepy, you may miss a key point.

   Alert (ə-lûrt′) means
   A. notes.   C. positive.
   B. quiet.   D. wide awake.

D. Use the **general sense of each sentence** to figure out the meaning of each italicized word or group of words. Then, on the answer line, write the letter of the meaning of the italicized word(s).

_____ 9. Certain foreign officials in this country have *immunity from* our laws; they can't be arrested even for murder.

   Immunity (ĭ-myōō′nĭ-tē) *from* means
   A. protection from.   C. fear of.
   B. punishment for.   D. lack of respect for.

_____10. If you were in the *vicinity* when the gasoline tank exploded, you must have heard the roar and seen smoke pouring into the sky.

   Vicinity (vĭ-sĭn′ĭ-tē) means
   A. area.   C. amount.
   B. country.   D. land.

VOCABULARY IN CONTEXT: Mastery Test 3

Using context clues for help, write the letter of the best meaning for each italicized word.

_____ 1. No one likes a *chronic* complainer like Simon, who criticizes everything all the time.

Chronic (krŏn'ĭk) means

A. rare.　　　　　　　　　C. messy.

B. constant.　　　　　　　D. educated.

_____ 2. In a hospital emergency room, it is common to see such *gruesome* sights as burned skin and bleeding wounds.

Gruesome (groo͞'səm) means

A. horrible.　　　　　　　C. false.

B. common.　　　　　　　D. amazing.

_____ 3. "Your paper needs to be more *coherent*," my English teacher wrote. "In places, it is poorly organized and lacking in logic."

Coherent (kō-hîr'ənt) means

A. disorganized.　　　　　C. organized and logical.

B. detailed.　　　　　　　D. critical.

_____ 4. Some people believe that they need to *supplement* their diet with large amounts of vitamins and minerals. The addition of these vitamins and minerals, they believe, is what keeps them in good health.

Supplement (sŭp'lə-mənt) means

A. substitute.　　　　　　C. flavor.

B. add to.　　　　　　　　D. vary.

_____ 5. Sometimes people with *contrary* qualities are attracted to each other. For example, a shy person may go out with someone who likes to talk.

Contrary (kŏn'trĕr'ē) means

A. similar.　　　　　　　　C. opposite.

B. unusual.　　　　　　　 D. respectable.

(Continues on next page)

_____ 6. To *prolong* your life, you should consider getting married. Married people tend to live longer than people who stay single.

Prolong (prə-lông′) means to
A. make shorter.   C. make duller.
B. make longer.   D. make more exciting.

_____ 7. Common *transactions* include buying food and clothing, going to the bank, and getting gas for the car.

Transactions (trăn-săk′shəns) are
A. reasons.   C. thrills.
B. business deals.   D. ways to relax.

_____ 8. Many cities have decided to *initiate* a recycling program so that their old newspapers, bottles, and cans will be re-used instead of dumped.

Initiate (ĭ-nĭsh′ē-āt′) means to
A. cancel.   C. start.
B. apologize for.   D. finish.

_____ 9. There is a special chair that eases the *ordeal* of giving birth. Most women who use the chair say they feel less pain and give birth more quickly than when lying down.

An *ordeal* (ôr-dēl′) is
A. a difficult experience.   C. a very short experience.
B. an enjoyable experience.   D. an educational experience.

_____10. On a warm summer day, you may say, "It is my opinion that the level of heat has gone beyond what I am able to consider comfortable." A *concise* way to say the same thing is "I'm hot."

Concise (kən-sīs′) means
A. different.   C. brief and clear.
B. confusing.   D. funny.

VOCABULARY IN CONTEXT: Mastery Test 4

Using context clues for help, write the letter of the best meaning for each italicized word.

_____ 1. Watching television seems to be as *vital* to some people as food and air.

Vital (vīt′l) means
A. difficult.
B. free.
C. unimportant.
D. necessary.

_____ 2. When an Asian volcano erupted in 1883—the largest volcanic explosion in modern history—the sound was *audible* 3,000 miles away.

Audible (ô′də-bəl) means
A. able to be seen.
B. able to be heard.
C. able to be felt.
D. talked about.

_____ 3. A headache can be so *severe* that it keeps a person from being able to work.

Severe (sə′vīr) means
A. serious.
B. new.
C. mild.
D. unusual.

_____ 4. One usually *rational* football fan became so crazy when his favorite team lost the Super Bowl that he shot the TV.

Rational (răsh′ə-nəl) means
A. insane.
B. very popular.
C. reasonable.
D. determined.

_____ 5. It was said that no *obstacle*—whether extreme heat, snow, or rocky land—could keep the Pony Express from delivering the mail on time. Once, when Indians killed the rider, the horse even went on to deliver the mail alone.

Obstacle (ŏb′stə-kəl) means
A. something that gets in the way.
B. temperature.
C. animal.
D. adventure.

(Continues on next page)

_____ 6. Ice is harder than most people think; its hardness is *comparable* to that of concrete.

Comparable (kŏm′pər-ə-bəl) *to* means
A. as thick as.
B. similar to.
C. different from.
D. not at all like.

_____ 7. My sister is such an *inept* cook that she never needs to call the family to supper. We just come to the table when the smoke alarm goes off.

Inept (ĭn-ĕpt′) means
A. excellent.
B. slow.
C. unskilled.
D. experienced.

_____ 8. When my friend asked, "Do you feel all right?" she *implied* that I did not look well.

Implied (ĭm-plīd′) means
A. suggested.
B. asked.
C. forgot.
D. pretended.

_____ 9. The small store had many hip-hop and rock recordings, but not much in the *category* of country music.

Category (kăt′ĭ-gôr′ē) means
A. goal.
B. feeling.
C. group.
D. plan.

_____10. During Mardi Gras in New Orleans, people like to dress up in *extravagant* costumes. Some wear silk or satin along with feathers and many-colored beads.

Extravagant (ĭk-străv′ə-gənt) means
A. showy.
B. plain.
C. athletic.
D. businesslike.

VOCABULARY IN CONTEXT: Mastery Test 5

A. Using context clues for help, write the letter of the best meaning for each italicized word.

_____ 1. My plants did poorly in the living room, but in the sunny kitchen window, they have *thrived*.

Thrived (thrīvd) means

A. needed more care.
B. grown weaker.
C. grown very well.
D. become overgrown.

_____ 2. Sometimes people in online personal ads are not very *candid*. They will say that they're attractive, slender, and young when they're really average-looking, overweight, and middle-aged.

Candid (kăn′dĭd) means

A. pleasing.
B. happy.
C. honest.
D. attractive.

_____ 3. People who *encounter* a wild animal in the woods should stay calm and try to back away as soon as possible.

Encounter (ĕn-koun′tər) means

A. admire.
B. meet.
C. get away from.
D. try to save.

_____ 4. A complicated lecture can be *clarified* with logical examples and down-to-earth explanations.

Clarified (klăr′ə-fīd′) means

A. made clear.
B. practiced.
C. confused.
D. shortened.

_____ 5. After a *thorough* search of my car, I finally found my contact lens.

Thorough (thûr′ō) means

A. quick.
B. careful.
C. exciting.
D. enjoyable.

(Continues on next page)

B. Read the entire paragraph below. Then, using context clues, write the letter of the meaning of each word in italics.

> [1]Here's a story which *illustrates* that good deeds can take on a life of their own. [2]In 1885, the same year he published *The Adventures of Huckleberry Finn*, noted author Mark Twain made a visit to Yale University. [3]There he was introduced to Warner T. McGuinn, one of the school's first black law students. [4]McGuinn was a brilliant student, but was having trouble making ends meet. [5]He held three part-time jobs just to get by. [6]When Twain learned of McGuinn's difficult situation, he offered to pay the young man's expenses. [7]With Twain's *assistance*, McGuinn was able to quit his jobs and *concentrate* on his studies. [8]He graduated from Yale Law School at the top of his class and became a well-known lawyer in Baltimore, a member of the city council, and an *advocate* of civil rights for African-Americans. [9]And he, in turn, became a *mentor* to a young lawyer named Thurgood Marshall, who would go on to become the first African-American to serve on the United States Supreme Court.

_____ 6. *Illustrates* (ĭl′ə-strāts′) means
     A. shows.   C. claims.
     B. decides.   D. replies.

_____ 7. *Assistance* (ə-sĭs′təns) means
     A. suggestions.   C. interest.
     B. dislike.   D. help.

_____ 8. *Concentrate* (kŏn′sən-trāt′) means
     A. locate.   C. pay close attention.
     B. describe.   D. educate.

_____ 9. *Advocate* (ăd′və-kĭt) means
     A. critic.   C. judge.
     B. supporter.   D. witness.

_____ 10. *Mentor* (mĕn′tôr′) means
     A. guide.   C. challenger.
     B. buddy.   D. researcher.

VOCABULARY IN CONTEXT: Mastery Test 6

A. Using context clues for help, write the letter of the best meaning for each italicized word.

_____ 1. It is hard to be *neutral* when you listen to two people arguing. Usually you want to take one person's side.

Neutral (nōō′trəl)means

A. interested.   C. not favoring one side over another.

B. friendly.   D. disgusted.

_____ 2. Many students begin college because they see only two *options*: either go to college and get a good-paying job, or work for minimum wages the rest of their life.

Options (ŏp′shəns) means

A. choices.   C. habits.

B. wishes.   D. opportunities.

_____ 3. Rob's *tolerance* for dogs that slobber, bark, and jump up on people is very low. He prefers well-behaved dogs, or cats.

Tolerance (tŏl′ər-əns) means

A. dislike.   C. acceptance.

B. worry.   D. experience.

_____ 4. Recently a college student had a choice of studying for a final or going out for pizza with her friends. She chose to study, and that turned out to be a *prudent* decision. She got an A on the exam, while her friends all got D's.

Prudent (prōōd′nt) means

A. generous.   C. unfortunate.

B. wise.   D. tricky.

_____ 5. If a prisoner shows no *remorse* at committing a crime, the judge is likely to sentence him to the longest possible prison term.

Remorse (rĭ-môrs′) means

A. regret.   C. purpose.

B. pleasure.   D. surprise.

B. Read the entire paragraph below. Then, using context clues, write the letter of the meaning of each word in italics.

[1]In several *locales* around the country, the United States Postal Service has set up a special room where postal clerks have an *extraordinary* job: they open and read your mail. [2]This room is called the "Dead Letter Office." [3]Reading people's mail is permitted because the clerks are trying to find out where the mail is supposed to go or who sent it. [4]Millions of letters each year are sent with incorrect addresses, no return addresses, or both. [5]Others are written in a scribble that must be *comprehended* or in a foreign language that must be translated. [6]Some envelopes are completely blank. [7]Specially trained clerks spend their time opening letters and packages to discover whether or not they can be sent to the intended *recipient* or returned to the sender. [8]Estimates are that only 30 percent of the mail that ends up at the Dead Letter Office *ultimately* finds its way to the sender or receiver.

_____ 6. *Locales* (lō-kălz′) means
    A. targets.   C. people.
    B. places.   D. boxes.

_____ 7. *Extraordinary* (ĭk-strôr′dn-ĕr′ē) means
    A. boring.   C. common.
    B. very unusual.   D. dangerous.

_____ 8. *Comprehended* (kŏm′prĭ-hĕnd′ĭd) means
    A. taken seriously.   C. understood.
    B. ignored.   D. listed.

_____ 9. A *recipient* (rĭ-sĭp′ē-ənt) is a
    A. letter carrier.   C. writer.
    B. receiver.   D. clerk.

_____10. *Ultimately* (ŭl′tə-mĭt-lē) means
    A. strangely.   C. illegally.
    B. finally.   D. sadly.

4

Main Ideas

THIS CHAPTER IN A NUTSHELL

- Recognizing a writer's **main idea**, or point, is the most important reading skill.
- Learn to think as you read by asking yourself, "What is the writer's point?"
- The main idea is a general idea supported by specific ideas and details.

WHAT IS THE MAIN IDEA?

College was not going well.

"What's the point?" People ask this question when they want to know what idea is being presented. Sometimes a main idea is clear right away, as in the cartoon above. What is the point of the cartoon?

Explanation:

The main idea is that "College was not going well." The support for the main idea is the list of specific grades showing on the student's grade report.

When you read, get in the habit of asking "What is the main point the writer is trying to make?" Recognizing the **main idea**, or point, is the most important key to better reading.

☑ Check Your Understanding

For example, read the following paragraph, asking yourself as you do, "What is the writer's point?"

> [1]Certain basic fears are part of our lives. [2]For one thing, we fear being disrespected. [3]Bullies play on this fear. [4]They cruelly tease their victims and take away their self-respect. [5]And we feel hurt and disrespected when someone doesn't return our phone calls or walks past us without saying hello. [6]Another of our deepest fears is being alone. [7]No matter how tough we act, we know that the poet who wrote "No man is an island" was telling the truth. [8]We need each other. [9]Not having other people in our lives makes us feel empty inside. [10]A third basic fear is of growing old. [11]Every year, Americans use plastic surgery to try to turn back the clock. [12]And our magazines and TV shows and movies are full of beautiful young people. [13]We do not want to be reminded that the clock keeps ticking.

Here is a good two-step way to find a writer's point, or main idea:

1 Look for a general statement.

2 Decide if that statement is supported by most of the other material in the paragraph. If it is, you have found the main idea.

Below are four statements from the passage about basic fears. Pick out the general statement that is supported by the other material in the passage. Write the letter of that statement in the space provided. Then read the explanation that follows.

Four statements from the passage:

    A. We fear being disrespected.

    B. Another of our deepest fears is being alone.

    C. A third basic fear is of growing old.

    D. Certain basic fears are part of our lives.

The general statement that expresses the main idea of the passage is: _____

Explanation:

Sentences A, B, and C all refer to specific fears that we have in life: being disrespected, being alone, and growing old. Only sentence D is a general statement that covers all of the specific fears described in the paragraph. Sentence D, then, is the sentence that expresses the main idea of the passage.

The Main Idea as an "Umbrella" Idea

Think of the main idea as an "umbrella" idea. The main idea is the writer's general point. The other material of the paragraph fits under the general point. That other material is made up of specific supporting details—evidence such as examples, reasons, or facts. The diagram below shows the relationship:

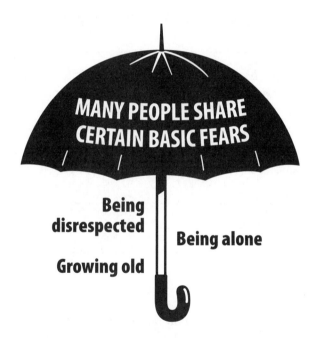

The explanations and activities on the following pages will deepen your understanding of the main idea.

GENERAL VERSUS SPECIFIC IDEAS

You saw in the paragraph on basic fears that the main idea is a *general* idea that is supported by *specific* ideas. To improve your skill at finding main ideas, then, it will be helpful to practice separating general from specific ideas.

☑ *Check Your Understanding*

See if you can do the following brief exercises. Then read the explanation that follows.

1. *Fish* is a general term. Write the names of three specific kinds of fish.

   _____   _____   _____

2. *Countries* is a general term. Write the names of three specific countries.

   _____   _____   _____

3. *Household chores* is a general term. Write three specific chores you sometimes have to do in your house or apartment.

   _____   _____   _____

4. Finally, *a bad day* is a general term. Write three specific reasons why you might say, "Today was a really bad day for me."

   _____

   _____

   _____

Explanation:

Three specific kinds of fish might be flounder, salmon, and tuna. Three specific countries might be the United States, Mexico, and Korea. Three specific chores might be preparing a meal, washing dishes, and taking out the trash. Finally, three specific reasons for a bad day might be "My cat died," "I came down with a cold," and "I missed the bus and was late for class."

Now do the practices that follow, which will give you more experience in telling the difference between general and specific ideas.

➤ *Practice 1*

Each cluster of words below consists of one general idea and four specific ideas. The general idea includes all the specific ideas. Identify each general idea with a **G** and the specific ideas with an **S**. Look first at the example.

Example   _S_ anger
              _S_ love
              _S_ fear
              _G_ emotion
              _S_ envy

(*Emotion* is the general idea because it includes anger, love, fear, and envy, which are specific kinds of emotions.)

1. ___ goldfish
    ___ parakeet
    ___ pet
    ___ dog
    ___ cat

2. ___ square
    ___ circle
    ___ triangle
    ___ shape
    ___ diamond

3. ___ up
    ___ down
    ___ direction
    ___ sideways
    ___ north

4. ___ soda
    ___ beer
    ___ orange juice
    ___ beverage
    ___ water

5. ___ high-risk job
    ___ astronaut
    ___ firefighter
    ___ policeman
    ___ miner

6. ___ sleeping bag
    ___ sheet
    ___ pillow
    ___ blanket
    ___ bedding

7. ___ "hello"
    ___ greeting
    ___ a wave
    ___ "hi"
    ___ open arms

8. ___ screech
    ___ noise
    ___ crash
    ___ off-key music
    ___ sirens

9. ___ jump
    ___ command
    ___ stop
    ___ move
    ___ sit down

10. ___ jail
    ___ hanging
    ___ suspension
    ___ fine
    ___ punishment

➤ *Practice 2*

In each item below, one idea is general and one is specific. The general idea includes the specific idea. In the spaces provided, write two more specific ideas that are covered by the general idea.

Example   *General idea:* containers
                    Specific ideas: box,   _____*can*_____,   _____*bottle*_____

(*Containers* is the general idea; *box* is a specific kind of container. *Can* and *bottle* are also specific kinds of containers.)

1. *General idea:* movie stars
   Specific ideas: Denzel Washington, _____, _____

2. *General idea:* wild animals
   Specific ideas: gorilla, _____, _____

3. *General idea:* furniture
   Specific ideas: rocking chair, _____, _____

4. *General idea:* desserts
   Specific ideas: ice cream, _____, _____

5. *General idea:* U.S. cities
   Specific ideas: Los Angeles, _____, _____

6. *General idea:* holidays
   Specific ideas: Thanksgiving, _____, _____

7. *General idea:* ball games
   Specific ideas: baseball, _____, _____

8. *General idea:* birds
   Specific ideas: hawk, _____, _____

9. *General idea:* vegetables
   Specific ideas: spinach, _____, _____

10. *General idea:* planets
    Specific ideas: Earth, _____, _____

Note: You will have more practice with general and specific ideas in "The Basics of Argument" on pages 437–454.

THE TOPIC AND MAIN IDEA

To find the main idea of a selection, you can look first for a general statement. If that statement is supported by most of the other material in the selection, you've found the main idea. Another approach to finding the main idea is to look for the topic of the selection.

The **topic** is the general subject of a selection. It can often be expressed in several words. Recognizing the topic can lead you to the writer's main point about that topic. To find the topic of a selection, ask this simple question:

Who or what is the selection about?

Then, to find the main idea, ask:

What is the main point being made about the topic?

☑ *Check Your Understanding*

For example, read the paragraph below and see if you can answer the questions that follow.

> [1]Spanking is a bad idea. [2]First of all, think about the lesson that a child learns when he is spanked. [3]He learns that physical violence is a way to deal with a problem. [4]Spanking tells him that bigger, stronger people are allowed to hit smaller, weaker people. [5]Secondly, a spanking often has more to do with a parent's emotions than with the child's behavior. [6]Parents under stress may spank a child to ease their own problems and frustrations. [7]And finally, spanking is just not effective discipline. [8]Children should be taught through careful and consistent explanations to behave in a certain way. [9]They will develop better self-control than children who behave only to avoid getting hit.

_____ 1. Write the letter of the *topic* of the paragraph. To find the topic, ask yourself what the paragraph is about.

     A. Spanking

     B. Lessons

     C. Children's behavior

_____ 2. Write the number of the sentence that states the *main idea* of the paragraph. In other words, what point is the writer making about the topic? (Remember that the main idea will be supported by the other material in the paragraph.)

Explanation:

As the first sentence of the paragraph suggests, the topic is "spanking." Continuing to read the paragraph, you see that, in fact, everything in it is about spanking. And the main idea is clearly sentence 1: "Spanking is a bad idea." This is a general idea that sums up what the entire paragraph is about. It is the "umbrella" statement under which all the other material in the paragraph fits. The parts of the paragraph could be shown as follows:

Topic: Spanking

Main idea: Spanking is a bad idea.

Supporting details:
1. Spanking teaches physical violence.
2. Spanking often has more to do with the parent than with the child.
3. Spanking is not effective discipline.

The following practices will sharpen your sense of the difference between a topic, the point about the topic (the main idea), and the supporting details.

➤ Practice 3

Below are groups of four items. In each case, one item is the topic, one is the main idea, and two are details that support and develop the main idea. Label each item with one of the following:

T — for the **topic** of the paragraph
MI — for the **main idea**
SD — for the **supporting details**

Note that an explanation is provided for the first group; reading it will help you do this practice.

Group 1

_____ A. Binge buyers go shopping on a regular basis to buy huge numbers of things.

_____ B. Daily shoppers cannot miss a single day at the stores or on online shopping sites.

_____ C. Shopping addicts.

_____ D. There are two types of shopping addicts.

Explanation:

All of the statements in Group 1 involve shopping addicts, so item C must be the topic. (A topic is expressed in a single word or short phrase and is not a complete sentence.) Statements A and B each describe one specific type of shopping addict. Statement D is a general statement: that there are two types of shopping addicts. Therefore, it is the main idea.

Group 2

_____ A. Headaches can be caused by changes in the supply of blood to the head.

_____ B. Headaches can result from muscle tension.

_____ C. Headaches can have two main causes.

_____ D. Causes of headaches.

Group 3

_____ A. Remedies for too much sun.

_____ B. You can soothe a case of sunburn by spreading plain yogurt over the burnt area for ten minutes.

_____ C. Several remedies for too much sun can be found in your kitchen.

_____ D. If your eyes have been irritated by the sun, cover them for five minutes with chilled tea bags or a paper towel soaked in milk.

Group 4

_____ A. Drinking excessively can lead to problems other than alcoholism.

_____ B. Excessive drinking.

_____ C. People who drink too much often develop liver disease.

_____ D. Damage to brain cells results from heavy drinking.

➤ *Practice 4*

Following are four paragraphs. Read each paragraph and then choose what you think are the correct topic and main idea for that paragraph.

Here is how to proceed:

1 Ask yourself, "What seems to be the topic of the paragraph?" (It often helps to look for and even circle a word or idea that is repeated in the paragraph.)

> *Hint:* When looking for the topic, make sure you do not pick one that is either **too broad** (covering a great deal more than is in the selection) or **too narrow** (covering only part of the selection). The topic and the main idea of a selection must include everything in that selection—no more and no less.

2 Next, ask yourself, "What point is the writer making about this topic?" This will be the main idea. In this practice, it is stated in one of the sentences in the paragraph.

3 Then test what you think is the main idea by asking, "Is this statement supported by all or most of the other material in the paragraph?"

Paragraph 1

   [1]Male and female children are sometimes treated and viewed differently from birth on. [2]First, boys get a blue blanket and girls get pink. [3]Also, although more male than female babies fall ill, studies say a number of parents are more likely to consider a baby strong if it is male. [4]Similarly, such parents urge boys to take part in rough-and-tumble play. [5]But these parents prefer that girls watch and talk rather than be physically active. [6]When questioned, the parents say they want their sons to be successful and independent, and they want their daughters to be loving and well-behaved.

_____ 1. The topic of the paragraph is
   A. males and females.
   B. male and female children.
   C. childhood illness.

_____ 2. Write the number of the sentence that states the main idea of the paragraph.

Paragraph 2

[1]An enlarged heart can be a sign that the heart is having trouble pumping blood. [2]This condition could be caused by a bad heart valve or by high blood pressure. [3]An enlarged heart could also be caused by a high level of exercise. [4]Athletes such as long-distance runners frequently have larger than average hearts. [5]However, their hearts operate at a high rate of efficiency. [6]An enlarged heart, then, can be a sign of bad health or good health.

_____ 3. The topic of the paragraph is
     A. pumping blood.
     B. athletes and their hearts.
     C. an enlarged heart.

_____ 4. Write the number of the sentence that states the main idea of the paragraph.

Paragraph 3

[1]Researchers who do surveys depend on what people tell them. [2]People who are surveyed, however, sometimes lie. [3]In one survey, for instance, people were asked if they used seat belts. [4]Later, researchers checked to see how many people really did use their seat belts. [5]It turned out that almost 40 percent of those who said they buckled up did not. [6]Also, researchers once asked people about their smoking habits. [7]Then they tested the people's saliva to find a chemical that is found in the mouths of smokers. [8]The tests showed that 6 percent of the women and 8 percent of the men had lied about smoking.

_____ 5. The topic of the paragraph is
     A. researchers.
     B. people who are surveyed.
     C. people who are surveyed about smoking.

_____ 6. Write the number of the sentence that states the main idea of the paragraph.

Paragraph 4

¹As you speak with someone, you can gather clues as to whether he or she understands you. ²Then you can adjust what you say accordingly. ³But when you write, you must try to predict the reader's reactions without such clues. ⁴You also have to give stronger evidence in writing than in conversation. ⁵A friend may accept an unsupported statement such as "My boss is awful." ⁶But in most writing, the reader would expect you to back up such a statement with proof. ⁷Obviously, effective writing requires more attention to detail than everyday conversation does.

_____ 7. The topic is
   A. proof.
   B. conversation.
   C. effective writing versus conversation.

_____ 8. Write the number of the sentence that states the main idea of the paragraph.

A Note on the Central Point

In selections made up of many paragraphs, the overall main idea is called the **central point**. You can find a central point in the same way that you find a main idea. First, identify the topic (which is often suggested by the title of the selection). Then look at the supporting material. The paragraphs within the longer reading will provide supporting details for the central point.

CHAPTER REVIEW

In this chapter, you learned the following:

- The main idea is the key to good comprehension. The main idea is a general "umbrella" idea. The specific details of a passage fit under it.

- To find the main idea, look for a general statement that is supported by specific details in a passage.

- The topic—the general subject of a selection—can also help lead you to the main idea. Ask yourself, "What point is being made about the topic?"

The next chapter—Chapter 5—will increase your understanding of the specific details that writers use to support and develop their main ideas.

On the Web: If you are using this book in class, you can visit our website for additional practice in recognizing main ideas. Go to **www.townsendpress.com** and click on "Online Exercises."

➤ Review Test 1

To review what you've learned in this chapter, answer each of the following questions by filling in the blank or writing the letter of the correct answer.

1. The supporting details are always more *(general or specific?)* _____ than the main idea.

2. The umbrella statement that covers all of the material in a paragraph is the *(topic or main idea?)* _____.

3. To help yourself find the *(topic or main idea)* _____ of a paragraph, ask yourself, "Who or what is this paragraph about?"

_____ 4. TRUE OR FALSE? To help you decide if a certain sentence is the main idea of a paragraph, ask yourself, "Is this sentence supported by all or most of the other material in the paragraph?"

➤ Review Test 2

A. Each group of words below consists of one general idea and four specific ideas. The general idea includes all the specific ideas. Underline the general idea in each group.

1. uncle	sister	relative	cousin	grandmother
2. vanilla	flavor	chocolate	strawberry	butterscotch
3. poker	baseball	hide and seek	game	Monopoly
4. sandals	boots	sneakers	footwear	high heels

B. In each item below, one idea is general and one is specific. In the spaces provided, write two more specific ideas that are covered by the general idea.

5–6. *General idea:* means of transportation
Specific ideas: train, _____, _____

7–8. *General idea:* musical instruments
Specific ideas: guitar, _____, _____

C. (9–16.) Below are groups of four items. In each case, one item is the topic, one is the main idea, and two are details that support and develop the main idea. Label each item with one of the following:

   T — for the **topic** of the paragraph
   MI — for the **main idea**
   SD — for the **supporting details**

Group 1

_____ A. Single children have their problems.

_____ B. Single children have little privacy from their parents.

_____ C. Single children.

_____ D. Single children can be lonely without the companionship of brothers and sisters.

Group 2

_____ A. Television can be educational, with news programs and nature shows.

_____ B. Television is relaxing and entertaining after a stressful day.

_____ C. Television has its good points.

_____ D. Television.

D. Following are two paragraphs. Read each paragraph, and then choose what you think are the correct topic and main idea for that paragraph.

Paragraph 1

   ¹The crocodile and a small bird called the plover have a surprisingly friendly relationship. ²A crocodile's jaws are strong, and its teeth are razor sharp. ³Yet the plover dares to step inside the croc's mouth. ⁴You see, after eating, the crocodile opens his mouth. ⁵This allows his "living toothbrush" to step in and clean uneaten food from his teeth. ⁶In return for his service, the plover gets a free meal.

_____ 17. The topic is
   A. the crocodile's habits.
   B. the crocodile and the plover.
   C. friendly relationships between animals.

_____ 18. Write the number of the sentence that states the main idea of the paragraph.

Paragraph 2

    ¹It's well known that trees provide shade, beauty, and wind protection. ²However, there are also two lesser-known benefits of trees. ³First, trees clean the air. ⁴Their leaves actually filter out pollution in the air. ⁵One large sugar maple, for example, can remove as much pollution as is put in the air by cars burning a thousand gallons of gas. ⁶The second lesser-known benefit of trees is that they reduce stress. ⁷Experiments show that people relax more when they are shown scenes with trees than when they are shown city scenes without natural greenery.

_____ 19. The topic is
      A. nature.
      B. lesser-known benefits of trees.
      C. anti-stress benefits of trees.

_____ 20. Write the number of the sentence that states the main idea of the paragraph.

➤ Review Test 3

Here is a chance to apply your understanding of main ideas to a full-length reading. This selection tells you about a study skill that can mean the difference between success and failure in college. Read it and then answer the questions that follow.

Words to Watch

Below are some words in the reading that do not have strong context support. Each word is followed by the number of the paragraph in which it appears and its meaning there. These words are indicated in the selection by a small circle (°).

concepts (4): ideas
vividly (4): in a clear and lively way
legible (8): easily read
global warming (11): an increase in the world's temperatures

CLASSROOM NOTETAKING

Robin White

1   How would you feel if you were forced to spend 1800 hours—the equivalent of 75 days in a row—sitting in a hard-backed chair, eyes wide open, listening to the sound of someone else's voice? You wouldn't be allowed to sleep, eat, or smoke. You couldn't leave the room. To make matters worse, you'd be expected to remember every important point the speaker made, and you'd be punished for forgetting. And, to top it off, you'd have to pay many thousands of dollars for the experience.

2   Sound like a torture scene from a spy movie? Actually, it's nothing of the kind. It's what all college students do who take a full load of five courses for four years. Those 1800 hours are the time they'll spend listening in class.

3   Unfortunately, many students *do* regard these hours as torture. Many of them will let their attention wander. They'll spend a lot of time daydreaming or scribbling on the edges of their notebooks. Maybe they'll sit in the back of the room and prepare for some other class or jot a note to a friend. Some students will reduce the pain to a minimum by not even coming to class. These students do not realize that if they don't listen in class—and take notes—they're putting their college life in danger.

WHY TAKE CLASS NOTES?

4   One reason you should take class notes is that the information in the classroom adds to what you might find in textbooks. Good teachers keep up to date with their subjects and can include the latest facts and ideas in their presentations. They needn't wait for the next edition of the book to come out. They can provide additional examples or simplify difficult concepts°, making it easier for you to master hard material. And the best teachers combine knowledge with showmanship. They can make any subject, from world history to computers, leap vividly° to life.

5   True, you say, but isn't it good enough just to listen to these wonderful people without writing down what they say? Actually, it isn't, which leads us to another reason for taking lecture notes. Studies have shown that after two weeks, you'll forget 80 percent of what you heard. And you didn't come to the lecture room just to be entertained. You came to learn. The only way to keep the material in your head is to get it down in permanent form—in the form of class notes.

HOW TO TAKE CLASS NOTES

6   There are three steps to mastering the art of taking good lecture notes: getting yourself to the classroom, taking good notes, and reviewing those notes.

Getting to Class

7   Your attitude should be, "Here I am in college. So I've got to go to class and learn all I can." Remember, you're not going to class to be bored, tortured, or entertained; you're going there to learn. Get to class on time and get a good seat

near the front of the room. You'll hear better there and be less tempted to let your mind wander.

Taking Good Notes

8 When you take class notes, always use 8½″ × 11″ paper, preferably in a loose-leaf notebook so you can insert handouts. Write on only one side of the paper. Later, you might want to spread all your notes out in front of you. Have a pen to write with rather than a pencil, which moves more slowly across a page and is not as legible°.

9 Be prepared to do a good deal of writing in class. A good rule of thumb for taking notes is "When in doubt, write it down." After class, you will have time to go over your notes and make decisions about what is important enough to study and what is not. But during a lecture, you don't always have time to decide what is really important and what is not. You don't want to miss getting down a valuable idea that the instructor might not repeat later.

10 Be sure to *always* write down what the instructor puts on the board. If he or she takes the time to write something on the board, the material is probably important. And don't fall into the trap that some students fall into. They write down what is on the board, but nothing more. They just sit and listen while the instructor explains all the connections between those words that have been chalked on the board. Everything may be perfectly clear to a student at that moment. However, several days later, chances are that all the connecting material will be forgotten. If you write down the explanations in class, it will be much easier for you to make sense of the material and to study it later.

11 As much as possible, organize your notes by starting main points at the margin. Indent secondary points under the main points, and indent examples even further. Skip lines between main sections. Wherever possible, number the points. If the instructor explains three reasons for poverty, or four results of global warming°, make sure you number each of those reasons or results. The numbers help organize the material and make it easier for you to study and remember it.

12 Here are some other hints for taking good classroom notes:

- *If you miss something, don't panic.* Leave space for it in your notes and keep going. Later, get the missing information from a classmate or your textbook.

- *Be alert for signals of importance.* If you get a definition with an example, that is important. If you get a numbered list of items, it is probably important. If your instructor says, "The point I am trying to make is . . . ," that point is important. Get all such things down in your notes.

- *Use abbreviations in order to save time.* Put a key for abbreviated words in the top margin of your notes. For instance, in a business class, *com* could stand for *communication*; *info* for *information*. In a psychology class, *beh* could stand for *behavior*; *mot* for *motivation*. You can also abbreviate certain common words, using a "+" for *and*, a "*w/*" for *with*, and an "*ex*" for *example*.

- *Finally, don't ignore the very beginning and end of class.* Often, instructors spend the first five minutes of a class either reviewing material they've already covered or giving a preview of the day's lecture. The last five minutes of a class may be a summary of the important ideas covered that day. Don't spend the first five minutes of class getting your materials out and the last five minutes putting them away. If you do, you'll probably miss something important.

Reviewing Class Notes

17 If you have taken good notes, you're ready to really learn the material back at home.

18 As soon as you have time, sit down and reread your notes. Fill in anything unclear or missing while it's still fresh in your mind. Then, in the left-hand column of each page, write a few key words and phrases from the day's notes. Cover your notes, and, using only these key words, try to recall as much of the material as you can. This review will help you remember the material and prepare for exams.

To sum all this up, be prepared to 19 go into class and be an active notetaker. Going to class and taking good notes while you are there are keys to success in college.

Questions about the Reading

For each question, write the letter of your answer in the space provided.

_____ 1. In the sentences below, the word *showmanship* (shō′mən-shǐp) means
    A. dramatic skill.   C. research ability.
    B. handwriting.   D. popularity.

    "And the best lecturers combine knowledge with showmanship. They can make any subject, from world history to computers, leap vividly to life." (Paragraph 4)

_____ 2. Which subject is the topic of the entire selection?
    A. Students
    B. Success in school
    C. College lectures
    D. Taking lecture notes

_____ 3. Which sentence expresses the selection's central point (the main idea of the entire reading)?
    A. Students can learn more from lectures than from reading textbooks.
    B. Taking lecture notes is an important skill involving three main steps.
    C. College lectures are more than just entertainment.
    D. There are various ways to achieve success in school.

_____ 4. The main idea of paragraph 4 is stated in its
    A. first sentence.   C. third sentence.
    B. second sentence.   D. last sentence.

_____ 5. Which sentence expresses the main idea of paragraph 18?
    A. Notetaking allows you to bring a copy of the lecture home with you.
    B. Always fill in the blanks in your notes as soon as class ends.
    C. Completing and reviewing lecture notes soon after class will help you remember the material.
    D. Reread your notes soon after class.

_____ 6. According to the author, good teachers
    A. include material in their lectures that is not found in the textbook.
    B. organize their lectures so clearly that notetaking is not necessary.
    C. write everything on the blackboard.
    D. are careful not to say anything important at the beginning or end of class.

_____ 7. A good general rule for taking notes is:
    A. Write down only what is written on the board.
    B. Listening carefully is more important than taking notes.
    C. Write your notes in one big paragraph.
    D. When in doubt, write it down.

_____ 8. Which of the following is **not** recommended by the author?
    A. Take notes with a pen, not a pencil.
    B. Take notes on only one side of the paper.
    C. Tape record your instructor's lectures.
    D. Use abbreviations in your notes.

_____ 9. From reading this selection, you can guess that
    A. many students can do well in a class without taking notes.
    B. even if you listen carefully, it is almost impossible to remember everything you hear in a lecture.
    C. students who sit in the back row are less distracted by activity in the classroom.
    D. students who take good notes do not need to read their textbooks.

_____ 10. Which of the following statements might the author agree with?
  A. Good notetaking can make the difference between low and high grades.
  B. Taking notes in class is not as important as listening to the lecture.
  C. It is the instructor's responsibility to make sure that each student learns.
  D. If you've done a good enough job taking notes, you should not have to ever review them.

Discussion Questions

1. How would you rate yourself as a classroom notetaker? Would you give yourself an A, a B, a C, or a failing grade? Explain why.

2. According to the reading, part of a student's preparation for classroom notetaking should be to examine his or her attitude (paragraph 7). Why do you think the author feels examining one's attitude is so important?

3. Of all the advice in this selection, which three points will probably be the most helpful for you to use?

Note: Writing assignments for this selection appear on page 560.

Check Your Performance   **MAIN IDEAS**

Activity	Number Right	Points	Score
Review Test 1 (4 items)	_____	× 5 =	_____
Review Test 2 (20 items)	_____	× 2 =	_____
Review Test 3 (10 items)	_____	× 4 =	_____
	TOTAL SCORE	=	_____%

Enter your total score into the **Reading Performance Chart: Review Tests** on the inside back cover.

MAIN IDEAS: Mastery Test 1

A. Each group of words below consists of one general idea and four specific ideas. The general idea includes all the specific ideas. Underline the general idea in each group.

1. jazz   blues   rap   music   rock

2. coffee maker   dishwasher   microwave   household   clothes
                                              appliance   dryer

3. fry   boil   cook   bake   steam

4. protection   burglar alarm guard dog   insurance   suntan
                                                            lotion

5. Detroit   New Orleans   Boston   Cleveland   city

6. murder   crime   stealing   speeding   kidnapping

7. steel   copper   iron   metal   silver

8. newspaper   editorials   sports   comics   classified
                                                            ads

(Continues on next page)

B. In each item below, one idea is general and one is specific. In the spaces provided, write **two** more specific ideas that are covered by the general idea.

9–10. *General idea:* sandwich
Specific ideas:
peanut butter and jelly,   _____, _____

11–12. *General idea:* singer
Specific ideas: Gloria Estefan, _____, _____

13–14. *General idea:* flowers
Specific ideas: tulip,   _____, _____

15–16. *General idea:* tools
Specific ideas: drill,   _____, _____

17–18. *General idea:* floor coverings
Specific ideas: carpet,   _____, _____

19–20. *General idea:* TV or radio talk show
Specific ideas:
The *Tonight Show*,   _____, _____

MAIN IDEAS: Mastery Test 2

A. Each group of words below consists of one general idea and four specific ideas. The general idea includes all the specific ideas. Underline the general idea in each group.

1. helmet   turban   hat   baseball cap   sombrero

2. granola   oatmeal   raisin bran   cereal   bran flakes

3. debt   credit-card bill   mortgage   child support   car loan

4. burnt toast   minor problems   flat tire   boring date   a cold

5. poker   card game   canasta   hearts   blackjack

6. Dracula   Wolfman   monster   Frankenstein   King Kong

7. silk   nylon   wool   cotton   fabric

8. microwaves   take-out food   time savers   high-speed   express
                                              trains   mail

(Continues on next page)

B. In each item below, one idea is general and one is specific. In the spaces provided, write two more specific ideas that are covered by the general idea.

9–10. *General idea:* fruit
Specific ideas: apple, _____ , _____

11–12. *General idea:* sports
Specific ideas: basketball, _____ , _____

13–14. *General idea:* relaxing activities
Specific ideas:
listening to music, _____ , _____

15–16. *General idea:* medicine
Specific ideas: cough syrup, _____ , _____

17–18. *General idea:* ways to pay
Specific ideas: check, _____ , _____

19–20. *General idea:* sources of stress
Specific ideas: poor health, _____ , _____

MAIN IDEAS: Mastery Test 3

Below are groups of four items. In each case, one item is the topic, one is the main idea, and two are details that support and develop the main idea. Label each item with one of the following:

> **T** — for the **topic** of the paragraph
> **MI** — for the **main idea**
> **SD** — for the **supporting details**

Group 1

_____ A. I think I am getting the flu.

_____ B. The flu.

_____ C. I have a fever of 102.

_____ D. My throat is sore and my nose keeps running.

Group 2

_____ A. Some people are active and find a way to deal with conflict.

_____ B. People deal with conflict in different ways.

_____ C. Some people are passive and hope the conflict will go away on its own.

_____ D. Conflict.

Group 3

_____ A. Good teachers often leave teaching because of low salaries.

_____ B. Problems in schools.

_____ C. Children who are troublemakers can prevent other students from learning in class.

_____ D. There are many problems in our schools.

(Continues on next page)

Group 4

_____ A. Some foods may protect against certain diseases.

_____ B. Some fish oils contain a substance that may lower blood pressure.

_____ C. Protective foods.

_____ D. A substance in garlic and onions appears to reduce cholesterol.

Group 5

_____ A. Working mothers, students, and older people find work-sharing positions very practical.

_____ B. Work-sharing—full-time jobs shared by two or more workers— can benefit both employees and employers.

_____ C. Employers are pleased that the turnover rate is lower and productivity is high.

_____ D. Work sharing.

MAIN IDEAS: Mastery Test 4

Following are five paragraphs. Read each paragraph and do two things:
1. Choose what you think is the correct topic of the paragraph.
2. Write the number of the sentence that states the main idea of the paragraph.

A. [1]Men are more likely than women to have health problems. [2]In almost all parts of the world, men die at an earlier age than women do. [3]In America, men are more likely than women to die from lung disease or heart disease. [4]Men are also more likely to deal with diseases in which stress is a factor—diseases such as ulcers and asthma. [5]In addition, men go to the hospital for mental illness far more often than women. [6]Men are also three times more likely to take their own life than women are.

_____ 1. The topic is
   A. health problems.
   B. men and women.
   C. health problems in men.

_____ 2. Write the number of the sentence that states the main idea of the paragraph.

B. [1]Although people dream of being celebrities, the disadvantages of fame are great. [2]First, these famous people are expected to look perfect all the time. [3]There's always someone ready to photograph a celebrity looking dumpy in old clothes. [4]Famous people also give up their privacy. [5]Their divorces and other problems end up on the evening news and in headlines. [6]Even worse, celebrities are often in danger. [7]They get threatening letters and are sometimes attacked.

_____ 3. The topic is
   A. the dangers of fame.
   B. the disadvantages of fame.
   C. the advantages and disadvantages of fame.

_____ 4. Write the number of the sentence that states the main idea of the paragraph.

(Continues on next page)

C.   ¹Losers in presidential elections often fade away after one attempt at the White House. ²But some unsuccessful presidential nominees try more than once. ³Richard Nixon was defeated by John F. Kennedy in 1960, yet was successful eight years later. ⁴Adlai Stevenson lost to Dwight Eisenhower in 1952 and then tried again in 1956. ⁵He was unsuccessful again. ⁶But Henry Clay and William Jennings Bryan can top that. ⁷Each was nominated three times and lost each time.

_____ 5. The topic is
     A. some unsuccessful presidential nominees.
     B. Richard Nixon and John F. Kennedy.
     C. nominees for the presidency.

_____ 6. Write the number of the sentence that states the main idea of the paragraph.

D.   ¹Flea markets and garage sales appeal to people for a couple of reasons. ²First, of course, a used item costs less than a new one. ³Many people on a budget have wonderful wardrobes they have assembled with good used clothing. ⁴Second, many who shop at flea markets and garage sales are collectors. ⁵There are people who collect old hats, 1950s toasters, salt and pepper shakers, comic books, and just about anything else you can think of.

_____ 7. The topic is
     A. collecting old hats.
     B. flea markets and garage sales.
     C. places to shop.

_____ 8. Write the number of the sentence that states the main idea of the paragraph.

E.   ¹Secondhand smoke—smoke from someone else's cigar or cigarette—can cause breathing illnesses and even lung cancer. ²According to the government, the dangers of secondhand smoke can be avoided in a few ways. ³First, don't allow smoking at all in your home. ⁴Second, if someone smokes outdoors, it should not be in areas where nonsmokers pass by. ⁵Third, in restaurants that still allow smoking, ask to be seated as far away from the smoking area as possible.

_____ 9. The topic is
     A. smoking.
     B. the smoking area in restaurants.
     C. secondhand smoke.

_____10. Write the number of the sentence that states the main idea of the paragraph.

MAIN IDEAS: Mastery Test 5

Following are five paragraphs. Read each paragraph and do two things:
1. Choose what you think is the correct topic of the paragraph.
2. Write the number of the sentence that states the main idea of the paragraph.

A.   [1]Many employees steal small items from their workplaces. [2]The most common stolen goods are office supplies. [3]People who would never steal a pen from a supermarket shelf think nothing of taking one home from work. [4]Also, many office workers consider personal use of the office copying machine a benefit of the job. [5]And then there are specialists. [6]One famous story concerns an appliance plant worker. [7]He regularly helped himself to parts from the assembly line. [8]Eventually, he had enough to build his own refrigerator.

_____ 1. The topic is
   A. crime.
   B. employee theft.
   C. employee theft of office supplies.

_____ 2. Write the number of the sentence that states the main idea of the paragraph.

B.   [1]Businesses leave the United States for various reasons. [2]Lower cost for plants and labor is a major reason. [3]Being purchased by a foreign company is another reason for a business to leave the United States. [4]Some companies feel that the taxes in the United States are too high. [5]Also, a host country might be offering special benefits.

_____ 3. The topic is
   A. businesses that leave the United States.
   B. business in America.
   C. taxes in different countries.

_____ 4. Write the number of the sentence that states the main idea of the paragraph.

(Continues on next page)

C. ¹Harmful chemicals are often found around the house. ²However, harmful household chemicals can be replaced with safer ones. ³For instance, baking soda can be used in place of harsh oven cleaners and stain removers. ⁴Instead of a chemical cleaner, a mixture of vinegar and water can be used to clean windows and glass. ⁵Vinegar and salt can remove mildew. ⁶And skim milk can be used to polish linoleum floors.

_____ 5. The topic is
  A. skim milk.
  B. the love of the environment.
  C. harmful household chemicals.

_____ 6. Write the number of the sentence that states the main idea of the paragraph.

D. ¹Motion sickness is caused by mixed messages sent by the eyes and ears to the brain. ²When a vehicle is moving, the body moves up and down. ³The eyes usually sense this and send the brain a message that everything is okay. ⁴But the ears may not be so sure, and can send the brain a worry message. ⁵The brain relays these messages to the rest of the body. ⁶When the messages reach the stomach, sickness results.

_____ 7. The topic is
  A. the stomach.
  B. motion sickness.
  C. a moving vehicle.

_____ 8. Write the number of the sentence that states the main idea of the paragraph.

E. ¹Twenty years ago, most dentists advised patients not to chew gum. ²It was thought that chewing gum would increase tooth decay. ³Ten years ago, chewing gum became more accepted by dentists. ⁴Today, there is evidence that chewing gum can actually assist in the fight against tooth decay. ⁵As a result, more dentists are recommending that their patients chew gum daily. ⁶Over the years, then, dentists' advice on chewing gum has changed greatly.

_____ 9. The topic is
  A. dentists.
  B. tooth decay.
  C. dentists' advice on chewing gum.

_____ 10. Write the number of the sentence that states the main idea of the paragraph.

MAIN IDEAS: Mastery Test 6

Following are five paragraphs. Read each paragraph and do two things:
1. Choose what you think is the correct topic of the paragraph.
2. Write the number of the sentence that states the main idea of the paragraph.

A. ¹Fairy tales are often thought to be charming and lovely stories for children. ²Yet the original versions of some familiar fairy tales are shockingly violent. ³"Cinderella" is the story of a handsome prince who searched for Cinderella with a glass slipper worn by Cinderella at a ball. ⁴In the original version, Cinderella's sisters cut off their toes to make the slipper fit. ⁵"Little Red Riding Hood" is another familiar fairy tale that has become less shocking. ⁶In the original version, a wicked queen sent a hunter to kill Red Riding Hood and bring back her heart and lungs.

_____ 1. The topic is
  A. fairy tales.
  B. original versions of some fairy tales.
  C. "Little Red Riding Hood."

_____ 2. Write the number of the sentence that states the main idea of the paragraph.

B. ¹The EPA (Environmental Protection Agency) estimates that American cars use over 200 million gallons of motor oil per year. ²Only 10 percent of this is recycled. ³The rest is dumped. ⁴It eventually makes its way into streams, rivers, lakes, and oceans. ⁵The amount of motor oil dumped is ten times more than the worst oil spill this country has ever known. ⁶Recycling the motor oil your car uses, then, is a very good way to help the environment.

_____ 3. The topic is
  A. motor oil.
  B. the EPA.
  C. oil spills.

_____ 4. Write the number of the sentence that states the main idea of the paragraph.

C. ¹The average amount of body fat in individuals differs according to gender and athletic ability. ²In general, between 15 and 18 percent of men's body weight is fat. ³In contrast, women have between 23 and 27 percent of their weight as fat. ⁴Athletes of both sexes generally have less body fat. ⁵Among the best male athletes, less than 10 percent of their total weight is fat. ⁶Among women athletes, generally between 12 and 15 percent of their weight is fat. *(Continues on next page)*

_____ 5. The topic is
   A. body fat.
   B. body fat of athletes.
   C. the best male athletes.

_____ 6. Write the number of the sentence that states the main idea of the paragraph.

D. [1]Children who don't read during summer vacation will lose six months of their reading level by September. [2]There are several things parents can do to help children maintain their reading levels during summer vacation. [3]First, turn the TV off when it is not being watched. [4]Second, set up a daily reading time for children. [5]Third, be a role model by reading novels, magazines, or newspapers. [6]Leave them around the house so that children will see these reading materials. [7]Fourth, show an interest in what your child is reading by asking questions or by taking turns reading out loud. [8]Also, remember that writing and reading go together. [9]Leave notes for your child that require a written response. [10]Buy a notebook for children in which they can record their daily activities and thoughts.

_____ 7. The topic is
   A. reading.
   B. children's reading levels.
   C. reading out loud.

_____ 8. Write the number of the sentence that states the main idea of the paragraph.

E. [1]Biologists recently discovered that the common field mouse has a surprisingly complicated social structure. [2]Among California field mice, for instance, males and females stay with each other for as long as they both live. [3]In addition, a chemical produced by the female encourages the male to take care of the young. [4]Finally, older siblings take care of younger ones. [5]When the female gives birth to one litter, she immediately gets pregnant, and another litter is born soon thereafter. [6]Those born in the first litter take care of the next generation.

_____ 9. The topic is
   A. biology.
   B. the common field mouse.
   C. field-mouse siblings.

_____ 10. Write the number of the sentence that states the main idea of the paragraph.

5

Supporting Details

THIS CHAPTER IN A NUTSHELL

- Supporting details are the evidence—such as reasons or examples—that backs up main ideas. Those details help you understand main ideas.
- Outlines and maps can show you a main idea and its major and minor supporting details at a glance.

Look at the following cartoon and see if you can answer the questions that follow.

Copyright 2006 by Randy Glasbergen.
www.glasbergen.com

GLASBERGEN

"First my ball rolled under the sofa, then my water dish was too warm, then the squeaker broke on my rubber pork chop. *I've had a horrible day and I'm totally stressed out!!!*"

- What is the dog's main idea, or point?
- What is his support for his point?

Explanation:

The dog's main idea, or point, is that he has had a horrible day and is stressed out. He supports his point by providing three examples (lost ball, warm water dish, and broken squeaker toy) of just why the day was so terrible for him.

WHAT ARE SUPPORTING DETAILS?

Supporting details are reasons, examples, facts, or other kinds of evidence that explain a main idea, or point.

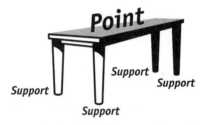

In the model paragraph in Chapter 4, the supporting details appear as a series of examples:

> [1]Certain basic fears are part of our lives. [2]For one thing, we fear being disrespected. [3]Bullies play on this fear. [4]They cruelly tease their victims and take away their self-respect. [5]And we feel hurt and disrespected when someone doesn't return our phone calls or walks past us without saying hello. [6]Another of our deepest fears is being alone. [7]No matter how tough we act, we know that the poet who wrote "No man is an island" was telling the truth. [8]We need each other. [9]Not having other people in our lives makes us feel empty inside. [10]A third basic fear is of growing old. [11]Every year, Americans use plastic surgery to try to turn back the clock. [12]And our magazines and TV shows and movies are full of beautiful young people. [13]We do not want to be reminded that the clock keeps ticking.

☑ *Check Your Understanding*

See if you can complete the basic outline below by writing in the three examples that support the main idea. The first one has been added for you.

Main idea: Certain basic fears are part of our lives.

Supporting detail: 1. Being disrespected

Supporting detail: 2. _____

Supporting detail: 3. _____

Explanation:

You should have added "Being alone" and "Growing old" as the two other supporting details. Notice that the supporting details provide the added information—specific examples of basic fears—that is needed to fully understand the main idea. To read effectively, then, you must recognize both main ideas and the details that support those ideas.

In the previous paragraph about basic fears, the supporting details are *examples.* Now look at the paragraph below, in which the main idea is explained by *reasons.* In the outline provided, write in the main idea and the three reasons that serve as supporting details.

> [1]My wife and children love our dog Punch, but I have several reasons for wanting to get rid of him. [2]First of all, Punch hates me. [3]Every time I walk past him, he gives me an evil look and curls his top lip back to show me his teeth. [4]The message is clearly, "Someday, I'm going to bite you." [5]Another reason to get rid of Punch is his shedding. [6]Every surface in our house is covered with white Punch hair. [7]I spend more time brushing it off my clothes than I do mowing the lawn. [8]Finally, Punch is an early riser, while I am not. [9]Even on weekends, he starts barking and whining to go outside at 7 a.m. [10]Somehow or other, I seem to be the only family member that hears him. [11]When I told my family that I had a list of good reasons for getting rid of Punch, they said they would make up a list of reasons to get rid of Dad.

Main idea: _____

Supporting detail: 1. _____

Supporting detail: 2. _____

Supporting detail: 3. _____

Explanation:

The main idea is that the writer wants to get rid of the family's dog, and the supporting details are the three reasons that he gives (Punch hates him, sheds everywhere, and wakes him up early).

➤ *Practice 1*

Each group of items below includes a main idea and two supporting details. In the space provided, label each item with one of the following:

MI—for the **main idea**
SD—for a **supporting detail**

Group 1

_____ A. In Italian, the word for "mother" is "mamma."

_____ B. The word for "mother" is similar in many languages.

_____ C. In Mandarin Chinese, the word for "mother" is "ma."

Group 2

_____ A. School uniforms make it easy and worry-free for students to get dressed every day.

_____ B. When students wear uniforms, it eliminates competition over who is better dressed.

_____ C. Requiring students to wear school uniforms has definite advantages.

Group 3

_____ A. People who do not exercise regularly after age 30 suffer the consequences.

_____ B. Inactive people lose nearly one pound of muscle each year after age 30.

_____ C. After age 30, inactive people lose about 5 percent of their strength every decade.

Group 4

_____ A. Some parents have tried to ban *The Adventures of Huckleberry Finn* from the classroom.

_____ B. Attempts have been made to ban *To Kill a Mockingbird* from schools.

_____ C. Efforts have been made to ban many great American novels from school libraries.

OUTLINING

Preparing an outline of a passage will help you see clearly the relationship between a main idea and its supporting details. Notice how the outlines on this page and the next page help you see and understand material at a glance.

Outlines begin with a main idea, followed by supporting details. There are often two levels of supporting details—major and minor. The **major details** explain and develop the main idea. In turn, the **minor details** help fill out the major details and make them clear.

Once you know how to outline, you can use this skill to prepare very useful study notes. Instead of studying fact after fact in sentence after sentence, you can organize the material into outlines. Good outlines tie ideas together clearly, making them easier to understand and remember.

Below is a more detailed outline of the paragraph on basic fears. This outline shows both major and minor details:

> [1]Certain basic fears are part of our lives. [2]For one thing, we fear being disrespected. [3]Bullies play on this fear. [4]They cruelly tease their victims and take away their self-respect. [5]And we feel hurt and disrespected when someone doesn't return our phone calls or walks past us without saying hello. [6]Another of our deepest fears is being alone. [7]No matter how tough we act, we know that the poet who wrote "No man is an island" was telling the truth. [8]We need each other. [9]Not having other people in our lives makes us feel empty inside. [10]A third basic fear is of growing old. [11]Every year, Americans use plastic surgery to try to turn back the clock. [12]And our magazines and TV shows and movies are full of beautiful young people. [13]We do not want to be reminded that the clock keeps ticking.

Main idea: Certain basic fears are part of our lives.

Major detail: 1. Being disrespected.
Minor details: a. Bullies tease us.
    b. We're hurt when phone calls are not returned or people don't say hello.

Major detail: 2. Being alone.
Minor details: a. "No man is an island."
    b. Not having other people in our lives makes us feel empty inside.

Major detail: 3. Growing old.
Minor details: a. We use plastic surgery to turn back the clock.
    b. Our magazines, TV shows, and movies are full of beautiful young people.

The main idea is supported and explained by the major details, and in turn, the major details are supported and explained by the minor details. For example, the major detail of "being disrespected" is supported by the details about the teasing by bullies and people not calling or saying hello.

☑ *Check Your Understanding*

See if you can fill in the missing major and minor supporting details in the outline of the following paragraph.

> [1]Clapping and applause serve a number of purposes. [2]First of all, sometimes people clap to show encouragement. [3]For example, think of a child nervously walking onto a stage to perform a magic trick for an audience. [4]Often, audience members will clap in support even before the child begins to perform. [5]A second reason people clap is out of joy or excitement. [6]This can be seen, for instance, at concerts when people begin to suddenly clap in time with the music. [7]Another reason for applause is as a sign of respect. [8]Famous and admired people usually receive big rounds of applause simply for being introduced. [9]Last of all, people clap to show appreciation. [10]After a speaker has delivered a talk or a performer has sung or played, people will applaud to show their gratitude.

Main idea: Clapping and applause serve a number of purposes.

1. To show encouragement
Example—Supporting a child performer

2. _____
Example—Clapping in time to music at a concert

3. _____
Example—_____

4. _____
Example—_____

Explanation:

You should have added three major details: (2) out of joy or excitement; (3) as a sign of respect; (4) to show appreciation. And for the third and fourth major supporting details, you should have added minor details in the form of examples. As a sign of respect, people applaud when famous or admired people are introduced. To show appreciation, people applaud after a talk or performance.

Notice that just as the main idea is more general than its supporting details, major details are more general than minor ones.

Outlining Tips

The following tips will help you prepare outlines:

TIP **Tip 1 Look for words that tell you a list of details is coming.** Here are some common list words:

List Words

several kinds of	various causes	a few reasons
a number of	a series of	three factors
four steps	among the results	several advantages

For example, look again at the main ideas shown below from two of the paragraphs already discussed, and circle the list words:

- Certain basic fears are part of our lives.
- Clapping and applause can serve a number of purposes.

Explanation:

In the main ideas above, the words *certain basic fears* and *a number of purposes* tell us that a list of major details is coming. You will not always be given such helpful signals that a list of details will follow. However, be ready to take advantage of them when they are present. Such list words can help you quickly understand the basic organization of a passage.

TIP **Tip 2 Look for words that signal major details.** Such words are called **addition words**; they tell us writers are adding to their thoughts. Here are some common addition words:

Addition Words

one	to begin with	in addition	last
first	another	next	last of all
first of all	second	moreover	final
for one thing	also	furthermore	finally

For example, look again at the selection on basic fears, shown on the following page, and answer the questions that follow.

¹Certain basic fears are part of our lives. ²For one thing, we fear being disrespected. ³Bullies play on this fear. ⁴They cruelly tease their victims and take away their self-respect. ⁵And we feel hurt and disrespected when someone doesn't return our phone calls or walks past us without saying hello. ⁶Another of our deepest fears is being alone. ⁷No matter how tough we act, we know that the poet who wrote "No man is an island" was telling the truth. ⁸We need each other. ⁹Not having other people in our lives makes us feel empty inside. ¹⁰A third basic fear is of growing old. ¹¹Every year, Americans use plastic surgery to try to turn back the clock. ¹²And our magazines and TV shows and movies are full of beautiful young people. ¹³We do not want to be reminded that the clock keeps ticking.

• Which words signal the first major detail? _____

• Which word signals the second major detail? _____

• Which word signals the third major detail? _____

Look also at the selection on clapping and applause, shown below, and answer the questions that follow.

¹Clapping and applause serve a number of purposes. ²First of all, sometimes people clap to show encouragement. ³For example, think of a child nervously walking on to a stage to perform a magic trick for an audience. ⁴Often, audience members will clap in support even before the child begins to perform. ⁵A second reason people clap is out of joy or excitement. ⁶This can be seen, for instance, at concerts when people begin to suddenly clap in time with the music. ⁷Another reason for applause is as a sign of respect. ⁸Famous and admired people usually receive big rounds of applause simply for being introduced. ⁹Last of all, people clap to show appreciation. ¹⁰After a speaker has delivered a talk or a performer has sung or played, people will applaud to show their gratitude.

• Which words signal the first major detail? _____

• Which word signals the second major detail? _____

• Which word signals the third major detail? _____

• Which words signal the fourth major detail? _____

Explanations:

In the first selection, on basic fears, the addition word signals are *for one thing*, *another*, and *third*. In the second selection, on clapping and applause, the word signals are *first of all, second, another,* and *last of all*.

➤ *Practice 2*

Read each passage. Then complete the outline that follows by filling in the missing major and minor details. Finally, answer the questions that follow each outline.

Passage 1

¹There are different ways to handle embarrassing moments. ²One way is not to make a big deal of your mistake. ³For instance, if you spill your coffee, just casually clean it up and continue your conversation. ⁴Another way is to respond with humor. ⁵After spilling the coffee, say something like, "And for my next trick, I'll knock over a water glass!" ⁶And a third way to handle an embarrassing moment is to get help, without making a big fuss. ⁷For example, if you spill a cup of coffee at a restaurant, don't crawl under the table to clean it up yourself. ⁸Just politely tell the waiter, "Sorry; I need some help cleaning up here."

Main idea: There are different ways to handle embarrassing moments.

1. _____

    Ex.—If you spill coffee, clean it up and keep talking.

2. _____

    Ex.—Say "And for my next trick, I'll knock over a water glass!"

3. _____

    Ex.—_____

Questions about the passage:

• Which words in the main idea tell you that a list is coming?

    _____

• Which word signals the first major detail? _____

• Which word signals the second major detail? _____

• Which word signals the last major detail? _____

Passage 2

^{1}In high school, almost every student belongs to one of three subcultures, or social groups, within the student body. ^{2}The first subculture is the delinquent group, the least popular of the subcultures. ^{3}Members of this group dislike authority figures and hate school in general. ^{4}The next step up the ladder of popularity is the academic subculture. ^{5}These students are known for their high regard for education. ^{6}They also have the reputation of being hard-working students. ^{7}Last of all, the most popular group is the fun subculture. ^{8}Members of this group are interested in their social status at the school. ^{9}They also focus on material things like clothes and cars.

Main idea: In high school, almost every student belongs to one of three subcultures.

1. _____
   a. Dislike authority figures
   b. Hate school in general

2. _____
   a. Known for high regard for education
   b. Known as hard-working

3. _____
   a. _____
   b. _____

Questions about the passage:

• Which words in the main idea tell you that a list of details is coming?

   _____

• Which word signals the first major detail? _____

• Which word signals the second major detail? _____

• Which words signal the third major detail? _____

PREPARING MAPS

Students sometimes find it helpful to use maps rather than outlines. **Maps,** or diagrams, are visual outlines in which circles, boxes, or other shapes show the relationship between main ideas and supporting details. Each major detail is connected to the main idea. If minor details are included, each is connected to the major detail it explains.

☑ *Check Your Understanding*

Read the following passage and then see if you can complete the map and answer the questions that follow.

¹In our busy lives, there are different steps we take to save time. ²First, we use modern inventions to help us do more in less time. ³For instance, we use a microwave oven to cook a baked potato instead of baking it in the oven. ⁴Or we use the self-checkout option at the grocery store rather than waiting for a cashier. ⁵We also save time by doing more than one thing at a time. ⁶For example, a student may finish writing a paper while eating breakfast. ⁷Or we may take a shower and brush our teeth at the same time. ⁸Finally, of course, we may simply rush. ⁹We may save time simply by gulping a meal or running to catch to a bus.

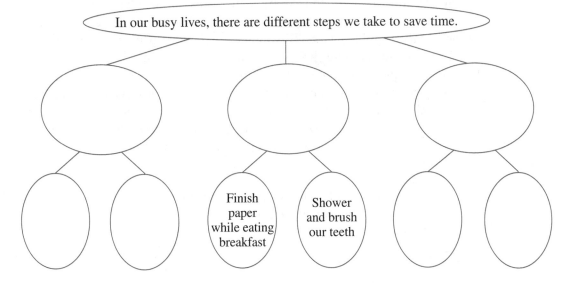

Questions about the passage:

• Which words in the main idea tell you that a list of details is coming?

_____

• Which word signals the first major detail? _____

• Which word signals the second major detail? _____

• Which word signals the third major detail? _____

Explanation:

The first major detail is "Use modern inventions," and the minor details are "Microwave" and "Self-checkout option." The second major detail is "Do more than one thing at a time." The third major detail is "Rush," and the minor details are "Gulp a meal" and "Run to catch a bus."

➤ **Practice 3**

Read each passage. Then complete the map that follows by filling in the missing major and minor details. Finally, answer the questions that follow each map.

Passage 1

[1]A recent poll identified Americans' four most popular hobbies. [2]The number one hobby enjoyed by Americans is reading. [3]Fiction is the favorite category, especially the kind of thrillers written by John Grisham and Mary Higgins Clark. [4]Biographies of famous people are next in line. [5]The second favorite hobby is photography. [6]Especially with digital cameras and camcorders becoming less expensive, Americans love documenting their lives in photographs. [7]The next most popular category is gardening. [8]From growing roses to raising their own tomatoes, Americans like playing in the dirt. [9]The final category is collecting things. [10]And what do Americans collect most? [11]Stamps and beer cans.

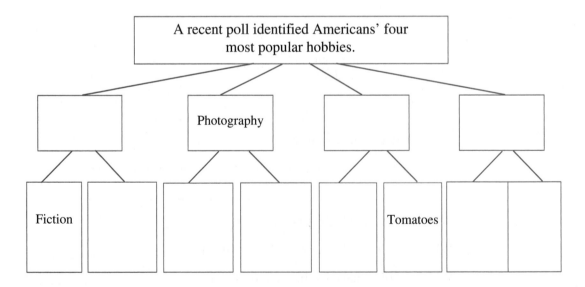

Questions about the passage:

- Which words in the main idea tell you that a list of details is coming?

  _____

- Which word signals the first major detail? _____

- Which word signals the second major detail? _____

- Which word signals the third major detail? _____

- Which word signals the fourth major detail? _____

Passage 2

¹Here are several suggestions to help you do better on tests. ²To begin with, go to class and take a lot of notes. ³Teachers tend to base their exams on the material they present in class. ⁴You must be there and write down that material. ⁵Another key suggestion is to study regularly. ⁶Learn new material on a daily basis. ⁷At the same time, review everything often. ⁸Finally, use test-taking strategies. ⁹Answer the easier questions on an exam first; then go back and tackle the hard ones. ¹⁰Also, for an essay question, make a brief outline before beginning to write.

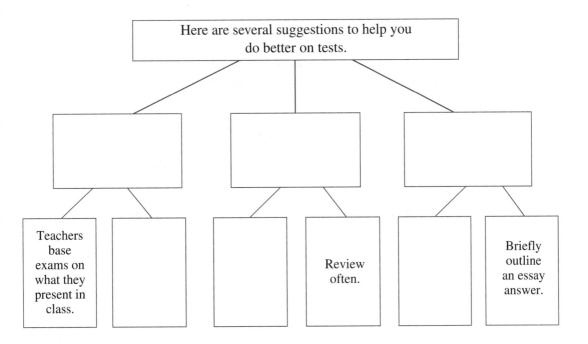

- Which words in the main idea tell you that a list of details is coming?

  _____

- Which words signal the first major detail? _____
- Which word signals the second major detail? _____
- Which word signals the third major detail? _____

A Final Note

This chapter has looked at supporting details in well-organized paragraphs. But keep in mind that supporting details are part of readings of any length, including selections that may not have an easy-to-follow list of one major detail after another. Starting with the reading at the end of this chapter (page 291), you will be given practice in answering questions about key supporting details. These questions will develop your ability to pay close, careful attention to what you are reading.

CHAPTER REVIEW

In this chapter, you learned the following:

- Supporting details go hand in hand with main ideas. They provide the added information you need to make sense of a main idea.
- List words and addition words can help you to find major and minor supporting details.
- Outlining and mapping are useful note-taking strategies.
- Outlines and maps, or diagrams, show the relationship between the main idea, major details, and minor details of a passage.

The next chapter—Chapter 6—will deepen your understanding of the relationship between main ideas and supporting details.

On the Web: If you are using this book in class, you can visit our website for additional practice in identifying supporting details. Go to **www.townsendpress.com** and click on "Online Exercises."

➤ Review Test 1

To review what you've learned in this chapter, fill in the blank or write the letter of your answer.

1. Supporting details are reasons, examples, facts, steps, or other kinds of evidence that explain a _____.

2. A _____ is a visual outline; it shows at a glance the relationship between a main idea and its supporting details.

_____ 3. Words such as *several reasons, a number of causes,* and *three steps* tell you that a series of details is coming; such words are known as
   A. addition words.
   B. list words.

_____ 4. Words such as *first, also, another,* and *finally* often tell you that a new supporting detail is being introduced; such words are known as
   A. addition words.
   B. list words.

➤ Review Test 2

A. (1–6.) Complete the outline below by filling in the missing major and minor details. Then answer the questions that follow the outline.

¹Good speakers "talk" with their bodies in several ways. ²For one thing, they use eye contact. ³Looking directly into people's eyes helps speakers build a warm bond with the audience. ⁴Eye contact can also tell speakers whether or not they are keeping the audience's interest. ⁵Head and face motions are another way speakers use their bodies. ⁶A shaking of one's head can show dislike for an idea. ⁷A nod or a smile can show acceptance of a concept. ⁸Finally, good speakers can use hand movements to accent what is being said. ⁹Upraised hands can show a positive emphasis to one's words. ¹⁰And a clenched fist can demonstrate anger.

Main idea: Good speakers "talk" with their bodies in several ways.

1. _____.

   a. Looking directly into people's eyes helps speakers build a warm bond with the audience.

   b. Eye contact tells speakers if they are keeping the audience's interest.

2. _____.

   a. Head shaking can show dislike for an idea.

   b. _____

3. _____

   a. _____

   b. _____

B. Now answer the following questions about the passage you have outlined.

   7. Which words tell you that a list of details is coming?

   _____

   8. Which words introduce the first major detail? _____

   9. Which word signals the second major detail? _____

   10. Which word signals the third major detail? _____

➤ Review Test 3

Here is a chance to apply your understanding of supporting details to a full-length reading. Job interviews, like final exams, can cause self-doubts and upset stomachs. You may feel that interviews are even worse than finals since you can't prepare for them. In the selection below, however, the author explains that there is much you can do to get ready for job interviews. You can make yourself stand out from the crowd of other applicants.

Read the selection and then answer the questions that follow. You'll find questions on vocabulary in context and main ideas as well as on supporting details.

Words to Watch

Below are some words in the reading that do not have strong context support. Each word is followed by the number of the paragraph in which it appears and its meaning there. These words are marked in the reading by a small circle (°).

personable (1): friendly
conservative (4): traditional
flustered (5): nervously confused
potential (14): possible

WINNING THE JOB INTERVIEW GAME

Marcia Prentergast

1   Few things in everyday life are dreaded more than going to a job interview. First you have to wait in an outer room, which may be filled with other people all applying for the same job you want. You look at them and they look at you. Everyone knows that only one person is going to get the job. Then you are called into the inter-viewer's office, where you have to sit in front of a complete stranger. You have to try to act cool and personable° while you are asked all sorts of questions. The questions are highly personal, or confusing, or both. "What are your strengths and weaknesses?" "Where do you see yourself in five years?" The interview may take twenty minutes, but it may seem like two hours. Finally, when you're done, you get to go home and wait a week or so to find out if you got the job.

2   The job-interview "game" may not be much fun, but it is a game you can win if you play it right. The name of the game is standing out of the crowd—in a positive way. If you go to the interview in a Bozo the Clown suit,

you may stand out of the crowd, all right, but not in a way that is likely to get you hired.

3   A few basic hints can help you play the interview game to win:

4   **1. Dress like you're in charge.** That means wearing business clothing: usually a suit and tie or a conservative° dress or skirt suit. Don't dress casually or sloppily, but don't overdress—remember, you're going to a business meeting, not a social affair. Business attire will impress the interviewer. More than that, it will actually help you to feel more businesslike, more in charge. As the old saying goes, the clothes make the man (or woman).

5   **2. Plan to arrive early.** This will keep you from getting hurried and flustered°, and also help you avoid the disaster of being late. Give yourself a few minutes to catch your breath and mentally go over your application or resumé.

6   **3. Expect to do some small talk first.** Knowing what to expect can put you ahead of the game. When the interviewer calls you in, you will probably spend a minute or so in small talk before getting down to the actual interview questions. This small talk is a good time to make a positive impression, though. Follow the interviewer's lead, and if he or she wants to discuss the weather, let's say, by all means do so for a little bit.

7   **4. Be prepared.** Certain questions come up regularly in job interviews. You should plan for all these questions in advance! Here are common questions, what they really mean, and how to answer them:

• *"Tell me about yourself."* This question   8
is raised to see how organized you are. If you give a wandering, aimless answer, the interviewer may put you down as a scatterbrain. You might talk briefly about where you were born and raised, where your family lives now, where you went to school, what jobs you've had, and how you happen to be here now looking for the challenge of a new job. You should have planned and rehearsed your answer, so you can present this basic information about yourself quickly and smoothly.

This question can also give you a   9
chance to show that you're right for the job. If you're applying for a sales job, for example, you might want to point out that you like being around people.

• *"What are your weaknesses?"* This   10
question is asked to put you off your guard, perhaps making you reveal things you might not want to. A good ploy is to admit to a "weakness" that employers might actually like—for example, admit to being a workaholic or a perfectionist.

• *"Why did you leave your last job?"* This   11
can be a "killer" question, especially if you were fired, or if you quit because you hated your boss. According to the experts, never badmouth anyone when asked this question. If you were fired, talk about personality conflicts, but without blaming anyone. If you hated your boss, say you quit for some other reason—to find a position with more growth opportunities, for example.

• *"Why did you apply for this job?"* This   12
question is really asking how eager an employee you will be. The simple answer might be "I need the money"—but that is not what job interviewers and

employers want to hear. They want employees who will work hard and stay with the company. So be honest, but give a suitable response. You might say that this is the sort of work you've always wanted to do, or that you see this company as the kind of place where you would like to create a career.

13   Other typical questions are pure softball—if you're ready. If you are asked, "Are you creative?" or "Are you a leader?" give some examples to show that you are. For instance, you may want to discuss your organizational role in one of your college clubs. Perhaps you helped recruit new members or came up with ideas to increase attendance at events. If you are asked, "What are your greatest strengths?" be ready to talk about your abilities that fit the job. Perhaps you'll mention your ability to learn quickly, your talent for working with others, your skill with organizing time efficiently, or your ability to solve problems.

No amount of preparation is ever   14 going to make job interviews your favorite activity. But if you go in well-prepared and with a positive attitude, your potential° employer can't help but think highly of you. And the day will come when you will be the one who wins the job.

Questions about the Reading

For each question, write the letter of your answer in the space provided.

Vocabulary in Context

_____ 1. In the sentences below, the word *attire* (ə-tīr′) means
    A. notes.
    B. answers.
    C. clothing.
    D. posture.

      "Business attire will impress the interviewer. . . . As the old saying goes, the clothes make the man (or woman)." (Paragraph 4)

_____ 2. In the sentence below, the word *ploy* (ploi) means
    A. question.
    B. mistake.
    C. approach.
    D. wish.

      "A good ploy is to admit to a 'weakness' that employers might actually like—for example, admit to being a workaholic or à perfectionist." (Paragraph 10)

_____ 3. In the sentences below, the word *badmouth* (băd′mouth′) means
   A. answer.
   B. criticize.
   C. recognize.
   D. imitate.

   > "'Why did you leave your last job?' . . . According to the experts, never badmouth anyone when asked this question. If you were fired, talk about personality conflicts, but without blaming anyone." (Paragraph 11)

Central Point and Main Ideas

_____ 4. Which statement best expresses the central point of the selection?
   A. Interviewers may ask some difficult and highly personal questions.
   B. When going to an interview, dress in business clothing, mentally go over your application or resumé, and go in with a positive attitude.
   C. There are several things you can do to make yourself stand out in a positive way at job interviews.
   D. Employers may ask you why you left your last job.

_____ 5. Which sentence expresses the main idea of paragraph 1?
   A. First sentence
   B. Second sentence
   C. Third sentence
   D. Last sentence

Supporting Details

_____ 6. According to the author, some advantages of arriving early to an interview are
   A. you will not be flustered or late, and you'll have time to review your application or resumé.
   B. you will have time for small talk with the interviewer.
   C. you will have time to see all the other people applying for the same job.
   D. you will have time to check your appearance and to speak to the interviewer's secretary.

7–10. Complete the following outline of "Winning the Job Interview Game" by filling in the main idea and the missing major and minor details, which are listed below in random order.

Items Missing from the Outline

- Tell me about yourself.

- There are ways to do well at job interviews.

- What are your greatest strengths?

- Plan to arrive at the interview a few minutes early.

Main idea: _____

1. To look like you're in charge, dress in business clothing.

2. _____

3. Expect to do some small talk at the beginning of the interview.

4. Be prepared to answer certain questions that are often asked in job interviews.

    a. _____
    b. What are your weaknesses?
    c. Why did you leave your last job?
    d. Why did you apply for this job?
    e. Are you creative?
    f. Are you a leader?

    g. _____

Discussion Questions

1. Have you ever had a job interview? What did you learn from it?

2. If you were asked by a job interviewer, "What is your greatest weakness?" and "What is your greatest strength?" how would you answer?

3. In terms of a career, where do you see yourself in five years? How are you preparing for that goal?

Note: Writing assignments for this selection appear on page 560.

Check Your Performance		SUPPORTING DETAILS	
Activity	*Number Right*	*Points*	*Score*
Review Test 1 (4 items)	_____	× 5 =	_____
Review Test 2 (10 items)	_____	× 4 =	_____
Review Test 3 (10 items)	_____	× 4 =	_____
	TOTAL SCORE	=	_____%

Enter your total score into the **Reading Performance Chart: Review Tests** on the inside back cover.

SUPPORTING DETAILS: Mastery Test 1

A. (1–6.) Each group of items below includes a main idea and two major supporting details. In the space provided, label each item with one of the following:

> **MI**—for the **main idea**
> **SD**—for a **supporting detail**

Group 1

_____ 1. There are far more deaths in automobile accidents than in airplane accidents.

_____ 2. The fear of flying is not based in reality.

_____ 3. Six times as many people die in train wrecks as in commercial airline crashes.

Group 2

_____ 1. American families have changed a great deal during the last few decades.

_____ 2. Since 1970, single-parent families have increased by more than 300 percent.

_____ 3. In 1970, over 40 percent of American households were made up of married parents with children; today fewer than 25 percent of them are.

(Continues on next page)

B. (7–10.) In the spaces provided, complete the outline of the paragraph by filling in the two missing major details. Then answer the questions that follow the outline.

> [1]Many people continue to work after "retiring." [2]There are two main reasons many senior citizens continue to work. [3]The first reason, of course, is for the money. [4]Many senior citizens need to add to what they receive from Social Security and pensions. [5]According to one survey, one-third of older workers fall into this category. [6]The other reason many senior citizens continue to work is that they like to. [7]One retiree, a former mechanic, loves his $5.15-an-hour job at a fast-food restaurant because it gives him the chance to meet people. [8]And a teacher who had always wanted to be a doctor went into medicine after her retirement. [9]She went back to school to become a nurse.

Main idea: There are two main reasons many senior citizens continue to work.

1. _____

2. _____

   9. Which word signals the first major detail?

     _____

  10. Which word signals the second major detail?

     _____

SUPPORTING DETAILS: Mastery Test 2

A. (1–6.) Each group of items below includes a main idea and two major supporting details. In the space provided, label each item with one of the following:

> **MI**—for the **main idea**
> **SD**—for a **supporting detail**

Group 1

_____ 1. To make sure your application is easy to read, use a pen and print or write clearly.

_____ 2. Come prepared to fill in the details of your educational and employment backgrounds.

_____ 3. There are certain things to remember when filling out a job application.

Group 2

_____ 1. At the time of the Civil War, the average adult male was 5 feet 7 inches tall; today the average adult male is nearly 5 feet 10 inches.

_____ 2. The average American male is much bigger than the average American male was at the time of the Civil War.

_____ 3. Today the average adult male weighs about 190 pounds; at the time of the Civil War, the average adult male weighed less than 150 pounds.

(Continues on next page)

B. (7–9.) In the spaces provided, complete the outline of the paragraph by filling in the **three** missing major details. Then answer the question that follows the outline.

> [1]When you die, what will happen to your body? [2]Most people end up underground in a metal coffin. [3]But a traditional burial is expensive and takes up valuable land. [4]Fortunately, there are less costly ways than a traditional burial to dispose of your remains. [5]One popular option is cremation. [6]This low-priced option involves burning your body until it is reduced to a pile of ash. [7]Your ash can be kept by loved ones or sprinkled in a special spot. [8]Another option is natural burial. [9]In this case, your body is buried in a cardboard box or cloth blanket that decays rapidly in soil, leaving no metals or chemicals in the ground. [10]A final option is to donate your body to science. [11]This option is free and allows you to contribute to medical science and to the welfare of humankind long after your death.

Main idea: There are less costly ways than a traditional burial to dispose of your remains.

1. _____

2. _____

3. _____

10. Which word signals the second major detail?

_____

SUPPORTING DETAILS: Mastery Test 3

A. Read the paragraph and answer the questions that follow. In the space provided, write the letter of each answer.

To help you focus on the supporting details of the paragraph, the main idea has been boldfaced.

> [1]**Parts of our environment affect the way we behave and feel.** [2]For one thing, there is temperature. [3]Most of us prefer temperatures in the 70s. [4]When it is hotter than the 70s, we become less active and less alert. [5]Lighting also affects us. [6]In the classroom or on the job, bright light encourages work. [7]In contrast, the low lighting of a restaurant relaxes us and encourages informal conversation. [8]Last is color. [9]For example, red is felt as exciting, blue as calming, and yellow as cheerful.

_____ 1. As the main idea in the first sentence suggests, the major details of this paragraph are
   A. various temperatures.
   B. places where we work and relax.
   C. parts of our environment that affect our behavior and moods.

_____ 2. Specifically, the major details of this paragraph are
   A. cool, hot, and just-right temperatures.
   B. the classroom, the job, and the restaurant.
   C. temperature, lighting, and color.

_____ 3. The addition words that introduce the major details are
   A. *for one thing, also,* and *last.*
   B. *most, when,* and *and.*
   C. *in contrast, for example,* and *as.*

_____ 4. According to the paragraph, most people become less alert
   A. in bright light.
   B. in temperatures greater than the 70s.
   c. in restaurants with low lighting.

_____ 5. The last sentence of the paragraph provides
   A. a major detail.
   B. minor details.
   c. both major and minor details.

(Continues on next page)

B. Read the paragraph and answer the questions that follow. In the space provided, write the letter of each answer.

To help you focus on the supporting details of the paragraph, the main idea has been boldfaced.

> [1]**Intelligence includes several basic mental abilities.** [2]One is language skill. [3]People who have this ability do well on reading tests and have large vocabularies. [4]Another such ability is a quick memory. [5]People with this skill may learn the words to a popular song after hearing it only once or twice. [6]A third basic mental skill allows us to make sense of visual information. [7]People who have this ability are skilled at reading maps or understanding diagrams.

_____ 6. The major details of this paragraph are types of
  A. mental abilities.
  B. language abilities.
  C. similarities and differences.

7. Fill in the blank: The addition words that introduce the major details are *one, another,* and _____.

_____ 8. According to the paragraph, the ability to learn the words to a popular song quickly shows a strong
  A. language ability.
  B. memorizing ability.
  C. visual ability.

_____ 9. According to the paragraph, the ability to make sense of maps and diagrams shows a strong
  A. language ability.
  B. memorizing ability.
  C. visual ability.

_____10. Write the letter of the better outline of the paragraph.

  A. Intelligence
    1. Doing well on reading tests
    2. Having large vocabularies
    3. Quickly learning the words to a popular song
    4. Seeing similarities and differences between designs and pictures

  B. Some basic mental abilities that make up intelligence
    1. Language skill
    2. A quick memory
    3. The ability to make sense of visual information

SUPPORTING DETAILS: Mastery Test 4

A. (1–4.) Complete the map of the following paragraph. First complete the main idea sentence at the top, and then fill in the three missing major details.

> [1]Heart disease is the number one killer of Americans. [2]The American Heart Association has identified the major causes of heart disease. [3]Up until recently, it had listed three factors. [4]Smoking was the number one cause. [5]It was closely followed by high blood levels of cholesterol. [6]The next most common cause of heart disease was high blood pressure. [7]Recently a fourth cause was identified. [8]Inactivity was added because evidence showed that people need to move to keep the heart stimulated.

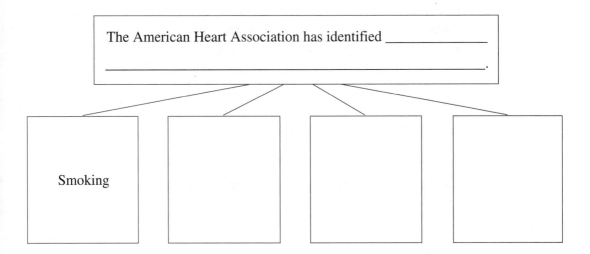

The American Heart Association has identified _____
_____.

Smoking

5. What words in the main idea tell you that a list of details is coming?

_____

(Continues on next page)

B. (6–10.) Complete the outline of the following paragraph by filling in the missing major and minor details.

> [1]Storytelling can be a good way to calm down a restless child. [2]Here are some tips on how to involve your child in a story you are telling. [3]First, grab the child's interest from the start. [4]If the story is imaginary, you might start with "Once upon a time, ..." [5]If the story is true, you might begin with "Many years ago, . . ." or "Before you were born, ..." [6]Second, have a setting for your story. [7]For a fictional story, a phrase such as "in the forest" gives children a useful frame of reference. [8]For a nonfiction story, even something like "outside of town" gives children a frame of reference. [9]Third, appeal to the senses. [10]Describe how things look. [11]For instance, you might mention colors that characters are wearing. [12]Or imitate the sounds of parts of your story—for instance, a train whistle or a birdcall. [13]When appropriate, also include descriptions of how things smelled and felt. [14]Finally, don't worry if the child appears to be daydreaming as you tell the story—he or she may be imagining the story as you speak.

Main idea: Here are some tips on how to involve your child in a story you are telling.

1. Grab the child's interest from the start.

    a. _____

    b. If the story is true, begin with "Many years ago, . . ." or "Before you were born, ..."

2. _____

    a. For a fictional story, a phrase such as "in the forest" gives children a useful frame of reference.

    b. _____

3. _____

    a. _____

    b. Imitate the sounds of parts of your story.

    c. When appropriate, also include descriptions of how things smelled and felt.

4. Don't worry if the child appears to be daydreaming as you tell the story—he or she may be imagining the story as you speak.

SUPPORTING DETAILS: Mastery Test 5

A. (1–4.) Fill in the major details needed to complete a map of the following passage.

[1]A respectful parent guides and instructs more than he or she punishes. [2]To be a respectful parent, there are several "don'ts" you should remember. [3]First, don't yell a lot at children. [4]Yelling will tell a child that the parent is out of control. [5]Or it will result in a shouting match that loses respect. [6]Second, don't make too many rules. [7]Growing up is not a boot camp. [8]Too many rules will prevent children from understanding what is really important. [9]Third, don't show disrespect to a child. [10]This will create resentment. [11]Fourth, don't order children around. [12]They will not learn responsibility if they feel they have to do what you want at the instant you command it. [13]Finally, don't neglect to acknowledge good behavior. [14]Praise and hugs work wonders in promoting responsibility and respect.

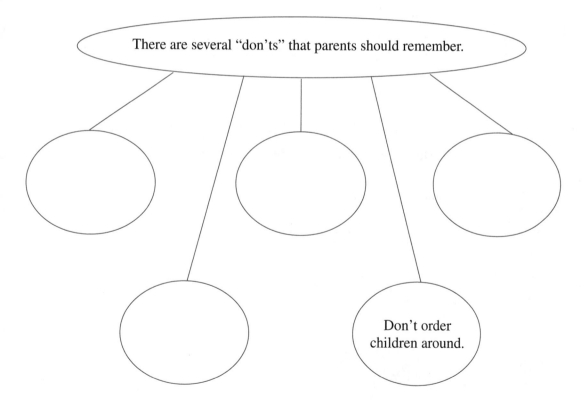

There are several "don'ts" that parents should remember.

Don't order children around.

(Continues on next page)

B. (5–10.) Complete the outline of the following paragraph by filling in the missing major and minor details.

> ¹Certain kinds of employee behavior are likely to lead to dismissal. ²First is dishonesty. ³For example, if a boss thinks an employee is lying, that employee is not likely to be on the job long. ⁴Similarly, if a worker is believed to be stealing, he or she may not last long. ⁵A second type of unacceptable behavior is irresponsibility. ⁶For instance, most bosses dislike workers taking too many breaks. ⁷Just as bad is an employee doing personal business during the workday. ⁸Finally, a poor attendance record can lead to dismissal. ⁹Employees cannot afford to be absent frequently. ¹⁰And on some jobs, an employee who is even fifteen minutes late will have some serious explaining to do.

Main idea: Certain kinds of employee behavior are likely to lead to dismissal.

1. _____

    a. Lying

    b. _____

2. _____

    a. _____

    b. Doing personal business during the workday

3. Poor attendance

    a. _____

    b. _____

SUPPORTING DETAILS: Mastery Test 6

A. (1–5.) Read the paragraph and answer the questions that follow. In the space provided, write the letter of each answer.

To help you focus on the supporting details of the paragraph, the main idea has been boldfaced.

> [1]**The National Board of Medical Examiners released a number of alarming facts about doctors.** [2]To begin with, the amount of time doctors spend examining patients is down dramatically from previous years. [3]Twenty years ago, doctors spent eleven minutes with patients. [4]Today they take only seven minutes. [5]Next, it was found that a large number of patients have been switching doctors. [6]In one recent year, for instance, 25 percent of patients reported changing doctors. [7]The most common reason given was that patients did not feel comfortable with the doctor they left. [8]Finally, medical students' reasons for wanting to become a doctor were unexpected. [9]The most common reason given was to make a good living. [10]Working with people ranked third.

_____ 1. The opening words that tell you a list of details is coming are

    A. "The National Board of Medical Examiners."

    B. "a number of alarming facts about doctors."

    C. "the amount of time doctors spend examining patients."

_____ 2. The first major supporting detail is signaled by the words

    A. *a number of.*   B. *previous years.*   C. *to begin with.*

_____ 3. The second major detail is introduced in sentence

    A. 3.   B. 5.   C. 6.

_____ 4. The third major detail is introduced in sentence

    A. 7.   B. 8.   C. 9.

_____ 5. Write the letter of the better outline of the paragraph.

    A. Main idea: The National Board of Medical Examiners recently released a number of alarming facts about doctors.

      1. Twenty years ago, doctors spent eleven minutes examining patients.

      2. Today, on the average, doctors spend seven minutes examining patients.

      3. Within the past year, 25 percent of patients reported changing doctors, in most cases because of discomfort with the doctor.

      4. The reasons medical students give for wanting to become a doctor were unexpected.

(Continues on next page)

B. Main idea: The National Board of Medical Examiners recently released a number of alarming facts about doctors.

1. Doctors today spend less time examining patients than they did twenty years ago.
2. A large number of patients have been switching doctors.
3. Medical students rank making a good living as a more important reason to become a doctor than working with people.

B. (6–9.) In the spaces provided, complete the map of the paragraph by filling in the four missing major details. Then answer the question that follows the map.

¹Very often, the more mysterious something is, the more false ideas there are surrounding it. ²There are several incorrect ideas about the human brain, a mysterious object. ³One false idea is that the brain itself is firm and grey. ⁴In reality, the living brain is deep red, darker than blood, and is soft and shaky like jelly. ⁵Next, the idea that new brain cells can't be created after damage or loss is not true. ⁶Cells continue to reproduce throughout one's life, and the ability to learn and create is unending. ⁷A third false idea is that humans use only 10 percent of their brains. ⁸Since this idea first appeared in the early 1900s, scientists have gone on to show that we use all of our brains. ⁹The final mistaken idea is that we have "right brain" and "left brain" abilities. ¹⁰It is true that some abilities are located in specific areas of the brain. ¹¹However, most skills are spread out equally on both sides. ¹²In fact, if one side of the brain in injured at a young age, skills often just transfer to the other side of the brain.

```
┌─────────────────────────────────────────────────┐
│  There are several incorrect ideas about the human brain, │
│                a mysterious object.               │
└─────────────────────────────────────────────────┘
   ┌──────────┐  ┌──────────┐  ┌──────────┐  ┌──────────┐
   │          │  │          │  │          │  │          │
   │          │  │          │  │          │  │          │
   │          │  │          │  │          │  │          │
   └──────────┘  └──────────┘  └──────────┘  └──────────┘
```

10. What words in the main idea tell you that a list of details is coming?

_____

6

Finding Main Ideas

THIS CHAPTER IN A NUTSHELL

- The main idea most often appears in the first sentence of a paragraph.

- The main idea may include such list words as *various kinds* and *a number of*. Supporting details may be introduced with such addition words as *first of all, next,* and *finally*.

- Sometimes the first sentence or two of a paragraph acts only as an introduction to the main idea. The main idea then appears in the second or third sentence. Often a word like *but* or *however* signals such a main idea.

- The main idea may also appear in the middle or at the end of a paragraph.

Look at the following cartoon:

"Location, location, location."

Real estate agents (even a pigeon real-estate agent talking to a pigeon couple) are fond of using the words "Location, location, location" to sell a property.

What they mean is that location is the most important thing—in fact, the three most important things—about a house or an apartment. In a paragraph, location is also important, as you will learn in this chapter.

In the previous chapters, most of the main ideas were in the first sentence of each paragraph. But the main idea may appear elsewhere in the paragraph as well. This chapter begins by describing common locations of the main idea. The chapter will then give you practice in finding the main idea in a series of paragraphs.

As you work through this chapter, remember what you have already learned about finding main ideas:

1 Look for a **general idea** and ask yourself, "Is this idea supported by all or most of the other material in the paragraph?"

2 See if you can decide on the **topic**—the general subject of the paragraph—and then ask, "What point is the paragraph making about this topic?"

3 Look for **list words** such as *several reasons* or *various factors* or *three steps*; such words often appear in the main idea sentence. (See page 281.) Also, look for **addition words** such as *first, another, also,* and *finally*; such words may introduce details that support the main idea. (See page 281.)

MAIN IDEA AT THE BEGINNING

Main Idea
Supporting Detail
Supporting Detail
Supporting Detail
Supporting Detail

Writers often begin a paragraph with the main idea. The rest of the paragraph then supports the main idea with details.

☑ *Check Your Understanding*

See if you can underline the main idea in the following paragraph.

> [1]My desk is well organized. [2]I keep pencils and pens in the top left drawer. [3]Typing and writing paper are in the middle left drawer. [4]The bottom left side has all the other supplies I might need, from paper clips to staples. [5]The top of the desk is clear, except for a study light and a blotter.

⁶The right side of the desk has two drawers. ⁷The bottom one is a file drawer, where I keep my notes for each class. ⁸And in the top drawer? ⁹That's where I keep nuts, raisins, small pretzels, and M&M's that I snack on while I work.

Explanation:

This paragraph follows a very common pattern: The main idea is presented in the *first* sentence. The following sentences support the main idea with details of just how the desk is organized.

But a main idea does not always appear in the very first sentence of a passage. See if you can underline the main idea in this paragraph:

> ¹Many people say they have a problem sleeping. ²But in many cases, sleep problems can be avoided by following a few simple guidelines. ³First, don't drink alcoholic beverages or drinks with caffeine close to bedtime. ⁴Next, do not exercise within three hours of bedtime. ⁵Finally, plan a sleep routine. ⁶Every day, go to bed at the same time and get up at the same time.

Explanation:

In the above paragraph, the main idea is stated in the *second* sentence. The first sentence introduces the topic (sleeping problems), but it is the idea in the second sentence—that sleep problems can be avoided by following a few simple guidelines—that is supported in the rest of the paragraph. So keep in mind that the first sentence may simply introduce or lead into the main idea of a paragraph. **Very often, a word like** *but* **or** *however* **then signals the main idea.** In the above paragraph, the word *but* helps mark the main idea.

MAIN IDEA IN THE MIDDLE

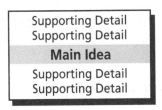

Sometimes the first few sentences of a paragraph act as an introduction to the main idea. The main idea then appears in the middle of the paragraph.

☑ *Check Your Understanding*

Here is an example of a paragraph in which the main idea is somewhere in the middle. Try to find and underline it. Then read the explanation that follows.

> ¹Today we take world-wide communication for granted. ²Through TV and radio, we learn almost instantly what happens throughout the world. ³In Roman times, however, military leaders communicated with each other through a more down-to-earth method—pigeons. ⁴Homing pigeons have a strong instinct to return home from just about anywhere. ⁵The birds were kept in cages at the military camps. ⁶When a message had to be sent, a soldier strapped it to the bird's leg. ⁷The bird was then released, and it flew home, delivering the message.

Explanation:

If you thought the third sentence contains the main idea, you were correct. The two sentences before the main idea introduce the topic: communication. Then the writer presents the main idea, which is that in Roman times pigeons were used for military communications. The rest of the paragraph develops that idea with supporting details that explain just how the pigeons were used.

MAIN IDEA AT THE END

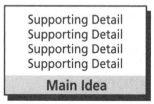

Sometimes all the sentences in a paragraph will lead up to the main idea, which is stated at the end.

☑ *Check Your Understanding*

See if you can underline the main idea in the following paragraph:

> ¹One common belief is that damp weather or a "chill" causes people to catch a cold. ²The truth is that exposure to a cold virus—not weather—is what causes the sickness. ³A related idea is that vitamin C can help prevent

the common cold. [4]While vitamin C can help with other conditions, there is no evidence that it stops or relieves colds. [5]Another medical myth is that chocolate causes acne. [6]Researchers who have studied this skin condition have not been able to connect acne to a diet rich in chocolate. [7]Finally, many people believe they should drink eight glasses of water a day for good health. [8]But the only result you can expect from this much water is a need to visit the bathroom. [9]Many popular ideas about health are simply false.

Explanation:

Here the supporting details (beliefs and ideas about health) appear first, and the point of the supporting details—that many popular ideas about health are false—appears at the end.

> ## Practice 1

The main idea may appear at any place within each of the four paragraphs that follow. Write the number of each main idea sentence in the space provided.

> *Hints:* Remember the three ways to find main ideas:
>
> **1** Look for a general idea and ask yourself, "Is this idea supported by all or most of the other material in the paragraph?"
>
> **2** See if you can decide on the topic—the general subject of the paragraph—and then ask, "What point is the paragraph making about this topic?"
>
> **3** Look for list words such as *several reasons* or *various factors* or *three steps*; such words often appear in the main idea sentence. Also, look for addition words such as *first, another, also,* and *finally*; such words may introduce details that support the main idea.

_____ 1. [1]What you consider a "normal" diet depends upon where you live. [2]For example, horse meat is on the menu in many French restaurants. [3]In Korea, dogs are raised to be eaten. [4]Rabbits are popular food in Italy. [5]Fried grasshoppers are eaten in rural Mexico. [6]In much of Asia, giant waterbugs are roasted and eaten whole. [7]Sheep's head is popular in Norway, lizards are eaten in South America, and whale blubber is consumed in the Arctic. [8]While we may think these foods are unusual or even disgusting, remember that people of the Hindu religion think it is disgusting that we eat beef.

_____ 2. ¹If you are like 70 million Americans, you don't get enough sleep. ²Lack of sleep affects people in a number of harmful ways. ³For one thing, too little sleep affects our concentration and judgment. ⁴We are more likely to make mistakes, whether taking a test or driving a car. ⁵Also, lack of sleep harms our body. ⁶Our level of stress increases and our immune system weakens, leaving us at risk for illness. ⁷Last, lack of sleep has negative psychological effects, such as irritability, impatience, and an increased risk of depression. ⁸The good news: these effects can be erased—with about eight hours of sleep a night.

_____ 3. ¹Shooting deaths are all too common on our city streets. ²And after the shooting, bystanders often say, "I didn't see anything." ³The sad truth is that witnesses to a crime are often afraid to speak up, even if they know who pulled the trigger. ⁴Some feel that what happens in the neighborhood is nobody else's business. ⁵Others stay silent because they don't want to be seen as "snitches," helping the police or other authorities. ⁶A few even fear that if they do say something, they will become the next victims. ⁷And so their neighborhood continues to be a hopeless and dangerous place, where killers are allowed to walk freely.

_____ 4. ¹Robotic surgeons are becoming a reality. ²One of the most promising surgical robots is called the Da Vinci. ³It is a 1,200-pound, $1.5 million gadget that already sits in some operating rooms. ⁴A human surgeon works at a nearby control board to guide Da Vinci's multiple arms. ⁵Those arms are so long, slender, and flexible that they can reach deep into a patient's body, perform difficult tasks, and withdraw, leaving only a tiny scar. ⁶Surgical robots that are even "smarter" than the Da Vinci are being developed.

➤ Practice 2

The main idea may appear at any place within each of the four paragraphs that follow. Write the number of each main idea sentence in the space provided.

_____ 1. ¹In the deep South, where it is often very hot, people tend to speak slowly. ²They draw out their words, making a one-syllable word like "down" sound as if it has two syllables. ³On the other hand, people living in the New England states, where it gets very cold, often speak quickly. ⁴Sometimes they clip their words as though they are in a hurry to get out of an icy wind blowing around them. ⁵Meanwhile, people living in parts of the country that don't usually have extreme temperatures, such as the West Coast and the Midwest, are often said to have no accent at all. ⁶They just talk "regular." ⁷It seems possible that the climate in an area actually influences how the local residents speak.

_____ 2. ¹America should put an end to the death penalty. ²There is no evidence that the death penalty stops people from committing crimes. ³A person about to murder another person does not stop to think, "No, I might be executed for this." ⁴Also, the death penalty is unfairly applied. ⁵Poor or minority people are put to death far more often than wealthier white people. ⁶The more well-off people can pay for better lawyers and therefore escape the death penalty. ⁷Last, the death penalty is immoral. ⁸The Bible says "Thou shalt not kill," and our society should honor that commandment.

_____ 3. ¹There is much that people can do for their pets. ²But the opposite is also true—numerous studies have shown that owning a pet can improve a person's mental and physical well-being. ³A pet that a person feels attached to improves the owner's frame of mind. ⁴In addition, a pet gives a feeling of being needed to the person who takes care of it. ⁵Pets also give an unconditional love that makes coming home after a rotten day more bearable. ⁶Even being in the same room as a pet can lower one's blood pressure and heart rate.

_____ 4. ¹Several kinds of changes can warn that a teenager is considering suicide. ²Some changes are physical. ³The youngster may have no energy or may show a sudden gain or loss in weight. ⁴Other changes are emotional. ⁵There can be unexpected outbursts, usually for no obvious reason. ⁶Also, the youngster may stop communicating with family or may even withdraw from people in general. ⁷The most dramatic signs of suicide are changes in old habits and interests. ⁸These signs often include new sleeping patterns and giving away favorite possessions.

CHAPTER REVIEW

In this chapter, you learned the following:

- The first place to check for the main idea is the first sentence. But the main idea can appear anywhere within a paragraph.

- At times the first sentence or two serve as an introduction to the main idea, which then appears in the second or third sentence. In such cases, a word like *but* or *however* often signals the main idea.

The next two chapters—Chapters 7 and 8—explain how writers use signal words to connect their ideas.

  On the Web: If you are using this book in class, you can visit our website for additional practice in finding main ideas. Go to **www.townsendpress.com** and click on "Online Exercises."

➤ *Review Test 1*

To review what you've learned in this chapter, complete each of the following sentences.

1. The main idea appears most often in the *(first, second, final)*

   _____ sentence of a paragraph.

2. Sometimes the first sentence or so of a paragraph may simply introduce

   or lead into the _____, which may appear in the second or third sentence.

3. When a sentence early in a paragraph begins with a word such as

   however or _____, look closely at that sentence to see if it is the main idea.

4. The main idea may occur at the beginning, in the middle, or at the

   _____ of a paragraph.

➤ *Review Test 2*

The main idea may appear at any place within each of the four paragraphs that follow. Write the number of each main idea sentence in the space provided.

_____ 1. ¹Wood was once the only material used in a home's framework. ²However, some homebuilders now have good reasons for using steel in constructing house frames. ³First, wood is not always available. ⁴Also, the cost of steel is often 20 percent less than that of wood. ⁵Furthermore, unlike wood, steel is termite-proof. ⁶Steel will not shrink, warp, or split. ⁷Steel will not catch on fire, as wood will. ⁸And steel is stronger and more durable than wood.

_____ 2. [1]Highway maintenance workers must be prepared to clean up just about any mess you can think of. [2]Once, twenty thousand gallons of molasses leaked from a tanker truck. [3]Highway workers spent hours scraping up the gooey mess. [4]Another time, a load of live chickens escaped from an overturned truck. [5]Workers ran all over trying to catch the birds. [6]Some escaped and are still living in bushes near the accident site. [7]One highway crew had to stop traffic to pick up a safe that someone had dropped. [8]A highway crew in California reported that in one month they picked up fifty mattresses, twenty ladders, fifteen chairs, ten refrigerators, and three bathtubs.

_____ 3. [1]Lightning usually strikes outdoors. [2]We've all heard about people who were struck by lightning while walking or working outside. [3]But lightning can be harmful inside as well as outside. [4]It can come in through an open window or door and then bounce around a room until it finds a way outside again. [5]Also, any electrical appliance which conducts electricity can act as a magnet for dangerous lightning. [6]Lightning can even be conducted through telephone wires and strike a person talking on the phone.

_____ 4. [1]It is becoming more and more common for single women to bear children. [2]In 1960, only 5.3 percent of children had single moms. [3]By 2004, that figure had increased to 35.8 percent. [4]Among ethnic groups, African-American women are most likely to have children outside of marriage. [5]Sixty-nine percent of African-American children are born to single mothers. [6]Next are American Indian and native Alaskan women. [7]Sixty-two percent of births to those women are outside of marriage. [8]Forty-six percent of births to Hispanic women are to single women. [9]Twenty-four percent of babies born to non-Hispanic white women are to single moms. [10]And 15 percent of births to Asian or Pacific Island women are to unmarried women.

➤ Review Test 3

Here is a chance to apply your understanding of signal words to a full-length reading. This selection was written by a former community college student who has strong opinions about what students really need to know as they begin their college careers. Read the selection and then answer the questions that follow. You'll find questions on vocabulary in context, main ideas, and supporting details.

Words to Watch

Below are some words in the reading that do not have strong context support. Each word is followed by the number of the paragraph in which it appears and its meaning there. These words are indicated in the selection by a small circle (°).

> *paralegal assistant* (7): a person trained to assist a lawyer
> *persist* (10): continue on
> *endured* (13): carried on in spite of hardship
> *projected* (22): gave the impression of

LEARNING SURVIVAL SKILLS

Jean Coleman

1   For four years I was a student at a community college. I went to night school as a part-time student for three years, and I was able to be a full-time student for one year. My first course was a basic writing course because I needed a review of grammar and the basics of writing. I did well in that course, and that set the tone for everything that followed.

2   It is now eleven years since I started college, and I have a good job with a Philadelphia accounting firm. When I was invited to write this article, the questions put to me were "What would you want to say to students who are just starting out in college? What advice would you give? What experiences would it help to share?" I thought a lot about what it took for me to be a successful student. Here, then, are my secrets for survival in college and, really, for survival in life as well.

"Be Realistic."

3   The first advice that I'd give to beginning students is this: "Be realistic about how college will help you get a job." Some students believe that once they have college degrees, the world will be waiting on their doorsteps, ready to give them wonderful jobs. But

the chances are that unless they've planned, there will be *nobody* on their doorsteps.

4   I remember the way my teacher in a study skills course dramatized this point in class. He played a student who had just been handed a college degree. He opened up an imaginary door, stepped through, and peered around in both directions outside. There was nobody to be seen. I understood the point he was making immediately. A college degree in itself isn't enough. We've got to prepare while we're in college to make sure our degree is a marketable one.

5   At that time I began to think seriously about (1) what I wanted to do in life and (2) whether there were jobs out there for what I wanted to do. I went to the counseling center and said, "I want to learn where the best job opportunities will be in the next ten years." The counselor gave me some ideas. If I had that question today, I'd just go to the Internet. Using the search engine Google, I'd type in "best jobs," and I would quickly have plenty of information about good future jobs.

6   The result of my personal career planning was that I eventually graduated from community college with a degree in accounting. I then got a job almost immediately, for I had chosen an excellent employment area. The firm that I work for paid my tuition as I went on to get my bachelor's degree. It is now paying for my work toward becoming a certified public accountant, and my salary increases regularly.

7   By way of contrast, I know a woman named Sheila who earned a bachelor's degree with honors in French. After graduation, she spent several unsuccessful months trying to find a job using her French degree. Sheila eventually wound up going to a specialized school where she trained for six months as a paralegal assistant°. She then got a job on the strength of that training—but her years of studying French were of no practical value in her career at all.

8   I'm not saying that college should serve only as a training ground for a job. People should take some courses just for the sake of learning. At the same time, they should take courses with a career in mind.

9   In my own case, I started college at the age of twenty-seven. I was divorced, had a six-year-old son to care for, and was working full time as a hotel night clerk. I was in school getting ready for the solid job I desperately needed. I am saying, then, that students must be realistic. If they will need a job soon after graduation, they should be sure to study in an area where jobs are available.

"Persist."

10   The older I get, the more I see that life lays on us some hard experiences. There are times for each of us when simple survival becomes a deadly serious matter. We must then learn to persist°—to struggle through each day and wait for better times to come—as they always do.

11   I think of one of my closest friends, Neil. After graduating from high school with me, Neil spent two years working as a stock boy at a local department store in order to save money for college tuition. He then went to the guidance office at the small

college in our town. Incredibly, the counselor there told him, "Your IQ is not high enough to do college work." Thankfully, Neil decided to go anyway and earned his degree in five years—with a year out to care for his father, who had had a stroke one day at work.

12   Neil then got a job as a manager of a regional beauty supply firm. He met a woman who owned a salon, got married, and soon had two children. Three years later he found out that his wife was having an affair. I'll never forget the day Neil came over and sat at my kitchen table and told me what he had learned. He always seemed so much in control, but that morning he lowered his head into his hands and cried. "What's the point?" he kept saying in a low voice over and over to himself.

13   But Neil has endured°. He divorced his wife, won custody of his children, and learned how to be a single parent. Recently, Neil and I got letters informing us of the twentieth reunion of our high-school graduating class. Included was a short questionnaire for us to fill out that ended with this item: "What has been your outstanding accomplishment since graduation?" Neil wrote, "My outstanding accomplishment is that I have survived." I have a feeling that many of our high-school classmates, twenty years out in the world, would have no trouble understanding the truth of his statement.

14   I can think of people who started college with me who had not yet learned, like Neil, the basic skill of endurance. Life hit some of them with unexpected low punches and knocked them to the floor. There was Alan, whose girlfriend broke off their relationship. Alan stopped coming to class, and by the end of the semester he was failing most of his courses. I also recall Nelson, whose old car kept breaking down. After Nelson put his last $200 into it, the brakes failed and needed to be replaced. Overwhelmed by his continuing car troubles, Nelson dropped out of school. And there was Rita, discouraged by her luck of the draw with teachers and courses. In sociology, she had a teacher who wasn't able to express ideas clearly. She also had a math teacher who talked too fast and seemed not to care at all about whether his students learned. To top it off, Rita's adviser had enrolled her in an economics course that put her to sleep. Rita told me she had expected college to be an exciting place, but instead she was getting busywork assignments and trying to cope with hostile or boring teachers. Rita decided to drop her math course, and that must have set something in motion in her head, for she soon dropped her other courses as well.

15   In my experience, younger students seem more likely to drop out than do older students. I think some younger students are still in the process of learning that life slams people around without warning. I'm sure they feel that being knocked about is especially unfair because the work of college is hard enough without having to cope with other hardships.

16   In some situations, withdrawing from college may be the best response. But there are going to be times in college when students—young or old—must simply decide, "I am going to persist." They should remember that there are many other people out there

who are quietly having hard times. I think of Dennis, a boy in my introductory psychology class who lived mostly on peanut butter and discount store loaves of white bread for almost a semester in his freshman year. And I remember Estelle, who came to school because she needed a job to support her sons when her husband, who was dying of leukemia, would no longer be present.

"Grow."

17   I don't think that people really have much choice about whether to grow in their lives. To not be open to growth is to die a little each day. Grow or die—it's as simple as that.

18   I have a friend, Jackie, who, when she's not working, can almost always be found at home or at her mother's. Jackie eats too much and watches TV too much. I sometimes think that when she swings open her apartment door in response to my knock, I'll be greeted by her familiar chubby body with an eight-inch-screen television set occupying the place where her head used to be.

19   Jackie seems quietly desperate. There is no growth or plan for growth in her life. I've said to her, "Go to school and study for a job you'll be excited about." She says, "It'll take me forever." Once Jackie said to me, "The favorite time of my life was when I was a teenager. I would lie on my bed listening to music and I would dream. I felt I had enormous power, and there seemed no way that life would stop me from realizing my biggest dreams. Now that power doesn't seem possible to me anymore."

20   I feel that Jackie must open some new windows in her life. If she does not, her spirit is going to die. There are many ways to open new windows, and college is one of them. For this reason, I think people who are already in school should stay long enough to give it a chance. No one should turn down lightly such an opportunity for growth.

"Enjoy."

21   For all its challenges, college is often a wonderful experience. If school had not been something I really enjoyed, I would not have made it.

22   In high school I felt I was shy, clumsy, and average. But in college, I was free to present myself in any way I chose. I decided from my first week in school that my college classmates and instructors were going to see the new, improved Jean. I projected° a confidence I didn't always feel. I sat near the front in every class. I took part in discussions. Instead of slipping away after class, I made a point to chat with my teachers and invite other students to have coffee with me. Soon I realized that my "act" had worked. People saw me as a confident, outgoing woman. I really liked this new image of myself as a successful college student.

23   Another of the pleasures of college was the excitement of walking into a class for the first time. As it turned out, some courses were more memorable than others. However, I rarely had a course that didn't have some real rewards to offer me.

24   I even enjoyed the physical preparation for a new class. I loved going to the bookstore and finding the textbooks I'd need. I liked to sit down with them,

crack open their bindings, and smell their new-book scent. I made a habit of buying a new spiral-bound notebook for each of my classes. Writing the new course's name on the notebook cover and seeing those fresh, blank sheets waiting inside helped me feel organized and ready to tackle a new challenge.

25   One of the best parts of college was the people I've met. Some of them became friends I hope I'll keep forever. Even the ones I just knew briefly helped make my life richer. One of my best friends was Charlotte. Like me, she came back to school after her marriage broke up. When I first met Charlotte, she was scared to death. She was sure that she could never keep up with the younger students. She felt she would be over her head in returning to college. I'll never forget one day about three weeks into the term when she turned to me and broke into a silly grin. "You know, Jean," she said, "I'm doing as well in class as anyone else!" Seeing Charlotte's growing confidence helped me believe in my own ability to succeed.

Getting to know my instructors was   26 a pleasure as well. I had more of a relationship with them than with my high-school teachers. They weren't perfect or all-knowing—but they were mostly good people who really cared about helping me get where I wanted to go.

In Conclusion

College helped me make it. I now   27 have a secure job future. My son is doing well in school. I have friends. I am proud and happy. I still have my fears and my problems, but I have survived and done more than survive. I'm in control of my life. I believe college can do the same for you.

Questions about the Reading

For each question, write the letter of your answer in the space provided.

Vocabulary in Context

_____ 1. In the sentences below, the word *peered* (pîrd) means
  A. joked.   C. raced.
  B. looked.   D. hid.

> "He opened up an imaginary door, stepped through, and peered around in both directions outside. There was nobody to be seen." (Paragraph 4)

_____ 2. In the sentence below, the word *overwhelmed* (ō-vər-hwĕlmd′) means
  A. overlooked.   C. defeated.
  B. strengthened.   D. unconcerned.

> "Overwhelmed by his continuing car troubles, Nelson dropped out of school." (Paragraph 14)

Central Point and Main Ideas

_____ 3. Which sentence best expresses the central point of the selection?
  A. All people experience great problems in the course of their lives.
  B. Following certain guidelines will help you succeed in school and in life.
  C. Divorce can be the beginning of a new and better life.
  D. Certain survival skills can help you become a successful accountant.

_____ 4. Which sentence best expresses the main idea of paragraphs 3–8?
  A. Students should make sure that college prepares them for a career that they will enjoy and in which jobs are available.
  B. If the author was planning her career today, she would simply check the Internet for good job opportunities.
  C. The author's friend Sheila ended up with a job that had nothing to do with her college degree.
  D. The author is now working as an accountant and also toward becoming a certified public accountant.

_____ 5. Which sentence best expresses the main idea of paragraphs 11–13?
   A. Neil's story makes the point that sometimes the most important thing in life is to simply continue on.
   B. The author's friend, Neil, suffered through some very hard times.
   C. The author and Neil have kept in touch long after graduating together.
   D. Even if someone tells you that you shouldn't go to college, you should still go.

_____ 6. Which sentence best expresses the main idea of paragraphs 18–20?
   A. The author believes that her friend, Jackie, eats too much and watches too much TV.
   B. The author's friend, Jackie, has lost her belief that she will realize her biggest dreams.
   C. The author realizes that attending college is simply one way to grow as a person.
   D. The author believes that her friend, Jackie, should stop sitting around the house and go to college in order to grow as a person.

_____ 7. Which sentence best expresses the main idea of paragraph 26?
   A. The author realized that her college instructors had private lives of their own.
   B. The author enjoyed working with and getting to know her college instructors.
   C. In high school, the author thought her teachers had no private lives.
   D. The author realized that most of her college instructors weren't perfect.

Supporting Details

_____ 8. The author
   A. took a straight liberal arts curriculum.
   B. switched from being a French major to an accounting major.
   C. took accounting classes and ended up with a degree in art.
   D. took some general interest classes, but ended up with a degree in accounting.

_____ 9. The author saw herself as shy, clumsy, and average, but decided to
   A. project a confidence she didn't always feel.
   B. sit in the middle of the class so no one would notice her.
   C. get involved in school clubs.
   D. drop out of any classes that seemed worthless.

_____10. The author states in paragraphs 14–16 that successful students
A. have better luck with teachers than unsuccessful students.
B. are often younger students.
C. face fewer hardships than unsuccessful students.
D. make up their minds to keep trying despite hardships.

Discussion Questions

1. The author's "secrets" for survival in college and in life are "be realistic," "persist," "grow," and "enjoy." Which of these points do you feel are most important for you to remember, and why?

2. Jean Coleman gives a lot of advice to students just starting college. Is there anything she does *not* mention that you think beginning students need to know? What is it?

3. The author suggests that students should find out what jobs will be available in the future and then get a degree in a related field. What type of career do you think you'd be interested in, and why? What degree will help you enter that field?

Note: Writing assignments for this selection appear on pages 560–561.

Check Your Performance   **FINDING MAIN IDEAS**

Activity	Number Right	Points	Score
Review Test 1 (4 items)	_____	× 5 =	_____
Review Test 2 (4 items)	_____	× 5 =	_____
Review Test 3 (10 items)	_____	× 6 =	_____

TOTAL SCORE   =   _____%

Enter your total score into the **Reading Performance Chart: Review Tests** on the inside back cover.

FINDING MAIN IDEAS: Mastery Test 1

The main idea may appear at any place within each of the five paragraphs that follow. Write the number of each main idea sentence in the space provided.

_____ 1. [1]In many homes, the refrigerator door is the family bulletin board. [2]On it, people place things they don't want to lose. [3]These may include the phone number of the local police or of a favorite baby sitter. [4]Also kept there are reminders, including notes about social events. [5]In addition, the refrigerator is a favorite spot to display things, such as a child's art work.

_____ 2. [1]The first frost in Montana occurs around September 15. [2]Colorado gets its first frost about October 1. [3]Oklahoma's first frost is near the end of October. [4]Louisiana can expect a frost around the middle of November. [5]And Florida can look for a frost about the middle of December. [6]Clearly, the farther south you go, the later the first frost date is likely to be.

_____ 3. [1]Have you ever wondered why we are attracted to certain people as friends and lovers? [2]Several factors help explain our attraction to other people. [3]One key is physical closeness. [4]We are more likely to be interested in people we see often. [5]What we think of as good looks is also important. [6]We tend to like people we find physically attractive. [7]In addition, we are drawn to people with whom we share similar backgrounds, interests, and values.

_____ 4. [1]Marta is fourteen and lives in a village in San Salvador. [2]As in most peasant families there, every day the women prepare tortillas, thin round pancakes made from mashed corn. [3]In San Salvador, the tortillas are made in a few steps, the same way they were made hundreds of years ago. [4]Marta collects the corn and puts it in a pot of water to soak. [5]The next day, she puts the wet corn through a hand grinder. [6]Her mother then puts the ground corn on a block of stone and mashes it back and forth many times until it is a pasty dough. [7]This dough is then patted into tortillas, which are cooked on a flat griddle over an open fire. [8]They are eaten with salt and a portion of beans.

(Continues on next page)

_____ 5. ¹When people think of "Frankenstein," they usually think of a dangerous monster with a stitched-on head. ²However, the original creature, presented in the 1818 novel by Mary Shelley, was nothing like the modern Hollywood version. ³First of all, his appearance is described as "hideous" in the novel, but he doesn't have a flat head or bolts sticking out of his neck. ⁴In addition, the creature in the book is to be pitied, not feared. ⁵He sits and cries over the fact that people reject him. ⁶He is ultimately driven to violence because he wants to be loved, and no one will love him. ⁷He has human emotions even though he is not a human. ⁸Finally, "Frankenstein" isn't even the monster's name. ⁹Dr. Frankenstein is the scientist who created the monster. ¹⁰The novel is named after him, not his creation.

FINDING MAIN IDEAS: Mastery Test 2

The main idea may appear at any place within each of the five paragraphs that follow. Write the number of each main idea sentence in the space provided.

_____ 1. ¹You might assume that television programs are similar around the world. ²However, TV programming varies from country to country. ³Some countries such as Sweden and Zimbabwe permit television to be broadcast only at certain times during the day. ⁴Other countries limit the number of hours that entertainment shows can be on the air. ⁵Poland, for example, insists that news shows be on the air for more time than entertainment shows. ⁶And some countries, including Argentina, ban advertising.

_____ 2. ¹Being a judge may be an important job, but judges often face the down-to-earth problem of fighting off sleepiness during a long trial. ²One reason is that arguments made by attorneys are usually routine. ³They are also often long and boring. ⁴Another reason is that judges must remain seated throughout a trial. ⁵This can slow the body down, especially after lunch. ⁶Also, courtrooms are usually stuffy. ⁷Air circulation is poor, there are no windows, and lighting is dim.

_____ 3. ¹As people get older, their physical and mental capabilities decline. ²Yet research has shown that as people age, they are likely to feel happier. ³One poll found that two-thirds of people over 65 were happy with their lives. ⁴In contrast, only about half of the people between the ages of 18 and 49 said that they were pleased with their lives.

_____ 4. ¹Some foreign students are uncomfortable with the casual relationship that exists between American teachers and students. ²In many countries, students treat teachers much more formally. ³In addition, foreign students have the language problem to deal with. ⁴Their English classes may not have prepared them to understand fast-paced conversations filled with slang expressions. ⁵Foreign students' social lives can be difficult as well. ⁶Having a background so different from that of other students can make it hard to find friends. ⁷Obviously, life in America can be hard on foreign students.

(Continues on next page)

_____ 5. [1]William Henry Harrison had one of the most fascinating careers of all the presidents of the United States. [2]He was the only president to study medicine. [3]Before getting his degree, he left school and joined the Army, where he rose to the rank of general. [4]He was elected president at age 68. [5]Until Ronald Reagan, he was the oldest man ever elected president. [6]He gave one of the longest inaugural addresses on record, close to two hours. [7]Shortly after his speech, he caught pneumonia. [8]Harrison died a little more than a month after taking office.

FINDING MAIN IDEAS: Mastery Test 3

The main idea may appear at any place within each of the five paragraphs that follow. Write the number of each main idea sentence in the space provided.

_____ 1. [1]Velcro is a fastening tape that was first seen as a replacement for the zipper. [2]The ease in opening and closing Velcro has given it some interesting uses. [3]For instance, astronauts have used it to keep objects —and themselves—from floating off into space. [4]They also have had small pieces of Velcro stuck inside their helmets so they could scratch an itchy nose. [5]Today, the fabric is used to fasten the fireproof suits of race-car drivers. [6]This allows a driver to jump out of a suit in seconds if necessary. [7]Velcro is also used to join two parts of the artificial heart.

_____ 2. [1]According to a medical journal, there are some important guidelines for having your ears or other body parts pierced. [2]First, let a professional who uses sterile instruments perform the task. [3]Second, do not pierce your ears if you have a serious medical condition, including heart disease, blood disorder, or diabetes. [4]Also, for six weeks, do not wear rings that contain nickel or a gold alloy or that are gold-plated. [5]Next, avoid the risk of infection by washing the pierced area twice a day with cotton dipped in rubbing alcohol. [6]Finally, if the area becomes red, swollen, or sore, see a doctor immediately.

_____ 3. [1]Every week, guns kill several hundred Americans. [2]To cut down on these deaths, some say we should stop the sale of guns, or at least of the worst kinds of guns. [3]Since so many people already own guns, others suggest we require a permit to carry one outside the home. [4]Many gun owners call for yet another solution: tough penalties for those who use guns in crimes. [5]These are just several of many ideas on how to reduce the dangers of guns in America.

(Continues on next page)

_____ 4. ¹A single computer chip can hold a great deal of information. ²For several reasons, veterinarians are implanting computer microchips under the skin of pets. ³First, the chips can be used to recognize an animal that has been lost or stolen. ⁴Second, they can be used to identify purebred animals that have come from breeders. ⁵Breeders who guarantee that an animal is free from defects can identify the animal later in life. ⁶And third, the animal's history can be kept on the chip. ⁷This means that if a pet changes vets, the new doctor can see what treatments the animal has undergone.

_____ 5. ¹There are various ways to stay informed about important events in the world. ²One is to read newspapers. ³Good daily papers such as _The New York Times_ and the _Los Angeles Times_ are available in many cities across the country. ⁴_USA Today_ is sold nationally and provides state and national coverage. ⁵Another way to stay informed is to subscribe to a weekly newsmagazine. ⁶_Time_ and _Newsweek_ are the most popular. ⁷A third way to keep informed is to watch TV news shows. ⁸Each network broadcasts morning and evening news shows. ⁹News reports of varying lengths can be found on cable channels such as CNN at all times of the day. ¹⁰Last but not least, many people today use the Internet to get up-to-the-minute news.

FINDING MAIN IDEAS: Mastery Test 4

The main idea may appear at any place within each of the five paragraphs that follow. Write the number of each main idea sentence in the space provided.

_____ 1. [1]Before much was known about germs, doctors unknowingly caused much illness and death by spreading germs. [2]Before the twentieth century, doctors did not wash their hands between tasks. [3]Little was known about germs and how they were spread. [4]Doctors would finish one operation, then immediately start on another. [5]Then they would examine patients, never realizing that they were carrying bacteria from one person to another. [6]In many cases, they seriously infected the very people they were trying to cure.

_____ 2. [1]Instincts are animal behaviors that don't need learning. [2]One example of instinct is the way birds build nests. [3]Birds don't stop to think about which type of nest to build. [4]All robins, for instance, build their nests the same way. [5]Also, ants don't think about how to get food. [6]Without lessons, they gather food in the same way that every other ant in the hill does. [7]A third example is that all cats lick themselves clean without learning to do so.

_____ 3. [1]Husbands once had more power in marriages: they earned more, were better educated, and had jobs with more prestige. [2]But as more women finish college, get better jobs, and earn more, they gain power at home. [3]Another factor in the balance of power is whether or not both partners care equally about the marriage. [4]If the husband, for example, cares more about staying married than the wife does, the wife will have more power. [5]That is because the husband will do more to please her. [6]Thus the power structure of marriage has become more complicated in recent years.

(Continues on next page)

_____ 4. [1]What steps can you take if you turn an ankle or strain a muscle? [2]Many sports physicians recommend the "RICE" formula for sprains and strains: Rest, Ice, Compression, and Elevation. [3]First, rest the joint or muscle that hurts. [4]Secondly, apply ice to the injured area. [5]Ice may be used at regular times for two days. [6]A compression bandage, such as an Ace bandage, will also ease the pain. [7]Finally, elevating an injured ankle or knee will keep pressure off it and prevent further damage. [8]Of course, if the pain continues or if the injury swells, you should see a doctor at once.

_____ 5. [1]Sometimes it's hard to remember that cats and dogs are descended from wild animals. [2]Even though these house pets have been tame for many centuries, they still have some leftover wild qualities. [3]For example, watch a cat when she drinks water. [4]You'll notice that her ears are turned around to listen for any sounds behind her. [5]This is the result of a wild cat's (lions, tigers, leopards) instinct of listening for approaching animals while drinking at a water hole. [6]Or perhaps you've seen a dog turn around and around before settling down for a nap. [7]Wild dogs (wolves, coyotes, foxes) are often observed trotting around in circles in order to flatten out resting spots in tall grasses and scratchy weeds. [8]Although Rover may actually be preparing to stretch out on the sofa, this old instinct still remains.

FINDING MAIN IDEAS: Mastery Test 5

The main idea may appear at any place within each of the five paragraphs that follow. Write the number of each main idea sentence in the space provided.

_____ 1. ¹There are six major problems that students bring into the high-school classroom, says the National Education Association. ²First, about a quarter of all students smoke marijuana regularly, and more than two-thirds use alcohol. ³Also, 40 percent of today's fourteen-year-old girls will get pregnant in their teens, and 80 percent of these will drop out of high school. ⁴A third problem is that 30 percent of all students now in high school will drop out. ⁵In addition, one out of three girls and one out of eight boys under eighteen years old have reported being sexually abused. ⁶Fifth, 15 percent of girls will suffer an eating disorder during part or all of their teenage years. ⁷Finally, suicide is the second most common cause of death among fifteen- through nineteen-year-olds.

_____ 2. ¹In California, a "Victim's Bill of Rights" law was passed recently. ²This law broadened the type of evidence that could be used in court. ³The idea was to keep criminals from going free because of legal loopholes. ⁴But defense lawyers soon learned that they, too, could use this law. ⁵In rape trials especially, the new law could be used to move part of the blame onto the victim. ⁶This was done by presenting evidence, not permitted before, that the victim was careless or sexually "loose." ⁷Therefore, a law intended to protect crime victims turned out to have just the opposite effect.

_____ 3. ¹The far inland parts of Antarctica seem more like a different planet than part of our Earth. ²Because this area of Antarctica is at the very bottom of the world, the temperatures often fall below -100 degrees. ³Sustained winds of 80 miles per hour or more can howl across the icy land for days on end. ⁴There are no trees, buildings, or hills to block or slow down the winds. ⁵Obviously, there are no signs of any kind of life present, and total darkness covers the land from April to October! ⁶And although there *is* land in Antarctica, most of it is buried more than a mile beneath the ever-present snow and ice. ⁷Because temperatures always remain well below freezing, some of this ice pack that makes up the strange land of Antarctica is estimated to be more than a million years old.

(Continues on next page)

_____ 4. [1]Our life stages—for example, birth, puberty, death—may be set by biology. [2]However, how we view those stages is shaped by society. [3]During the Middle Ages, for example, children dressed—and were expected to act—like little adults. [4]Adolescence became a separate stage of life only fairly recently, when a teenage subculture appeared. [5]Before that, young people were "children" until about age 16. [6]Then they went to work, married, and had their own children. [7]Today, young adulthood has become a new stage of life, covering about ages 20 to 30. [8]And now that people live longer and spend many years in active retirement, older adulthood has also become a distinct life stage.

_____ 5. [1]Police raids on "massage parlors" are often reported in the newspapers. [2]Women are arrested for working as prostitutes. [3]Their clients risk arrest as well. [4]The prostitutes often have a long record of similar arrests. [5]A better way to solve this social problem might be to simply legalize prostitution. [6]It could be a woman's—or man's—right to sell her or his sexual services, if that is what she or he wants to do. [7]If prostitution were legalized, the business would be safer for everyone involved. [8]Prostitutes could be required to have regular health checks. [9]They would also have legal protection if their clients acted abusively.

FINDING MAIN IDEAS: Mastery Test 6

The main idea may appear at any place within each of the five paragraphs that follow. Write the number of each main idea sentence in the space provided.

_____ 1. [1]According to one researcher, the distance we like to keep between ourselves and other people depends on who the other people are. [2]The space within about one foot from us is "intimate" space. [3]We share it willingly only with loved ones. [4]If forced to share it with strangers (in a crowded elevator, for instance), we feel uncomfortable. [5]Between one and four feet away is our "personal" space, which we share with friends. [6]This is about how far apart we sit at a restaurant, for example. [7]Between about four and ten feet away is "social" space. [8]This is the distance we keep from strangers at parties and other gatherings. [9]Finally, over ten feet away is "public" space, a distance at which we can pretty much ignore others.

_____ 2. [1]A bullfighter usually kneels in front of the bull before a fight begins. [2]Audience members are amazed at his courage. [3]However, the truth is that by kneeling, the bullfighter tricks the bull into being gentle. [4]Among some animals, when two males fight, one can signal he gives up by taking a yielding position. [5]The animal drops to the ground and raises his backside. [6]This position tells the other male that he has won and thus reduces his instinct to fight. [7]For this reason, the bull thinks the kneeling bullfighter is giving up. [8]Therefore, the bull does not attack.

_____ 3. [1]The reason we shiver and get goosebumps when we are frightened has to do with our animal nature. [2]When animals see or hear something threatening, their fur stands on end. [3]This reaction makes them look larger and thus more dangerous to an enemy. [4]In addition, extra blood flows to their muscles, getting them ready for action. [5]Humans react in the same way. [6]When we sense danger, goosebumps appear where our fur would stand on end—if we had fur. [7]Also, since more blood is going to our muscles, less blood flows to our skin, making us feel cold. [8]We shiver, then, to get warm.

(Continues on next page)

_____ 4. [1]If you want to, you can jump in your car and *drive* to Alaska. [2]The Alcan Highway (short for Alaska-Canada) stretches for 1422 miles from British Columbia, Canada, to Delta Junction, Alaska. [3]Along the way, you'll see amazing mountains, ancient ice packs, and the occasional moose or grizzly bear. [4]You'll stop at small frontier towns in the Yukon and meet all sorts of interesting people. [5]However, you'll also have to deal with very rough patches of road the further north you go. [6]Nearly everyone who drives the entire Alcan Highway experiences at least one flat tire along the way. [7]Also, towns may be more than 100 miles apart and may contain little more than a closed gas station and an empty campground once you reach them. [8]So, while driving the Alcan Highway can be an exciting adventure, it can also be a difficult journey.

_____ 5. [1]The Dionnes were the first quintuplets to survive their infancy. [2]They were born on May 28, 1934, in a tiny Canadian town. [3]The five identical girls were born to a poor farming couple who already had six children. [4]The story of the Dionnes is a strange and even tragic one. [5]The Canadian government took custody of the quints away from their parents. [6]The government then built a sort of theme park called "Quintland," to house the five little girls. [7]As many as 6,000 visitors a day visited Quintland, where they could watch the Dionnes through a one-way mirror. [8]When they were 18, the girls moved back to their parents' home. [9]But soon they broke off contact with their parents, claiming that their father was molesting them. [10]As adults, the Dionnes were very poor, having never learned any way to support themselves. [11]They sued the Canadian government to share in the profits that it had made on Quintland.

7

Signal Words I

THIS CHAPTER IN A NUTSHELL

- To help make their ideas clear, writers use **signal words**, also known as **transitions**—words that carry the reader from one idea to the next.

- Typical addition words are *for one thing, second, also, another, in addition,* and *finally.*

- Typical time words are *first, next, then, after,* and *last.*

You will become a better reader if you notice **signal words**. These are the words that writers provide to make the connections between their ideas clear. There are two common kinds of signal words, also known as **transitions**:

- Words that show addition
- Words that show time

ADDITION WORDS

Put a check (✓) beside the item that is easier to read and understand:

___ I hate my job because of the long hours. My boss is often rude to me.

___ I hate my job because of the long hours. Also, my boss is often rude to me.

As you probably noted, the second item is easier to understand. The word *also* makes it clear that the writer is presenting two reasons for hating his or her job. One reason is that the hours are long. *Another* reason is that the boss is rude. *Also* and words or phrases like it are known as addition words.

Addition words (and other signal words) are like signs on the road that guide travelers. They are also known as "bridge" words, carrying the reader across from one idea to the next:

I hate my job because of the long hours.  , my boss is often rude to me.

Addition words tell us that writers are *adding to* their thoughts. They help writers organize their information and present it clearly to readers. Here are some common addition words:

Addition Words

one	to begin with	in addition	last
first	another	next	last of all
first of all	second	moreover	final
for one thing	also	furthermore	finally

Examples:

The following examples contain addition words. Notice how these words introduce ideas that *add to* what has already been said.

- A good dinner and a glass of wine at the end of the day relax me. *In addition,* they make my problems seem smaller.

- Americans spend the biggest portion of their money on medical and dental care. The *next* biggest area of spending is on groceries.

- In 1870, the Constitution was amended to guarantee men of any race the right to vote. *Another* amendment in 1920 granted women the right to vote.

➤ *Practice 1*

Complete each sentence with a suitable addition word from the box below. Try to use each transition once. Then, in the space provided, write the letter of the transition you have chosen.

A. also	B. another	C. finally
D. in addition	E. second	

Hint: Make sure that each addition word or phrase that you choose fits smoothly into the flow of the sentence. Test each choice by reading the sentence aloud.

_____ 1. There are three reasons why top athletes make so much money. For one thing, they receive big salaries just for playing their sport. Second, they earn huge fees for personal appearances. _____, they make even more money by endorsing products.

_____ 2. Desert plants such as cactus store up water so they can survive long periods without rain. Desert animals _____ find a way to survive with little water.

_____ 3. Paper and plastics are two products that many communities ask people to recycle. _____ is used motor oil.

_____ 4. Bats are gentle creatures that will bite another animal only in self-defense. _____, a single bat can eat more than 1,200 mosquitoes an hour.

_____ 5. Many couples today are busier than ever. First of all, they must raise their own children. Their _____ responsibility is to care for aging parents.

➤ *Practice 2*

A. Below is a paragraph that is organized with the help of addition words. Underline the **three** addition words. They will help you then complete the outline of the paragraph.

[1]A recent study suggested that parents should be on the lookout for stress in their children. [2]There are several signs of stress in young people. [3]Unusual tiredness in a child is one sign. [4]Another is temper tantrums. [5]And a third is the child forgetting known facts, which may result from mental exhaustion.

Main idea: There are several signs of stress in young people.

1. _____

2. _____

3. _____

B. Again, underline the **three** addition words. Then complete the outline of the paragraph.

[1]Most people think of pizza as junk food, but pizza contains healthful ingredients. [2]First of all, the crust is rich in B vitamins, which keep the nervous system humming smoothly. [3]Also, the tomato sauce is an excellent source of vitamin A, which is essential for good vision, among other things. [4]And finally, the mozzarella cheese contains protein and calcium, each of which supports good health in many ways, including keeping bones strong.

Main idea: Pizza contains healthful ingredients.

1. _____

   _____

2. _____

   _____

3. _____

   _____

C. Once again, underline the **three** addition words. Then complete the outline of the paragraph.

> [1]Walking can be a rewarding experience. [2]To begin with, walking lets you chat with your neighbors and see for yourself what's going on in your neighborhood. [3]In addition, a brisk walk is an excellent and inexpensive form of exercise. [4]Moreover, physical exercise such as walking acts as a natural anti-depressant.

Main idea: Walking can be a rewarding experience.

1. _____

2. _____

3. _____

TIME WORDS

Check (✓) the item that is easier to read and understand.

___ I let the cooked turkey sit for thirty minutes. I carved it.

___ I let the cooked turkey sit for thirty minutes. Then I carved it.

The word *Then* in the second item makes the relationship between the sentences clear. *After* letting the cooked turkey sit for a while, the writer carves it. *Then* and words like it are time words.

I let the cooked turkey sit for thirty minutes. I carved it.

Time words tell us *when* something happened in relation to when something else happened. They help writers organize and make clear the order of events, stages, and steps in a process. Here are some common time words:

Time Words

before	next	while	later
previously	soon	during	after
first	often	until	eventually
second	as	now	finally
third	when	then	last

Note: Additional ways of showing time are dates ("In 1850…"; "Throughout the 20th century…"; "By 2010…") and other time references ("Within a week…"; "by the end of the month…"; "in two years…").

Examples:

The following items contain time words. Notice how these words show us *when* something takes place.

- I quickly shut the back door *after* the mouse ran out.
- *Before* their baby daughter was born, my sister and her husband were sure it was a boy.
- Some teenagers giggled loudly *during* the movie's love scenes. *Then* an usher asked them to leave.

➤ Practice 3

Complete each sentence with a suitable time word from the box. Try to use each transition once. Then, in the space provided, write the letter of the transition you have chosen.

A. after	B. before	C. then
D. until	E. when	

Hint: Make sure that each time word you choose fits smoothly into the flow of the sentence. Test each choice by reading the sentence aloud.

_____ 1. _____ John Kennedy served as a United States Senator from Massachusetts, he was elected president.

_____ 2. Here is a good way to prepare for a test: Study hard for an hour or so. _____ take a ten-minute break.

_____ 3. James had difficulty learning to swim _____ he learned how to float.

_____ 4. _____ Washington, D.C. was chosen, the capital of the United States was Philadelphia.

_____ 5. _____ she runs out of any grocery item, Gail writes it on her shopping list.

➤ *Practice 4*

A. Below is a paragraph that is organized with the help of time words. Underline the **three** time words.

> [1]A psychologist placed a banana just outside the cage of a chimpanzee and a stick inside the cage. [2]Soon, the chimp grabbed the stick and poked it through the bars of the cage. [3]Next, the chimp dragged the banana within reach. [4]Finally, the chimp took the banana and ate it.

B. Below is another paragraph that is organized with the help of time words. Underline the **three** time words. Then complete the outline of the paragraph.

> [1]Take the following steps to find the right boyfriend or girlfriend. [2]First, trust your own instincts. [3]Don't be distracted by what your best friend thinks you should be looking for in a partner. [4]Your tastes are what matters here. [5]The next step is to widen your social circle. [6]Use e-mail, the phone, parties, clubs, church, and volunteer activities to be in touch with as many people as possible. [7]You're not going to run into the right person by sitting at home watching TV. [8]And last, don't settle for just anyone who is willing to date you. [9]If you're hanging onto a so-so relationship just so you aren't alone, you won't be ready if someone really special comes along.

Main idea: Use the following tips to find the right boyfriend or girlfriend.

1. _____

2. _____

3. _____

C. Underline the **five** time words. Then complete the outline of the paragraph.

> ¹Do you have a noticeable stain or burn in your carpeting? ²It's a problem you can correct. ³First, use a sharp utility knife to cut out the damaged area (but not the padding underneath). ⁴Second, cut a patch the same size and shape from a leftover piece of carpet or a spot of carpeting that's not noticeable, such as under a sofa. ⁵Next, cut a piece of cardboard a little larger than the patch. ⁶Then place the cardboard where you cut out the damaged piece of carpet. ⁷Last, glue the carpet patch to the cardboard.

Main idea: A noticeable stain or burn in a carpet can be corrected.

1. _____

_____

2. _____

_____

3. _____

_____

4. _____

_____

5. _____

_____

Two Final Points about Signal Words

1 Some signal words have the same meaning. For example, *also, moreover*, and *furthermore* all mean "in addition." Writers like to use different signal words to avoid repetition.

2 Certain words can serve as two different types of signal words, depending on how they are used. For example, the word *first* may be used as an addition word to show that the writer is presenting a list of details:

- My sister has some unusual shopping habits. *First*, she will never shop at a store unless there is a sale going on. *Moreover*, she . . .

First can also be used to signal a time order:

- The coach was unhappy with the way his team was playing. *First*, he called for a time-out. *Then* . . .

CHAPTER REVIEW

In this chapter, you learned how writers use signal words, also called transitions, to help make their ideas clear. You also learned two common kinds of signal words:

- **Addition words**
  - Writers use addition words to present a list of reasons, examples, or other details that support an idea. The items have no time order, but are listed in whatever order the writer chooses.
  - Words that signal addition include *for one thing, second, also, in addition,* and *finally.*

- **Time words**
  - Writers use time words to discuss a series of events or steps in the order in which they happen.
  - Words that signal time order include *first, next, then, after,* and *last.*

The next chapter—Chapter 8—will help you learn three other important kinds of signal words: words that show examples, contrast, and cause-effect.

 On the Web: If you are using this book in class, you can visit our website for additional practice with words that signal addition and time. Go to **www.townsendpress.com** and click on "Online Exercises."

➤ *Review Test 1*

To review what you've learned in this chapter, complete each item by filling in the blank or writing the letter of the correct answer.

1. Signal words are also known as _____. They are words or phrases (like *also* or *another* or *then* or *last of all*) that show the relationships between ideas.

_____ 2. TRUE OR FALSE? Signal words are like bridges that connect one idea with another.

3. Typical (*addition* or *time*) _____ words are *for one thing, also, moreover,* and *another.* Such words tell us the writer is presenting one or more ideas that add to the same line of thought as a previous idea.

4. Typical (*addition* or *time*) _____ words are *then, next, later,* and *after.* They tell us when something happened in relation to when something else happened.

➤ *Review Test 2*

A. Fill in each blank with one of the signal words in the box. Use each word once. Then write the letter of the word in the space provided.

A. after	B. also	C. finally	D. in addition

_____ 1. An ideal apartment should be close to work and school. It should _____ be in a safe area. In addition, it should be reasonably priced.

_____ 2. A butterfly goes through four life stages. It is an egg, then a caterpillar. It next becomes a cocoon and _____ emerges as a butterfly.

_____ 3. Pearls are so soft that they can be scratched during cleaning. _____ , they will dissolve if dropped into vinegar.

_____ 4. One way to start writing is to just get anything at all down on paper. Don't worry about spelling or punctuation or even making much sense. _____ you have broken the ice by getting a lot of words on the page, you can start to shape your paper.

B. (5–7.) Fill in each blank with an appropriate signal word from the box. Use each transition once.

soon	then	when

[1]A city in California made out a $26,000 check to Thomas Russell, a tax collector in the city. [2]But the check was mistakenly sent to an inmate by the same name. [3](5) _____ it was delivered to the Tracy County jail, the inmate cashed the check, posted bond, and left jail. [4]Officials (6) _____ discovered their mistake. [5]They quickly tracked down the offender, and he was (7) _____ put back in jail.

another	one	third

C. (8–10.) Fill in each blank with an appropriate signal word from the box. Use each transition once.

[1]Humans developed several physical features that make them differ from other animals. [2](8) _____ human feature is the ability to stand and walk upright. [3]With their eyes at a high level, humans are able to see distant objects. [4](9) _____ distinctive human feature is their teeth and jaws. [5]Human beings have smaller, more even teeth than other animals. [6]A (10) _____ human feature is the most important: a large brain. [7]The human brain, for instance, is almost three times as large as the chimpanzee's.

➤ Review Test 3

Here is a chance to apply your understanding of signal words to a full-length reading. Maria Cardenas grew up in a family of migrant workers. The family moved from state to state, following the fruit and vegetable harvest. Maria became used to backbreaking labor, poverty, and violence. Her hard times, as well as her own lack of education, could have ended her hopes for a better life. But, as this selection will show, Maria has found the courage both to dream and to make her dreams become reality.

Read the selection and then answer the questions that follow. You'll find questions on vocabulary in context, main ideas, supporting details, and signal words.

Words to Watch

Below are some words in the reading that do not have strong context support. Each word is followed by the number of the paragraph in which it appears and its meaning there. These words are marked in the reading by a small circle (°).

shattered (17): broken into pieces; destroyed
abducted (18): taken away by force
taunted (22): cruelly teased
overwhelmed (24): overpowered
briskly (24): in a lively manner
GED (24): general equivalency diploma (equal to a high-school diploma)
eligible (27): qualified

MIGRANT CHILD TO COLLEGE WOMAN

Maria Cardenas

1   As I walk into the classroom, the teacher gazes at me with her piercing green eyes. I feel myself shrinking and burning up with guilt. I go straight to her desk and hand her the excuse slip. Just like all the other times, I say, "I was sick." I hate lying, but I have to. I don't want my parents to get in trouble.

2   I'm not a very good liar. She makes me hold out my hands, inspecting my dirty fingernails and calluses. She knows exactly where I've been the past several days. When you pick tomatoes and don't wear gloves, your hands get rough and stained from the plant oils. Soap doesn't wash that out.

3   In the background, I can hear the students giggling as she asks her usual questions: "What was wrong? Was your brother sick, too? Do you feel better today?" Of course I don't feel better. My whole body aches from

those endless hot days spent harvesting crops from dawn to dusk. I was never absent by choice.

4   That year, in that school, I think my name was "Patricia Rodriguez," but I'm not sure. My brother and I used whatever name our mother told us to use each time we went to a new school. We understood that we had to be registered as the children of parents who were in the United States legally, in case Immigration ever checked up.

5   My parents had come to the States in the late '60s to work in the fields and earn money to feed their family. They paid eight hundred dollars to someone who smuggled them across the border, and they left us with our aunt and uncle in Mexico. My five-year-old brother, Joel, was the oldest. I was 4, and then came Teresa, age 3, and baby Bruno. The other kids in the neighborhood teased us, saying, "They won't come back for you." Three years later, our parents sent for us to join them in Texas. My little heart sang as we waved good-bye to those neighbor kids in Rio Verde. My father did love us!

6   My parents worked all the time in the fields. Few other options were open to them because they had little education. At first, our education was important to them. They were too scared to put us in school right away, but when I was 8 they did enroll us. I do remember that my first-grade report card said I was "Antonietta Gonzales." My father made sure we had everything we needed—tablets, crayons, ruler, and the little box to put your stuff in. He bragged to his friends about his children going to school. Now we could talk for our parents. We could translate their words for the grocer, the

doctor, and the teachers. If Immigration came by, we could tell them we were citizens, and because we were speaking English, they wouldn't ask any more questions.

In the years to come, I often   7 reminded myself that my father had not forgotten us like the fathers of so many kids I knew. It became more important for me to remember that as it became harder to see that he loved us. He had hit my mother once in a while as I was growing up, but when his own mother died in Mexico in 1973, his behavior grew much worse. My uncles told me that my father, the youngest of the family, had often beaten his mother. Maybe it was the guilt he felt when she died, but for whatever reason, he started drinking heavily, abusing my mother emotionally and physically, and terrorizing us kids. The importance of our education faded away, and now my papa thought my brother and I should work more in the fields. We would work all the time—on school vacations, holidays, weekends, and every day after school. When there were lots of tomatoes to pick, I went to school only every other day.

8 If picking was slow, I stayed home after school and cooked for the family. I started as soon as I got home in the afternoon. I used the three large pots my mother owned: one for beans, one for rice or soup, and one for hot salsa. There were also the usual ten pounds of flour or *maseca*, ground corn meal, for the tortillas. I loved this cooking because I could eat as much as I wanted and see that the little kids got enough before the older family members finished everything. By this time there were three more children in our family, and we often went to bed hungry. (My best subject in school was lunch, and my plate was always clean.)

9 Other than lunchtime, my school life passed in a blur. I remember a little about teachers showing us how to sound words out. I began to stumble through elementary readers. But then we'd move again, or I'd be sent to the fields.

10 Life was never easy in those days. Traveling with the harvest meant living wherever the bosses put us. We might be in little houses with one outdoor toilet for the whole camp. Other times the whole crew, all fifty or one hundred of us, were jammed into one big house. Working in the fields meant blistering sun, aching muscles, sliced fingers, bug bites, and my father yelling when we didn't pick fast enough to suit him.

11 But we were kids, so we found a way to have some fun. My brother and I would make a game of competing with each other and the other adults. I never did manage to pick more than Joel, but I came close. One time I picked 110

baskets of cucumbers to Joel's 115. We made thirty-five cents a basket.

12 Of course, we never saw any of that money. At the end of the week, whatever the whole family had earned was given to my father. Soon he stopped working altogether. He just watched us, chatted with the field bosses, and drank beer. He began to beat all of us kids as well as our mother. We didn't work fast enough for him. He wanted us to make more money. He called us names and threw stones and vegetables at us. The other workers did nothing to make him stop. I was always scared of my father, but I loved him even though he treated us so badly. I told myself that he loved us, but that alcohol ruled his life.

13 I knew what controlled my father's life, but I never thought about being in control of my own. I did as I was told, spoke in a whisper, and tried not to be noticed. Because we traveled with the harvest, my brothers and sisters and I attended three or four different schools in one year. When picking was good, I went to the fields instead of school. When the little kids got sick, I stayed home to watch them. When I did go to school, I didn't understand very much. We spoke only Spanish at home. I don't know how I got through elementary school, much less to high school, because I only knew how to add, subtract, and multiply. And let's just say I got "introduced" to English writing skills and grammar. School was a strange foreign place where I went when I could, sitting like a ghost in a corner alone. I could read enough to help my mother fill out forms in English. But enough to pick up a story and understand it? Never. When a

teacher told the class, "Read this book, and write a report," I just didn't do it. I knew she wasn't talking to me.

14   In 1978, my mother ran away after two weeks of terrible beatings. Joel and I found the dime under the big suitcase, where she had told us it would be. We were supposed to use it to call the police, but we were too scared. We stayed in the upstairs closet with our brothers and sisters. In the morning, I felt guilty and terrified. I didn't know whether our mother was alive or dead. Not knowing what else to do, I got dressed and went to school. I told the counselor what had happened, and she called the police. My father was arrested. He believed the police when they said they were taking him to jail for unpaid traffic tickets. Then the police located my mother and told her it was safe to come out of hiding. My father never lived with us again although he continued to stalk us. He would stand outside the house yelling at my mother, "You're gonna be a prostitute. Those kids are gonna be no-good drug addicts and criminals. They're gonna end up in jail."

15   My father's words made me deeply angry. I had always had a hunger for knowledge, always dreamed of a fancy job where I would go to work wearing nice clothes and carrying a briefcase. How dare he try to kill my dream! True, the idea of that dream ever coming true seemed unlikely. In school, if I asked about material I didn't understand, most of the teachers seemed annoyed. My mother would warn me, "Please don't ask so many questions."

16   But then, somehow, when I was 14, Mrs. Mercer noticed me. I don't remember how my conversations with

Maria Cardenas poses with her husband, Alfonso, after a day in the orange fields.

this teacher started, but it led to her offering me a job in the Western clothing store she and her husband owned. I helped translate for the Spanish-speaking customers who shopped there. I worked only Saturdays, and I got paid a whole twenty-dollar bill. Proudly, I presented that money to my mother. The thought "I can actually do more than field work" began to make my dreams seem like possibilities. I began to believe I could be something more. The month of my sixteenth birthday, Mrs. Mercer recommended me for a cashier's job in the local supermarket. I worked there for six weeks, and on Friday, January 16, 1981, I was promoted to head cashier. I was on top of the world! I could not believe such good things were happening to me. I had a good job, and I was on my way to becoming my school's first Spanish-speaking graduate. I thought nothing could go wrong, ever again.

     But that very night, my dreams 17 were shattered° again—this time, I thought, permanently. The manager let me off at nine, two hours early. I didn't have a ride because my brother was not picking me up until 11:00 p.m. But I was in luck! I saw a man I knew, a friend of my brother's, someone I had worked with in the fields. He was a trusted family friend, so when he offered me a lift, I said, "Of course." Now I could go home and tell everybody about the promotion.

18   I never made it home or to my big promotion. The car doors were locked; I could not escape. I was abducted° and raped, and I found myself walking down the same abusive road as my mother. My dreams were crushed. I had failed. In my old-fashioned Mexican world, I was a "married woman," even if I wasn't. To go home again would have been to dishonor my family. When I found I was pregnant, there seemed to be only one path open to me. I married my abductor, dropped out of tenth grade, and moved with him to Oklahoma.

19   "My father was right," I thought. "I am a failure." But dreams die hard. My brother Joel was living in the same Oklahoma town as I was. He would see me around town, my face and body bruised from my husband's beatings. But unlike the workers in the fields who had silently watched our father's abuse, Joel spoke up. "You've got to go," he would urge me. "You don't have to take this. Go on, you can make it."

20   "No!" I would tell him. I was embarrassed to have anyone know what my life had become. I imagined returning to my mother, only to have her reprimand me, saying, "What's the matter with you that you can't even stay married?"

But Joel wouldn't give up. Finally 21 he told me, "I don't care what you say. I am going to tell Mother what is going on."

And he did. He explained to our 22 mother that I had been forced to go with that man, that I was being abused, and that I was coming home. She accepted what he told her. I took my little girl and the clothes I could carry, threw everything into my car, and left Oklahoma for Florida. My husband taunted° me just as my father had my mother: "You'll be on food stamps! You can't amount to anything on your own!" But I proved him wrong. I worked days in the fields and nights as a cashier, getting off work at midnight and up early the next day to work again. I don't know how I did it, but I kept up the payments on my little car, I didn't go on food stamps, and I was happy.

But as Antonietta grew up and 23 started school, I began to think my little triumphs were not enough. I was thrilled to see her learning to read, doing well in school. And when she would bring me her simple little books and trustingly say, "Read with me!" it filled me with joy. But I realized the day would come, and come soon, that I would be unable to read Antonietta's books. What would she think of me when I said, "I can't"? What would I think of myself?

Teaching myself to read became 24 the most important goal in my life. I began with Antonietta's kindergarten books. I thought sometimes how people would laugh if they saw me, a grown woman, a mother, struggling through *The Cat in the Hat*. But with no one to watch me, I didn't care. Alone in my house, after my daughter was asleep, I read. I read everything we had in the house—Antonietta's books, cereal boxes, advertisements that came in the mail. I forced myself through them, stumbling again and again over unfamiliar words. Eventually I began to feel ready to try a real story, a grown-up story. But my fears nearly stopped me again. We lived near a library. Antonietta had asked again and again to go there. Finally I said "all right." We walked in, but panic overwhelmed° me. All those people, walking around so briskly°, knowing where to find the books they wanted and how to check them out! What was someone like me doing there? What if someone asked me what I wanted? Too intimidated to even try, I insisted that we leave. I told Antonietta to use the library at her school. I struggled on in private, eventually earning my GED°.

25   The years passed, and I married a wonderful man who loved me and my daughter. He was proud that I had some real education, and he knew that I wanted more. But I couldn't imagine that going on in school was possible.

26   Then, in 1987, I was working for the Redlands Christian Migrant Association. They provided services for migrant children. One day, in the office, I spotted something that made my heart jump. It was a book called *Dark Harvest*. It was filled with stories about migrant workers. Although my reading skills had improved, I had still never read a book. But this one was about people like me. I began reading it, slowly at first, then with more and more interest. Some of the people in it had gone back for a GED, just as I had! Even more—some had gone on to college and earned a degree in education. Now they were teaching. When I read that book, I realized that my dream wasn't crazy.

27   My husband and I took the steps to become legally admitted residents of

With the help of her English teacher, Johanna Seth, Maria uses a word processor to edit one of her papers.

the United States. Then, my husband found out about a federal program that helps seasonal farm workers go to college. I applied and found I was eligible°. When I took my diagnostic tests, my reading, English, and math levels turned out to be seventh-grade level. Not as bad as I thought! The recruiter asked if I would mind attending Adult Basic Education classes to raise my scores to the twelfth-grade level. Mind? I was thrilled! I loved to study, and in spite of a serious illness that kept me out of classes for weeks, my teacher thought I was ready to try the ABE exams early. Her encouragement gave my confidence a boost, and I found my scores had zoomed up to a 12.9 level.

28   Then, in the fall of 1994, I took the greatest step of my academic life. Proud and excited, I started classes at Edison Community College in Florida. Of course, I was also terrified, trembling inside almost like that scared little girl who used to tiptoe up to the teacher's desk with her phony absence excuses. But I'm wasn't a scared little kid anymore. My self-confidence was growing, even if was growing slowly.

29   I laugh when I look back at that day I fled in terror from the library. My family and I might as well live there now. We walk in with me saying, "Now, we have other things to do today. Just half an hour." Three hours later, it's the kids saying to me, "Mom, are you ready yet?" But it's so exciting, knowing that I can learn about anything I want just by picking up a book! I've read dozens of how-to books, many of them about gardening, which has become my passion. I can't put down motivational books, like Ben Carson's *Gifted Hands*

and *Think Big*. I love Barbara Kingsolver's novels. One of them, *The Bean Trees*, was about a young woman from a very poor area in Kentucky whose only goal, at first, was to finish school without having a child. I could understand her. But my favorite author is Maya Angelou. Right now, I'm re-reading her book *I Know Why The Caged Bird Sings*. She writes so honestly about the tragedy and poverty she's lived with. She was raped when she was little, and she had a child when she was very young. And now she's a leader, a wonderful writer and poet. When I saw her read a poem at President Clinton's inauguration, I was very moved. And I can't talk about my life now without mentioning Kenneth and Mary Jo Walker, the president of Edison Community College and his wife. They offered me a job in their home, but so much more than that: they became my friends, my guardian angels. I am constantly borrowing books from them, and they give me so much encouragement that I tell them, "You have more faith in me than I do myself."

30   Sometimes I have to pinch myself to believe that my life today is real. I have a hard-working husband and three children, all of whom I love very much. All of them—Antonietta, Korak, and Jasmine—have grown up to be passionate readers, like me. Also like me, the children have worked in the fields, but there is little similarity between their lives and mine as a child. They grew up going to only one school the whole year long. They worked at their own pace, learning the value of work and of money—and they kept what they earned. Antonietta, who inspired me to begin reading, is a gifted

writer, whose teachers encouraged her to become a journalist.

31   And guess what! My teachers compliment my writing too. When I enrolled in my developmental English class at Edison, my teacher, Johanna Seth, asked the class to write a narrative paragraph. A narrative, she explained, tells a story. As I thought about what story I could write, a picture of a scared little girl in a schoolroom popped into my head. I began writing:

32   *As I walk into the classroom, the teacher gazes at me with her piercing green eyes. I feel myself shrinking and burning up with guilt. I go straight to her desk and hand her the excuse slip. Just like all the other times, I say, "I was sick." I hate lying, but I have to. I don't want my parents to get in trouble.*

33   I finish my narrative about giving my phony excuses to my grade-school teachers and hand it in. I watch Mrs. Seth read it and, to my horror, she begins to cry. I know it must be because she is so disappointed, that what I have written is so far from what the assignment was meant to be that she doesn't know where to begin to correct it.

34   "Did you write this?" she asks me. Of course, she knows I wrote it, but she seems disbelieving. "You wrote this?" she asks again. Eventually I realize that she is not disappointed. Instead, she is telling me something incredible and wonderful. She is saying that my work is good, and that she is very happy with what I've given her. She is telling me that I can succeed here.

35   And now I know she was right. I graduated from Edison as a member of Phi Theta Kappa, the national academic

Posing with Maria at graduation are President and Mrs. Walker and their daughter Keri; Maria's husband, Alfonso; and the children, Antonietta, Korak, and Jasmine.

honor society for junior colleges. Then I earned my bachelor's degree in elementary education from Florida Gulf Coast University. I've had the joy of seeing Antonietta doing well in law school, Korak starting college at Edison, and Jasmine studying in high school. Unfortunately, health problems have gotten in the way of my plans to become a full-time teacher. But I am still sometimes able to meet with groups of migrant children and encourage them to stand on their own two feet. I have achieved so much! What once seemed like impossible dreams have become my reality.

Questions about the Reading

For each question, write the letter of your answer in the space provided.

Vocabulary in Context

_____ 1. In the sentences below, the word *options* (ŏp′shənz) means
   A. opinions.
   B. pleasures.
   C. gifts.
   D. choices.

   "My parents worked all the time in the fields. Few other options were open to them because they had little education." (Paragraph 6)

_____ 2. In the sentence below, the word *reprimand* (rĕp′rə-mănd′) means
   A. scold.
   B. ignore.
   C. compliment.
   D. support.

   "I imagined returning to my mother, only to have her reprimand me, saying, 'What's the matter with you that you can't even stay married?'" (Paragraph 20)

_____ 3. In the sentences below, the word *intimidated* (ĭn-tĭm′ĭ-dā′tĕd) means
   A. thoughtful.
   B. bored.
   C. fearful.
   D. critical.

   "We walked in, but panic overwhelmed me. . . . What was someone like me doing there? What if someone asked me what I wanted? Too intimidated to even try, I insisted that we leave." (Paragraph 24)

Central Point and Main Ideas

_____ 4. Which sentence best expresses the central point of the entire selection?

       A. Maria's goal was to graduate from college and teach migrant children to achieve their dreams.

       B. With hard work and courage, Maria was able to overcome great difficulties to build a wonderful family and go to college.

       C. Some books are filled with inspirational stories that can help us all.

       D. Maria's story shows us that certain skills, including writing and mathematical abilities, are necessary if we want to succeed in college.

_____ 5. The main idea in paragraph 10 is its

       A. first sentence.

       B. second sentence.

       C. third sentence.

       D. last sentence.

_____ 6. Which sentence best expresses the main idea of paragraph 26?

       A. In 1987, Maria worked for the Redlands Christian Migrant Association.

       B. The book *Dark Harvest* convinced Maria that her dream for a better education wasn't crazy.

       C. The Redlands Christian Migrant Association provided services for migrant children.

       D. The book *Dark Harvest* contained stories about migrant workers, including some who had gone on to college and became teachers.

Supporting Details

_____ 7. Maria's father began to drink heavily and abuse his wife more than ever after

       A. he lost his job.

       B. his children began going to school.

       C. Immigration came to the house.

       D. his mother died.

_____ 8. Maria was encouraged to leave her abusive husband by her

       A. mother.

       B. daughter.

       C. brother.

       D. employer.

Signal Words

_____ 9. The first word of the sentence below signals a relationship of
A. addition.   B. time.

"When the little kids got sick, I stayed home to watch them."
(Paragraph 13)

_____10. The relationship of the second sentence below to the first is one of
A. addition.   B. time order.

"Proud and excited, I started classes at Edison Community College
in Florida. Of course, I was also terrified. . . ." (Paragraph 28)

Discussion Questions

1. Maria's children worked in the fields, as their mother had. In what ways
were those children's lives different from Maria's life when she was a child
working in the fields?

2. Why do you think Mrs. Seth cried when she read Maria's narrative about
giving phony excuses to her grade-school teacher? Why might Maria have
thought that Mrs. Seth was disappointed with what she had written?

3. What do you think Maria means when she says she encourages migrant
children to "stand on their own two feet"? What do you think *all* children
must learn in order to "stand on their own two feet"?

Note: Writing assignments for this selection appear on pages 561–562.

Check Your Performance   **SIGNAL WORDS I**

Activity	*Number Right*	*Points*	*Score*
Review Test 1 (4 items)	_____	× 5 =	_____
Review Test 2 (10 items)	_____	× 4 =	_____
Review Test 3 (10 items)	_____	× 4 =	_____

TOTAL SCORE   =   _____%

Enter your total score into the **Reading Performance Chart: Review Tests** on the inside back cover.

SIGNAL WORDS I: Mastery Test 1

A. Fill in each blank with an appropriate signal word from the box. Use each transition once. Then, in the space provided, write the letter of the signal word you have chosen.

A. also	B. first of all	C. in addition
D. until	E. while	

Hint: Make sure that each word or phrase that you choose fits smoothly into the flow of the sentence. Test your choices by reading each sentence to yourself.

_____ 1. To avoid drunk drivers, some people stay off the road late at night. They _____ stay home on New Year's Eve.

_____ 2. Some scientists worry that we will not pay enough attention to global warming _____ it is too late.

_____ 3. _____ he was digging in his garden, Lonnie discovered an old tin box full of coins.

_____ 4. That family really believes in volunteering. The mother delivers food to shut-ins, and the father works with the Boy Scouts on weekends. _____, their daughter plays the piano at nursing homes.

_____ 5. Be careful to avoid spreading bacteria when you are handling raw meat in the kitchen. _____, wash your hands frequently with soap and hot water. You should also scrub chopping boards, knives, and dishes immediately after using them.

(Continues on next page)

B. Fill in each blank with an appropriate transition from the box. Use each transition once.

before	finally	then	when

¹Recently a man in Kansas got in trouble (6) _____ he created his own form of hot-air balloon. ²He strapped forty-two weather balloons to a lawn chair and (7) _____ inflated the balloons. ³Sitting in the chair, he took off and climbed to sixteen thousand feet (8) _____ shooting some of the balloons with a BB gun. ⁴He descended faster than he expected and (9) _____ crashed into some power lines. ⁵He was uninjured, but spent the next few days in jail.

_____10. This paragraph uses
    A. addition words.
    B. time words.

SIGNAL WORDS I: Mastery Test 2

A. Fill in each blank with an appropriate transition from the box. Use each transition once. Then, in the space provided, write the letter of the transition you have chosen.

A. after	B. also	C. during
D. moreover	E. second	

_____ 1. _____ buying his girlfriend a huge box of candy, Jared learned she was allergic to chocolate.

_____ 2. Duct tape was invented for use in plumbing. People _____ use it to mend toys, seal holes in garden hoses, create a secure grip on rakes, repair books, and hundreds of other tasks.

_____ 3. The First Amendment in the Bill of Rights says that the government will not establish a state religion. The _____ Amendment guarantees the right of the people to bear arms.

_____ 4. _____ the Salem (Massachusetts) Witch Trials of 1692, twenty people were executed for supposedly being witches.

_____ 5. Alzheimer's disease is a cruel illness that robs its victims of their memories. _____, it sometimes causes drastic personality changes.

(Continues on next page)

B. Fill in each blank with an appropriate transition from the box. Use each transition once.

during	last	next
then	to begin with	

¹Arranged marriages are still very common in much of the world, especially India. ²Most modern arranged marriages go through the same typical stages. ³(6) _____, the parents choose several possible mates for the adult child. ⁴(7) _____, meetings between the two families are then scheduled. ⁵(8) _____ those meetings, the young people have their first chance to meet and chat. ⁶If they seem to like each other, the man and woman might (9) _____ spend some brief time alone, perhaps going for a walk in their neighborhood. ⁷(10) _____, the young people decide if they wish to marry, or to continue meeting other possible mates.

SIGNAL WORDS I: Mastery Test 3

A. Fill in each blank with an appropriate addition word from the box. Use each transition once.

another	one

¹The U.S. Census Bureau reports that close to 40 percent of the country's citizens live in states other than where they were born. ²Two main factors are involved. ³(1) _____ is economic. ⁴People who are looking for work tend to move where the jobs are. ⁵(2) _____ consideration is weather. ⁶People seem to enjoy the warmer states. ⁷This is especially true of senior citizens. ⁸When given the chance to move from a snowy state to a sunny state, many older Americans will do so.

B. Fill in each blank with an appropriate time word from the box. Use each transition once.

finally	first	second	then

¹People infected with rabies develop a series of alarming symptoms. ²At (3) _____ they feel achy and miserable, as if they were getting the flu. ³A (4) _____ symptom is that they begin behaving oddly. ⁴They may act extremely anxious, irritable, depressed, and even aggressive. ⁵They (5) _____ become extremely sensitive to sound, touch, and light. ⁶(6) _____ they develop hallucinations and seizures. ⁷Rabies is a dreadful disease that is almost always fatal.

(Continues on next page)

C. Fill in each blank with an appropriate transition from the box. Use each transition once.

also	for one thing	furthermore

[1]A steroid is a type of drug that is taken to build muscle and improve physical performance. [2]A steroid can help an athlete compete in certain sports. [3]However, the medical profession has raised various concerns about steroid use. [4](7) _____ , a steroid can raise blood pressure. [5]Studies have shown that it can (8) _____ cause violent mood swings. [6](9) _____ , a steroid may lead to heart disease, liver cancer, and kidney failure. [7]The dangers of using steroids far outweigh the benefits, which is why they are banned in most athletic contests.

_____ 10. This paragraph uses
    A. addition words.
    B. time words.

SIGNAL WORDS I: Mastery Test 4

A. Fill in each blank with an appropriate transition from the box. Use each transition once.

after	during

[1]Nuclear weapons have been used in war only twice, both times being in Japan (1) _____ World War II. [2]On August 6, 1945, the United States dropped the first atomic bomb on Hiroshima, Japan. [3]Over 140,000 people were killed, both by the bomb itself and from the radiation that followed. [4]Three days later, a second bomb was dropped on another Japanese city. [5](2) _____ these two bombings, Japan surrendered unconditionally, and the war ended.

_____ 3. This paragraph uses
    A. addition words.
    B. time words.

B. Fill in each blank with an appropriate transition from the box. Use each transition once.

another	one

[1]Books can be grouped in a variety of ways. [2](4) _____ familiar type is fiction. [3]Fictional books are books whose contents are made up. [4]The author invents all the characters and incidents. [5](5) _____ well-known type is the nonfiction book. [6]In nonfiction, the author writes truthfully about real people and real events. [7]There is a third type of book that falls somewhere between fiction and nonfiction. [8]That is the historical novel. [9]In a historical novel, the author writes about real people who lived at a particular time and place, but makes up what those people say and do.

_____ 6. This paragraph uses
    A. addition words.
    B. time words.

(Continues on next page)

C. Fill in each blank with an appropriate transition from the box. Use each transition once.

during	finally	then

¹In 1968, a 3M company scientist named Spencer Silver developed an unusual new glue. ²The glue was strong enough to cling to objects, but weak enough that it could be removed and re-stuck elsewhere. ³(7) _____ the next few years, Dr. Silver tried to find a practical use for his strange new glue. ⁴Nothing happened until the early 1970s. ⁵(8) _____ a co-worker of Dr. Silver's named Art Fry was sitting in church, wishing that he had a bookmark that would not either fall out of his hymnal or damage it. ⁶He realized that Dr. Silver's adhesive would be the perfect solution. ⁷(9) _____, in 1979, 3M combined Dr. Silver's and Art Fry's ideas to create Post-It Notes. ⁸The product has become one of 3M's biggest sellers.

_____10. This paragraph uses
   A. addition words.
   B. time words.

SIGNAL WORDS I: Mastery Test 5

Read each textbook passage and then answer the questions that follow.

A. ¹To become a group leader, behave in certain ways in group discussions. ²First, be well informed about the work. ³Group members are more willing to follow someone who really knows the subject. ⁴Second, work harder than anyone else in the group. ⁵Leadership is often a question of setting an example, and you can do so with hard work. ⁶Third, be open to an exchange of ideas with others in the group. ⁷Listen to their ideas, and react with ones of your own. ⁸Finally, help the group work together smoothly. ⁹Make others in the groups feel good about themselves, and give credit where it is due.

_____ 1. This paragraph uses
   A. addition words.
   B. time words.

2–3. Two of the transitions that signal major details of the paragraph are

_____ and _____.

4–6. Complete the outline of the selection.

Main idea: Your chances of becoming a group leader are increased if you behave in certain ways during group discussions.

1. _____

   _____

2. _____

   _____

3. _____

   _____

4. Help the group work together smoothly.

(Continues on next page)

B. ¹Although the exact cause of childhood obesity is not known, there are a number of theories. ²One cause may be a child's genes. ³A study of 540 adopted adults found that their weight was more like their biological parents than their adoptive ones. ⁴A second cause is environment. ⁵Children tend to eat the same kinds of foods and develop the same kinds of habits as the people around them. ⁶Third, heavier children are less active. ⁷But are they less active because they are fat, or do they become fat because they are less active? ⁸So far, there is no final answer. ⁹But some support the conclusion that children become fat because they are less active. ¹⁰Last of all, too much television may also be a factor. ¹¹According to studies, every hour a day spent watching TV results in a 2 percent increase in the frequency of obesity. ¹²Children who watch a lot of TV tend to eat more snacks, especially the high-calorie ones they see in ads. ¹³They are also less active than other children.

_____ 7. This paragraph uses
      A. addition words.
      B. time words.

8–10. Complete the map of the selection.

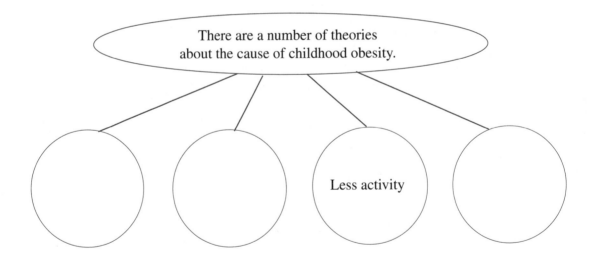

SIGNAL WORDS I: Mastery Test 6

Read each textbook passage and then answer the questions that follow.

A. ¹Perhaps surprisingly, physical good looks are only part of what makes us attractive to others. ²For one thing, attractiveness can change with age. ³How a person looks at the age of 17 is not always a sign of how he or she will look at age 30 or 50. ⁴Sometimes an average-looking adolescent, especially one with a warm, attractive personality, becomes a quite attractive middle-aged adult. ⁵Secondly, the longer we know and like someone, the more attractive we think that person is. ⁶Perhaps you can recall individuals who, as you grew to like them, became more attractive. ⁷Their physical imperfections were no longer so noticeable. ⁸Finally, love sees loveliness. ⁹The more in love a woman is with a man, the more physically attractive she finds him. ¹⁰And the more in love people are, the less attractive they find all others of the opposite sex.

_____ 1. This paragraph uses
   A. addition words.
   B. time words.

2–3. Two of the transitions that signal major details of the paragraph are

   _____ and _____.

4–5. Complete the outline of the selection.

Main idea: Physical good looks are only part of what makes us attractive to others.

1. _____

   _____

2. The longer we know and like someone, the more attractive we think that person is.

3. _____

   _____

(Continues on next page)

B. ¹We communicate with each other for various reasons. ²One reason is to meet needs. ³Psychologists tell us that we are social animals; that is, we need other people just as we need food, water, and shelter. ⁴Two people may converse happily for hours gossiping and chatting about unimportant matters that neither remembers afterward. ⁵When they part, they may have exchanged little real information, but their communication met an important need—simply to talk with another human being. ⁶Another reason we communicate is to develop relationships. ⁷We get to know others through our communication with them. ⁸A third reason we communicate is to exchange information. ⁹We may be trying to decide how warmly to dress or whom to vote for in the next presidential election. ¹⁰All of us have countless exchanges that involve sending and receiving information.

_____ 6. This paragraph uses
     A. addition words.
     B. time words.

7–8. Two of the transitions that signal major details of the paragraph are

_____ and _____.

9–10. Complete the map of the selection.

8

Signal Words II

THIS CHAPTER IN A NUTSHELL

- To help make their ideas clear, writers use **signal words**, also known as **transitions**—words that carry the reader from one idea to the next.
  - Typical illustration transitions are *for example* and *for instance*.
  - Typical contrast transitions are *but* and *however*.
  - Typical cause and effect transitions are *reasons*, *because*, and *as a result*.

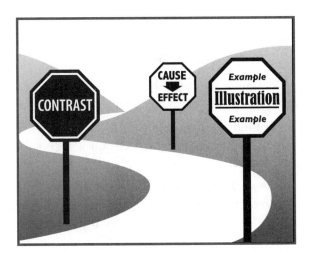

The previous chapter explained two common types of signal words (or *transitions*) that writers use to help make their ideas clear. This chapter looks at three other common types of signal words:

- Example words
- Contrast words
- Cause and effect words

EXAMPLE WORDS

Check (✓) the item that is easier to read and understand:

___ Be careful when buying an old house. The plumbing, wiring, and roof may need to be replaced.

___ Be careful when buying an old house. For instance, the plumbing, wiring, and roof may need to be replaced.

The second item is easier to understand. The words *for instance* make it clear that the plumbing, wiring, and roof are among a number of things that may need to be replaced. *For instance* and other words and phrases like it are example words, also known as illustration words.

Example words tell us that a writer will provide one or more *examples* to make a given idea clear. Here are some common example words:

Example Words

(for) example	(for) instance	to illustrate
including	such as	once

Examples:

The following sentences contain example words. Notice how these words signal that one or more *examples* will follow.

- At least nine states get their names from rivers that flow through them. *For example,* Minnesota is named after the Minnesota River.

- Some English phrases don't make much sense to people just learning the language. *For instance,* if you tell a non-native speaker to "keep an eye out" for somebody, he probably won't know what you're talking about.

- President John F. Kennedy was famous for his sense of humor. *To illustrate,* once during a lecture he was asked how he had become a hero during World War II. He answered that he had no choice: "They sank my boat."

➤ *Practice 1*

Complete each item with a suitable example word or phrase from the box below. Try to use each transition once. Then, in the space provided, write the letter of the transition you have chosen.

> A. for example   B. for instance   C. including
> D. once   E. such as

> *Hint:* Make sure that each example word you choose fits smoothly into the flow of the sentence. Test each choice by reading the sentence aloud.

_____ 1. Many health claims are made for certain foods. _____, olive oil is said to reduce heart disease.

_____ 2. Nita's parents speak Spanish when they don't want their children to understand them, _____ when they are planning a birthday party.

_____ 3. Governments own some businesses. _____, local governments often own parking areas and water systems.

_____ 4. Certain months of the year, _____ January, March, and June, are named for Roman gods.

_____ 5. President Abraham Lincoln was famous for his honesty. _____, when he worked at a store, he walked several miles to return change to a customer.

➤ *Practice 2*

Very often textbook authors will define terms the reader may not know. Then, to make sure a definition is clear, an author may give one or more examples. Below are some paragraphs from textbooks. Read each and answer the questions that follow.

A. [1]A phobia is an irrational and extreme fear of some object or situation. [2]One example is a fear of heights that is so extreme that one cannot drive over bridges without trembling. [3]Other common phobias include fears of snakes, water, and enclosed places.

1. Which sentence gives a definition? _____

2. Which sentence provides an example? _____

B.   [1]Functional illiteracy is the inability to read and write at a level required for success in daily life. [2]The problem is wide-ranging. [3]For instance, it is estimated that one in five adults is unable to read warning labels on containers of harmful substances. [4]Other examples are the many adults that cannot read the headlines in a newspaper or fill out a job application. [5]Yet another illustration of this problem is the half of the adult population in this country that is unable to read a book written at an eighth-grade level.

1. Which sentence gives a definition? _____

2. Which sentence provides an example? _____

C.   The following paragraph has a definition-example pattern. Complete the map of the paragraph. First, write the definition in the heading. Then fill in the two missing supporting details—examples of the term that is defined.

[1]Regeneration is the ability some animals have to renew lost body parts. [2]This ability can come in very handy when a limb is lost in an accident or in a fight. [3]For instance, an octopus can regrow lost tentacles. [4]The sea star is another example of an animal that can regenerate. [5]Even one leg of a sea star that includes part of the center of the body can regenerate a whole new body. [6]Also, some lizards can regrow their tails. [7]When such a lizard is caught by its tail, it releases the tail and runs away. [8]A new tail is then grown.

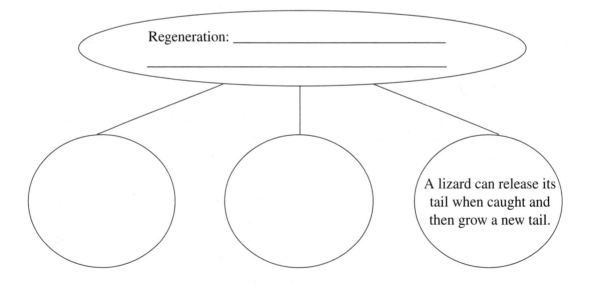

Regeneration: _____

_____

A lizard can release its tail when caught and then grow a new tail.

CONTRAST WORDS

Check (✓) the item that is easier to read and understand.

___ The dog next door is lovable. She barks a lot at night.

___ The dog next door is lovable although she barks a lot at night.

The first item suggests that one of the lovable things about the dog is that she barks at night. The word *although* in the second item shows a contrast: the dog is lovable *even though* she barks so much at night. *Although* and words like it are contrast words.

Contrast words signal that a writer is pointing out differences between subjects. A contrast word shows that two things *differ* in one or more ways. Contrast words also inform us that something is going to *differ from* what we might expect. Here are some common words that show contrast:

Contrast Words

but	instead	still	difference
yet	in contrast	as opposed to	different(ly)
however	on the other hand	in spite of	differs from
although	on the contrary	despite	unlike
nevertheless	even though	rather than	while

Examples:

The following items contain contrast words. Notice how these words signal that one idea is *different from* another idea.

- Alberto was angry when he didn't get a raise. His wife, *however,* took the news calmly.

- Tarantulas are scary-looking, *but* they are actually quite harmless.

- A cup of coffee can give you a quick energy boost. *On the other hand,* coffee can also make you irritable and unable to sleep at night.

➤ *Practice 3*

Complete each sentence with a suitable contrast word or phrase from the box. Try to use each transition once. Then, in the space provided, write the letter of the transition you have chosen.

A. even though	B. however	C. in contrast
D. in spite of	E. rather than	

> *Hint:* Make sure that each contrast word you choose fits smoothly into the flow of the sentence. Test each choice by reading the sentence aloud.

_____ 1. _____ the day started with sunshine, the weather forecast was for rain by evening.

_____ 2. Dennis always votes Democratic, _____ to the other members of his family.

_____ 3. _____ the long winters in Alaska, many people enjoy living there.

_____ 4. _____ buying ready-made curtains, Elena made her bedroom curtains out of pretty sheets.

_____ 5. Some cats will wait patiently to be fed. Others, _____, will follow their owner around the house meowing when they are hungry.

➤ *Practice 4*

A. Below is a paragraph that is organized with the help of contrast words. Underline the **two** contrast words. Then complete the outline of the paragraph.

¹There are two different views of the value of computers in the classroom. ²Some people feel that computers will soon take over many of the teachers' duties. ³One writer states, "Computers make do-it-yourself education downright efficient. ⁴Your child can probably learn spelling or arithmetic or a foreign language faster on a computer" than from a teacher in a crowded classroom. ⁵But others warn that too much technology may harm children. ⁶One psychologist says that computers, as well as video games and TV, may weaken children's language skills.

Main idea: There are two different views of the value of computers in the classroom.

1. Positive view: _____

2. Negative view: _____

B. Again, underline the **two** contrast words. Then complete the outline of the paragraph.

> ¹Doctors and scientists do not agree about when a person is truly dead. ²Some of them think that a person should be declared legally dead when blood circulation and breathing have stopped. ³Then organs that are still in good working order can be removed and donated to critically ill patients in need of a new liver, heart, or kidney. ⁴However, there are those who say that death does not occur until the entire brain stops functioning. ⁵These people admit that waiting for brain death means organs may stop working and not be in condition to be donated. ⁶But they point out that some individuals have awakened months after going into a state that seems like death.

Main idea: Doctors and scientists do not agree about when a person is truly dead.

1. _____

2. _____

C. Once again, underline the **two** contrast words. Then complete the outline of the paragraph.

> ¹Do you like to gamble? ²If so, you have plenty of company. ³Whether it's making a friendly bet on a football game or visiting the Las Vegas casinos, many people like to gamble. ⁴For most people, gambling is a bit of harmless fun. ⁵They win or lose a few dollars at the card table or slot machine, and they enjoy the process. ⁶Yet for others, gambling is a serious addiction. ⁷Unlike most of us, they bet money they cannot afford to lose. ⁸Even if they win, they cannot stop; they then bet their winnings. ⁹Eventually they suffer a big loss and have to beg, borrow, or steal money to try to win it back. ¹⁰That sort of gambling has ruined many people's lives.

Main idea: There are two kinds of gamblers.

1. _____

2. _____

CAUSE AND EFFECT WORDS

Check (✓) the item that is easier to read and understand.

___ The baby refused to eat her breakfast. I was in a bad mood all morning.

___ The baby refused to eat her breakfast. As a result, I was in a bad mood all morning.

In the first item, we are not sure of the relationship between the two ideas. Were there two problems: the baby refusing to eat and the bad mood? Or did the first problem cause the second one? The phrase *as a result* makes clear that the baby's behavior *caused* the bad mood.

Cause and effect words show that the writer is discussing one or more *reasons* or *results*. Here are some common cause and effect words:

Cause and Effect Words

therefore	so	because (of)	thus
(as a) result	effect	(as a) consequence	results in
cause	explanation	consequently	lead to
affect	due to	since	reason

Examples:

The following examples contain cause and effect words. Notice how these words introduce a *reason* for something or the *result* of something.

- Students who work full-time sometimes nap before classes *because* they are tired after work.

- One *reason* for our lower electric bills is that we use less air conditioning.

- The lifeguard thought she spotted a shark. *As a result,* the beach was closed for the rest of the day.

➤ Practice 5

Complete each sentence with a suitable cause and effect word or phrase from the box. Try to use each transition once. Then, in the space provided, write the letter of the transition you have chosen.

> *Hint:* Make sure that each cause or effect word you choose fits smoothly into the flow of the sentence. Test each choice by reading the sentence aloud.

A. because	B. effect	C. result
D. so	E. therefore	

_____ 1. Drinking large amounts of carrot juice can _____ in a person's skin turning orange.

_____ 2. The contract offer made by management did not satisfy union members. _____, they decided to go on strike.

_____ 3. Scientists in the Antarctic no longer wear fur _____ they have discovered that quilted, layered clothing keeps them warmer.

_____ 4. Most baseball stadiums have lights _____ that day games that run late don't need to be called off.

_____ 5. American-style fast food has become popular all over the world. The _____ is that people around the world are developing American-style problems like diabetes, high blood pressure, and obesity.

➤ Practice 6

A. Below is a paragraph that is organized with the help of cause and effect words. Underline the **three** cause and effect words. Then complete the outline of the paragraph.

> [1]Researchers have learned that laughing can be good for you. [2]Laughing relaxes the facial muscles, causing you to look and feel less tense. [3]It also increases the oxygen in the brain, resulting in a light-headed sense of well-being. [4]In addition, laughing is a proven stress-reducer; it therefore decreases your chances of getting stress-related illnesses.

Main idea: Laughing can be good for you.

1. _____

2. _____

3. _____

B. Underline the **two** cause and effect words. Then complete the outline of the paragraph.

> [1]Changes at the end of the 1800s created more work for women. [2]In both the home and the workplace, there was a greater emphasis on being clean. [3]As a result, women spent more time washing, dusting, and scrubbing. [4]Another change in the late 1800s was the availability of a greater variety of foods. [5]Consequently, women spent more time on such food preparation as plucking feathers from chickens, roasting coffee beans, grinding whole spices and sugar, and cooking meals. [6]By 1900, the typical housewife worked six hours a day on just two tasks: cleaning and meal preparation.

Main idea: Changes at the end of the 1800s created more work for women.

1. _____

   _____

2. _____

   _____

C. The following passage uses the cause-effect pattern. Complete the map of the paragraph on the following page: First write in the main idea. Then fill in the two missing supporting details.

> [1]Being unemployed can have harmful effects on health. [2]In poor countries especially, unemployment may result in little or no medical care. [3]The experience of unemployment itself can affect one's health. [4]Studies have shown anxiety and depression can result from the loss of a job. [5]Alcohol and tranquilizer abuse is another effect of unemployment. [6]And being without work can also lead to high blood pressure and a rise in heart disease.

_____ can have harmful health effects.

| Especially in poor countries, little or no medical care | Anxiety and depression | | |

CHAPTER REVIEW

In this chapter you learned about three additional kinds of signal words that writers use:

- **Example words**
  - — Writers may provide examples to help make an idea clear.
  - — Words that signal examples include *for example* and *for instance.*
- **Contrast words**
  - — Writers often discuss how two things are different from each other.
  - — Words that signal contrast include *but* and *however.*
- **Cause and effect words**
  - — Writers often discuss the reasons why something happens or the effects of something that has happened.
  - — Words that signal causes include *reason* and *because.*
  - — Words that signal effects include *therefore* and *as a result.*

The next chapter—Chapter 9—will develop your skill in making inferences about what you read.

On the Web: If you are using this book in class, you can visit our website for additional practice with words that signal examples, contrast, and cause and effect. Go to **www.townsendpress.com** and click on "Online Exercises."

➤ Review Test 1

To review what you've learned in this chapter, complete each item by filling in the blank.

1. This chapter presented more transitions—signal words or phrases like *for example, however,* and *therefore* that help carry the reader from one *(chapter, page, idea)* _____ to the next.

2. Typical *(example, contrast, cause and effect)* _____ words are *such as, including,* and *for instance.* These words try to make a given idea clear.

3. Typical *(example, contrast, cause and effect)* _____ words are *but, on the other hand,* and *however.* These words tell us that two things differ in one or more ways.

4. Typical *(example, contrast, cause and effect)* _____ words are *because, reason,* and *as a result.* These words tell us the reason why something happened or the results of something.

➤ Review Test 2

A. Fill in each blank with one of the signal words in the box. Use each word once.

for instance	however	therefore

1. A stereotype is an overly generalized image of members of a group. One common stereotype, _____, is the image of all professors as being absent-minded.

2. Researchers have discovered that people with certain speech problems lack feeling in their tongues. _____, they have trouble placing their tongues in the correct position for certain sounds.

3. In the northern half of the world, the months of July through September are warmest. _____, in the southern half of the world, those are the coldest months.

B. (4–5.) Fill in each blank with an appropriate transition from the box. Use each transition once.

different	however

[1]Glossy and flat paints have (4) _____ advantages. [2]A glossy paint is easier to keep clean than a flat paint; (5) _____, a flat paint covers flaws in the wall better than a glossy one does. [3]The cost for both paints is about the same. [4]The choice of which is better depends on the buyer's need and preference.

(6–8.) Fill in each blank with an appropriate transition from the box. Use each transition once.

example	for instance	such as

[1]A mutant is a plant or animal with a brand-new characteristic. [2](6) _____, one mutant that was born not too long ago was a two-headed calf. [3]Another (7) _____ was a recently hatched chicken with four legs. [4]Some mutants turn out to be useful, (8) _____ an orange plant that appeared in a field of normal white cauliflower. [5]It led to the production of a new vegetable—an orange cauliflower.

C. (9–10.) Fill in each blank with an appropriate transition from the box. Use each transition once.

as a result	reason

[1]The United States Postal Service has set up a special room in several locations around the country. [2]This room is known as the "Dead Letter Office." [3]Here postal clerks open and read mail. [4]Why do they open private mail? [5]One (9) _____ is that millions of letters are sent each year with wrong addresses and no return address. [6]These letters are opened so that clerks can find out where to return the mail. [7]Also, some envelopes are completely blank, with no address at all. [8](10) _____, postal clerks must also open these letters to try to discover where they should be sent. [9]According to estimates, only 30 percent of the opened letters find their way to the sender or the person the letter was meant to reach.

➤ *Review Test 3*

Here is a chance to apply your understanding of signal words to a full-length reading. The following selection tells what happens when the author decides to stop and move a cat lying in the middle of the road. It turns out the cat is still alive, and his day becomes a complicated one.

Read the selection and then answer the questions that follow. You'll find questions on vocabulary in context, main ideas, supporting details, and signal words.

Words to Watch

Below are some words in the reading that do not have strong context support. Each word is followed by the number of the paragraph in which it appears and its meaning there. These words are marked in the reading by a small circle (°).

> *grimaced* (2): made a twisted face to express pain or disgust
> *ligament* (5): a band of tissue which connects bones or supports organs
> *tendon* (5): a tissue which connects muscles to bones and other parts of
> > the body
> *good Samaritan* (6): someone who helps others unselfishly
> *resignation* (9): acceptance without resistance
> *dejected* (11): depressed
> *pathetic* (11): pitiful

LIFE OVER DEATH

Bill Broderick

1   My reaction was as it always is when I see an animal lying in the roadway. My heart sank. And a lump formed in my throat at the thought of a life unfulfilled. I then resolved to move him off the road, to ensure that one of God's creations did not become a permanent part of the pavement. Some might ask what difference it makes. If it's already dead, why not just leave it there? My answer is that I believe in death with dignity, for people and for animals alike.

2   So I pulled my car over to the side of the road and walked back to where the cat lay motionless. Two cars passed over him, managing to avoid running him over. With no other cars in sight, I made my way to the lifeless form just as a jogger went by. The jogger grimaced° at the sight of the cat, blood dripping from his mouth. "How'd it happen?" he asked. I replied that I didn't know; he probably got hit by some careless driver. I just wanted to get him off the road. I

reached down for the cat and got the surprise of my life. The little creature lifted his head ever so slightly and uttered a pitiful, unforgettable little "meow." He was still alive.

3   What was I going to do now? I was already late for work. All I had intended to do was move the cat off the road. I didn't need this. But I knew I had no choice. I sighed deeply, then reached down and carefully cradled the cat in my hands. I asked the jogger to open my car trunk and remove the things from a small box. Then I gently placed the cat in the box. He was in shock, so he probably could not feel the pain from his obvious injuries. "Kinda funny lookin', isn't he?" asked the jogger. I was annoyed by his question, but I had to admit that he was right. This cat looked peculiar. Not ugly, mind you. But he seemed to have a comical look on his face, even at such a dreadful time.

4   "What are you gonna do with him?" the jogger asked. I told him I would take the cat to the local vet and let him decide what to do.

5   The vet was only five minutes away. My wife and I had been taking our animals to him for several years, and I knew I could rely on him to do what was best for the cat. I took the cat into the reception room and placed it on the counter. As this was an emergency, the vet was summoned right away. He examined the cat thoroughly, listing the injuries for his assistant to write down. "Broken jaw, that'll have to be set. Two teeth broken. A couple more loose. Possible internal injuries, but they don't look too bad. Uh-oh. This doesn't look good. He doesn't appear to have any movement in his right front leg.

Possible break, definite ligament° and tendon° damage."

6   The vet completed his examination, then looked at me and asked what I wanted to do. I knew what he meant. Did I want to have the cat "put to sleep"? I became uneasy. I clumsily explained that I was hoping to get advice from him on what to do. Fair enough. The jaw would have to be wired shut for six weeks, and the cat would have to wear a cast on his leg for three months. There was no way of knowing if the damage to the leg was permanent. He could have the cast removed and still not be able to use the leg. The cost of all the surgery would be high, but I would get a 50 percent "good Samaritan°" discount if I went ahead with it.

7   Now I was really at a loss. If I went ahead with the surgery, I'd be paying for a cat that wasn't mine, whose owner I'd probably never find, and who might end up with the use of only three legs. And on top of it, this was one of the funniest-looking cats ever born. Black and white, spotted where it shouldn't be, twisted tail, and a silly half-smile on its face. I chuckled at that and the entire situation.

8   "What do you want to do, Bill?" asked the vet.

9   I shrugged my shoulders in resignation°. "Dan, I'll choose life over death every time. Let's give it our best shot."

10   I called back later in the day and learned that the surgery had been successful. "You can pick up your cat tomorrow morning," I was told. My cat. I started to say that he was not my cat, but I knew otherwise.

11   The next morning, my wife and I drove to the vet and picked up the cat.

He looked ghastly. His jaw was now bandaged, and a cast covered one leg entirely and wrapped around his midsection. We were dejected°. But, as we drove him home, we began thinking that perhaps this cat was not as pathetic° as he looked. As frightened as he must have been, as much pain as he must have felt, he sat calmly in my wife's lap. He purred and stared out the window with his curious half-smile.

12   When we got home, we introduced him to our two Siamese cats, who stared in disbelief at this strange creature. They sensed it might be a cat, but they had never seen one like this. It took him very little time to get used to his new surroundings. It took him longer to get used to the cast, which made even walking a chore. Surely he must have been embarrassed. After all, an animal normally able to glide around quietly should not make a scraping sound every time he moves.

13   In due time, the cast came off. To our relief, Pokey, as we now called him, had about 90 percent mobility in the leg. He got around okay, but he limped whenever he tried to move any faster than a slow walk.

14   All this occurred four years ago. Pokey is still with us today. In fact, he has become our most beloved cat. Because of his injury, he is strictly an indoor cat. This does not seem to bother him at all. It is hard to believe that any cat has ever enjoyed himself more. Maybe it's because he had been slowed after being hit by a car, or perhaps he just has a special individuality. He is never bored. At times he will race around the house like

After surgery, Pokey had to wear a cast on one leg for three months.

he is leading the Indy 500. Or he'll leap into the air at an imaginary foe. Or he'll purr loudly at the foot of our bed, staring into space with that silly grin on his face. And he couldn't care less that he still looks funny.

It would have been easy to let 15 Pokey lie in the middle of the road. And it would have been just as simple to have the vet put him to sleep. But when I think of all the pleasure this cat has given us, and of how much fun he has living with us, I know the right decision was made. And I'd do it again in a second. I'll take life over death every time.

Questions about the Reading

For each question, write the letter of your answer in the space provided.

Vocabulary in Context

_____ 1. In the sentence below, the word *resolved* (rĭ-zŏlvd′) means
   A. forgot.
   B. hid.
   C. decided.
   D. drove.

> "I then resolved to move him off the road, to ensure that one of God's creations did not become a permanent part of the pavement." (Paragraph 1)

_____ 2. In the sentences below, the word *summoned* (sŭm′ənd) means
   A. paid.
   B. called for.
   C. written to.
   D. ignored.

> "As this was an emergency, the vet was summoned right away. He examined the cat thoroughly. . . ." (Paragraph 5)

_____ 3. In the sentences below, the word *ghastly* (găst′lē) means
   A. threatening.
   B. appealing.
   C. terrible.
   D. marvelous.

> "He looked ghastly. His jaw was now bandaged, and a cast covered one leg entirely and wrapped around his midsection." (Paragraph 11)

Central Point and Main Ideas

_____ 4. Which sentence best expresses the central point of the selection?
   A. Drivers need to be alert to dangers on the road.
   B. Every life is valuable.
   C. Cats make wonderful pets.
   D. Pokey is strictly an indoor cat because of his injury.

_____ 5. Which sentence best expresses the main idea of paragraph 6?
    A. The author wanted to know if the damage to the cat's leg was permanent.
    B. The vet didn't know what to do with the cat.
    C. To help the author decide what to do, the vet explained what could be done for the cat and what it would cost.
    D. The author expected the vet to say that the cat should be "put to sleep."

_____ 6. Which sentence best expresses the main idea of paragraph 14?
    A. Pokey is beloved and enjoys life a great deal now.
    B. Pokey sometimes leaps into the air at imaginary enemies.
    C. Pokey must spend the rest of his life indoors.
    D. Pokey was injured four years ago.

Pokey, now fully recovered, is the author's favorite cat.

Key Supporting Details

_____ 7. The author

A. saw a car hit the cat.

B. thought that the cat was ugly.

C. was surprised that the jogger came by.

D. was very surprised that the cat was still alive.

_____ 8. The author

A. had heard about the vet.

B. looked for the nearest vet.

C. knew and trusted the vet.

D. drove for hours till he found a vet.

Signal Words

_____ 9. In the sentence below, the word *but* signals

A. an example.

B. contrast.

C. cause and effect.

"The cost of all the surgery would be high, but I would get a . . . discount if I went ahead with it." (Paragraph 6)

_____10. In the sentence below, the word *because* signals

A. an example.

B. contrast.

C. cause and effect.

"Because of his injury, he is strictly an indoor cat." (Paragraph 14)

Discussion Questions

1. In the first paragraph, the author uses the expression "death with dignity." What do you think he means by that expression?

2. Why do you think that Pokey has become, in Broderick's words, "our most beloved cat"? Do you think Pokey's injuries had an effect on how the author ended up feeling about him? Why or why not?

3. Can—and should—something be done to make the world a better place for hurt and homeless animals like Pokey? Or should our priorities lie elsewhere? Explain your answer.

Note: Writing assignments for this selection appear on page 562.

Check Your Performance			SIGNAL WORDS II
Activity	*Number Right*	*Points*	*Score*
Review Test 1 (4 items)	_____	× 5 =	_____
Review Test 2 (10 items)	_____	× 4 =	_____
Review Test 3 (10 items)	_____	× 4 =	_____
		TOTAL SCORE =	_____ %

Enter your total score into the **Reading Performance Chart: Review Tests** on the inside back cover.

SIGNAL WORDS II: Mastery Test 1

A. Fill in each blank with an appropriate signal word from the box. Use each transition once. Then, in the space provided, write the letter of the transition you have chosen.

A. as a result	B. but	C. for instance
D. however	E. so that	

_____ 1. Audiences usually dislike film monsters, _____ some moviegoers who see *King Kong* shed tears at the big ape's death.

_____ 2. The chef stuffed steel wool into the cracks in the kitchen corners _____ mice could no longer get into the cooking area.

_____ 3. People can insure just about anything. _____, comedians Abbott and Costello once insured themselves against any member of the audience dying of laughter.

_____ 4. In the 2000 presidential election, Al Gore received more popular votes than George W. Bush. _____, Bush was awarded the presidency.

_____ 5. The baby was sick most of the night. _____, the parents got very little sleep.

(Continues on next page)

B. Fill in each blank with an appropriate signal word from the box. Use each transition once.

caused	due to	lead to	result

[1]Teens and young adults lose hair for various reasons. [2]As part of the normal changes in the body, they can expect to lose about one hundred hairs per day. [3]Medical problems may (6) _____ more hair loss. [4]Abnormal hair loss may also be (7) _____ by undernourishment, so teens should be mindful of their diet. [5]Fevers can also (8) _____ in more hair falling out than usual. [6]Significant hair loss may also be (9) _____ allergic reactions to dyes or hair straighteners.

_____10. This paragraph uses
    A. example words.
    B. contrast words.
    C. cause and effect words.

SIGNAL WORDS II: Mastery Test 2

A. Fill in each blank with an appropriate signal word from the box. Use each transition once. Then, in the space provided, write the letter of the transition you have chosen.

A. although	B. because	C. example
D. for instance	E. instead	F. reason

_____ 1. _____ we think of spaghetti as an Italian food, it was probably first invented in China.

_____ 2. _____ of federal cutbacks, many schools have lost their physical education, art, and music programs.

_____ 3. A raptor is a bird that hunts and kills live animals. Hawks, eagles, and owls are _____s of raptors.

_____ 4. _____ of admitting he'd broken the vase, the little boy hid the pieces behind his grandmother's sofa.

_____ 5. Mary and Marie are identical twins with different birthdays. The _____ is that one girl was born before midnight and the other just after midnight.

_____ 6. Camping in the woods is not like sleeping in your bed at home. _____, you have to worry about insects, snakes, and about what to use as a bathroom in the middle of the night.

(Continues on next page)

B. Fill in each blank with an appropriate signal word from the box. Use each transition once.

consequently	due to	result

[1]Pigs do not save money. [2]They don't even save food. [3]So why do we save our coins in things called "piggy banks"? [4]Our use of the term "piggy banks" is actually (7) _____ a mistake. [5]Back in the Middle Ages, metal was too expensive to be used for most household items. [6](8) _____, ordinary containers were made of an inexpensive earthen clay called "pygg." [7]People would save their extra money in "pygg jars," which eventually became "pygg banks." [8]Over the next few hundred years, people forgot that "pygg" meant clay, and began thinking of the word as "pig." [9]Potters began making coin-holding containers in the shape of a pig. [10]The (9) _____ was that the "piggy bank" was born.

_____ 10. This paragraph uses
   A. example words.
   B. contrast words.
   C. cause and effect words.

SIGNAL WORDS II: Mastery Test 3

A. Fill in each blank with an appropriate signal word from the box. Use each transition once.

different	however

¹There are interesting differences between honeybees and bumblebees. ²First of all, they have contrasting living circumstances. ³Honeybees live in large colonies and need a lot of space to build their hives. ⁴Bumblebees, (1) _____, live in small underground colonies and require little territory to nest. ⁵Honeybees and bumblebees are also (2) _____ in their stinging behavior. ⁶Honeybees will sting with little reason. ⁷In contrast, bumblebees rarely sting, even if they are accidentally disturbed. ⁸However, their sting is far more painful than that of a honeybee.

_____ 3. This paragraph uses
   A. example words.
   B. contrast words.
   C. cause and effect words.

(Continues on next page)

B. Fill in each blank with an appropriate signal word from the box. Use each transition once.

because of	resulted	therefore

[1]During the Middle Ages, people in Europe hated and feared ordinary house cats, which they thought were used by witches to contact demons. [2]Unfortunately, this fear of cats (4) _____ in many more deaths from the bubonic plague than should have occurred. [3](5) _____ their fear, people drove cats away from their houses and villages. [4]Rats were (6) _____ totally free to breed there and spread disease. [5]Millions of people died from the bubonic plague, which was carried by diseased rats. [6]If more cats had been allowed to stay, they could have killed many of these rats.

_____ 7. This paragraph uses
   A. example words.
   B. contrast words.
   C. cause and effect words.

C. Fill in each blank with an appropriate transition from the box. Use each transition once.

example	for instance

[1]A "tell sign" is a nonverbal clue that a person may be lying. [2](8) _____, if a person is making more obvious hand gestures than normal, or scratching the head or neck, he may not be telling the truth. [3]These gestures suggest a subconscious effort to rub out an untrue statement. [4]Another (9) _____ of a tell sign is a repeated shrugging of the shoulders, which may be a subconscious way to contradict what has been said.

_____ 10. This paragraph uses
   A. example words.
   B. contrast words.
   C. cause and effect words.

SIGNAL WORDS II: Mastery Test 4

A. Fill in each blank with an appropriate signal word from the box. Use each transition once.

consequence	result in	therefore

[1]When United States coins were originally produced, the dollar, half-dollar, 25-cent, and 10-cent coins were made of gold and silver. [2]People sometimes tried to enrich themselves by filing down the edges, which would (1) _____ their getting a little of the precious metal. [3](2) As a _____, the government began making those coins with ridged edges. [4]That way, it was obvious if someone had filed off some of the coin. [5]Later, the government stopped using precious metals for coins. [6]But blind people pointed out that the ridged edges on certain coins helped them to identify those coins by touch. [7](3) _____, dimes, quarters, half-dollars, and dollar coins still have ridged edges.

_____ 4. This paragraph uses
   A. example words.
   B. contrast words.
   C. cause and effect words.

(Continues on next page)

B. Fill in each blank with an appropriate signal word from the box. Use each transition once.

on the other hand	while

¹Do you consider yourself an introvert—or an extrovert? ²Introverts are people who gain energy from solitary activities. ³They often enjoy reading, writing, watching movies at home, or spending time with just one or two friends. ⁴Extroverts, (5) _____, draw energy from spending time with others. ⁵They like being with a crowd, taking part in group activities, and hanging out with lots of people. ⁶Introverts figure things out by thinking quietly about them, (6) _____ extroverts prefer to talk things out.

_____ 7. This paragraph uses
   A. example words.
   B. contrast words.
   C. cause and effect words.

C. Fill in each blank with an appropriate signal word from the box. Use each transition once.

example	for instance

¹A dictionary may seem solid and unchanging, like a rock. ²However, that is not the case at all. ³Dictionaries are constantly changing, just as language itself is. ⁴(8) _____, the latest edition of the *Merriam-Webster Dictionary* includes ten thousand words that the previous edition did not. ⁵One (9) _____ of a new word is *google*. ⁶It comes from the Internet search engine called Google. ⁷When someone says, "I googled for information about headaches," she means she spent time searching that topic on the Internet.

_____ 10. This paragraph uses
   A. example words.
   B. contrast words.
   C. cause and effect words.

SIGNAL WORDS II: Mastery Test 5

A. Fill in each blank with an appropriate signal word from the box. Use each transition once. Then complete the outline that follows.

because of	lead to	reason
result	so	

¹Most victims of house fires are poor people. ²In a very real sense, you could say that poverty is the (1) _____ that fires happen. ³Poor people tend to live in the oldest, most badly maintained buildings in a city. ⁴(2) _____ their poor maintenance, these houses often have faulty electrical wiring that can (3) _____ fires. ⁵Also, the poor often rely on open flames—whether using candles for light or gas stoves for heat. ⁶Any time there is an open flame nearby, a fire can easily (4) _____. ⁷Finally, poor people may not have money to spend on smoke detectors, (5) _____ they do not have any warning when a fire breaks out.

_____ 6. This paragraph uses addition words and
   A. example words.
   B. contrast words.
   C. cause and effect words.

7–9. Complete the outline of the selection.

Main idea: Poverty can be seen as the cause of house fires.

1. _____

2. _____

3. _____

(Continues on next page)

B. Read the following paragraph and answer the question that follows.

> [1]People hotly debate the issue of whether live animals should be used in testing medical products. [2]People who oppose animal testing say there is no excuse for making animals experience the pain and fear that is associated with live testing. [3]They say that animal testing is of limited value, since animals and humans respond differently to medications and medical procedures. [4]On the other hand, supporters of animal testing say that many of the medicines and surgical procedures we use today would not exist without lab testing on animals. [5]They claim that devices like heart and lung machines and pacemakers could never have been invented without animal testing.

_____10. This paragraph
   A. gives examples of animals that are used in product tests.
   B. contrasts two views on animal testing of medical products.
   C. states reasons why live animals should not be used to test medical products.

SIGNAL WORDS II: Mastery Test 6

A. Read the paragraph below. Then answer the question and complete the outline that follows.

> [1]Stress can lead to extreme behaviors. [2]Some people react to stress by trying to escape from their problems through drug abuse. [3]These people use drugs as a desperate way to deal with the difficulties of their lives. [4]Another extreme behavior caused by stress is aggression, including child abuse and other violence between family members. [5]Stress may also lead people to fall into a depression so deep that they fear it will never go away. [6]The result is a suicide attempt.

_____ 1. This paragraph uses
   A. example words.
   B. contrast words.
   C. cause and effect words.

2–5. Outline the paragraph, writing in the main idea and the three major supporting details.

Main idea: _____

1. _____

2. _____

3. _____

(Continues on next page)

B. Read the following paragraph and answer the questions that follow.

[1]Obsessive-compulsive behavior is a disorder in which people have repeated thoughts and actions they cannot control. [2]One example involves an extreme fear of germs. [3]After doing a routine action such as opening a book or eating a sandwich, one man would wash his hands for fifteen minutes. [4]Another instance of this disturbing disorder is a constant focus on money. [5]One man was so consumed by the thought of becoming a millionaire at age 30 that he worked day and night. [6]Eventually he collapsed and was taken to a hospital, where he tried to pull out his gold fillings and sell them to an attendant.

_____ 6. This paragraph uses
   A. example words.
   B. contrast words.
   C. cause and effect words.

7–10. Complete the map of the paragraph: Fill in the missing major and minor supporting details.

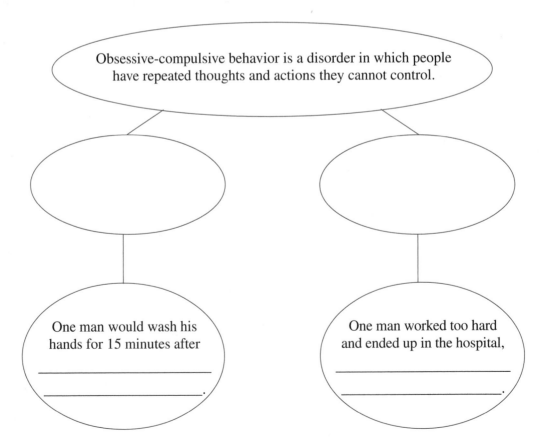

Obsessive-compulsive behavior is a disorder in which people have repeated thoughts and actions they cannot control.

One man would wash his hands for 15 minutes after

One man worked too hard and ended up in the hospital,

9

Inferences

THIS CHAPTER IN A NUTSHELL

- Ideas are often suggested rather than being stated directly. We must **infer**, or figure out, those ideas.

- To make logical inferences, we must look closely at the information available and use our own experience and common sense.

Inferences are ideas that are not stated directly. They are conclusions that we come to based on what we see, hear, and read.

Look at the cartoon below. What can you figure out about it? Check (✓) the **two** inferences that are most logically based on the information suggested by the cartoon. Then read the explanation on the next page.

© 2000 Randy Glasbergen.

GLASBERGEN

"Relax, Mom ... it's macaroni."

_____ The boy's mother approves of body piercings.

_____ The boy had not warned his mother what he was going to do.

_____ In the past, the boy had asked if he could get body piercings.

_____ The boy did not really get body piercings.

_____ The boy's mother has a few body piercings of her own.

Explanation:

1. The boy's mother would not seem so shocked by her son's appearance if she approved of body piercings. Also, her son is telling her to relax, a sign that she is upset.

2. If the boy had warned his mother what he was going to do, her hair would not be standing on end and her eyes bugging out. She is clearly shocked by her son's appearance. You should have checked this item.

3. Nothing suggests that the boy had asked if he could get body piercings.

4. The boy is telling his mother that what appear to be body piercings are only macaroni. You should have checked this item.

5. Nothing in the picture or words suggests that the boy's mother has body piercings of her own.

With visual material such as cartoons, book covers, and photographs, we can infer a great deal from all the clues provided. With written material, we can "read between the lines" and pick up ideas the writer only suggests, or implies. This chapter will give you practice in making inferences from both visual and reading materials.

INFERENCES ABOUT VISUAL MATERIALS

Cartoon

Look at the cartoon on the next page. Put a check (✓) by the **two** inferences that are most logically based on the information given in the cartoon. Then read the explanation that follows.

"Class, who can tell me what I have preserved in this jar?
No, it's not a pig or a baby cow...it's the last student
who got caught cheating on one of my tests!"

____ The class has just finished taking a test.

____ The specimen in the jar is really a baby pig.

____ The teacher is strict about cheating in his class.

____ The teacher wants his students to be afraid to cheat.

____ More students cheat in biology class than in other classes.

Explanation:

1. Experience tells us that teachers give warnings like this *before* the test begins, not after.

2. We can safely assume that the specimen in the jar is not really a student, since teachers are not permitted to "preserve" students. It may be a baby pig, a baby cow, or just a "pretend" animal. However, we don't know exactly what it is.

3. From the stern warning the teacher gives the class as he holds up the jar, we can infer that he is strict about cheating in his class. You should have checked this item.

4. Holding up the preserved "cheating student" is a sign the teacher wants his students to be afraid to cheat. You should have checked this item.

5. Nothing in the cartoon suggests that students are any more likely to cheat in a biology class than in other classes.

Book Cover

Look at the following cover of a book titled *Surviving Abuse: Four True Stories* by Beth Johnson. Put a check (✓) by the **two** inferences that are most logically based on the information given on the cover.

___ The people pictured here are all abuse survivors.

___ Men are seldom abuse victims.

___ Some of the people pictured are abusers, and some are abuse victims.

___ Abuse is a problem for more than one ethnic group.

___ Once a person has been abused, his or her life is ruined.

Explanation:

1. The title *Surviving Abuse: Four True Stories* suggests that the four people pictured on the cover are all abuse survivors. You should have checked this item.

2. Two of the abuse victims are men and two are women. There is nothing to suggest that more women than men are victims of abuse.

3. The title indicates that the stories tell of surviving abuse, not being an abuser. Also, an abuser would not want to be pictured on the cover of a book.

4. The people on the cover represent three ethnic groups, suggesting that the problem of abuse cuts across all ethnic boundaries. You should have checked this item.

5. The smiling faces of the people on the cover suggest that being the victim of abuse need not ruin a person's life. So does the title, *Surviving Abuse.*

Photograph

Look at the following photograph. Put a check (✓) by the **two** inferences that are most logically based on the information given in the photograph.

____ The man is a drug addict.

____ The man in the photo is homeless.

____ A passing child gave the stuffed animal to the man.

____ The stuffed animal helps keep the man warm.

____ The man does not have any legs.

Explanation:

1. Although experience tells us that people who sleep in the streets are often drug addicts, we can't say for sure that the man is a drug addict.

2. Common sense tells us that a man who has a home would not be sleeping in a trash-strewn area. You should have checked this item.

3. Nothing in the photo indicates that the man got the stuffed animal from a passing child. Most parents would probably not allow their child to interact with a homeless man.

4. The man appears to have wrapped himself in a blanket or sleeping bag in order to keep warm. The stuffed animal which rests on top of him suggests that he is also using it to keep warm. You should have checked this item.

5. Although the nearby wheelchair suggests that the man has a physical disability, we can't say for certain that the man has no legs.

A Final Comment about Visual Materials

As the preceding examples—the cartoons, the book cover, and the photograph—make clear, we live in a world full of images, and we make inferences about such visual materials all the time. In other words, making inferences is a skill all of us already possess. This chapter will now go on to strengthen your ability to make good inferences when reading.

INFERENCES ABOUT READING MATERIALS

You have already practiced making inferences while reading an earlier chapter in this book. Do you remember the following sentence from the "Vocabulary in Context" chapter?

> **Assets** such as good health, a loving family, and an enjoyable job make life worth living.

The sentence does not tell us exactly what *assets* means. However, it does suggest that assets are valuable things such as good health, a loving family, and an enjoyable job. We can then infer that *assets* means "things of value." For all the sentences in chapter 3, you inferred the meanings of words by looking closely at the surrounding context.

In our everyday reading, we often "read between the lines" and pick up ideas that are not directly stated in print. To make such inferences, we use clues provided by the writer, and we also apply our own experience, logic, and common sense.

Inferences in Passages

☑ *Check Your Understanding*

Read the following passage and then check (✓) the **two** inferences that are most firmly based on the given information.

> [1]My wife is a murderer. [2]I got her a plant as a surprise one-month anniversary gift, and she proceeded to kill it. [3]She wasn't trying to kill it, but she doesn't exactly have a green thumb. [4]In the belief that all living things require water, she began flooding the plant on a daily basis. [5]"Be careful not to overwater it," I warned. [6]"Plants need air as well as water." [7]"Okay," she replied, and then dumped on another gallon of water. [8]The sicker the plant got, the more she watered it. [9]Finally, it melted away into an oozing heap. [10]One day I returned home to see that the plant and its pot had simply disappeared. [11]We had not been married that long yet, but I figured the safest thing to do was to say nothing.

_____ 1. The woman did not believe the man's advice.

_____ 2. The women intentionally killed the plant.

_____ 3. The man knows more about plants than his wife does.

_____ 4. The man is very angry at his wife.

_____ 5. The man was surprised that the plant died.

Explanation:

1. The woman continues to water the plant heavily after her husband's warning; she obviously did not believe his advice. You should have checked this item.

2. The man says that his wife wasn't trying to kill the plant, but that she simply lacks a green thumb. We can infer that she accidentally, not intentionally, killed the plant. The man states that his wife is a "murderer" for comic effect. People cannot "murder" plants.

3. Since the man knows that overwatering is not good for plants, he must know more about plants than his wife does. You should have checked this item.

4. The man says that "the safest thing to do was to say nothing." His words suggest that he fears her reaction if he says something about the dead plant. If he had been very angry at her, he probably would have said something.

5. The wife's continued overwatering of the plant, which the man notices and comments upon, suggests that he is not surprised that the plant died.

➤ Practice 1

Read each passage and then check (✓) the **two** inferences that are most firmly based on the given information.

A. [1]In the 1600s, the word _spinster_ referred to any female. [2]Spinning thread or yarn for cloth was something every woman did at home. [3]By 1700, _spinster_ had become a legal term for an unmarried woman. [4]Such women had to work to survive, and spinning was their most common job. [5]Before long, however, spinning was done in factories. [6]_Spinster_ then suggested someone who was "left over" or "dried up," just as the job of home spinning had dried up for women. [7]Today, with so many women working and marrying later and later, most single women consider the word _spinster_ an insult.

_____ 1. Women who could spin were thought to make especially good wives.

_____ 2. The word *spinster* was not originally an insulting term.

_____ 3. Today's single women should be proud to be called spinsters.

_____ 4. At one time in history, unmarried women were looked down upon.

_____ 5. Today, single women are no longer called spinsters.

B. [1]Sentenced to execution, some condemned American criminals have used their last moments to share a witty last word with observers. [2]George Appel was electrocuted in 1928. [3]Just before the switch was pulled, he joked with the onlookers: "Well, folks, soon you'll see a baked Appel." [4]James W. Rodgers was shot by firing squad in 1960. [5]When asked if he had a last request, he replied, "Why, yes—a bullet-proof vest." [6]James French was sent to the electric chair in 1966. [7]On the way to his execution, he caught the attention of a nearby reporter. [8]"I have a terrific headline for you in the morning," he said; "French Fries." [9]Jesse Bishop was sentenced to die by gas chamber in 1979. [10]His last words were: "I've always wanted to try everything once . . . Let's go!"

_____ 1. Different methods of execution are used in the United States.

_____ 2. Appel, Rodgers, and Bishop were innocent of the crimes they were accused of.

_____ 3. Appel, Rodgers, and Bishop all wanted to die.

_____ 4. There are generally witnesses watching an execution.

_____ 5. People watching the executions were shocked by the convicted men's remarks.

C. [1]In 1857, a group of Egyptian salesmen tried to convince Congress that camels should be used in desert outposts in the West. [2]The salesmen pointed out that camels could carry up to 1,000 pounds more than an elephant. [3]They said a camel's energy was almost limitless. [4]As proof, they had a camel race a horse across difficult land covering 110 miles. [5]The horse won the race, but died of fatigue shortly afterward. [6]To show how much staying power the camel had, the salesmen had the camel run again the next day. [7]The camel covered the same area at the same speed. [8]The salesmen then pointed out how little water camels need. [9]Camels barely sweat, and they regulate their body temperatures depending on the heat. [10]Congress was convinced and bought seventy-five camels for soldiers to use. [11]However, soldiers hated the beasts and turned them loose in the desert. [12]Most disappeared, but there are still occasional sightings of camels in remote desert regions today.

_____ 1. Camels are bad-tempered animals.

_____ 2. The Egyptian salesmen were trying to cheat Congress.

_____ 3. Camels could have been valuable in the American West.

_____ 4. Camels travel at a steady pace without using much energy.

_____ 5. The camels could never have survived in the American desert.

INFERRING MAIN IDEAS

Sometimes a paragraph does not have a main idea. In such cases, the writer has decided to let the supporting details suggest the main idea. The main idea is unstated, or **implied**, and you must **infer** it—figure it out—by deciding upon the point of the supporting details.

Asking two questions will help you to determine the writer's main idea:

- What is the topic, or subject, of the paragraph? In other words, what is the whole paragraph about?

- What is the main point being made about the topic?

The following paragraph has no stated main idea. Ask the two questions above to help you decide which of the four answers that follow the paragraph states the implied main idea. In the space provided, write the letter of that answer. Then read the explanation that follows.

> [1]When you have a relationship with someone, it is almost certain that you will argue now and then. [2]To keep an argument from causing hard feelings, listen to the other person's point of view. [3]Don't just hear what you want to hear, but focus on what the person is saying. [4]Also try to identify with his or her point of view as much as you can, remembering that a view other than your own may be valid. [5]Another way to keep an argument from causing hard feelings is to concentrate on behavior that is annoying you, not on the other person's character. [6]For example, say, "This bothers me a lot," not, "Only a stupid idiot would act the way you are!" [7]Finally, when the argument is over, put it behind you.

_____ The **unstated main idea** is:

A. People often argue with each other.

B. When you have a relationship with someone, you should try not to argue with him or her.

C. There are guidelines you can follow to ensure that an argument does not cause hard feelings.

D. The most important point in knowing how to argue is to put an argument behind you once it is over.

Explanation:

If you answered the question "Who or what is the paragraph about," you probably found the topic: arguing. The next question to ask is "What is the main point being made about arguing?" To answer that question, consider the supporting details:

- The details of the paragraph are not about how often people argue or the importance of trying not to argue, so answers A and B are wrong.

- The details of the paragraph are specific guidelines for keeping an argument from causing hard feelings: "listen to the other person's point of view," "try to identify with his or her point of view," "concentrate on behavior that is annoying you, not on the other person's character," and "when the argument is over, put it behind you." Therefore answer C is correct—it makes a general statement that covers the specific guidelines listed.

- Answer D is wrong because it is too narrow: it is about only one of the guidelines.

➤ Practice 2

The following paragraphs have implied main ideas, and each is followed by four sentences. In the space provided, write the letter of the sentence that best expresses the implied main idea.

_____ 1. ¹Because turnips were often eaten by the poor, other people often turned up their noses at them. ²Carrots were also once held in low esteem. ³They grew wild in ancient times and were used then for medicinal purposes. ⁴But they weren't considered fit for the table in Europe until the thirteenth century. ⁵Similarly, in the early seventeenth and eighteenth centuries, some Europeans considered potatoes fit only for animals. ⁶They were thought to cause leprosy in humans.

The **unstated main idea** is:
A. Vegetables are a healthy addition to any diet.
B. In previous centuries, some Europeans thought potatoes were unhealthy for humans.
C. Through the centuries, people have had mistaken ideas about certain vegetables.
D. While potatoes were once considered unhealthy, carrots were once used as medicine.

_____ 2. [1]A minister in Louisiana gave his cat away to a granddaughter who lived in New Orleans. [2]Three weeks later, the cat showed up at the minister's home. [3]It had traveled 300 miles and crossed the Mississippi and Red Rivers on its own. [4]A German man took his cat on a family vacation from Germany to Turkey. [5]At the border, the cat was nowhere to be found. [6]However, two months and 1,500 miles later, the cat returned to his home in Germany. [7]An American man took his cat with him when he moved from Utah to Washington. [8]Soon after arriving in his new home, the cat disappeared. [9]Over a year later, the cat showed up on the front porch of the man's Utah home 850 miles away. [10]The man's former neighbors recognized the animal and offered him a new home.

The **unstated main idea** is:

A. Cats do not adjust well to new homes.

B. Lost pets are often found thanks to the kindness of people.

C. People should not get a cat unless they are sure they will not be moving.

D. Cats can have an incredible sense of direction.

_____ 3. [1]To become president of the United States, a person must be at least thirty-five years of age. [2]He or she must have lived in the United States for the last fourteen years. [3]In addition, he or she must be a natural-born citizen of the country. [4]A convicted felon cannot be president of the United States.

The **unstated main idea** is:

A. There is an age limit to becoming president.

B. There are specific rules about who can become an elected official of a country.

C. The requirements for becoming a president of the United States are too limiting.

D. There are certain requirements for becoming president of the United States.

CHAPTER REVIEW

In this chapter, you learned the following:

- Making inferences is a skill we practice all the time with much of what we see and read.

- Important ideas in reading may not be stated directly, but must be inferred.

- To make good inferences, we must use the information presented, our own experience, and common sense.

The final chapter in Part One—Chapter 10—will deepen your ability to think in a clear and logical way.

 On the Web: If you are using this book in class, you can visit our website for additional practice in making inferences. Go to **www.townsendpress.com** and click on "Online Exercises."

➤ *Review Test 1*

To review what you've learned in this chapter, answer each of the following questions by filling in the blanks.

1. To fully understand a cartoon, book cover, ad, or other visual image, we often must make _____.

2. When we read, we often "read between the lines" and pick up ideas that are implied rather than directly _____.

3. When making inferences, it is (*a mistake, useful*) _____ to draw upon our own experience as well as clues provided.

4. When the _____ of a paragraph is not stated directly, you can often figure it out by looking at the paragraph's supporting details.

➤ *Review Test 2*

A. (1–2.) Put a check (✓) by the **two** inferences that are most logically based on the information given in the following cartoon.

© 1997 Randy Glasbergen.
www.glasbergen.com

GLASBERGEN

"Whenever something goes wrong,
I just push this little button and restart.
I wish my whole life was like that!"

_____ 1. The woman dislikes using a computer.

_____ 2. The woman spends too much time in front of a computer.

_____ 3. Something has gone wrong on the computer, but the woman knows what to do about it.

_____ 4. The woman knows that many problems in life have no easy solutions.

_____ 5. The man and the woman are not getting along with each other.

B. (3–4.) Read the following passage and then check (✓) the **two** inferences that are most firmly based on the given information.

> ¹Because children have to attend school until they are 16, our classes are crowded with troublemakers who do not want to be there. ²These troublemakers make it difficult for serious students to get an education. ³Teachers must spend most of their time merely trying to keep the troublemakers under control, rather than actually teaching the good students. ⁴By the time a student is 13, it is clear whether he or she is serious about school or is only going to play the fool there. ⁵At that age, the troublemakers should be allowed to drop out, so that the good students can get on with their education.

_____ 1. Required attendance in school creates more problems than it solves.

_____ 2. Students today are creating more problems than they ever did in the past.

_____ 3. Students who are troublemakers at age 13 often mature and turn out to be good students.

_____ 4. If troublemakers were allowed to drop out at age 13, serious students would get a better education.

_____ 5. Students want to drop out of school because schools and teachers are not doing a good job.

C. Read the following paragraph and then, in the space provided, write the letter of the sentence that best expresses the implied main idea.

> ¹Most American parents wait until their children are at least two years old before teaching them how to use the toilet. ²Teaching infants to use the toilet early will help keep them comfortable and happy. ³The young children will not have to deal with irritating moisture and uncomfortable diaper rash. ⁴Early toilet training can also save parents and communities a lot of cash. ⁵Parents can save up to $3,000 on disposable diapers, and communities will not have to deal with the expenses caused by so much trash. ⁶In addition, toilet training may help parents form early bonds with their infants. ⁷Parents must pay close attention to their children's signals so that they know when their children need to use the toilet. ⁸By giving their children more attention and learning how to understand these signals, parents can start building a strong relationship with their children at a very early age.

_____ 5. The **implied main idea** of this paragraph is:
  A. It is extremely difficult to toilet-train an infant.
  B. Most parents are too busy to toilet-train an infant.
  C. There are real benefits to toilet-training children at younger ages.
  D. Forcing infants to use the toilet makes them angry and resentful of adults.

> ## Review Test 3

Here is a chance to apply your understanding of inferences to a full-length reading. The selection is by Dr. Ben Carson, who grew up poor with his single mother in inner-city Detroit. He was considered the "dummy" of his fifth-grade class until he realized he could learn and do well in school. Today, he is one of the world's most respected surgeons. In this excerpt from his book *The Big Picture*, he shares a message with young people of today.

Following the reading are questions on inferences. There are also questions on the skills taught in previous chapters.

Words to Watch

Below are some words in the reading that do not have strong context support. Each word is followed by the number of the paragraph in which it appears and its meaning there. These words are marked in the reading by a small circle (°).

deplorable (2): wretchedly bad; miserable
cavernous (4): resembling a cave
spontaneous (5): unplanned; impulsive
graphically (8): vividly
gratification (8): satisfaction
bevy (9): group

DARE TO THINK BIG

Dr. Ben Carson

1   I do not speak only to parent groups. I spend a lot of time with students, such as those I encountered not long ago on a memorable visit to Wendell Phillips High School, an inner-city school on Chicago's south side.

2   Before I spoke, the people who invited me to the Windy City held a reception in my honor. There I met and talked with school officials and local religious leaders, many of whom informed me about the troubled neighborhood where the school is located. They indicated that gang influence was prevalent, living conditions were deplorable° in the surrounding public housing developments, dropout statistics were high, and SAT scores were low.

3   It sounded like a lot of other high schools I have visited around the country. Yet so dire were these warnings that, on the crosstown drive to the school, I could not help

wondering what kind of reception I would receive from the students.

4   I need not have worried. When I walked into Wendell Phillips High School, its long deserted hallways gave the building a cavernous°, empty feel. The entire student body (1,500 to 2,000 strong) had already been excused from class and was assembled quietly in the school's auditorium. A school administrator, who was addressing the audience, noted my entrance through a back door and abruptly interrupted his remarks to announce, "And here's Dr. Carson now!"

5   All eyes turned my way. Immediately students began to applaud. Some stood. Suddenly they were all standing, clapping, and cheering. The applause continued the entire time I walked down the aisle and climbed the steps onto the auditorium stage. I couldn't remember ever receiving a warmer, more enthusiastic, or more spontaneous° reception anywhere in my entire life.

6   I found out later that a local bank had purchased and distributed paperback copies of my autobiography, *Gifted Hands*, to every student at Wendell Phillips. A lot of those teenagers had evidently read the book and felt they already knew me. By the time I reached the microphone, the noise faded away. I felt overwhelmed by their welcome.

7   I did what I often do when facing such a young audience. I wanted them thinking seriously about their lives and futures. So I quickly summarized my earliest years as a child, about my own student days back at Southwestern High School in Detroit. I referred briefly to the incident when my anger nearly caused a tragedy that would have altered my life forever. I recounted my struggles with peer pressure, which sidetracked me for a time.

Then I talked about the difference   8 between being viewed as cool and being classified as a lowly nerd. I find that serves as a graphically° relevant illustration for my message on delayed gratification°—a theme I hit almost every time I speak to young people.

The cool guys in every school are   9 the ones who have earned a varsity letter in some sport—maybe several sports. They wear the latest fashions. They know all the hit tunes. They can converse about the latest blockbuster movies. They drive sharp cars and seem to collect a bevy° of beautiful girlfriends.

The nerds are the guys always   10 hauling around an armload of books, with more in their backpacks. They wear clean clothes—and often big, thick glasses. They even understand the science experiments. They ride the school bus, or worse yet, their parents drive them to school. Most of the popular girls would not be caught dead speaking to them in the hallway between classes.

The years go by, and graduation   11 draws near. Often the cool guy has not done well in school, but his personality wins him a job at the local fast-food franchise, flipping hamburgers and waiting on customers. The nerd, who has won a scholarship, goes off to college.

A few more years go by. The cool   12 guy is still flipping burgers. Maybe he has even moved up to Assistant Shift Manager by now. The girls who come in to eat lunch may notice and smile at him. He is still cool.

13   The nerd finishes up at college and does very well. Upon graduation he accepts a job offer from a Fortune 500 company. With his first paycheck, he goes to the eye doctor, who replaces those big, old, thick glasses with a pair of contacts. He stops at the tailor and picks out a couple of nice suits to wear. After saving a big chunk of his first few paychecks, he makes a down payment on a new Lexus. When he drives home to visit his parents, all the young women in the old neighborhood say, "Hey, don't I know you?" Suddenly, they do not want to talk to the guy behind the fast-food counter anymore.

14   The first guy—the cool guy—had everything back in high school. So what did he get for all that?

15   The other guy was not cool at all—but he was focused. Where did he go in the long run?

16   "And that," I told my audience, "is how we have to learn to think about life! With a long-term view. A Big-Picture perspective!"

17   Those students at Chicago's Wendell Phillips High School could not have been more attentive as I recounted the things this former nerd has seen and done. They listened to me explain and illustrate the incredible potential that resides in the average human brain. They even seemed receptive to my challenge that they begin to use those brains to plan and prepare for the future. So, as I wrapped up my talk by daring them to THINK BIG, I did something I had never done before, though I realized it could backfire if I had read this audience wrong. But since they had been such a responsive group, I decided to risk it.

18   I concluded by asking that auditorium full of high school students for a show of hands. "How many of you are ready, here today, to raise your hands and say to me, to your teachers, and to your peers, 'I want to be a nerd'?"

19   Although many of them laughed, almost all the students of Wendell Phillips High School raised their hands as they stood and applauded and cheered even louder than when I had walked in.

Questions about the Reading

For each question, write the letter of your answer in the space provided.

Vocabulary in Context

_____ 1. In the sentences below, the word *prevalent* (prĕv′ə-lənt) means
  A. absent.
  B. widely present.
  C. desirable.
  D. unimportant.

> "There I met and talked with school officials and local religious leaders . . . about the troubled neighborhood where the school is located. They indicated that gang influence was prevalent. . . ." (Paragraph 2)

_____ 2. In the sentences below, the word *dire* (dīr) means
  A. alarming.
  B. misleading.
  C. reassuring.
  D. amusing.

> "They indicated that . . . living conditions were deplorable in the surrounding public housing developments, dropout statistics were high, and SAT scores were low. . . . [S]o dire were these warnings that, on the crosstown drive to the school, I could not help wondering what kind of reception I would receive from the students." (Paragraphs 2–3)

Central Point and Main Ideas

_____ 3. Which sentence best expresses the central point of the entire selection?
  A. Dr. Ben Carson, a famous surgeon, was considered a nerd in high school.
  B. The student body of a tough inner-city high school listened politely to Dr. Ben Carson's talk.
  C. In a talk to high-school students, Dr. Ben Carson encouraged them to focus on long-term goals.
  D. Guys who earn varsity letters, know all the current music, and drive sharp cars seem to collect the most girlfriends in high school.

_____ 4. Which sentence best expresses the main idea of paragraph 13?
   A. The nerd does well in college and even lands a job with a Fortune 500 company.
   B. After a well-paying job lets him afford contacts, nice clothes, and a nice car, the nerd becomes more attractive to women.
   C. When the nerd graduates from college, he can afford a cool wardrobe.
   D. Later in life the cool guy is sure to envy the nerd's accomplishments.

Key Supporting Details

_____ 5. Dr. Carson arrived at Wendell Phillips High School
   A. worried about how the students would respond to him.
   B. confident that his speech would be a big success.
   C. favorably impressed by what he had heard from community leaders.
   D. very late.

_____ 6. The students at Wendell Phillips High School
   A. worked in fast-food restaurants.
   B. had unusually high SAT scores.
   C. skipped school on the day that Dr. Carson spoke.
   D. had been excused from class to hear Dr. Carson speak.

_____ 7. Peer pressure
   A. sidetracked Dr. Carson for a while during his teenage years.
   B. never affected Dr. Carson during his teenage years.
   C. was less of a problem during Dr. Carson's teen years than it is now.
   D. affected Dr. Carson in positive ways during his teenage years.

Inferences

_____ 8. From the article, the reader might conclude that
   A. Dr. Carson was considered cool in high school.
   B. Dr. Carson hardly ever speaks to parent groups.
   C. planning for the future can mean giving up some pleasure today.
   D. the visit to Wendell Phillips High School was Dr. Carson's first to Chicago.

_____ 9. Dr. Carson implies that
   A. girls in high school aren't impressed by cool guys.
   B. the cool guy in high school wasn't thinking about his future.
   C. the cool guy in school had a "Big Picture" perspective on his life.
   D. when the nerd got his first paycheck, he should have saved it instead of spending it on clothes and contact lenses.

_____10. What audience did Dr. Carson seem to have in mind when he wrote
this essay?
   A. High-school administrators
   B. High-school students
   C. Parents of high school students
   D. High-school dropouts

Discussion Questions

1. It doesn't seem likely that Dr. Carson, a highly educated adult, often uses words like "cool" and "nerd" in his own conversation. Why, then, do you think he chose to use such language in his speech at Wendell Phillips High School? What effect do you think it had on the students?

2. Although Dr. Carson was a good student, he admits that peer pressure and his own hot temper sometimes got in the way of his success. What are some obstacles—internal and external—that stand in the way of your being the best student you can be? What are some ways you might overcome these obstacles?

3. Dr. Carson speaks frequently to high school students because he has learned something about life that he believes can be of value to them. If you were asked to give a single piece of advice to a group of younger students, what would you say?

Note: Writing assignments for this selection appear on page 563.

Check Your Performance   **INFERENCES**

Activity	*Number Right*	*Points*	*Score*
Review Test 1 (4 items)	_____	× 5 =	_____
Review Test 2 (5 items)	_____	× 4 =	_____
Review Test 3 (10 items)	_____	× 6 =	_____

TOTAL SCORE = _____%

Enter your total score into the **Reading Performance Chart: Review Tests** on the inside back cover.

INFERENCES: Mastery Test 1

A. (1–3.) Look at the following book cover and then put a check (✓) by the **three** inferences that are most logically based on the information given on the cover.

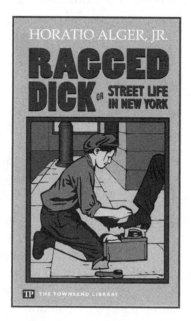

_____ A. Ragged Dick is a shoeshine boy.

_____ B. Shining shoes is a well-paying job.

_____ C. Ragged Dick is lazy.

_____ D. The story takes place many years ago.

_____ E. Ragged Dick is poor.

_____ F. Ragged Dick sometimes cheats his customers.

B. (4–7.) Put a check (✓) by the **two** inferences that are most logically based on each of the sentences below.

• When a blind man carries a lame man, both go forward.

_____ A. When people combine their strengths, they make progress.

_____ B. Only people with disabilities need the help of others.

_____ C. Disabled people should try to be as independent as possible.

_____ D. Nobody is perfect, but by working together, people can make up for each other's weaknesses.

(Continues on next page)

• If you get a lemon, make lemonade.

_____ E. Everyone gets more lemons in life than lemonade.

_____ F. Attitude and effort can turn around a bad situation.

_____ G. Sugar can make everything taste better.

_____ H. Even bitter things can be made into something sweet.

C. (8–10.) Read the following passage and then check (✓) the **three** inferences that are most firmly based on the given information.

¹Recently, a friend and I were at Universal Studios in Florida waiting to be seated for a show called *Raiders of the Lost Ark*. ²We stood there munching ice cream bars and people-watching when my eye was drawn to a tall woman near the front of our line. ³The woman, puffing away at a cigarette, looked to be in her late 50s. ⁴She was flashily dressed, with a beaded pink jacket and tight white pants, and her white-blonde hair was curled and styled like a young woman's. ⁵She smiled as she spoke to someone near her. ⁶With all of her makeup, she looked to me like a clown.

⁷"That woman near the front has no idea of how ridiculous she is," I commented to my friend. ⁸"She should act her age."

⁹Then the line started to move, and I noticed that she walked with a crutch. ¹⁰It hooked up under one arm and supported what was obviously a very weak leg. ¹¹The woman moved as briskly as she could, but still more slowly than other people. ¹²And then I realized that she was alone as I saw her take a seat by herself a few rows in front of us.

¹³The show started, but for quite a while I didn't pay any attention to it. ¹⁴Instead, I shook my head in self-disgust. ¹⁵And I thought about how many tests there are in our lives—how many chances we have to be either kind or cruel. ¹⁶On this particular test, I had just scored a zero.

_____ A. The woman injured her leg in an auto accident.

_____ B. The woman is trying to enjoy life despite her disability.

_____ C. The woman pitied herself because she had to use a crutch.

_____ D. The woman has a different idea of what it means to "act one's age" than the narrator.

_____ E. The narrator regrets that he prejudged the woman.

_____ F. The woman is a widow.

INFERENCES: Mastery Test 2

A. (1–3.) Look at the following cartoon and put a check (✓) by the **three** inferences that are most logically based on the information given.

THE JOKE'S ON YOU — by Phil Ryder & YOU

"Whoa...hold on a minute. You're not supposed to tell them the truth. For goodness sake, man, you're a politician; show some self-respect."

- Racer X • Jamaica Plain, MA

_____ A. Both men are politicians.

_____ B. The two men are brothers.

_____ C. The man who is speaking often lies to the public.

_____ D. The man who is listening will continue to tell the truth.

_____ E. The man who is listening is inexperienced.

_____ F. The audience is not interested in what the two men have to say.

B. (4–7.) Put a check (✓) by the **two** inferences that are most logically based on each of the sentences below.

• May your coffin be built out of the wood of a hundred-year-old oak tree, which I shall plant tomorrow.

_____ A. The speaker is wishing someone a long life.

_____ B. The speaker is an undertaker.

_____ C. The speaker is talking to a young person, perhaps a child.

_____ D. The speaker dislikes the person he or she is talking to.

(Continues on next page)

- You've got to do your own growing, no matter how tall your grandfather was.

    ____ E. People with successful relatives have an easier time in life.

    ____ F. Whatever your family background, no one can live your life for you.

    ____ G. Family background is more important than character.

    ____ H. The effort you make as an individual is more important than your family background.

C. (8–10.) Read the following passage and then check (✓) the **three** inferences that are most firmly based on the given information.

> [1]Sharon is a person whose life seems filled with conflict. [2]I rarely talk with her without being reminded of that fact. [3]For example, she constantly complains to me that people "do her wrong." [4]"And I thought she was my friend!" is her constant complaint. [5]Before I knew Sharon well, I sympathized with her incredible bad luck. [6]Now, however, I think I understand the situation better. [7]Sharon expects her friends to show her unconditional love and acceptance, no matter how she behaves. [8]Even when she stands her friends up, tells them lies, and takes advantage of them, she is amazed when they withdraw their friendship. [9]Despite her constant experience of losing friends, she doesn't realize that she is responsible for the situation.

    ____ A. The writer has gained insight into Sharon's life, but Sharon hasn't.

    ____ B. People like Sharon never change.

    ____ C. Sharon has many good qualities.

    ____ D. Sharon doesn't always treat her friends well.

    ____ E. The writer no longer believes that Sharon's problems are due to bad luck.

    ____ F. The writer of the passage is Sharon's sister.

INFERENCES: Mastery Test 3

A. (1–3.) Look at the following cartoon and put a check (✓) by the **three** inferences that are most logically based on the information given.

Shoe

_____ A. A mistake has been made on Bob's tombstone.

_____ B. Both characters were probably friends of Bob.

_____ C. The two characters are Bob's brothers.

_____ D. Bob died as the result of a foolish accident.

_____ E. Bob took pride in being a good proofreader.

_____ F. Bob is not really buried in the grave.

B. (4–7.) Put a check (✓) by the **two** inferences that are most logically based on each of the sentences below.

- It is easier for a camel to go through the eye of a needle than it is for a rich man to enter the kingdom of heaven.

    _____ A. Rich men are favored by God.

    _____ B. Poor people are more likely to enter the kingdom of heaven than rich people.

    _____ C. Rich men should share their wealth with others.

    _____ D. Rich men don't care about entering the kingdom of heaven.

(Continues on next page)

• Kindness is the language which the deaf can hear and the blind can see.

____ E. You don't need to see and hear to appreciate kindness.

____ F. Kindness is a powerful form of communication.

____ G. Only the disabled can truly appreciate kindness.

____ H. People should be especially kind to deaf and blind people.

C. (8–10.) Read the following passage and then check (✓) the **three** inferences that are most firmly based on the given information.

> [1]At the very bottom of the American social ladder are the homeless. [2]They are people whose worldly goods fill a few shopping bags. [3]Social workers usually find that these people once were better off, but that some misfortune led to their losing their home. [4]An apartment building, for example, is sold to a developer, and its poor tenants are evicted. [5]A breadwinner loses his or her job because of a plant closing or a long illness. [6]A woman leaves an abusive husband but cannot afford an apartment of her own. [7]Whatever the cause, the result is the same: a person, a couple, a mother and her children, or an entire family living on the street. [8]Having fallen from a higher rung on the social ladder, many of the homeless are unable to regain their position.

____ A. People become homeless for a variety of reasons.

____ B. People are usually homeless for only a short period of time.

____ C. Most homeless people are women.

____ D. Homeless people are often unfortunate, not lazy.

____ E. The cost of renting even a modest apartment is often more than poor people can afford.

____ F. Homeless people usually only have themselves to blame for their homelessness.

INFERENCES: Mastery Test 4

A. (1–2.) Look at the following cartoon and put a check (✓) by the **two** inferences that are most logically based on the information given.

Copyright 2004 by Randy Glasbergen.
www.glasbergen.com

GLASBERGEN

**"Yes, I think I have good people skills.
What kind of idiot question is that?"**

_____ A. The man is being interviewed for a job.

_____ B. The woman will probably hire the man.

_____ C. The woman asked the man a foolish question.

_____ D. The man probably does not have good people skills.

(Continues on next page)

B. (3–4.) Put a check (✓) by the **two** inferences that are most logically based on the passage below.

> ¹Although most everyone knows that eating sensibly and exercising regularly are the keys to healthy weight loss, the America fad diet industry continues to receive millions of dollars from people looking for a faster, easier solution. ²Eating sensibly and exercising regularly involve both education and commitment, neither of which is easy. ³And results, though proven, may not come quickly. ⁴Many people are anxious to lose weight right away. ⁵In addition, they are not willing to do the work that healthy eating and regular exercise require. ⁶That is why the fad diet industry continues to succeed every year. ⁷People want to believe there is a quick and easy fix. ⁸But no such pill, powder, or program has ever been found to match the success rate of a healthy lifestyle.

___ A. Many Americans lack self-discipline when it comes to losing weight.

___ B. Some fad diets are better than others.

___ C. Americans tend to be impatient.

___ D. If people ate sensibly, they wouldn't need to exercise.

C. In the space provided, write the letter of the sentence that best expresses the implied main idea in the paragraph that follows.

_____ 5. ¹To make your clothes last longer, avoid using the dryer. ²Over time, the heat will fade colors and weaken fabrics. ³Instead, hang your clothing to dry inside the house in cold weather and outside (but away from direct sunlight, which can also fade colors) when it's warm. ⁴Also, don't use bleach more than absolutely necessary. ⁵Bleach contains strong chemicals that can weaken fibers. ⁶Never store knitted clothes on hangers—the clothing can stretch out of shape. ⁷Instead, keep them folded in a drawer. ⁸Finally, get rid of stains promptly—if you let them set, they are much harder, if not impossible, to remove.

The **unstated main idea** is:
A. Most people don't know how to make their clothes last longer.
B. There are several ways to make your clothes last longer.
C. Dryers and bleach are bad for your clothes.
D. There are several reasons to avoid using your dryer.

INFERENCES: Mastery Test 5

A. Read each passage and check (✓) the **two** inferences that are most firmly based on the given information.

1–2. ¹Many people have suggested that opposites attract. ²People are more comfortable with those who look and act like themselves. ³They are naturally attracted to people that they can relate to. ⁴99% of people marry someone who is of the same race. ⁵75% of people marry someone who is of the same religion. ⁶Most people marry someone who lives a short car ride away from their home and who has a similar level of attractiveness. ⁷People tend to marry someone who is within four years of their age, is around the same height as they are, and is in the same health. ⁸Rich people usually marry rich people, and poor people usually marry poor people. ⁹Smokers tend to marry other people who smoke. ¹⁰People who are outgoing, argumentative, or stubborn tend to end up with others who have those same qualities.

_____ A. Most people marry someone who is very similar to themselves.

_____ B. Marriages between people of different races and/or religions frequently end in divorce.

_____ C. Physical attraction is still one of the most important things to consider when choosing a mate.

_____ D. When it comes to marriage, opposites don't attract.

3–4. ¹Politicians who make the decisions to go to war are rarely personally affected by those decisions. ²They themselves do not do the fighting. ³They do not risk their lives on the battlefield. ⁴They do not run the danger of leaving their spouses widowed or their children parentless. ⁵Here's a suggestion. ⁶Before a politician can cast a "yes" vote to go to war, he or she should have to choose one member of his or her immediate family who will fight in that war. ⁷If politicians knew that a son or daughter, a brother or sister, would actually be part of the battle, they might find better ways to deal with the world's conflicts. ⁸As a result, there might be less war between countries and more peace.

_____ E. The writer believes that wars should be avoided.

_____ F. Most wars are unavoidable.

_____ G. Politicians need reminders that every person who dies in a war is a human being who probably has loved ones.

_____ H. Politicians have often risked their own lives in wars.

(Continues on next page)

B. In the space provided, write the letter of the sentence that best expresses the implied main idea in the paragraph that follows.

_____ 5. ¹Housework is the first thing to fall by the wayside in the time-pressured lives of professional women. ²In a survey by a women's magazine, over 80 percent of full-time working women said the only way they could balance job, home, and family was to sacrifice high cleaning standards. ³The next thing to get put on the back burner was sex. ⁴Almost 75 percent said that by the end of the day, they or their spouses were too tired for anything but TV. ⁵Fifty percent reported that friends and social occasions were third in line to get squeezed off the calendar.

The **unstated main idea** is:
A. Women who work full-time say they must sacrifice high cleaning standards.
B. According to a women's magazine survey, full-time working women would be better off if they took on part-time jobs instead.
C. Half of all full-time working women report that working full-time has meant less time for getting together with friends.
D. According to a women's magazine survey, full-time working women have to cut back on several customary activities.

INFERENCES: Mastery Test 6

A. After reading each passage, check (✓) the **two** inferences that are most firmly based on the information given.

1–2. [1]According to recent national studies, men are now less likely than women to get bachelor's degrees. [2]And those men who do finish college take longer to get their degrees than women. [3]Also, men get lower grades than women. [4]The studies show that college men study less and socialize more. [5]As a result, women are walking off with a higher share of the honors degrees. [6]The enrollment of men is also down. [7]Today they make up only 42 percent of the nation's college students. [8]Women have also become a majority in graduate schools and professional schools.

_____ A. Women are more intelligent than men.

_____ B. Women are doing better in college than men are.

_____ C. The enrollment of men in colleges will continue to decline.

_____ D. In general, young women today take college more seriously than young men do.

3–4. [1]The famous writer Dorothy Parker (1893–1967) once ran into a movie star after the star's most recent and highly publicized suicide attempt. [2]Parker patted the woman's arm and murmured, "Better luck next time." [3]When Parker heard that President Calvin Coolidge, known as "Silent Cal," was dead, she asked, "How can they tell?" [4]In her review of one Broadway play, she wrote that *The House Beautiful* is the play lousy." [5]And she remarked of the actress Katherine Hepburn in another play that she showed a range of emotions "from A to B."

_____ E. Dorothy Parker really wanted the "suicidal" movie star to kill herself.

_____ F. Parker thought that Katherine Hepburn's acting was dull.

_____ G. Katherine Hepburn never got over Parker's remark about her acting.

_____ H. Parker believed that bad plays and performances should be criticized.

(Continues on next page)

B. In the space provided, write the letter of the sentence that best expresses the implied main idea in the paragraph that follows.

_____ 5. [1]Patients should always be aware of a prescription drug's possible side effects. [2]Unexpected side effects, such as nausea or dizziness, can be frightening and even dangerous. [3]Consumers should ask, too, if they can take the medication along with other drugs they are using. [4]Some combinations of drugs can be deadly. [5]Finally, medication should always be stored in its own labeled bottle and never moved to another bottle. [6]Accidental mix-ups of drugs can have tragic results.

The **unstated main idea** is:
A. Consumers may use drugs carelessly.
B. Drugs can have dangerous side effects.
C. There are several guidelines for taking prescription medications safely.
D. To avoid tragic mix-ups, medications should always be stored in their own labeled bottles.

10

The Basics
of Argument

THIS CHAPTER IN A NUTSHELL

- A good thinker understands what it means to *make* a point.
- A good thinker understands what it means to *support* a point.

Look at the following cartoon and see if you can answer the questions that follow.

"I'm out in the fresh air and sunshine, my lungs are getting plenty of exercise and I'm consuming a leafy vegetable...this has to be good for me!"

- What is the man's argument here? That is, what is his point?
- What is his support for his point?

Explanation:

The man's point is that smoking is good for him. But his supporting reasons are *not* convincing ones. He's outside in the fresh air but putting cigarette smoke into his lungs, his lungs are not getting a healthy workout, and tobacco is not a leafy "vegetable." He makes a clear point—that smoking is good for him—but fails to support it. To make a good argument and prove a point, you must offer solid support.

EVALUATING ARGUMENTS

A critical thinker is someone who can look at an **argument**—a point and its support—and decide whether the support is solid or not. Look at the following point:

>   **Point:** It's more fun to watch movies at home than in a theater.

Now, is there solid support for this point? In other words, is the person who made it thinking clearly and logically? Let's say the person goes on to provide these details:

>   *Support:*
>   • When you are in a theater, you have to put up with rude adults and crying children.
>   • At home, you can "pause" a movie when you want to leave the room.
>   • It's great to watch movies in your pajamas while sitting in your favorite chair.

As you can see, the details do provide solid support for the point. They give us a basis for understanding and agreeing with the point that watching movies at home has its own special appeal.

This is a small example of what critical thinking is about: recognizing a point and deciding whether there is support that effectively backs up the point.

PRACTICE IN EVALUATING ARGUMENTS

Point and Support

This first activity will review and sharpen your sense of the difference between a point and its support. As you learned earlier in the book, a **point** is a general idea; **support** is the specific information that backs up the point.

☑ *Check Your Understanding*

Look at the following group of items. It is made up of a point and three statements that logically support the point. See if you can put a **P** in front of the point and an **S** in front of the three supporting statements.

_____ A. A six-foot snapping turtle lives on the bottom of the lake.

_____ B. Rattlesnakes have nests on the shoreline and often swim in the lake.

_____ C. Someone dumped scrap metal in the lake, and you could cut yourself badly.

_____ D. You should not go swimming in that lake.

Explanation:

Statements A, B, and C all describe specific dangers of swimming in the lake. Statement D—that you should not swim in the lake—is the point that all of the other sentences support.

➤ *Practice 1*

In each of the following groups, one statement is the point, and the other statements are support for the point. Identify each point with a **P** and each statement of support with an **S**.

Group 1

_____ A. Soda has no nutritional value.

_____ B. Most cans of regular soda contain 10 teaspoons of sugar.

·_____ C. Caffeinated sodas make hyperactive kids even more hyper.

_____ D. People should cut down on drinking soda.

Group 2

_____ A. The puppy chewed on everything from my sneakers to the living room sofa.

_____ B. It took the puppy weeks to learn that he was supposed to go outside, not on the kitchen floor.

_____ C. The new puppy was very difficult to train.

_____ D. At night the puppy would whine for hours, begging us to let him into our bedroom.

Group 3

_____ A. The majority of lottery winners are broke within five years.

_____ B. Family members often fight bitterly over how the money will be spent.

_____ C. Many lottery winners finally say they wish they had never won the money.

_____ D. Winning the lottery is not always a dream come true.

Logical Support I

Once you identify a point and its support, you need to decide if the support really applies to the point. The critical thinker will ask, "Is this support logical and relevant? Or is it beside the point?" In trying to make a point, people often bring up support that does not apply.

For example, say that a person claims that the people in the apartment next door are bad neighbors. To support that point, the person might say, "They play loud music late at night. In addition, they drive an old car." A critical thinker will realize that (1) playing loud music late at night may make them bad neighbors; (2) driving an old car does *not* make them bad neighbors. Driving an old car has nothing to do with whether or not they are bad neighbors. The first reason for disliking the people next door is relevant support, but the second reason is beside the point.

The following activity will sharpen your ability to decide whether evidence truly supports a point.

☑ Check Your Understanding

Read the following point and the three items of "support" that follow. Then put a check (✓) next to the **one** item that logically supports the point.

Point: The teacher takes a personal interest in her students.

_____ A. Her lectures are always well-prepared, and she always follows her class syllabus. When asked a question in class, she answers promptly and fully. She has co-written a textbook on the subject that she's teaching.

_____ B. She is lots of fun in class, always joking around and making wisecracks. On Halloween, she came in dressed as a witch. Once she handed out test booklets that said inside, "April fool!"

_____ C. She has a one-on-one interview with each student at least twice a year. She makes a point of knowing their families and often asks how their parents or siblings are doing. If a student is having a special problem, she often visits him or her at home.

Explanation:

A. The teacher described here knows her subject and is skilled at teaching, but nothing that she does shows that she takes a personal interest in her students. You should not have chosen this item.

B. The teacher described here is cheerful and fun-loving, but does nothing to show that she takes a personal interest in her students. You should not have chosen this item.

C. The teacher described here clearly goes out of her way to establish and maintain a personal connection to each of her students. If you checked the letter of this item, you were correct.

➤ Practice 2

Below is a point followed by three items of information. Put a check (✓) next to the **one** item that logically supports the point.

1. **Point:** The applicant for the job did not seem as though he really wanted to be hired.

_____ A. He showed up wearing brand-new blue jeans and a freshly ironed shirt. He greeted the receptionist politely and asked if he could have a cup of water while he was waiting to be interviewed. While he waited, he leafed through an old copy of *Time* magazine.

_____ B. He arrived fifteen minutes late for his interview, with no explanation. He looked rumpled and sleepy, as if he had just gotten out of bed. He answered the interviewer's questions with "Yeah" or "No." When the interviewer asked if he had any questions, he said, "Not really."

_____ C. He called the day before the interview to ask if he should bring anything along. When he arrived, he was ten minutes early, and he brought flowers for the receptionist. After the interview, he sent the interviewer a thank-you note.

2. **Point:** My classmate, Gina, is very kind.

_____ A. When the rest of the class was making fun of the music teacher, she refused to join in. When a boy from China joined the class, she did her best to make him feel welcome. She is a volunteer math tutor after school.

_____ B. She's always looking at her face in her compact mirror. She constantly worries that she's getting fat. If someone wears the same thing she's wearing to class, she flips out. She won't be seen in public without makeup.

_____ C. She participates in most classroom discussions. She spends at least two hours a night on her homework. She's doing an extra credit science project on solar energy. She was elected to the National Honor Society.

3. **Point:** Obesity is a growing health problem.

_____ A. Thirty or so years ago, people were more active and, therefore, thinner because they didn't have computers and cable TV to sit in front of for hours on end. There were also fewer fast-food restaurants and a smaller variety of junk food.

_____ B. Some diets are dangerous because they involve taking pills that contain large amounts of caffeine. Other diets are unhealthy since they cut out necessary nutrients like fat and carbohydrates. Most hazardous are diets that require starving one's self.

_____ C. Because 30 percent of our population is very overweight, there has been a huge increase in physical problems such as diabetes and heart disease. Emotional problems such as depression and anxiety have also increased. As a result, the cost of health insurance has gone up.

Logical Support II

☑ *Check Your Understanding*

Below is a point followed by five statements. Three of the statements logically support the point; two of the statements do not. In the spaces provided, write the letters of the **three** logical statements of support.

> *Point:* Those parents are careless about their child's health and safety.
>
> A. They leave him alone in the house at night, sometimes not returning at all.
>
> B. They drop him off at the home of people they barely know, then disappear for days.
>
> C. They rarely take him to see the doctor or dentist.
>
> D. They never check to see if he has done his schoolwork.
>
> E. They do not allow him to have any pets.
>
> *Items that logically support the point:* _____   _____   _____

Explanation:

Items A, B, and C all support the point that the parents are careless about their child's health and safety. Items D and E do not directly involves the child's safety, so neither supports the point.

➤ *Practice 3*

Each point is followed by three statements that provide logical support and two that do not. In the spaces, write the letters of the **three** logical statements of support.

> 1. *Point:* Returning to school as an older student can be challenging.
>
>   A. Studies show that more and more adults are returning to school.
>
>   B. It takes a lot of work to re-learn study habits.
>
>   C. Many older students have family and job responsibilities in addition to classes.
>
>   D. Some older students are afraid of not "fitting in."
>
>   E. It is never too late to gain new knowledge.
>
>   *Items that logically support the point:* _____   _____   _____

2. *Point:* Eating fish is good for your health.

    A. Fish offers as much protein as beef, but with far fewer calories.

    B. Fish contains omega-3 fatty acids, which have been shown to reduce cholesterol and lower blood pressure.

    C. Fish is low in sodium and is a good source of vitamins and minerals.

    D. If fish is fried or prepared with a creamy sauce, it can have as many calories as beef.

    E. Because of overfishing by commercial fisheries, some popular ocean fish are becoming scarce.

Items that logically support the point: _____ _____ _____

3. *Point:* Workers in early American factories led difficult lives.

    A. The average work day was twelve hours long.

    B. Early factory workers were paid pennies an hour.

    C. Female factory workers often worked in textile mills.

    D. The first American factories were built in the late 1700s.

    E. All workers on power machines risked accidents that could maim or kill.

Items that logically support the point: _____ _____ _____

Making a Logical Point

This activity will develop your ability to look at evidence and then decide what point is supported by that evidence. This skill of coming to a logical conclusion is an important part of good thinking.

☑ Check Your Understanding

Look at the following three items of support:

Support:

• Although the boss gives very unclear directions for what he wants, he is furious if a job isn't done exactly as he intended.

• The boss has hired his lazy, incompetent niece, and no one is allowed to complain about anything she does.

• The boss takes two-hour lunches, while no one else is allowed to have more than a half hour.

Now check (✓) the **point** that is logically supported by the above evidence. Then read the explanation that follows.

_____ A. The boss is supportive of his family members.

_____ B. All bosses have their good and bad points.

_____ C. The boss does not care if his business succeeds or fails.

_____ D. The boss is an unpleasant person to work for.

Explanation:

A. Only one of the supports mentions a member of the boss's family. You should not have chosen this point.

B. None of the supports says anything about the boss's good points, only his bad points, so you shouldn't have chosen this point.

C. The fact that the boss becomes furious if a job isn't done exactly as he intended indicates that he cares whether his business succeeds or fails. So you should not have chosen this point.

D. All the details support the statement that the boss is an unpleasant person to work for. It is the one you should have chosen as the point.

➤ Practice 4

For each group, read the three items of supporting evidence. Then check (✓) the point that is most logically supported by that evidence.

Group 1

Support:

• In heavily overpopulated areas, infants and children die at far above the average rate.

• The more overpopulated an area, the higher the crime rate.

• Noise pollution in overpopulated areas leads to psychological distress.

Point: Which of the following conclusions is best supported by all the evidence above?

_____ A. Overpopulation leads to a number of social problems.

_____ B. The life expectancy for adults in overpopulated places is lower than average.

_____ C. The majority of the world's cities are overpopulated.

_____ D. Overpopulation causes crime and disease.

Group 2

Support:

- Many American girls undereat in order to become or stay thin.

- Some young men take steroids to try to look more muscular.

- Adolescents who smoke cigarettes do so partly because smoking reduces appetite.

Point: Which of the following conclusions is best supported by all the evidence above?

_____ A. It is dangerous to use steroids without a doctor's prescription.

_____ B. Some young people risk their health for the sake of looking good.

_____ C. There are many reasons why young people should not smoke.

_____ D. Our society encourages girls to value their appearance above all else.

Group 3

Support:

- Drinking coffee improves my ability to concentrate.

- I enjoy having a cup of coffee while chatting with a friend.

- I love the taste and aroma of fresh coffee.

Point: Which of the following conclusions is best supported by all the evidence above?

_____ A. Much of the coffee we drink is produced in Central and South America.

_____ B. Drinking coffee can have unpleasant effects.

_____ C. Sometimes when I drink coffee in the evening, I have a hard time falling asleep.

_____ D. Coffee is my favorite beverage.

CHAPTER REVIEW

In this chapter, you learned the following:

- A good argument is made up of a point, or a conclusion, and evidence to back it up.

- To think through an argument, you need to decide if each bit of evidence is relevant and logical.

- Sound thinking also includes looking at evidence and deciding what logical point, or conclusion, can be drawn from that evidence.

On the Web: If you are using this book in class, you can visit our website for additional practice in evaluating arguments. Go to **www.townsendpress.com** and click on "Online Exercises."

➤ Review Test 1

To review what you've learned in this chapter, fill in each of the blanks below.

1. A point is the (*main idea, evidence, logic*) _____ presented by a writer or speaker.

2. A good thinker is one who can look at an argument—a point and its support—and decide whether the _____ is solid or not.

3. In addition to asking "What is the point?" you must ask, "What is the _____ for that point?"

4. Specific evidence is logical only if it truly supports the _____.

➤ Review Test 2

A. (1–4.) In the following group, one statement is the point, and the other statements are support for the point. Identify the point with a **P** and each statement of support with an **S**.

_____ A. The first major improvement in automotive safety came in 1910 with the invention of safety glass windshields.

_____ B. Automotive safety has improved over the years.

_____ C. Seat belts became standard in cars in the 1960s.

_____ D. Air bags became common in the 1980s.

B. (5.) Below is a point followed by three items of information. Put a check (✓) next to the **one** item that logically supports the point.

Point: Even though he's wealthy, my uncle is stingy.

_____ A. He worked as a design engineer for IBM. He has a huge collection of books. He plays the piano. He can recite lines from Shakespeare off the top of his head.

_____ B. He spends several hours a week clipping coupons. He buys day-old bread. He says he doesn't have cable TV because it costs too much. On the rare times we go out to restaurants, he gives the server a small tip.

_____ C. He doesn't like people from other countries. He thinks my sister should get married and have kids. He says things in this country have gone downhill since when he was young.

C. (6–8.) The point below is followed by three statements that provide logical support and two that do not. In the spaces, write the letters of the **three** logical statements of support.

> **Point:** I need a bigger apartment.
>
> A. There's barely enough room in the kitchen to turn around.
> B. My living room is the size of a closet.
> C. Because there's no storage space, boxes are piled on the floor.
> D. My best friend has a huge apartment.
> E. Rents are higher on this side of town.
>
> *Items that logically support the point:* _____   _____   _____

D. (9–10.) Read the three items of supporting evidence. Then check (✓) the point that is most logically supported by that evidence.

Group 1

Support:

- The drummer had no rhythm, and the lead guitarist was out of tune.
- The sound system was so bad that people were covering their ears.
- The singer forgot half the words.

Point: Which of the following conclusions is best supported by all the evidence above?

_____ A. Musicians are strange people.
_____ B. The concert was really bad.
_____ C. Practice makes perfect.
_____ D. Concerts are a great source of entertainment.

Group 2

Support:

- Lack of vitamin C leads to bleeding gums.
- People who lack iron in their diet may lose red blood cells and feel fatigue.
- A disease that causes slow bone growth results from a lack of vitamin D.

Point: Which of the following conclusions is best supported by all the evidence above?

_____ A. People long ago knew little about healthy eating.
_____ B. It is important to get enough vitamins and minerals in your diet.
_____ C. Citrus fruits (such as oranges) are a good source of vitamin C.
_____ D. Milk, which contains vitamin D and iron, is good for you.

➤ Review Test 3

Here is a chance to apply your understanding of argument to a full-length reading. "Shopping" can mean something as basic as running out to the store for a few groceries. But for many Americans, shopping is something quite different. It is recreation, distraction—even therapy. This selection explores some of the realities behind America's favorite hobby. Following the selection are questions that cover all of the reading skills you've worked on in this book.

Words to Watch

Below are some words in the reading that do not have strong context support. Each word is followed by the number of the paragraph in which it appears and its meaning there. These words are marked in the reading by a small circle (°).

> *descend on* (2): to arrive at or attack in an overpowering manner
> *cliché* (4): an overused expression or idea
> *distracts* (9): takes away one's attention; sidetracks
> *media* (10): the communications industry

WHY WE SHOP

Anita Rab

1   "Let's go shopping!"

2   The words echo across America like a battle cry. Every day, we head for the mall or the superstore, cash and credit cards in hand. We scan the store ads like hungry people reading a menu. We descend on° the counters and racks of goods as if on a treasure hunt. We pick the counters and racks clean and go home exhausted, but fulfilled. We have just had another fix of our favorite drug: shopping.

3   Why is America a nation of consumer junkies? There are several reasons.

4   First of all, Americans believe in competition, even for possessions. The old sports cliché°, "Winning isn't everything—it's the only thing," also applies to our feelings about buying. We simply have to own the cars, appliances, clothes, and furniture our neighbors and friends own. If we don't, we feel like losers.

5   The Coopers' four-year-old car, for instance, seems fine until the Ballards next door buy a brand-new model. Suddenly every paint chip and dent on the older model seems enormous. The Coopers begin to wonder what their "old clunker" says about them. Are people pitying them for driving it? Are they whispering that the Coopers must not be doing too well? Do they think

the Coopers are cheap? Then the Coopers will show them! Determined to stay ahead in the game, the Coopers visit the new car lots. They "just have to" replace their car. Forget the fact that a few weeks ago they thought their car was okay. Their idea of an "okay car" changed when the Ballards purchased a new one.

6   The Coopers are victims of the competitive urge. That urge tells us that people's success in life is measured by what they own. So we admire the ones who own three cars or enough shoes to fill a walk-in closet. By buying a new car, the Coopers are satisfying that urge. The problem is that this urge never stays satisfied for long. Next week, the Ballards may install a swimming pool.

7   A second reason for America's need to shop is our belief that "newer is better." In other countries, poorer people make do with what they have. A sewing machine or bicycle will be lovingly repaired. Children play with toys made of "junk" that Americans would have put in the wastebasket. Many of us don't realize that it is possible to fix a broken toaster, mend torn clothing, or be awakened by an old-fashioned wind-up clock.

8   Manufacturers encourage this "newer is better" attitude—for a good reason. They'll make more money if we buy a new model as soon as the old one fails. They've even invented items that are meant to be used once and discarded. These items aren't limited to paper plates and napkins. Now there are also disposable razors, cameras, and contact lenses. Also, fix-it shops are getting rare. Why should we repair the old when we can buy the new? As a result, junkyards and dumps are filled with still-usable items we no longer want. We don't reuse or recycle, which would save us money. Instead, we throw away.

9   In addition, shopping distracts° us from our worries. Maybe we've had a fight with a loved one. Maybe the job isn't going well. Perhaps we're concerned about our increasing weight or blood pressure. Figuring out how to deal with those problems is hard and painful. So instead, we make ourselves feel better by buying a new pair of shoes or a large-screen TV. Of course, when the thrill of the new purchase wears off, the old problems are still there. So we have to buy something else to distract us a little longer.

10   Finally, our buying habit is encouraged by the media°. Television and print ads carry tempting messages. These ads tell us that we *deserve* the very best, and the "best" is, not surprisingly, the newest. Ads insist that a new game system, MP3 player, or laptop computer is what we need to be happy. Or they tell us that buying a certain product will make us more attractive. That same basic message is in every ad for toothpaste, makeup, and cologne. A single item, the ads promise, can transform us into someone more desirable.

11   In fact, the media never stop reminding us that more and newer are better. Unless a television show or movie is about poor people, the setting is almost always sparkling new. Houses are large and expensive and crammed with expensive furniture and appliances. The unspoken message is "This is how people are supposed to live. Are your home, your car, your belongings this nice? If not, there's something wrong with you."

12   In this country, shopping fills a psychological need. We are truly hooked on passing cash or plastic over a counter and receiving something new in return. Like any addiction, it's one that can never be fully satisfied. It just keeps on eating away at us. It will continue to do so until we see shopping once and for all as the drug that it is.

Questions about the Reading

Vocabulary in Context

_____ 1. In the sentences below, the word *discarded* (dĭ-skärd′ĭd) means
   A. used over again.
   B. thrown away.
   C. repaired.
   D. recycled.

   "They've even invented items that are meant to be used once and discarded . . . disposable razors, cameras, and contact lenses." (Paragraph 8)

_____ 2. In the sentences below, the word *transform* (trăns-fôrm′) means
   A. sell.
   B. talk.
   C. change.
   D. confuse.

   "[Ads] tell us that buying a certain product will make us more attractive. That same basic message is in every ad for toothpaste, makeup, and cologne. A single item, the ads promise, can transform us into someone more desirable." (Paragraph 10)

Central Point and Main Ideas

_____ 3. Which sentence best expresses the central point of the selection?
   A. The media encourage the public to want new things.
   B. Americans are addicted to shopping for several reasons.
   C. Shopping can be exhausting but rewarding.
   D. The common addiction to shopping helps manufacturers.

_____ 4. Which sentence best expresses the main idea of paragraphs 4–6?
   A. The competitive urge is one reason for Americans' shopping addiction.
   B. To avoid feeling like losers, the Ballards like to stay ahead of their neighbors.
   C. The Coopers decided their four-year-old car was a clunker.
   D. If the Ballards get a swimming pool, the Coopers will want one too.

_____ 5. Which sentence best expresses the main idea of paragraphs 10–11?
   A. Ads for many products suggest that the products will make us more attractive.
   B. The media play a major role in encouraging us to shop.
   C. Ads frequently suggest that "newer" means "better."
   D. TV shows and movies generally show fancy, expensive homes.

Supporting Details

_____ 6. The author states that to make more money, manufacturers
   A. keep raising prices.
   B. make toasters that cannot be fixed.
   C. recycle old clothing into new products.
   D. sell items meant to be used only once and then thrown away.

_____ 7. According to the author, what do we do when the thrill of a new purchase wears off?
   A. We recycle the item.
   B. We buy something else.
   C. We try to solve our personal problems.
   D. We realize that we are addicted to shopping.

Inferences

_____ 8. The author suggests that one reason Americans are addicted to shopping is to
   A. raise their self-esteem.
   B. get richer.
   C. support products that they can reuse or recycle.
   D. buy things they really need.

_____ 9. The author suggests that
   A. our shopping habit does not lead to happiness.
   B. shopping is essentially a harmless habit.
   C. young people shop less than older people.
   D. people in other countries shop more than Americans do.

Argument

_____10. Which statement best states the central point of the selection?
   A. Every day, Americans need to satisfy their urge to shop by heading for department stores, discount centers, and malls. They then go home exhausted, but temporarily fulfilled.
   B. Americans are addicted to shopping because of their urge to compete, their belief that new things are best, their need to be distracted from worries, and the media's encouragement to shop.
   C. People like the Coopers are victims of the urge to compete through what they buy.
   D. Addictions are caused by complicated psychological and social factors.

Discussion Questions

1. Do you shop only for things you really need, or do you shop for other reasons? What do you think those reasons are?

2. Do you agree that shopping can be an addiction? Or do you think it is an exaggeration to say people can be "hooked" on shopping?

3. Are advertisers to blame for encouraging people to over-shop? Are advertisers also to blame for making us place too much value on material things?

Note: Writing assignments for this selection appear on pages 563–564.

Check Your Performance		**THE BASICS OF ARGUMENT**		
Activity		*Number Right*	*Points*	*Score*
Review Test 1 (4 items)		_____	× 5 =	_____
Review Test 2 (10 items)		_____	× 4 =	_____
Review Test 3 (10 items)		_____	× 4 =	_____
		TOTAL SCORE	=	_____%

Enter your total score into the **Reading Performance Chart: Review Tests** on the inside back cover.

THE BASICS OF ARGUMENT: Mastery Test 1

In each of the following groups, one statement is the point, and the other statements are support for the point. Identify each point with a **P** and each statement of support with an **S**.

Group 1

_____ A. That neighborhood is a bad place to live.

_____ B. The schools do not have a good reputation.

_____ C. There is a lot of crime in the neighborhood.

_____ D. Gang members wearing different colors can be seen on the streets.

Group 2

_____ A. A number of problems are associated with credit cards.

_____ B. Having a credit card tempts people to spend far more than they should.

_____ C. Many credit cards charge a hefty annual fee and also charge penalties for late payments.

_____ D. More people fall victim to credit card fraud every year.

Group 3

_____ A. The Egyptians had no machinery or iron tools to cut the stones.

_____ B. Some of the stones used in the pyramids weighed several tons.

_____ C. 400,000 men worked each year for twenty years to build the Great Pyramid.

_____ D. The construction of the Egyptian pyramids was extraordinary.

Group 4

_____ A. Students can type and print out reports on a computer.

_____ B. The Internet provides an endless supply of information for research papers.

_____ C. Computers have made it easier for students to do their work.

_____ D. A computer can be used to take a class at home, rather than having to travel to campus.

(Continues on next page)

Group 5

_____ A. During the Civil War, soldiers faced many hardships.

_____ B. More soldiers died of disease during the Civil War than were killed in battle.

_____ C. In army hospitals, surgeons cut off injured limbs without the aid of painkillers.

_____ D. Soldiers had to wear woolen uniforms even in the heat of summer.

THE BASICS OF ARGUMENT: Mastery Test 2

A. (1–8.) In each of the following groups, one statement is the point, and the other statements are support for the point. Identify each point with a **P** and each statement of support with an **S**.

Group 1

_____ A. Shrimp is often served with the head still attached.

_____ B. For many people, raw fish is too scary-looking to eat.

_____ C. Raw octopus tentacles look like they're waving.

_____ D. Fish eggs are like spoonfuls of tiny eyeballs.

Group 2

_____ A. Drivers who fall asleep at the wheel are responsible for two out of every ten accidents.

_____ B. Too little sleep can contribute to dangerously high blood pressure.

_____ C. Getting too little sleep can have dangerous results.

_____ D. On-the-job accidents resulting from lack of sleep cost American industry $50 billion a year.

B. (9.) Below is a point followed by three items of information. Put a check (✓) next to the **one** item that logically supports the point.

Point: Pursuing a dream is important.

_____ A. Most people learn a lot about themselves when they go after what they really want. Even if their dreams don't come true, the experience will give them confidence and a better idea of what they want to do in life. People often regret not pursuing a dream.

_____ B. Dreams are usually unrealistic. It is hard for some people to face the fact that their dream of becoming a famous inventor, writer, or musician will never come true. It is better to be realistic than disappointed.

_____ C. As people get older, they are often unwilling to take the chances they might have taken when they were younger. Dreams of fame, fortune, and success begin to fade. Often, dreams are let go in favor of security and comfort.

(Continues on next page)

C. (10.) For the group below, read the three items of supporting evidence. Then put a check (✓) next to the point that is most logically supported by that evidence.

Support:

• Experiments have shown that convicts who are allowed to have pets become less violent.

• The attitude of patients in nursing homes improves when they have the opportunity to interact with cats and dogs.

• Children with mental and/or physical handicaps have benefited from learning to ride horses.

Point: Which of the following conclusions is best supported by all the evidence above?

_____ A. Everyone should own a pet.

_____ B. In general, cats require less care than dogs.

_____ C. Caring for a pet teaches responsibility.

_____ D. Animals have been shown to promote mental and physical health.

THE BASICS OF ARGUMENT: Mastery Test 3

A. Each point is followed by three statements that provide logical support and two that do not. In the spaces, write the letters of the **three** logical statements of support.

1–3. ***Point:*** I don't think we should take my car on a long trip.

    A. It stalls out in rainy weather.
    B. It has air conditioning and power windows.
    C. I recently had the muffler replaced.
    D. Whenever I shift gears, I hear a strange grinding sound.
    E. The odometer reads 174,286 miles.

Items that logically support the point: _____   _____   _____

4–6. ***Point:*** There are several reasons why women stay in abusive relationships.

    A. In some places, abused women can go to shelters when leaving an abusive relationship.
    B. Women are often economically dependent on their abusive partners.
    C. Abusive people must learn healthier ways of dealing with anger and frustration.
    D. Women fear that if they leave, their abusers will track them down and injure or even kill them.
    E. Some women with violent partners blame themselves for the abuse, instead of blaming their partners.

Items that logically support the point: _____   _____   _____

7–9. ***Point:*** There are several ways to tell an alligator from a crocodile.

    A. Alligators and crocodiles have stones and pebbles in their stomachs which help them grind up food.
    B. Both alligators and crocodiles lay eggs.
    C. In general, alligators have shorter snouts than crocodiles.
    D. When an alligator's jaws are closed, only the upper teeth can be seen.
    E. You can see a large bottom tooth on each side when a crocodile's jaws are closed.

Items that logically support the point: _____   _____   _____

(Continues on next page)

B. (10.) Below is a point followed by three items of information. Put a check (✓) next to the **one** item that logically supports the point.

Point: My grandmother is lonely.

_____ A. She has cooked the entire Thanksgiving dinner for fifteen people for more than twenty years. She never complains about it, and, in fact, she seems to enjoy doing it.

_____ B. Most of her friends have retired and moved away. She has a hard time getting out and meeting new people because of her poor eyesight. Usually, she just sits at home and listens to the radio.

_____ C. Even when it's raining, she spends an hour in her garden every day. She has memorized the names of at least 200 plants and flowers. She even talks to her flowers to help them grow.

THE BASICS OF ARGUMENT: Mastery Test 4

A. (1–8.) In each of the following groups, one statement is the point, and the other statements are support for the point. Identify each point with a **P** and each statement of support with an **S**.

Group 1

_____ A. A common dream involves taking a test you haven't prepared for.

_____ B. Many people dream about being in public only half dressed.

_____ C. Many people dream of falling from a great height and trying to wake up before they hit the ground.

_____ D. Certain themes appear in many people's dreams.

Group 2

_____ A. Drunk drivers are thrown violently from vehicles because they often do not wear seat belts.

_____ B. Drunk drivers do not realize how fast they are going and get into accidents at high speeds.

_____ C. Intoxicated victims bleed more heavily because of alcohol in the bloodstream.

_____ D. Drunk driving accidents are the most deadly.

B. (9.) Below is a point followed by three items of information. Put a check (✓) next to the **one** item that logically supports the point.

Point: Nelson is unfriendly.

_____ A. His family moved a lot as he was growing up. He went to four different schools during high school. As soon as he made new friends, he often had to leave them behind.

_____ B. He shows no interest in relationships. Even though he gets invited to parties and other get-togethers, he rarely shows up. He never smiles or makes an effort to start a conversation with anyone.

_____ C. He volunteers at the local pet shelter and cares for abandoned cats and dogs. He has adopted several of the animals he's cared for. Some of his best friends are stray animals.

(Continues on next page)

C. (10.) For the group below, read the three items of supporting evidence. Then put a check (✓) next to the point that is most logically supported by that evidence.

> ### Support:
> - Tickets to a movie theater cost more than renting a movie.
> - Long lines and too few parking spaces can be problems at a theater.
> - Rude people at a movie cough, laugh, or talk loudly.
>
> **Point:** Which of the following conclusions is best supported by all the evidence above?
>
> _____ A. Wide-screen televisions are becoming more popular.
>
> _____ B. Many theaters give a choice of 10 or more movies to see.
>
> _____ C. Watching a movie at home is better than going to the theater.
>
> _____ D. Watching a movie at home is one of life's great pleasures.

THE BASICS OF ARGUMENT: Mastery Test 5

Each point is followed by three statements that provide logical support and two that do not. In the spaces, write the letters of the three logical statements of support.

1–3. *Point:* The use of grades in school should be abolished.

    A. Students would learn for the sake of learning—not for the sake of grades.

    B. Teachers would have more time to spend on lesson planning.

    C. Some students may not be motivated without grades.

    D. The use of grades dates back to the 1500s.

    E. Grades don't always accurately measure a student's knowledge.

Items that logically support the point: _____ _____ _____

4–6. *Point:* Elephants are very intelligent animals.

    A. For years, hunters shot elephants to obtain the ivory from their tusks.

    B. Like chimps, elephants can recognize their reflections in mirrors.

    C. Elephants tear off branches of trees to use as fly swatters.

    D. Elephants have been seen keeping vigil over their dead companions.

    E. An elephant can live as long as sixty-five years.

Items that logically support the point: _____ _____ _____

7–9. *Point:* The great baseball player Roberto Clemente was a kind man.

    A. Roberto Clemente led the National League in batting average four times.

    B. Roberto Clemente often visited hospitalized children while traveling with his team, the Pittsburgh Pirates.

    C. In the off-season, Clemente spent much of his time involved in charity work.

    D. In 1972, Roberto Clemente was voted into the Major League Baseball Hall of Fame.

    E. Roberto Clemente died in a plane crash while taking relief supplies to earthquake victims in Nicaragua.

Items that logically support the point: _____ _____ _____

(Continues on next page)

B. (10.) For the group below, read the three items of supporting evidence. Then put a check (✓) next to the point that is most logically supported by that evidence.

Support:

• Medical advances such as vaccines and organ transplants have saved the lives of countless people.

• Pollution caused by cars and factories harms us and our environment.

• Sophisticated guns and bombs have killed millions of people in the 20th century alone.

Point: Which of the following conclusions is best supported by all the evidence above?

_____ A. Pollution is the biggest threat to human health today.

_____ B. Wars should be outlawed.

_____ C. Breakthroughs in science and technology have both helped us and harmed us.

_____ D. The future promises to bring new medical breakthroughs.

THE BASICS OF ARGUMENT: Mastery Test 6

A. (1–4.) In the following group, one statement is the point, and the other statements are support for the point. Identify each point with a **P** and each statement of support with an **S**.

_____ A. It is rude and distracting to use a cell phone while attending a concert or seeing a movie.

_____ B. Driving a car while using a cell phone is dangerous.

_____ C. There are times when cell phones should not be used.

_____ D. A student who uses a cell phone in class is not learning anything and is distracting others.

B. (5–7.) The point below is followed by three statements that provide logical support and two that do not. In the spaces, write the letters of the **three** logical statements of support.

Point: I am not the world's greatest housekeeper.

A. Piles of junk mail cover my desk and coffee table.

B. I would like to have my kitchen remodeled.

C. The inside of my refrigerator looks like an out-of-control biology experiment.

D. My house was built in 1951.

E. I only wash dishes when I run out of clean ones.

Items that logically support the point: _____   _____   _____

C. (8–10.) For each of the following groups, read the three items of supporting evidence. Then put a check (✓) next to the point that is most logically supported by that evidence.

Group 1

Support:

• Bats eat thousands of insects in an hour.

• Bats spread pollen to flowers and plants, which can then reproduce.

• Bats produce valuable fertilizer.

(Continues on next page)

Point: Which of the following conclusions is best supported by all the evidence on the previous page?

_____ A. Many people are frightened by bats.

_____ B. Some bats feed on animal or human blood.

_____ C. Researchers still have a lot to learn about bats.

_____ D. Bats are helpful to both plants and humans.

Group 2

Support:

• People who need new organs can get organ transplants.

• The polio vaccine has made getting polio almost unheard of.

• There are more effective ways to fight cancer.

Point: Which of the following conclusions is best supported by all the evidence above?

_____ A. The cost of medical care has skyrocketed.

_____ B. Young children are required to get certain vaccines.

_____ C. Unfortunately, not everyone can afford adequate medical care.

_____ D. Medical knowledge has greatly increased in the past century.

Group 3

Support:

• In the 1960s and 1970s, when murder rates were lower than today, the death penalty was hardly ever used.

• Today, the states that use the death penalty most also have the highest murder rates.

• Each death sentence costs taxpayers hundreds of thousands of dollars in appeals and lawyer's fees.

Point: Which of the following conclusions is best supported by all the evidence above?

_____ A. More criminals should receive the death sentence.

_____ B. Executions cost more than they are worth.

_____ C. Some states need to find ways to lower their murder rates.

_____ D. The death penalty costs too much and doesn't work.

Part III

FIVE READING SELECTIONS

1

Learning to Read: The Marvel Kretzmann Story
Mary Sherry

Preview

Here is a true story about a person with a learning disability—she was unable to read for almost twenty years. Being good at math, she was passed on from one grade to the next. Although she was able to get a good job after high school, her problems with reading made life difficult. Eventually, she decided it was better to face her disability and conquer it. This is Marvel Kretzmann's success story.

Words to Watch

poised (18): calm and confident
self-esteem (19): confidence
brush-up (21): review
IQ (22): abbreviation for "intelligence quotient," one measure of intelligence
memos (26): short written reminders
thesaurus (26): a book of synonyms
illiterate (30): unable to read or write
floored (31): shocked

1   Imagine a world where you can't read the street signs. You have to find your way by using only landmarks. When you see a sign or road map, you can't understand it, even though it is written in your own language. And when people give you oral directions, you cannot write quickly enough to take useful notes.

In this world, getting around isn't 2 your only challenge. You must struggle to read directions on packages of cake

mixes and cleaning products. Figuring out the doses of over-the-counter medicines actually gives you a headache. You keep faulty products rather than return them to the store because you cannot fill out a refund slip. The only jobs you dare apply for are those that do not require any reading or writing.

3   This was Marvel Kretzmann's world for almost twenty years. It was a very small world because she feared getting lost if she went beyond her place of work, familiar stores, and well-known routes to friends' and family's homes. She lived in daily fear that she would be asked to fill out a form or write something down for someone. Her world was a terrifying place.

4   Marvel's greatest fear of all was being found out. What if people *knew*

that she could barely read and couldn't write at all?

5   Marvel was in the fifth grade when it became clear to her that she was far behind her classmates in reading and writing, and that she would never be able to catch up.

6   "I remember hearing giggles in the classroom as soon as I was called on to read out loud. The kids knew what was going to happen, and so did I. Any word with an "s" sound in it was sure to make me stumble. As I hesitated, my teacher would say the words for me, over and over, urging me to repeat after her. But all I could hear was the laughing in the background.

7   "Finally, the teacher would give up and say, 'We'll move on.' Even though I felt relief, I also felt embarrassed. I was pulled out of class for extra work, but by that time—as I realize now—it was too late. I was already labeled by classmates and teachers as 'slow.'

8   "But I was pretty good in math. This helped me get passed from grade to grade. It also helped me to hide how serious my problem was from my parents. I didn't want to bring the problem to their attention. As a ten-year-old, I was more interested in having fun than working hard on reading and writing."

9   Marvel had two close friends who accepted her for what she was, and is today: kind, generous, and a lot of fun. They would take notes for her and coach her through courses, and they helped cover her disability.

10   But those friends couldn't be with her all the time. Marvel recalls how in the large junior and senior high schools she attended, classmates soon caught on to her problem when the teacher asked

students to take turns reading out loud. "Come on! Hurry up! She can't read!" she heard kids saying under their breath. Soon, rather than calling on students in order, up and down rows, teachers would skip around the class. That way, they wouldn't have to call on Marvel.

11 "In high school I learned to avoid classes that had writing assignments and heavy reading. I took the easiest courses I could. I kept quiet and tried not to be noticed. I never volunteered in class. I earned the reputation of being a 'good' child. So many classes had multiple-choice tests that I usually could guess and get by. In fact, I remember one time when I was the only one in my class to get an A on an exam. I just did what I always did with those tests I couldn't understand. I went down the pages and marked this one or that one, guessing all the way!"

12 Marvel's ability to manage her life got better and better. She received her high-school diploma and enrolled in a technical school where she was trained as a dental assistant. A tutor helped her get through her classes. After finishing the program, she found a job. She liked being a dental assistant and discovered she was good at it. In this job she was safe! She didn't have to write or read instructions to do her work.

13 Life outside of the dental office was another matter. Things she bought, such as appliances and other household items, came with instruction manuals. Expert at sewing, Marvel bought a fairly complicated sewing machine. "I thought I was going to lose my mind threading it and adjusting the tension. There were instructions in the manual, but they might as well have been in a foreign language."

14 "When I bought a computer, I practically burned out the phone lines dialing everyone I thought might be able to help me. I called the computer salesperson, friends, my sister, and 1-800-SOS-APPL day and night. I simply couldn't read the manual well enough to understand the computer's most basic uses. I would call and nervously ask, 'Why is this thing beeping at me? What did I do?' I needed to be walked though each disaster so I could keep on going."

15 The opportunities—and pitfalls— of the adult world seemed endless, requiring new and more complicated adjustments. Marvel wanted a checking account. Getting one was easy, because the bank officer simply asked her questions and filled out the forms. Marvel discovered, though, that writing out checks was stressful, especially when she had to do it in public. She developed a system of filling in store names on the checks at home or in the car before shopping—just so she wouldn't have to struggle in front of a clerk. Since spelling out "eleven" and "twelve" was always troubling, Marvel simply avoided writing checks for those amounts. As she shopped, she ran totals of her purchases in her head. Then she bought additional items or put some back on the shelves, just so the bill would be at least thirteen dollars or less than eleven.

16 Marvel's husband knew she had difficulty reading and writing, but he had no idea just how much difficulty. He knew she had never been an "A" student, but he realized that she could manage things. For example, she addressed their wedding invitations from carefully printed lists. She wrote

a form letter for her thank-you notes. Whenever a gift arrived, she copied that letter, simply filling in the blank for whatever the gift was. She had a "system," and it worked.

17   But sometimes she got caught. A few years ago Marvel won a radio contest sponsored by an insurance company. The prize was a free luncheon for all the people in her office at a restaurant of Marvel's choice. She stopped by a popular spot to check it out, thinking it would be a nice place to treat her fellow workers. A restaurant employee asked her to write down the name and address of the business so she could send a menu to Marvel's office. Marvel couldn't remember how to spell "Chicago"—the name of the street where her office is located. "I just blocked," she said. "I see 'Chicago' written out many times every day, but at that moment I froze. I turned and walked out—feeling defeated by such a simple thing as spelling 'Chicago.' I arranged to have the luncheon somewhere else."

18   Marvel Kretzmann tells about her struggle almost as though she were talking about someone else. She is upbeat, self-confident, poised°, open, and very friendly. Now in her late thirties, she realizes that difficulty reading and writing is a fairly wide-spread problem. "There are a lot of us out there," she says. "There are people who are afraid to travel because they can't read signs. Some won't apply for work because they can't fill out a job application. Others pretend they have left their glasses at home so they can take a form to someone who will read it to them. What is sad, though, is that many people assume people like us are lazy because we won't write things down in front of them. Sometimes when they see us struggle, they think we simply don't concentrate, or worse, that we are worthless. Once when I applied for a job, the person who interviewed me corrected my job application in front of me! Imagine how I felt! I told myself I couldn't work for that man, even if he offered me a job."

19   This remarkable openness and confidence did not come about by accident, nor did they come easily. After all, Marvel had spent years and years ashamed of her difficulty. How did she build her self-esteem° to such a high level? "I suddenly came face to face with the reality that life wasn't going to get any easier! In fact, it was getting harder." Marvel and her husband had bought a house, and she couldn't understand the legal papers involved. Furthermore, Marvel could see changes coming to the dental profession. One day her job would require taking notes and filling out forms. The thought also occurred to her that since she had no children, there might not be anyone around to take care of her when she was old or to cover for her when she needed help with reading or writing.

20   So Marvel decided to go back to school.

21   She found a community adult-education program that offered brush-up° classes in academic subjects. There she found just what she needed and received small-group and individual instruction. The work was intense. Teachers trained to deal with special learning needs drilled Marvel in phonics, spelling, and reading. Marvel

came to school right after work and usually got there before the teachers did. The staff members who arrived first always found Marvel deep in study in the hallway. Finally they gave her a key to the classroom!

22   According to her teacher, Marvel's difficulties are typical of learning-disabled students. Such a person has a normal or an above-normal IQ°, but for some reason is unable to process math or reading and spelling. Unfortunately, the problem often isn't identified until the student is well beyond the grade levels where it could and should be more easily addressed. The problem is made worse by youthful reactions, such as bad behavior—or, in Marvel's case, extremely good behavior—and covering up.

23   Marvel is unhappy that she slipped through the system. "As an adult I can see there were great gaps in communications between my teachers and my parents—and between me and my teachers, and me and my parents on this issue! I fell through all the cracks. My teachers failed to impress on my parents very early on that I was having trouble. I didn't want my parents to think I wasn't doing well. And I didn't have the guts to approach the teachers and say, 'Hey!' There were times I felt no teacher cared, as long as I didn't disrupt the class."

24   Marvel doesn't think much about the past, though. She is mastering her computer—by reading the instructions. She plans to attend school for another year or so to keep working on spelling and writing, "to keep it fresh." Since she went back to school five years ago, her reading has risen from the fourth-grade level to a level beyond high school.

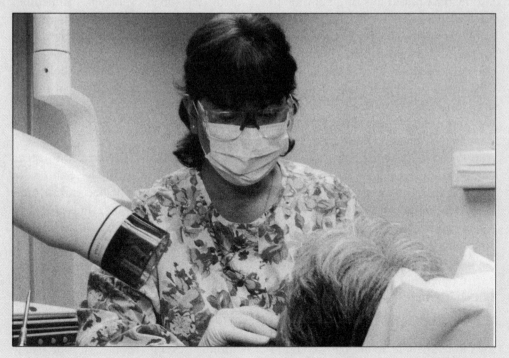

In her job as a dental assistant, Marvel works on a patient.

25   Writing is still a chore, and reading is work, too. "I'm never going to write a book," Marvel says. "I can't even read a three-hundred-page novel in a week—it might take me a month or two. But that doesn't bother me. I know I have made real progress when I can set small goals and achieve them. I was so proud one time when my husband asked me to read a manual to him while he worked on my car. He looked up from under the hood and told me I was doing a great job and that school was really helping me!

26   "Thankfully, I can write letters now and make lists for shopping and for packing for vacations. I can take notes and write memos° to others and know they will be understood. I have learned to use a lot of tools, including a dictionary, a thesaurus° (which I never knew existed), and a computer. I have also learned I need lots of quiet time to do these things well.

27   "I am able to read newspapers, magazine articles, and instruction manuals, even out loud if the situation calls for it. I feel more confident reading stories to my nieces and nephews and my friends' children. These are tremendous rewards—all the rewards I really need to make me feel good about going back to school.

28   "It hasn't been easy, despite all the wonderful help I've had. I will never forget my first night in a writing class after going to school for reading and phonics for a couple of years. The writing teacher gave the students fifteen minutes to write a short description about their favorite place. I could think of lots of places I would love to tell people about, but I couldn't write anything more than my name at the top of the paper! After the class my teacher and I agreed I wasn't ready for this yet. I didn't feel defeated, though. I returned to the phonics and reading group. A few months later I went back. By then I was able to handle the writing class. This class was another turning point for me. My teacher helped me break the silence. At last I was able to speak freely about the secret I had been hiding all these years. Now I feel good about writing something down and then reading it out loud."

29   Marvel believes it is important for her to encourage others who share her disability. "In the School for Adults, my teachers have asked me to reach out to people who they know have the same problem. I can spot them, too. They don't talk to anyone, they keep their heads buried in books they are struggling to read, and they never mix with the other students. Sometimes when I approach people who need a lot of help, they turn away because they don't want to admit how bad their problem is. I know how they feel. I also know that it is by taking many small steps that they will make progress. There are no miracles here, just a lot of hard work!

30   "Occasionally I am asked to speak to small groups about the School for Adults and how it helped me to meet this challenge. Sometimes I feel uncomfortable and feel I'm saying, in effect, 'Hi, I'm Marvel, and I am illiterate°!' However, I believe it is important to do what I can to get the word out to others who may benefit from the program.

31   "When school was ending last spring, several people in our study work group asked me if I would

Marvel is teaching herself how to use a Macintosh computer.

organize a little class for them during the summer. I was floored°! They were actually looking up to me! But I felt that if they thought I could help them, I knew they could push me, too, so why not? We met nearly every week and practiced reading out loud, and we worked on pronunciation and word definitions."

32   How far has Marvel come? Not long ago she was invited to serve on the Advisory Council for the School for Adults. She sits as an equal with the school's director, teacher representatives, business owners, and others from the community.

33   At one meeting, the secretary was absent, and the chairman asked if someone would take notes for her. Without a moment's thought, Marvel said, "I will."

And she did!   34

VOCABULARY QUESTIONS

A. Use context clues to help you decide on the best definition for each italicized word. Then, in the space provided, write the letter of your choice.

_____ 1. In the sentences below, the word *landmarks* (lănd′märks′) means
   A. street signs.
   B. familiar features of the surroundings.
   C. maps.
   D. written directions.

   "Imagine a world where you can't read the street signs. You have to find your way by using only landmarks." (Paragraph 1)

_____ 2. In the sentences below, the word *widespread* (wīd′sprĕd′) means
   A. unimportant.
   B. unusual.
   C. common.
   D. interesting.

   ". . . she realizes that difficulty reading and writing is a fairly widespread problem. 'There are a lot of us out there,' she says." (Paragraph 18)

_____ 3. In the sentences below, the word *intense* (ĭn-tĕns′) means
   A. rather easy.
   B. expensive.
   C. involving extreme effort.
   D. boring.

   "The work was intense. Teachers . . . drilled Marvel in phonics, spelling and reading. Marvel came to school right after work . . . ." (Paragraph 21)

_____ 4. In the sentence below, the word *disrupt* (dĭs-rŭpt′) means
   A. interfere with.
   B. attend.
   C. understand.
   D. skip.

   "There were times I felt no teacher cared, as long as I didn't disrupt the class." (Paragraph 23)

_____ 5. In the sentence below, the word *chore* (chôr) means
  A. fun activity.
  B. difficult task.
  C. mystery.
  D. surprise.

  "Writing is still a chore, and reading is work, too." (Paragraph 25)

B. Below are words, or forms of words, from "Words to Watch." Write in the one that best completes each sentence. Then write the letter of that word in the space provided.

A. brush-up	B. illiterate	C. memo
D. poised	E. self-esteem	

_____ 6. Although Marie was shy and giggly during her teens, she soon grew into a _____ and impressive young woman.

_____ 7. Before playing in the soccer game, Devon thought it wise to attend a _____ session on the rules.

_____ 8. The boss sent a _____ to all employees warning them that layoffs might soon occur.

_____ 9. Being able to figure out a complicated set of written directions is enough to boost anyone's _____.

_____ 10. If you are _____, it can be very difficult to get by in today's print-centered world.

READING COMPREHENSION QUESTIONS

Central Point and Main Ideas

_____ 1. Which sentence best expresses the central point of the selection?
  A. Learning disabilities of all types can be overcome with hard work.
  B. Marvel felt much shame and fear throughout her public-school education.
  C. Through hard work, Marvel gradually overcame her learning disability and the shame and fear it caused her.
  D. Students with learning disabilities should not have to attend the public schools in this country.

_____ 2. Which sentence best expresses the main idea of paragraph 12?

    A. The first sentence

    B. The second sentence

    C. The third sentence

    D. The last sentence

Supporting Details

_____ 3. The author states that in high school, she avoided classes that

    A. her close, helpful friends had not enrolled in.

    B. started early in the day.

    C. were too easy.

    D. had writing assignments and heavy reading.

_____ 4. According to one of Marvel's teachers, a typical learning-disabled student

    A. is poor at sports.

    B. has few talents.

    C. has an IQ of normal or above.

    D. has an IQ of normal or below.

_____ 5. Marvel is unhappy that she

    A. slipped through the public-school system.

    B. has never made the dean's list.

    C. is not paid more for her job as a dental assistant.

    D. never married.

Signal Words

_____ 6. In the sentence below, the words *such as* show a relationship of

    A. addition.

    B. contrast.

    C. time.

    D. illustration.

        "Things she bought, such as appliances and other household items, came with instruction manuals." (Paragraph 13)

_____ 7. In the sentences below, the word *but* shows a relationship of
   A. addition.
   B. time.
   C. contrast.
   D. illustration.

> "She had a 'system,' and it worked. But sometimes she got caught."
> (Paragraphs 16–17)

Inferences

_____ 8. Marvel's experience in the fifth grade suggests that
   A. children may not show sympathy toward other children with learning disabilities.
   B. elementary school teachers are quick to identify and help students who have trouble reading.
   C. the other students wanted to help Marvel learn to read better, but didn't know how.
   D. Marvel was not the only student in her class who had difficulty reading.

_____ 9. Paragraph 28 suggests that
   A. Marvel was not a very good student.
   B. Marvel did not allow short-term setbacks to keep her from learning to read and write.
   C. Marvel blamed her teacher for pushing her into a class she wasn't ready for.
   D. Marvel believed that the assignment to write about a favorite place was a silly one.

Argument

_____10. In the following group, one statement is the point, and the other statements are support for the point. Write the letter of the statement that is the **point** of the argument.
   A. People who are illiterate cannot read street signs or road maps.
   B. An inability to read limits a person's job opportunities.
   C. An inability to read makes it difficult for a person to function in today's world.
   D. Banking is difficult if one cannot read well enough to write checks.

MAPPING

Complete the map of this selection by filling in the letters of the missing major details, which are scrambled below. (Two of the items have already been filled in for you.)

Major Supporting Details Missing from the Diagram

A. Marvel learned to read at a level beyond high school.

B. Marvel decided to go back to school.

C. Marvel was in the fifth grade when she realized that she was far behind her classmates.

D. Marvel was trained as a dental assistant and then got a job as one.

E. Marvel avoided high-school classes that involved writing assignments and heavy reading.

F. Marvel was asked to join the Advisory Council of the School for Adults.

G. Marvel had two friends who took notes for her and coached her through her courses.

Central point: Marvel Kretzmann worked hard and eventually gained self-confidence and learned to read and write.

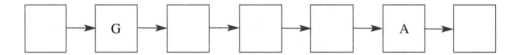

Marvel relaxes with some leisure reading.

DISCUSSION QUESTIONS

1. Should Kretzmann have been "passed from grade to grade" because she was good at math? Or should she have been made to stay at a lower grade until her reading and writing skills got better?

2. Do you know someone who has a learning disability? If so, how does that person's experience compare with Kretzmann's?

3. Kretzmann says that sometimes when she is called upon to speak to small groups, she feels "uncomfortable." Why do you think this is? Would you feel uncomfortable speaking to a group? Explain.

Note: Writing assignments for this selection appear on page 564.

Check Your Performance   LEARNING TO READ

Activity	Number Right	Points	Total
VOCABULARY			
Part A (5 items)	_____	× 10 =	_____
Part B (5 items)	_____	× 10 =	_____
		SCORE =	_____%
READING COMPREHENSION			
Central Point and Main Ideas (2 items)	_____	× 8 =	_____
Supporting Details (3 items)	_____	× 8 =	_____
Signal Words (2 items)	_____	× 8 =	_____
Inferences (2 items)	_____	× 8 =	_____
Argument (1 item)	_____	× 8 =	_____
Mapping (5 items)	_____	× 4 =	_____
		SCORE =	_____%

FINAL SCORES: Vocabulary _____%   **Comprehension** _____%

Enter your final scores into the **Reading Performance Chart: Five Reading Selections** on the inside back cover.

2

The Fist, the Clay, and the Rock
Donald Holland

Preview

Often the best teachers are the ones who challenge us the most. In this selection, the author describes such a teacher. Mr. Gery inspires his students to work hard using nothing more than his fist, a lump of clay, a rock—and a few well-chosen words. Read how he does it.

Words to Watch

mound (1): pile
squashed (6): flattened
wand (11): magic stick
segued (17): moved smoothly onto another subject
vivid (17): strikingly bright; true to life

1   The best teacher I ever had was Mr. Gery, who taught twelfth grade English. He started his class with us by placing on the front desk a large mound° of clay and, next to it, a rock about the size of a tennis ball. That got our attention quickly, and the class quieted down and waited for him to talk.

2   Mr. Gery looked at us and smiled and said, "If there were a pill I could give you that would help you learn, and help you want to learn, I would pass it out right now. But there is no magic pill. Everything is up to you."

3   Then Mr. Gery held up his fist and kind of shook it at us. Some of us looked at each other. What's going on?

we all thought. Mr. Gery continued: "I'd like you to imagine something for me. Imagine that my fist is the real world—not the sheltered world of this school but the real world. Imagine that my fist is everything that can happen to you out in the real world."

4   Then he reached down and pointed to the ball of clay and also the rock. He said, "Now imagine that you're either this lump of clay or the rock. Got that?" He smiled at us, and we waited to see what he was going to do.

5   He went on, "Let's say you're this ball of clay, and you're just sitting around minding your own business and then out of nowhere here's what happens." He made a fist again and he smashed his fist into the ball of clay, which quickly turned into a half-flattened lump.

6   He looked at us, still smiling. "If the real world comes along and takes a swing at you, you're likely to get squashed°. And you know what? The real world *will* come along and take a swing at you. You're going to take some heavy hits. Maybe you already have taken some heavy hits. Chances are that there are more down the road. So if you don't want to get squashed, you're better off if you're not a piece of clay.

7   "Now let's say you're the rock and the real world comes along and takes a swing at you. What will happen if I smash my fist into this rock?" The answer was obvious. Nothing would happen to the rock. It would take the blow and not be changed.

8   He continued, "So what would you like to be, people, the clay or the rock? And what's my point? What am I trying to say to you?"

9   Someone raised a hand and said, "We should all be rocks. It's bad news to be clay." And some of us laughed, though a bit uneasily.

10   Mr. Gery went on. "OK, you all want to be rocks, don't you? Now my question is, 'How do you get to be a rock? How do you make yourself strong, like the rock, so that you won't be crushed and beaten up even if you take a lot of hits?'"

11   We didn't have an answer right away, and he went on, "You know I can't be a fairy godmother. I can't pull out a wand° and say, 'Thanks for wanting to be a rock. I hereby wave my wand and make you a rock.' That's not the way life works. The only way to become a rock is to go out and make yourself a rock.

12   "Imagine you're a fighter getting ready for a match. You go to the gym, and maybe when you start you're flabby. Your whole body is flab, and it's soft like the clay. To make your body hard like a rock, you've got to train.

13   "Now if you want to train and become hard like the rock, I can help you. You need to develop skills, and you need to acquire knowledge. Skills will make you strong, and knowledge is power. It's my job to help you with language skills. I'll help you train to become a better reader. I'll help you train to be a better writer. But you know, I'm just a trainer. I can't make you be a fighter.

14   "All I can do is tell you that you need to make yourself a fighter. You need to become a rock. Because you don't want to be flabby when the real world comes along and takes a crack at you. Don't spend the semester just being Mr. Cool Man or Ms. Designer

Jeans or Mr. or Ms. Sex Symbol of the class. Be someone. *Be someone.*"

15   He then smashed that wad of clay one more time, and the thud of his fist broke the silence and then created more silence. He sure had our total attention.

16   "At the end of the semester, some of you are going to leave here, and you're still going to be clay. You're going to be the kind of person that life can smush around, and that's sad. But some of you, maybe a lot of you, are going to be rocks. I want you to be a rock. Go for it. And when this comes"—and he held up his fist— "you'll be ready."

17   And then Mr. Gery segued° into talking about the course. But his demonstration stayed with most of us.

And as the semester unfolded, he would call back his vivid° images. When someone would not hand in a paper and make a lame excuse, he would say, "Whatever you say, Mr. Clay" or "Whatever you say, Ms. Clay." Or if someone would forget a book, or not study for a test, or not do a reading assignment, he would say, "Of course, Mr. Clay." Sometimes we would get into it also and call out, "Hey, Clayman."

18   Mr. Gery worked us very hard, but he was not a mean person. We all knew he was a kind man who wanted us to become strong. It was obvious he wanted us to do well. By the end of the semester, he had to call very few of us Mr. or Ms. Clay.

VOCABULARY QUESTIONS

A. Use context clues to help you decide on the best definition for each italicized word. Then, in the space provided, write the letter of your choice.

_____ 1. In the sentences below, the word *sheltered* (shĕl′tərd) means
   A. protected.
   B. boring.
   C. exciting.
   D. dangerous.

   "I'd like you to imagine something for me. Imagine that my fist is the real world—not the sheltered world of this school but the real world." (Paragraph 3)

_____ 2. In the sentences below, the word *obvious* (ŏb′vē-əs) means
   A. difficult.
   B. nearby.
   C. easy to see.
   D. confusing.

   "'What will happen if I smash my fist into this rock?' The answer was obvious. Nothing would happen to the rock. It would take the blow and not be changed." (Paragraph 7)

_____ 3. In the sentences below, the word *acquire* (ə-kwīr′) means
   A. to ignore.
   B. to prevent.
   C. to question.
   D. to get by one's own efforts.

   " 'Now if you want to train and become hard like the rock, I can help you. You need to develop skills, and you need to acquire knowledge.' " (Paragraph 13)

_____ 4. In the sentence below, the word *wad* (wŏd) means
   A. mountain.
   B. lump.
   C. coating.
   D. package.

   "He then smashed that wad of clay one more time, and the thud of his fist broke the silence and then created more silence." (Paragraph 15)

_____ 5. In the sentence below, the word *lame* (lām) means
   A. reasonable.
   B. weak.
   C. amusing.
   D. crippled.

   "When someone would not hand in a paper and make a lame excuse, he would say, 'Whatever you say, Mr. Clay' or 'Whatever you say, Ms. Clay.' " (Paragraph 17)

B. Below are words, or forms of words, from "Words to Watch." Write in the one that best completes each sentence. Then write the letter of that word in the space provided.

A. mound	B. segued	C. squashed
D. vivid	E. wand	

_____ 6. After talking for a few minutes about the Bush presidency, our teacher _____ into a discussion of the 2008 presidential election.

_____ 7. The power-hungry dictator _____ all those who challenged his brutal policies.

_____ 8. The fairy tale was so _____ that when the child fell asleep, he dreamed about a house made of gingerbread and candy.

_____ 9. My little sister Vivien enjoys wearing a "magic" cape and waving her ruler around as if it were a _____.

_____ 10. That _____ of dirty clothes near the foot of the stairs really needs to be put in the washing machine.

READING COMPREHENSION QUESTIONS

Central Point and Main Ideas

_____ 1. Which sentence best expresses the central point of the selection?
   A. Mr. Gery forced his students to become fighters.
   B. Mr. Gery was good at getting his students to pay attention.
   C. Mr. Gery was not a mean person.
   D. Mr. Gery challenged his students to learn skills that would help them in the real world.

_____ 2. Which sentence best expresses the main idea of paragraph 6?
   A. Mr. Gery is in a bad mood.
   B. Mr. Gery wants his students to prepare themselves to take some heavy hits.
   C. Mr. Gery realizes that some of his students have already taken some heavy hits.
   D. Mr. Gery doesn't want his students to be like rocks.

Supporting Details

_____ 3. Mr. Gery compares his fist to
   A. a rock.
   B. a lump of clay.
   C. a magic wand.
   D. everything that can happen out in the real world.

_____ 4. Mr. Gery's job is to
   A. provide his students with shelter.
   B. help his students with language skills.
   C. train his students to become boxers.
   D. teach his students social studies.

Signal Words

_____ 5. Most of the signal words used in this selection are
   A. time words.
   B. addition words.

_____ 6. In the sentences below, the word *because* shows a relationship of
   A. contrast.   C. time.
   B. illustration.   D. cause and effect.

   "'You need to become a rock. Because you don't want to be flabby when the real world comes along and takes a crack at you.'" (Paragraph 14)

_____ 7. The relationship of the second sentence below to the first sentence is one of
   A. contrast.   C. time.
   B. cause and effect.   D. addition.

   "'You're going to be the kind of person that life can smush around, and that's sad. But some of you, maybe a lot of you, are going to be rocks.'" (Paragraph 16)

Inferences

_____ 8. This selection suggests that
   A. students who have poor reading and writing skills are going to be unprepared for real life.
   B. reading and writing skills are less important than being physically tough when facing the real world.
   C. using a computer is the best way to develop good reading and writing skills.
   D. good teachers can make their students into fighters.

_____ 9. We can infer that the author
   A. was one of the students that Mr. Gery called "Mr. Clay" at the end of the semester.
   B. became a English teacher like Mr. Gery.
   C. thought Mr. Gery should have been harder on the class.
   D. learned a great deal from Mr. Gery.

Argument

_____ 10. Write the letter of the statement that is the **point** of the following argument. The other statements are support for that point.
   A. Mr. Gery challenged his students to become like rocks, not like clay.
   B. An inspiring teacher, Mr. Gery worked hard to motivate his students to succeed.
   C. Mr. Gery told his students that he'd help them train to become better readers and writers and then worked them hard.
   D. Mr. Gery teased his students when they didn't complete their assignments by calling them "Mr. Clay" or "Ms. Clay."

OUTLINING

Prepare an outline of "The Fist, the Clay, and the Rock" by filling in the missing details, which are scrambled in the list below.

- By the end of the semester, Mr. Gery has to call very few of his students "Mr. or Ms. Clay."
- Mr. Gery smashes his fist into the lump of clay.
- Mr. Gery calls students who don't do their work "Mr. Clay" or "Ms. Clay."
- Mr. Gery holds up his fist and asks the class to imagine that it is the real world.

Central point: Mr. Gery captures his students' attention and helps them to acquire language skills that that they will need in the real world.

1. Mr. Gery places a mound of clay and a rock on his front desk.

2. _____

   _____

3. Mr. Gery asks the class to imagine that they're the lump of clay.

4. _____

   _____

5. Mr. Gery asks his class to imagine what would happen if he smashed his fist into the rock.

6. Mr. Gery tells the class that if they want to train and become hard like a rock, he can help them develop their language skills.

7. _____

   _____

8. _____

   _____

DISCUSSION QUESTIONS

1. What does Mr. Gery mean by saying that fists will come along in life? Give an example of a time you experienced a fist, or someone you know experienced a fist.

2. What does Mr. Gery mean by "clay"? What is the danger of being clay?

3. What does Mr. Gery mean by "rock"? How does a person become a rock?

Note: Writing assignments for this selection appear on page 565.

Check Your Performance   **THE FIST, THE CLAY, AND THE ROCK**

Activity	Number Right	Points	Total
VOCABULARY			
Part A (5 items)	_____	× 10 =	_____
Part B (5 items)	_____	× 10 =	_____
		SCORE =	_____ %
READING COMPREHENSION			
Central Point and Main Ideas (2 items)	_____	× 8 =	_____
Supporting Details (2 items)	_____	× 8 =	_____
Signal Words (3 items)	_____	× 8 =	_____
Inferences (2 items)	_____	× 8 =	_____
Argument (1 item)	_____	× 8 =	_____
Outlining (4 items)	_____	× 5 =	_____
		SCORE =	_____ %

FINAL SCORES: Vocabulary _____ %   **Comprehension** _____ %

Enter your final scores into the **Reading Performance Chart: Five Reading Selections** on the inside back cover.

3

Joe Davis
Beth Johnson

Preview

From age 14 on, Joe Davis followed a path that led him closer and closer to self-destruction. He lived in a world of drugs, guns, and easy money. In this world, he had no respect for himself or sympathy for others. Today Joe Davis is, in every way, a new man. Here is the story of how Joe saved his own life.

Words to Watch

option (6): choice
shown the ropes (10): shown how things should be done
rehabilitated (10): brought back to a good and healthy life
stickup man (11): someone who robs with a gun
went downhill (13): got worse
encountered (20): met
unruly (26): disorderly
hushed (27): quiet

1   Joe Davis was the coolest fourteen-year-old he'd ever seen.

2   He went to school when he felt like it. He hung out with a wild crowd. He started drinking some wine, smoking some marijuana. "Nobody could tell me anything," he says today. "I thought the sun rose and set on me." There were rules at home, and Joe didn't do rules. So he moved in with his grandmother.

Joe Davis was the coolest sixteen-year-old he'd ever seen.   3

4   Joe's parents gave up on his schooling and signed him out of the tenth grade. Joe went to work in his dad's body shop, but that didn't last long. There were rules there, too, and Joe didn't do rules. By the time he was in his mid-teens, Joe was taking pills that got him high and even using cocaine. He was also smoking marijuana all the time and drinking booze all the time.

5   Joe Davis was the coolest twenty-five-year-old he'd ever seen.

6   He was living with a woman almost twice his age. The situation wasn't great, but she paid the bills, and certainly Joe couldn't. He had his habit to support, which by now had grown to include heroin. Sometimes he'd work at a low-level job, if someone else found it for him. He might work long enough to get a paycheck and then spend it all at once. Other times he'd be caught stealing and get fired first. A more challenging job was not an option°, even if he had bothered to look for one. He couldn't put words together to form a sentence, unless the sentence was about drugs. Filling out an application was difficult. He wasn't a strong reader. He couldn't do much with numbers. Since his drug habit had to be paid for, he started to steal. First he stole from his parents, then from his sister. Then he stole from the families of people he knew. But eventually the people he knew wouldn't let him in their houses, since they knew he'd steal from them. So he got a gun and began holding people up. He chose elderly people and others who weren't likely to fight back. The holdups kept him in drug money, but things at home were getting worse. His woman's teenage daughter was getting out of line. Joe decided it was up to him to discipline her. The girl didn't like it. She told her boyfriend. One day, the boyfriend called Joe out of the house.

7   BANG.

8   Joe Davis was in the street, his nose in the dirt. His mind was still cloudy from his most recent high, but he knew something was terribly wrong with his legs. He couldn't move them; he couldn't even feel them. His mother came out of her nearby house and ran to him. As he heard her screams, he imagined what she was seeing. Her oldest child, her first baby, her bright boy who could have been and done anything, was lying in the gutter, a junkie with a .22 caliber bullet lodged in his spine.

9   The next time Joe's head cleared, he was in a hospital bed, blinking up at his parents as they stared helplessly at him. The doctors had done all they could; Joe would live, to everyone's surprise. But he was a paraplegic—paralyzed from his chest down. It was done. It was over. It was written in stone. He would not walk again. He would not be able to control his bladder or bowels. He would not be able to make love as he had before. He would not be able to hold people up, then hurry away.

10   Joe spent the next eight months being moved between several Philadelphia hospitals, where he was shown the ropes° of life as a paraplegic. Officially he was being "rehabilitated°"—restored to a productive life. There was just one problem: Joe. "To be *re*habilitated, you must have been *habilitated* first," he says today. "That wasn't me." During his stay in the hospitals, he found ways to get high every day.

11   Finally Joe was released from the hospital. He returned in his wheelchair to the house he'd been living in when he was shot. He needed someone to take care of him, and his woman friend was still willing. His drug habit was as strong as ever, but his days as a stickup man° were over. So he started selling drugs. Business was good. The money came in fast, and his own drug use accelerated even faster.

12   A wheelchair-bound junkie doesn't pay much attention to his health and cleanliness. Eventually Joe developed his first bedsore: a deep, rotting wound that ate into his flesh, overwhelming him with its foul odor. He was admitted to Magee Rehabilitation Hospital, where he spent six months on his stomach while the ghastly wound slowly healed. Again, he spent his time in the hospital using drugs. This time his drug use did not go unnoticed. Soon before he was scheduled to be discharged, hospital officials kicked him out. He returned to his friend's house and his business. But then police raided the house. They took the drugs, they took the money, they took the guns.

13   "I really went downhill° then," says Joe. With no drugs and no money to get drugs, life held little meaning. He began fighting with the woman he was living with. "When you're in the state I was in, you don't know how to be nice to anybody," he says. Finally she kicked him out of the house. When his parents took him in, Joe did a little selling from their house, trying to keep it low-key, out of sight, so they wouldn't notice. He laughs at the notion today. "I thought I could control junkies and tell them 'Business only during certain hours.'" Joe got high when his monthly Social Security check came, high when he'd make a

purchase for someone else and get a little something for himself, high when a visitor would share drugs with him. It wasn't much of a life. "There I was," he says, "a junkie with no education, no job, no friends, no means of supporting myself. And now I had a spinal cord injury."

14 Then came October 25, 1988. Joe had just filled a prescription for pills to control his muscle spasms. Three hundred of the powerful muscle relaxants were there for the taking. He swallowed them all.

15 "It wasn't the spinal cord injury that did it," he says. "It was the addiction."

16 Joe tried hard to die, but it didn't work. A sister heard him choking and called for help. He was rushed to the hospital, where he lay in a coma for four days.

17 Joe has trouble finding the words to describe what happened next.

18 "I had . . . a spiritual awakening, for lack of any better term," he says. "My soul had been cleansed. I knew my life could be better. And from that day to this, I have chosen not to get high."

19 Drugs, he says, "are not even a temptation. That life is a thing that happened to someone else."

20 Joe knew he wanted to turn himself around, but he needed help in knowing where to start. He enrolled in Magee Hospital's vocational rehabilitation program. For six weeks, he immersed himself in discussions, tests, and exercises to help him determine the kind of work he might be suited for. The day he finished the rehab program, a nurse at Magee told him about a receptionist's job in the spinal cord injury unit at Thomas Jefferson Hospital. He went straight to the hospital and met Lorraine Buchanan, coordinator of the unit. "I told her where I was and where I wanted to go," Joe says. "I told her, 'If you give me a job, I will never disappoint you. I'll quit first if I see I can't live up to it.'" She gave him the job. The wheelchair-bound junkie, the man who'd never been able to hold a job, the drug-dependent stickup man who "couldn't put two words together to make a sentence" was now the first face, the first voice that patients encountered° when they entered the spinal cord unit. "I'd never talked to people like that," says Joe, shaking his head. "I had absolutely no background. But Lorraine and the others, they taught me to speak. Taught me to greet people. Taught me to handle the phone." How did he do in his role as a receptionist? A huge smile breaks across Joe's face as he answers, "I did excellent."

21 Soon, his personal life also took a very positive turn. A month after Joe started his job, he was riding a city bus to work. A woman recovering from knee surgery was in another seat. The two smiled, but didn't speak.

22 A week later, Joe spotted the woman again. The bus driver sensed something was going on and encouraged Joe to approach her. Her name was Terri. She was a receptionist in a law office. On their first date, Joe laid his cards on the table. He told her his story. He also told her he was looking to get married. "That about scared her away," Joe recalls. "She said she wasn't interested in marriage. I asked, 'Well, suppose you did meet someone you cared about, who cared about you, and

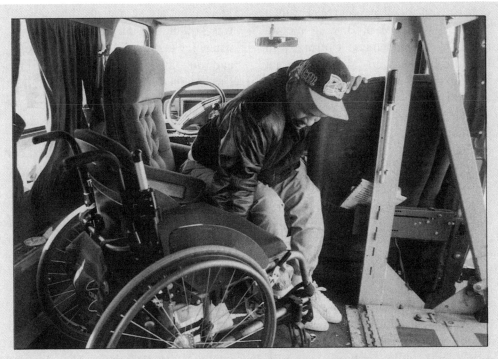

Joe Davis needs a specially equipped van for his wheelchair.

treated you well. Would you still be opposed to the idea of marriage?' She said no, she would consider it then. I said, 'Well, that's all I ask.'"

23   Four months later, as the two sat over dinner in a restaurant, Joe handed Terri a box tied with a ribbon. Inside was a smaller box. Then a smaller box, and a smaller one still. Ten boxes in all. Inside the smallest was an engagement ring. After another six months, the two were married in the law office where Terri works. Since then, she has been Joe's constant source of support, encouragement, and love.

24   After Joe had started work at Jefferson Hospital, he talked with his supervisor, Lorraine, about his dreams of moving on to something bigger, more challenging. She encouraged him to try college. He had taken and passed the high-school general equivalency diploma (GED) exam years before, almost as a joke, when he was recovering from his bedsores at Magee. Now he enrolled in a university mathematics course. He didn't do well. "I wasn't ready," Joe says. "I'd been out of school seventeen years. I dropped out." Before he could let discouragement overwhelm him, he enrolled at Community College of Philadelphia (CCP), where he signed up for basic math and English courses. He worked hard, sharpening study skills he had never developed in his earlier school days. Next he took courses toward an associate's degree in mental health and social services, along with a certificate in addiction studies. Five years later, he graduated from CCP, the first member of his family

ever to earn a college degree. He then went on to receive a B.A. in mental health from Hahnemann University in Philadelphia and an M.A. in social work from the University of Pennsylvania.

25   Today, Joe is employed as a psychotherapist at John F. Kennedy Mental Health Center in Philadelphia. He does his best to get into the "real world," the world of young men and women immersed in drugs, violence, and crime, Whenever he can, he speaks at local schools through a program called Think First. He tells young people about his drug use, his shooting, and his experience with paralysis.

26   At a presentation at a disciplinary school outside of Philadelphia, Joe gazes with quiet authority at the unruly° crowd of teenagers. He begins to speak, telling them about speedballs and guns, fast money and bedsores, even about the leg bag that collects his urine. At first, the kids snort with laughter at his honesty. When they laugh, he waits patiently, then goes on. Gradually the room grows quieter as Joe tells them of his life and then asks them about theirs. "What's important to you? What are your goals?" he says. "I was still in school at age 40 because when I was young, I chose the dead-end route many of you are on. But now I'm doing what I have to do to get where I want to go. What are *you* doing?"

27   He tells them more, about broken dreams, about his parents' grief, about the former friends who turned away from him when he was no longer a source of drugs. He tells them of the continuing struggle to regain the trust of people he once abused. He tells them about the desire that consumes him now, the desire to make his community a better place to live. His wish is that no young man or woman should have to walk the path he's walked in order to value the precious gift of life. The teenagers are now silent. They look at this broad-shouldered black man in his wheelchair, his head and beard close-shaven, a gold ring in his ear. His hushed° words settle among them like gentle drops of cleansing rain. "What are *you* doing? Where are *you* going?" he asks them. "Think about it. Think about me."

28   Joe Davis is the coolest fifty-one-year-old you've ever seen.

VOCABULARY QUESTIONS

A. Use context clues to help you decide on the best definition for each italicized word. Then, in the space provided, write the letter of your choice.

_____ 1. In the sentence below, the word *restored* (rĭ-stôrd′) means
   A. held back.
   B. punished.
   C. brought back.
   D. paid.

   "Officially he was being 'rehabilitated'—restored to a productive life." (Paragraph 10)

_____ 2. In the sentence below, the word *accelerated* (ăk-sĕl′ə-rā′td) means
   A. increased.
   B. grew less serious.
   C. disappeared.
   D. helped.

   "The money came in fast, and his own drug use had accelerated even faster." (Paragraph 11)

_____ 3. In the sentence below, the word *ghastly* (găst′lē) means
   A. quite small.
   B. very unpleasant.
   C. caused by a gun.
   D. illegal.

   " . . . he spent six months on his stomach while the ghastly wound slowly healed." (Paragraph 12)

_____ 4. In the sentences below, the word *notion* (nō′shən) means
   A. idea.
   B. joke.
   C. answer.
   D. cause.

   "When his parents took him in, Joe did a little selling from their house, trying to keep it low-key, out of sight, so they wouldn't notice. He laughs at that notion today. 'I thought I could control junkies . . . '" (Paragraph 13)

_____ 5. In the sentence below, the word *immersed* (ĭ-mûrst') means
  A. totally ignored.
  B. greatly angered.
  C. deeply involved.
  D. often harmed.

  "For six weeks, he immersed himself in discussions, tests, and exercises to help him determine the kind of work he might be suited for." (Paragraph 20)

B. Below are words, or forms of words, from "Words to Watch." Write in the one that best completes each sentence. Then write the letter of that word in the space provided.

A. encountered	B. hushed	C. option
D. rehabilitated	E. unruly	

_____ 6. Mr. Barris is the meanest-looking man I've ever _____ — his frown could freeze chili peppers.

_____ 7. Aunt Sarah _____ the children when their loud play made it hard for her to follow the soap opera.

_____ 8. His dad gave Carlos the _____ of working part-time in his store as a way of paying some of his college expenses.

_____ 9. The audience grew _____ after it was announced that the singer they had come to see had been delayed in traffic.

_____ 10. You'd never know it to look at him now, but the company president is a _____ drug addict.

READING COMPREHENSION QUESTIONS

Central Point and Main Ideas

_____ 1. Which sentence best expresses the central point of the selection?
  A. Most people cannot improve their lives after turning to drugs and crime.
  B. Joe Davis overcame a life of drugs and crime and a disability to lead a rich, productive life.
  C. The rules of Joe Davis's parents caused him to leave home and continue a life of drugs and crime.
  D. Joe Davis's friends turned away from him once they learned he was no longer a source of drugs.

_____ 2. A main idea may cover more than one paragraph. Which sentence best expresses the main idea of paragraphs 21–23?

    A. The first sentence of paragraph 21

    B. The second sentence of paragraph 21

    C. The first sentence of paragraph 22

    D. The first sentence of paragraph 23

_____ 3. Which sentence best expresses the main idea of paragraph 24?

    A. It was difficult for Joe to do college work after being out of school for so many years.

    B. Lorraine Buchanan encouraged Joe to go to college.

    C. Joe overcame a lack of academic preparation and eventually earned two college degrees and a master's degree.

    D. If students would stay in high school and work hard, they would not have to go to the trouble of getting a high-school GED.

Supporting Details

_____ 4. Joe Davis quit high school

    A. when he was 14.

    B. when he got a good job at a hospital.

    C. when he was in the tenth grade.

    D. after he was shot.

_____ 5. Joe tried to kill himself by

    A. swallowing muscle-relaxant pills.

    B. shooting himself.

    C. overdosing on heroin.

    D. not eating or drinking.

_____ 6. According to the selection, Joe first met his wife

    A. in the hospital, where she was a nurse.

    B. on a city bus, where they were both passengers.

    C. on the job, where she was also a receptionist.

    D. at the Community College of Philadelphia, where she was also a student.

_____ 7. Joe decided to stop using drugs

    A. when he met his future wife.

    B. right after he was shot.

    C. when he awoke from a suicide attempt.

    D. when he was hired as a receptionist.

Signal Words

_____ 8. The word *because* in the sentence below shows a relationship of

    A. addition.

    B. time.

    C. contrast.

    D. cause and effect.

> "'I was still in school at age 40 because when I was young, I chose the dead-end route many of you are on....'" (Paragraph 26)

Inferences

_____ 9. The author implies that

    A. Joe became a drug addict because his parents didn't care what happened to him.

    B. Joe tried hard to succeed in high school, but failed.

    C. Joe's parents turned their backs on him after he was shot.

    D. Joe was not as "cool" as he thought he was.

_____ 10. We can conclude that

    A. even longtime drug addicts like Joe can be rehabilitated.

    B. some drug addicts can never be rehabilitated.

    C. it's nearly impossible to go back to school after seventeen years.

    D. there are few resources available for people who are recovering from addiction.

OUTLINING

Following is an outline showing major events in Joe Davis's life. Complete the outline by filling in the missing events, which are scrambled in the list below.

- Joe takes a job as a receptionist.
- Joe gets shot, which paralyzes him from the chest down.
- Joe starts selling drugs.
- Joe earns a college degree.

Central point: From a life of drugs and crime, Joe Davis turned his life around in several positive ways.

   1. Joe leaves school.

2. _____

3. _____

4. Joe tries to commit suicide.

5. Joe gives up drugs and goes into a vocational rehabilitation program.

6. _____

7. Joe gets married.

8. _____

9. Joe earns a master's degree in social work.

10. Joe speaks to young people, using his experiences to inspire them to improve their lives.

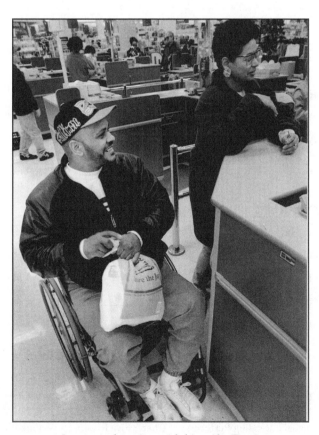

Joe goes shopping with his wife, Terri.

DISCUSSION QUESTIONS

1. What do you think was the main turning point in Joe's life, and why do you think it happened?

2. Why do you think the students Joe spoke to laughed at him as he tried to share his honest thoughts? Why did they become quieter as he continued to speak of his life? What effect do you think his presentation had on these students?

3. Joe wants young people to learn the lessons he did without having to go through what he went through. What lessons have you learned in your life that you would like to pass on to others?

Note: Writing assignments for this selection appear on pages 565–566.

Check Your Performance   **JOE DAVIS**

Activity	*Number Right*	*Points*	*Total*
VOCABULARY			
Part A (5 items)	_____	× 10 =	_____
Part B (5 items)	_____	× 10 =	_____
		SCORE =	_____ %
READING COMPREHENSION			
Central Point and Main Ideas (3 items)	_____	× 8 =	_____
Supporting Details (4 items)	_____	× 8 =	_____
Signal Words (1 item)	_____	× 8 =	_____
Inferences (2 items)	_____	× 8 =	_____
Outlining (4 items)	_____	× 5 =	_____
		SCORE =	_____ %

FINAL SCORES: Vocabulary _____ %   **Comprehension** _____ %

Enter your final scores into the **Reading Performance Chart: Five Reading Selections** on the inside back cover.

4

Rosa: A Success Story
Edward Patrick

Preview

This selection is about a woman who meets and conquers more obstacles than many of us have experienced. She does not spend a lot of time asking why these things are happening to her. She does what she must to make her life and the lives of her family better.

Words to Watch

plantation (1): large estate where crops are grown
to no avail (3): without success
trek (3): journey
conveyed (5): communicated
sentiment (5): attitude; thought
halting (6): awkward
preoccupied (16): not paying attention
collect myself (20): gain control of myself
immigrants (21): people who come to another country to live
oppressive (21): harsh and cruel

1   Up until six months before I met her, life for Rosa Perez had been easy. Her father was a wealthy plantation° owner in Nicaragua. Her family owned a large house with all the comforts of the rich. Then came the same type of violent civil war that has torn apart so many Latin American countries.

Rosa's father was identified as a 2 supporter of the rebel cause, and the family's plantation was seized. During the government takeover, her father was shot and killed. Her mother gathered as much money as she could and fled with Rosa and her two younger brothers, Adolpho and Roberto. Their destination was the United States. Rosa's mother knew a man who knew another man who could get them through Mexico and across the U.S. border into Texas or California. There was nothing to worry about, they were told. Rosa believed it.

3   At first, things went smoothly. Twelve others joined Rosa and her family. The group had no trouble getting into and across Mexico. But just before they were to cross into California, the guide said he could go no further. Another man would take them the rest of the way. Rosa's mother protested, but to no avail°. They were led across by a man they did not know. He told them to follow his every command. They must move quickly and silently or risk detection by the Border Patrol. It was a difficult trek°. It was dark. It was cold. Coyotes howled in what all hoped was the distance. Everyone was tired and frightened.

4   And then came the bright lights. Just as they were about to cross into the United States, the U.S. Border Patrol sighted the group and turned on the searchlights on their jeeps to track them down. People scattered. Rosa held on to Adolpho and Roberto. She looked back, but could not see her mother. *"Aqui. Ahora,"* commanded their guide, appropriately called a "coyote." Rosa blindly followed him and watched as the lights of the jeeps sped after the others. They waited quietly for what seemed like hours. Only when he was convinced that it was safe did their guide take the five

who had managed to follow him the rest of the way. Eleven were not with them, including Rosa's mother.

5   I first saw Rosa three months after this nightmare. I arrived at my office early, wanting only to unwind from the freeway drive before my first class. I was annoyed that someone was standing outside my office so early in the morning. But I spoke with her, and soon realized that there was something special about this slender, dark-skinned young woman with large, expressive brown eyes. I didn't know then what it was I saw in her. Now I know she revealed an inner strength, conveyed° an unspoken sentiment° that "You don't know me, but you can believe in me." It was magnetic. I knew that I would help in any way I could.

6   Rosa wanted to learn English. She wanted to do more than just get by. Her halting° English told me she could manage that already. She wanted to be able to read and write the language so that she could provide for her brothers. My basic reading class had been recommended to her. She asked what materials she could get to work on even before the semester started.

7   Eager students are always easy to work with, and Rosa proved to be one of my most enthusiastic students. She kept me on my toes and constantly challenged me. She prodded me to provide more information, additional examples, better explanations. If I used a word she didn't understand, she would stop me. She would make me explain it so that she and her classmates could grasp its meaning. If we looked for the main idea in a paragraph and her answer was different from mine, she insisted on giving the

reasons why she felt she was right and I was wrong. I could not always convince her that my answer was better. But I always encouraged her to ask questions whenever she was confused or unconvinced. While I looked forward to the class she had enrolled in, I was always exhausted at its conclusion.

8 Rosa advanced from our basic reading classes to the more difficult study-skills class. Then she moved through the writing classes offered in the department. She enrolled in the Early Childhood Program at the college. This is a program which can lead to certification as a child-care worker. Her progress in her classes was reflected in a steady stream of A's and B's.

9 It took Rosa three years to complete the course work that she needed to graduate. I made plans to attend the graduation ceremonies where she would receive her associate's degree. She insisted that I attend the graduation party her friend Alberto was giving. I said I would be honored to go.

10 The ceremony was typical, with boring speeches made for proud accomplishments. The party was something special. Rosa had come a long way in the three years I had known her. She had made some wonderful friends, had found a decent job at a nearby day-care center, and had provided a good home for her two brothers.

11 Rosa greeted me when I arrived. She wanted for me to meet everyone there, and she hinted at a surprise she had for me.

12 "Dr. P, may I present to you my brothers, Adolpho and Roberto."

13 *"Mucho gusto,"* I began.

14 "Right," said the smaller brother. "Call me Bobby. Nice to meet you, Doc. Say, you don't mind if me and Al 'mingle,' if you know what I mean?"

15 I knew, and encouraged them to meet and greet the others—especially the young ladies—in attendance.

16 I commented on how quickly her brothers had adjusted to life in the States. But Rosa seemed preoccupied°. I was puzzled until I saw that we were walking toward an older woman who had the same brown expressive eyes as Rosa. It was her mother.

17 Rosa's mother had been captured by the Border Patrol and deported to Nicaragua. There, she was jailed. Rosa had been depressed over her mother's lack of the freedom she and her brothers enjoyed. She had located her mother and worked for close to three years to get her released. I don't know all the details of how she did it. Perhaps it is best that I don't. At the moment I met her, I did not care at all about how she had attained freedom. I was just overjoyed that she was here with her children.

18 Rosa entered San Diego State University, some ninety miles away. As often happens with students who move on, I saw very little of her. She was working hard toward a degree in early childhood education, I was on leave for a year, and our paths rarely crossed. Sometimes she would come by right before Christmas or at the end of a school year. She stopped by the office again yesterday, with a purpose. She carried two babies in her arms. The six-month-old twins were hers. Their huge, expressive brown eyes told me that before she did.

19   Rosa proudly told what had happened in the five years since her graduation. I listened enthusiastically as she told me about receiving a Bachelor of Arts degree, marrying Alberto, opening a child-care center with him, and giving birth to their twin sons. "And now," she said, "I want to tell you their names. This is Alberto," she said, nodding toward the larger twin. Then she looked toward the smaller one. Her eyes smiled as much as her mouth. "He is smaller, yes, but obviously more intellectual. That is why we have chosen to name him Eduardo."

20   I gasped, tried to collect myself°, but did not succeed. Rosa came to the rescue. She calmly explained that Alberto and she decided to name the baby after me because of all the help I had provided when she needed it most. I babbled something about how proud I felt. It was true.

21   Some people, I know, object to the flow of immigrants° entering our country. They forget that almost all of us came to America from somewhere else. We need every so often to be reminded of success stories like Rosa's. Like many of our ancestors, she fled an oppressive° government and poor economic conditions. She then worked hard to create a new life for herself. Hers is not an uncommon story. Many others like her have come to enrich their lives, and they have enriched our country as well.

VOCABULARY QUESTIONS

A. Use context clues to help you decide on the best definition for each italicized word. Then, in the space provided, write the letter of your choice.

_____ 1. In the sentence below, the word *detection* (dǐ-tĕk′shən) means
A. assistance.
B. trust.
C. discovery.
D. noise.

"They must move quickly and silently or risk detection by the Border Patrol." (Paragraph 3)

_____ 2. In the sentences below, the word *prodded* (prŏd′ĭd) means
A. urged.
B. left.
C. prevented.
D. paid.

"[Rosa] kept me on my toes and constantly challenged me. She prodded me to provide more information, additional examples, better explanations." (Paragraph 7)

_____ 3. In the sentence below, the word _reflected_ (rĭ-flĕk′tĭd) means
   A. shown.
   B. given.
   C. sent back.
   D. hidden.

   "Her progress in her classes was reflected in a steady stream of A's and B's." (Paragraph 8)

_____ 4. In the sentence below, the word _deported_ (dĭ-pôr′tĭd) means
   A. saved.
   B. forced out of the country.
   C. kept in the country.
   D. invited.

   "Rosa's mother had been captured by the Border Patrol and deported to Nicaragua." (Paragraph 17)

_____ 5. In the sentence below, the word _attained_ (ə-tānd′) means
   A. remembered.
   B. lost.
   C. gained.
   D. defined.

   "At the moment I met her, I did not care at all about how she had attained freedom." (Paragraph 17)

B. Below are words, or forms of words, from "Words to Watch." Write in the one that best completes each sentence. Then write the letter of that word in the space provided.

A. conveyed	B. halting	C. oppressive
D. sentiment	E. trek	

_____ 6. In _____ English, Luis explained to me that he still had a number of relatives living in Mexico.

_____ 7. On September 11, 2001, TV and radio stations around the country _____ the shocking news that terrorists had attacked the World Trade Center.

_____ 8. When Mr. Davis retired from teaching after thirty-five years, many expressed the _____ that he had been one of the best teachers the school had ever had.

_____ 9. On our cross-country _____, we started in Brooklyn, New York and ended in Los Angeles.

_____10. Forcing a prisoner to stand for hours in a freezing room is an _____ form of punishment.

READING COMPREHENSION QUESTIONS

Central Point and Main Ideas

_____ 1. Which sentence best expresses the central point of the selection?
   A. Civil wars have destroyed many countries.
   B. Like many immigrants fleeing oppression, Rosa came to America and made a successful life for herself.
   C. Rosa finally brought her mother to the United States.
   D. Rosa married and gave birth to twins, one of whom she named after the author.

_____ 2. Which sentence best expresses the main idea of paragraph 4?
   A. The Border Patrol turned on bright searchlights.
   B. Rosa held on to her brothers but couldn't see her mother.
   C. Rosa and her brothers successfully crossed the border, but her mother was among those who did not.
   D. The guide was very cautious and waited for what seemed like hours until it seemed safe to continue crossing the border.

_____ 3. Which sentence best expresses the main idea of paragraphs 6–7?
   A. Rosa's English was not very good.
   B. Rosa always asked questions in class.
   C. The author encouraged Rosa to ask questions.
   D. Rosa was a very eager student.

Supporting Details

_____ 4. Of the group escaping Nicaragua with Rosa and her family,
   A. all members began a new life in the United States.
   B. the majority began a new life the United States.
   C. only five managed to begin a new life in the United States.
   D. only Rosa succeeded in reaching the United States.

_____ 5. According to the reading, Rosa's
   A. brothers had trouble adjusting to life in the United States.
   B. mother spent about three years in a Nicaraguan jail.
   C. graduation party was boring.
   D. husband has never met the author.

Signal Words

_____ 6. The relationship between the two sentences below is one of
   A. addition.
   B. time.
   C. example.
   D. contrast.

> "Rosa advanced from our basic reading classes to the more difficult study-skills class. Then she moved through the writing classes offered in the department." (Paragraph 8)

Inferences

_____ 7. We can conclude that Rosa
   A. came to America because she knew that she wouldn't have to work hard once she got here.
   B. believed that she would become rich in America.
   C. worked extremely hard to make a home for herself and her family in America.
   D. forgot about her mother in Nicaragua once she was in America.

_____ 8. We can infer that the author
   A. wishes that other immigrants were more like Rosa.
   B. thinks that there are too many immigrants flooding into America.
   C. realizes that he will probably never see Rosa again.
   D. deeply admires Rosa and other immigrants who are like her.

_____ 9. The selection suggests that
- A. it is easy to enter the United States illegally.
- B. it is risky to enter the United States illegally.
- C. few people attempt to enter the United States illegally.
- D. most of the people who attempt to enter the United States illegally are caught and sent back to where they came from.

Argument

_____ 10. Write the letter of the statement that is the **point** of the following argument. The other statements are support for that point.
- A. After fleeing war-torn Nicaragua, Rosa worked hard to become successful in America.
- B. Although Rosa could barely speak English when she began her college coursework, she received her associate's degree in three years.
- C. Rosa entered San Diego State University and received a Bachelor of Arts degree in early childhood education.
- D. Together with her husband, Alberto, Rosa opened a child-care center.

MAPPING

Major events of the selection are scrambled in the list below. Write them in their correct order in the diagram on the next page.

- Rosa's education toward a bachelor's degree
- Rosa's escape to the United States
- Rosa's education toward an associate's degree
- Rosa's visit with the twins
- Rosa's graduation and party

Central point: Rosa is an example of the many immigrants who come to America to escape oppression and then work hard to become productive citizens.

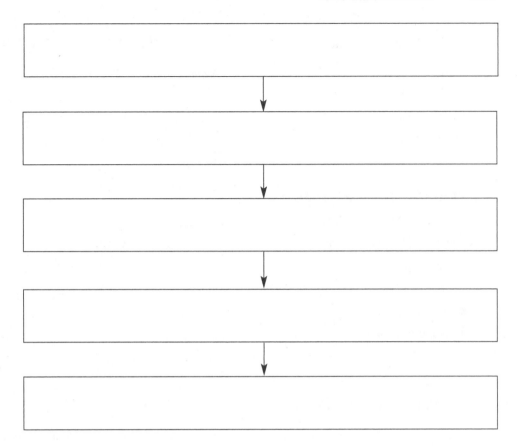

DISCUSSION QUESTIONS

1. As Rosa reached the border of the United States, she realized that her mother was not with her. Should she have looked for her mother, or was she right to cross into the United States when she did?

2. How did Rosa's education prepare her for her career? What interests and qualities would lead someone to want to work in childcare?

3. The author writes that "we need . . . to be reminded of success stories like Rosa's." Why do you think he feels this way? What can we learn from reading Rosa's story?

Note: Writing assignments for this selection appear on pages 566–567.

Check Your Performance   ROSA: A SUCCESS STORY

Activity	Number Right	Points	Total

VOCABULARY

Part A (5 items) _____   × 10 = _____

Part B (5 items) _____   × 10 = _____

SCORE = _____%

READING COMPREHENSION

Central Point and Main Ideas (3 items)   _____   × 8 = _____

Supporting Details (2 items)   _____   × 8 = _____

Signal Words (1 item)   _____   × 8 = _____

Inferences (3 items)   _____   × 8 = _____

Argument (1 item)   _____   × 8 = _____

Mapping (5 items)   _____   × 4 = _____

SCORE = _____%

FINAL SCORES: Vocabulary _____%   **Comprehension** _____%

Enter your final scores into the **Reading Performance Chart: Five Reading Selections** on the inside back cover.

5

The Lady, or the Tiger?
Frank R. Stockton

Preview

Imagine you are given this choice: The true love of your life will either die a violent death or leave you for another lover. Which would you choose? This is the decision that the princess in the following story has to make.

Words to Watch

smooth (1): pleasing; polished
opposite (3): located directly across from
choir (5): group of singers, often in a church
gasped (10): sharply drew in breath
charm (11): the power to delight or attract
pausing (15): stopping
Paradise (20): Heaven

1   Once upon a time, there was a king. He had smooth°, polite manners. But in his heart, he was very cruel.

2   He was a man who had many ideas, and he was sure that all of his ideas were right. One of his ideas was that he should give his people entertainment that would educate them. Here his cruel nature truly showed through. He loved the stories of the Roman soldiers of old. Those soldiers would fight with wild beasts to entertain an audience. The king decided to have contests like these, but to give them a special twist. Here is what the king did.

3   The king built a huge stadium, where all the people of the kingdom

could sit and look down on a sand-covered floor. When a man was accused of a crime, the king announced a holiday. Everyone came to the stadium. The king sat on his special golden throne. The accused man entered the stadium. After bowing respectfully to the king, the man walked to the opposite° side of the stadium. There he faced two doors, exactly alike. While all the people watched, the man opened one of those doors.

4   What was behind the door? That depended upon the man's choice. Behind one of them was something terrible. It was an angry, hungry tiger, who instantly jumped on the unlucky man and tore him to pieces. The watching crowd would scream in horror, then walk home sadly.

5   But if he opened the other door, he found a beautiful lady. Then he and she were immediately married as a reward for his innocence. It didn't matter if the man was already married. It didn't matter if he happened to be in love with someone else. The king had to have his way. The stadium was quickly filled with a priest, a choir°, and dancing girls playing golden horns. With the sound of happy bells ringing, the marriage was performed and the prisoner was freed. Children threw flowers on his path as he led his new bride home.

6   To the king, this seemed perfectly fair. The accused man made his own choice. When he opened a door, he did not know whether he was about to be eaten or married. What happened was entirely up to him!

7   Now, the king had a beautiful daughter who was as stubborn and strong-willed as he was. The young princess had fallen in love with a handsome young man, who loved her as well. Unfortunately, her young lover was a commoner, not highly-born enough to marry the daughter of a king. So the two met in secret.

8   Of course, the king learned about his daughter's lover. He had the young man arrested and thrown into prison. The date for the trial was set. The king had his servants search for the biggest and most ferocious tiger available. Other servants were sent out to find the most beautiful young lady in the kingdom.

9   Naturally, everyone was interested in this case. And everyone knew that the young man was guilty. He proudly admitted that he had loved the princess, and she admitted it as well. But the king didn't care about that. He still wanted his trial.

10   On the day of the trial, everyone came to the stadium. The king and his court took their places. Everything was ready. When the prisoner walked in, everyone gasped° and whispered admiring comments. He was so tall, so young, and so handsome! How sad that he might be dead soon!

11   The young man walked to the center of the stadium. He turned to bow to the king. But he did not look at the king. Instead, he looked straight at the princess, who sat beside her father. Are you surprised that she was there? You should not be. Remember that she was as strong-willed as her father. From the moment that her lover was arrested, she had thought of nothing but her plan. She had used all her money, charm°, and power to learn the secret of the two doors. And she had succeeded. She

knew which door hid the tiger, and which door hid the lady.

12 Not only that—she knew who the lady was. It was the prettiest of all the young girls in her own court, and the princess hated her. She imagined she had seen the girl and her lover look admiringly at one another. Once or twice she had seen the two speaking. With all the passion in her strong-willed heart, the princess hated the girl.

13 The moment her lover saw the princess's face, he saw that she knew the secret of the doors. With a flash of his eyes, he asked the silent question: "Which door?"

14 Her arm lay over the railing in front of her. She raised her hand ever so slightly and made a tiny, quick movement to the right. No one but her lover saw her. Every other eye in the place was fastened on him.

15 He turned and walked quickly to the doors. All the people held their breath. Without pausing° for a moment, he threw open the door on the right.

16 And now comes the point of the story. Did the tiger come out of the door? Or did the lady?

17 The more you think about the question, the harder it is to answer.

Think about it, reader. Try to put yourself in the shoes of this jealous, strong-willed woman. She had lost her man. But who should have him now?

18 During the past weeks, she had often imagined him opening the door to the tiger. What horror! What cruel, sharp teeth!

19 But even more often, she had imagined him opening the other door. She burned with anger as she imagined him rushing to meet the woman, his eyes sparkling with joy. She imagined the happy shouts and laughter from the crowd, the ringing of the wedding bells, and her own scream of misery lost in all that noise.

20 Wouldn't it be better for him to die, and to go wait for her in Paradise°?

21 And yet . . . that awful tiger! Those screams! That blood!

22 She had thought about her decision for many days and many nights. But she had finally made her choice. She knew for sure that when the moment came, she would move her hand to the right.

23 It is not an easy question, and I am not wise enough to answer it. And so I leave it to you to decide. Which came out of that door—the lady, or the tiger?

VOCABULARY QUESTIONS

A. Use context clues to help you decide on the best definition for each italicized word. Then, in the space provided, write the letter of your choice.

_____ 1. In the sentences below, the word *commoner* (kŏm'ə-nər) means
   A. prince.
   B. robber.
   C. rich man.
   D. ordinary person.

   "The young princess had fallen in love with a handsome young man, who loved her as well. Unfortunately, her young lover was a commoner, not highly-born enough to marry the daughter of a king." (Paragraph 7)

_____ 2. In the sentence below, the word *ferocious* (fĕ-rō'shəs) means
   A. pitiful.
   B. violent.
   C. weak with hunger.
   D. greedy.

   "The king had his servants search for the biggest and most ferocious tiger available." (Paragraph 8)

_____ 3. In the sentences below, the word *admiring* (ăd-mīr'ĭng) means
   A. nasty.
   B. intelligent.
   C. approving.
   D. silly.

   "When the prisoner walked in, everyone gasped and whispered admiring comments. He was so tall, so young, and so handsome! How sad that he might be dead soon!" (Paragraph 10)

_____ 4. In the sentences below, the word *passion* (păsh'ən) means
   A. love.
   B. respect.
   C. powerful emotion.
   D. interest.

   "She imagined she had seen the girl and her lover look admiringly at one another. Once or twice she had seen the two speaking. With all the passion in her strong-willed heart, the princess hated the girl." (Paragraph 12)

_____ 5. In the sentences below, the word *misery* (mĭz'ə-rē) means
    A. surprise.
    B. pleasure.
    C. sickness.
    D. deep unhappiness.

> "She burned with anger as she imagined him rushing to meet the woman, his eyes sparkling with joy. She imagined the happy shouts and laughter from the crowd, the ringing of the wedding bells, and her own scream of misery lost in all that noise." (Paragraph 19)

B. Below are words, or forms of words, from "Words to Watch." Write in the one that best completes each sentence. Then write the letter of that word in the space provided.

A. charm	B. gasp	C. opposite
D. pause	E. smoothly	

_____ 6. The salesman spoke to us so _____ that we almost bought a product we had no use for.

_____ 7. Sam _____ed when he saw that that his five-year-old nephew was playing with matches.

_____ 8. Beverly tried to _____ a co-worker into switching work shifts so she would be free to go to a party.

_____ 9. Every so often during the course of his talk, the speaker would _____ to take a drink of water.

_____10. In football, the two teams' goal posts stand at _____ ends of the field.

READING COMPREHENSION QUESTIONS

Central Point and Main Ideas

_____ 1. Which sentence best expresses the central point of the selection?
   A. A cruel king forces those accused of crimes to open one of two doors.
   B. A beautiful young princess falls in love with a commoner, but her father, the king, throws the young man into prison.
   C. A young princess decides whether to save her true love or see him torn apart by a tiger.
   D. The reader must decide whether a young princess will choose to let her lover marry another woman or see him torn apart by a tiger.

_____ 2. Which sentence best expresses the main idea of paragraph 12?
   A. The princess is jealous of a young girl in her own court.
   B. The princess has once seen the young girl and her lover look admiringly at one another.
   C. The princess knows that the young girl was the prettiest of all the young girls in her own court.
   D. Once or twice the princess has seen her lover speaking with the young girl.

Supporting Details

_____ 3. Which of his subjects does the king force to choose between the lady and the tiger?
   A. Known criminals.
   B. Men who had been accused of a crime.
   C. Unmarried men.
   D. Men who had spoken out against the king.

_____ 4. After entering the stadium, the young man immediately
   A. opens one of two doors.
   B. looks straight at the princess.
   C. begs the king for mercy.
   D. proudly admits to the king that he loves the princess.

Signal Words

_____ 5. In the excerpt below, the word *so* indicates a relationship of
   A. addition.
   B. time.
   C. cause and effect.
   D. contrast.

> "Unfortunately, her young lover was a commoner, not highly-born enough to marry the daughter of a king. So the two met in secret." (Paragraph 7)

_____ 6. The relationship between the two sentences below is one of
   A. cause and effect.
   B. comparison.
   C. illustration.
   D. contrast.

> "He proudly admitted that he had loved the princess, and she admitted it as well. But the king didn't care about that." (Paragraph 9)

_____ 7. In the sentences below, the word *when* indicates a relationship of
   A. addition.
   B. time.
   C. cause and effect.
   D. contrast.

> "Everything was ready. When the prisoner walked in, everyone gasped and whispered admiring comments." (Paragraph 10)

Inferences

_____ 8. The story suggests that the young man
   A. does not trust the princess.
   B. trusts the princess to save his life.
   C. has never really been in love with the princess.
   D. is a common criminal.

_____ 9. We can conclude that the king
   A. does not care about the happiness of his subjects.
   B. has a strong sense of right and wrong.
   C. loves his daughter very much.
   D. secretly hopes that the young man would choose the lady rather than the tiger.

Argument

_____ 10. Write the letter of the statement that is the **point** of the following argument. The other statements are support for that point.

    A. The king forces men to marry the ladies behind the door even if they are already married.

    B. The king throws his own daughter's lover in jail.

    C. The king does not care about the rights of others.

    D. The king orders unlucky men to be torn apart by tigers.

SUMMARIZING

Complete the following summary of "The Lady, or the Tiger?" by filling in each blank with one or more words.

A **summary** of a reading is a brief statement of its main ideas. The details in a summary follow the order of the original selection. That means the first answer can be found toward the beginning of the selection, and the later answers will be found further along in it. Fill in the answers after looking back at the story to find any you're not sure of.

Once upon a time, a cruel king built a huge stadium and forced any man who had been accused of a crime to open one of two doors. Behind one door was a beautiful lady, _____

_____

Behind the other door was a tiger who would tear the unlucky man to pieces.

Now, the king had a strong-willed daughter who had fallen in love with a young commoner. When the king found out that the two were seeing each other, he _____

_____

The date for the trial was set. While this was happening, the princess

_____

She also learned that the lady behind the door was to be the prettiest girl in her court. She had once imagined that _____

_____

She hated the girl.

On the day of her lover's trial, her lover bowed to the king, and then looked straight at the princess. He knew _____

_____

When the princess motioned to the right, the young man threw open that door. Did the tiger come out of the door? Or did the lady? It is up to the reader to decide.

DISCUSSION QUESTIONS

1. Do you think the tiger came out of the door, or the lady? Support your answer. If you were the princess, which door would you send your lover to?

2. The princess must choose between two strong feelings: love and jealousy. In your experience, which emotion is more powerful? Explain.

3. In this story, the princess must make an impossible choice in a "no-win" situation. Have you ever been faced with a difficult choice in which no matter what you decided, you would be unhappy? Explain.

Note: Writing assignments for this selection appear on page 567.

Check Your Performance   THE LADY, OR THE TIGER?

Activity	Number Right	Points	Total
VOCABULARY			
Part A (5 items)	_____	× 10 =	_____
Part B (5 items)	_____	× 10 =	_____
		SCORE =	_____%
READING COMPREHENSION			
Central Point and Main Ideas (2 items)	_____	× 8 =	_____
Supporting Details (2 items)	_____	× 8 =	_____
Signal Words (3 items)	_____	× 8 =	_____
Inferences (2 items)	_____	× 8 =	_____
Argument (1 item)	_____	× 8 =	_____
Summarizing (5 items)	_____	× 4 =	_____
		SCORE =	_____%

FINAL SCORES: Vocabulary _____% **Comprehension** _____%

Enter your final scores into the **Reading Performance Chart: Five Reading Selections** on the inside back cover.

Part IV

COMBINED-SKILLS TESTS

Following are twelve tests that cover many of the skills taught in Part II and reinforced in Part III of this book. Each test consists of a short reading passage followed by questions on any of the following: dictionary use, vocabulary in context, main ideas, supporting details, signal words, inferences, and argument.

SAMPLE ANSWER SHEET

Use the form below as a model answer sheet for the twelve combined-skills tests on the following pages.

Name _____

Section _____ Date _____

SCORE: (Number correct) _____ × 12.5 = _____%

COMBINED SKILLS: Test _____

1. _____

2. _____

3. _____

4. _____

5. _____

6. _____

7. _____

8. _____

COMBINED SKILLS: Test 1

Read the passage below. Then, in the space provided, write the letter of the best answer to each question that follows.

> [1]Many of us would probably pay huge amounts of money for everyday pleasures that are often taken for granted. [2]Imagine that you had 10 million dollars. [3]You would probably pay at least 2 million dollars to always have a guaranteed good night's sleep that would leave you feeling refreshed and great when you wake up in the morning. [4]To be forever free from pain (especially if you have had to deal with constant pain from headaches or an aching body), you would gladly part with 3 million. [5]To know that good friends would always be there for you, you might not hesitate to give up another 2 million dollars. [6]And in exchange for having satisfying work that you were good at and cared about and that paid you well, you would surrender your last 3 million.

_____ 1. In sentence 3, the word *guaranteed* means
   A. possible.
   B. necessary.
   C. sure.
   D. costly.

_____ 2. In sentence 5, the word *hesitate* means
   A. be slow to act.
   B. want.
   C. think.
   D. expect.

_____ 3. The sentence that best expresses the main idea of the passage is
   A. sentence 1.
   B. sentence 2.
   C. sentence 3.
   D. sentence 6.

_____ 4. According to the passage, satisfying work is work that
   A. pays huge amounts of money.
   B. you are good at, that you care about, and that pays you well.
   C. few other people are skillful enough to do.
   D. puts you in charge of many other people.

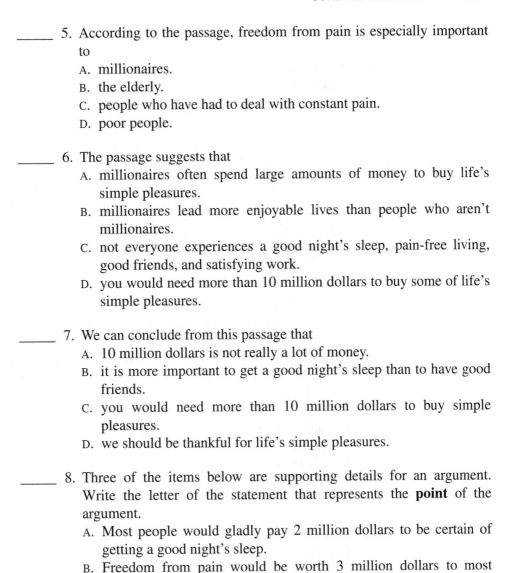

_____ 5. According to the passage, freedom from pain is especially important to
   A. millionaires.
   B. the elderly.
   C. people who have had to deal with constant pain.
   D. poor people.

_____ 6. The passage suggests that
   A. millionaires often spend large amounts of money to buy life's simple pleasures.
   B. millionaires lead more enjoyable lives than people who aren't millionaires.
   C. not everyone experiences a good night's sleep, pain-free living, good friends, and satisfying work.
   D. you would need more than 10 million dollars to buy some of life's simple pleasures.

_____ 7. We can conclude from this passage that
   A. 10 million dollars is not really a lot of money.
   B. it is more important to get a good night's sleep than to have good friends.
   C. you would need more than 10 million dollars to buy simple pleasures.
   D. we should be thankful for life's simple pleasures.

_____ 8. Three of the items below are supporting details for an argument. Write the letter of the statement that represents the **point** of the argument.
   A. Most people would gladly pay 2 million dollars to be certain of getting a good night's sleep.
   B. Freedom from pain would be worth 3 million dollars to most people.
   C. Most people would gladly pay millions to enjoy life's simple pleasures.
   D. To most people, having satisfying work would be worth 3 million dollars.

COMBINED SKILLS: Test 2

Read the passage below. Then, in the space provided, write the letter of the best answer to each question that follows.

¹In India, boys are valued as gifts from God. ²Girls, however, are considered at best a disappointment. ³Centuries of tradition determine that boys be given better treatment throughout life. ⁴In their parents' house they are, for instance, fed first so that they get the largest portions and choicest bits of food. ⁵In the recent past, strangling newborn girls was common in rural India, where there was not enough food to go around. ⁶Today, although the outright murder of girl babies may occur less often, female children are done away with in other ways. ⁷For instance, a baby girl who falls ill is often left untreated. ⁸On the other hand, her family would do anything possible to get medical care for their male children.

_____ 1. Which sentence best states the implied main idea of the selection?
  A. The way girls are treated has been improving in India.
  B. In India, boys have traditionally been favored over girls.
  C. In the past, newborn girls were sometimes strangled in rural India.
  D. Indian families do everything possible to get medical care for their male children.

_____ 2. According to the passage, the treatment of girls was worst in
  A. Indian cities.
  B. today's India.
  C. rural India.
  D. wealthy Indian families.

_____ 3. Indian parents display their preference for boys over girls by
  A. feeding their sons first.
  B. giving their sons the largest portions.
  C. giving their sons the choicest bits of food.
  D. all of the above.

_____ 4. The relationship of sentence 7 to sentence 6 is one of
  A. contrast.
  B. illustration.
  C. addition.
  D. time.

_____ 5. The relationship of sentence 8 to sentence 7 is one of
   A. contrast.
   B. time.
   C. cause and effect.
   D. illustration.

_____ 6. This passage suggests that in India
   A. girls have often been seen as an economic burden.
   B. many more girls are born than boys.
   C. parents were harshly punished for strangling newborn girls.
   D. there are far more adult males than females.

_____ 7. We can conclude from this passage that
   A. in India today, the economic position of women has greatly improved.
   B. most Indian parents do not want their sons to marry.
   C. India is a country with large numbers of poor people.
   D. even in India today, baby girls die more often than baby boys.

8. In the following group, one statement is the point, and the other three statements are support for the point. Identify the point with a **P** and each statement of support with an **S**.

   _____ A. In India, baby girls who fall ill are often left untreated, while parents will do anything possible to get medical care for their sons.

   _____ B. In India, boys are fed first and get the largest portions of food.

   _____ C. In India, boys are favored over girls.

   _____ D. In India, baby girls are sometimes strangled.

COMBINED SKILLS: Test 3

Read the passage below. Then, in the space provided, write the letter of the best answer to each question that follows.

[1]Traditionally, men preferred to be the only breadwinners in their families. [2]Men, however, have discovered several benefits to having a working wife. [3]First of all, of course, a working wife's income can raise her family's living standards. [4]Also, men with working wives are more free to try changing careers. [5]The woman's income can tide the family over economically during his career change. [6]Third, should a husband lose his job, some of the problems of unemployment are offset by his wife's earnings. [7]Among other things, her earnings provide him with the luxury of search time to locate the best job opportunity. [8]Finally, sharing the burden of earning a living has allowed men to discover the joys of fatherhood. [9]In earlier times, fathers were so busy earning a living that they had little chance to know their children.

_____ 1. In sentence 6, the words *offset by* mean
   A. made worse by.
   B. created through.
   C. shown in.
   D. made up for.

_____ 2. The main idea of the passage is stated in
   A. sentence 1.
   B. sentence 2.
   C. sentence 3.
   D. sentence 9.

_____ 3. According to the passage, in the past
   A. no women worked outside the home.
   B. women wanted their husbands to be the family's sole breadwinner.
   C. men wanted their wives to work outside the home, but few employers would hire them.
   D. fathers were so busy earning a living that they had little chance to know their children.

_____ 4. The relationship of sentence 2 to sentence 1 is
   A. cause and effect.
   B. contrast.
   C. time.
   D. illustration.

_____ 5. The relationship of sentence 8 to sentence 7 is one of
   A. cause and effect.
   B. time.
   C. addition.
   D. illustration.

_____ 6. We can conclude from this passage that
   A. in the past, most men stayed in the same job all their lives.
   B. women often earn more than men.
   C. women often earn less than men.
   D. most men want to go back to the old days when they were the sole breadwinners of their families.

_____ 7. We can infer from this passage that
   A. without a wife's income, most families would fall into poverty.
   B. in the past, many children spent more time with their mothers than with their fathers.
   C. in the past, most children never saw their fathers.
   D. with both parents working, children now see little of either parent.

8. In the following group, one statement is the point, and the other statements are support for the point. Identify the point with a **P** and each statement of support with an **S**.

   _____ A. Having a working wife frees men to try changing careers.

   _____ B. Having a working wife raises a family's standard of living.

   _____ C. Men have discovered several benefits to having a working wife.

   _____ D. Having a working wife enables men to discover the joys of fatherhood.

COMBINED SKILLS: Test 4

Read the passage below. Then, in the space provided, write the letter of the best answer to each question that follows.

[1]Many NBA basketball players may look like giants, but the tallest human who ever lived was nearly two feet taller than the average NBA star. [2]Robert Wadlow (1918-1940) grew to the height of just under 9 feet by the time he was twenty-one years old. [3]However, perhaps as impressive as his height was Robert's quiet determination to be seen as an ordinary and likable young man, rather than a freak of nature. [4]At age 13, Robert towered above his classmates at seven feet, four inches, but he did his best to blend in by becoming a Boy Scout and making friends through his everyday interests in stamp collecting and photography. [5]By the time Robert was 18, he was more than eight feet tall. [6]Strangers would stare, whisper, and even run from him, screaming in fear. [7]Rather than reacting angrily, Robert made an effort to speak kindly and quietly to everyone he met, even those who appeared afraid of him. [8]In time, his friendly ways earned him the nickname "The Gentle Giant." [9]Throughout his brief life, Robert continued to try to move attention away from his height and focus on his education, hobbies, and friends. [10]Sadly, medical complications related to his size claimed his life at 22. [11]Upon his death, his family honored the wish Robert had had to be seen as normal. [12]They had all of his clothes and personal items destroyed so that they would not be collected and displayed in a "freak" show.

_____ 1. In sentence 10, the word *complications* means
   A. practices.
   B. decisions.
   C. problems.
   D. improvements.

_____ 2. Which statement best states the main idea of the passage?
   A. Robert Wadlow, the tallest human who ever lived, wished to be seen as an ordinary and likable young man, not as a freak of nature.
   B. Robert Wadlow, who grew to the height of just under 9 feet, was the tallest human being who ever lived.
   C. Even though he was extremely tall, Robert Wadlow had rather everyday interests.
   D. Throughout his brief life, the "Gentle Giant," Robert Wadlow, struggled to overcome people's fear of him.

_____ 3. Robert Wadlow's interests included
   A. playing basketball.
   B. weight lifting.
   C. stamp collecting and photography.
   D. performing as "The Gentle Giant" in plays.

_____ 4. Upon his death, Robert Wadlow's parents honored his wish to be seen as normal by
   A. refusing to discuss his life with anyone outside the family.
   B. destroying his clothes and personal items so that they would not be collected and displayed in a freak show.
   C. publishing Robert's autobiography.
   D. burning all their photographs of Robert.

_____ 5. The relationship of sentence 3 to sentence 2 is one of
   A. addition.
   B. illustration.
   C. contrast.
   D. cause and effect.

_____ 6. This passage suggests that
   A. Robert liked to impress people with his great height.
   B. it was difficult for some people to view Robert as normal.
   C. Robert knew that his life would be brief.
   D. Robert's own family looked upon him as a freak.

_____ 7. We can conclude from this passage that
   A. Robert actually did not mind being treated like a freak.
   B. Robert was bitter at the treatment he received from others.
   C. Robert was sensitive and patient.
   D. Robert wanted to play professional basketball.

_____ 8. Three of the items below are supporting details for an argument. Write the letter of the statement that represents the **point** of the argument.
   A. Robert Wadlow became a Boy Scout.
   B. Robert Wadlow spoke kindly and quietly to everyone he met, even those who appeared afraid of him.
   C. Robert Wadlow wished to be seen as normal.
   D. Robert Wadlow tried to get people to focus on his education, hobbies, and friends rather than his height.

COMBINED SKILLS: Test 5

Read the passage below. Then, in the space provided, write the letter of the best answer to each question that follows.

¹When a forest burns, we expect to see firefighters trying to stop the flames. ²Despite past practices, park officials today sometimes allow forest fires to burn, or they even set fires themselves. ³During the 1900s, forest fires were put out immediately. ⁴That meant that fires did not grow very large. ⁵They didn't burn up all the dead trees and plants on the forest floor. ⁶So when a fire did start, a huge amount of fuel—those dead trees—was waiting right there on the ground. ⁷Today, officials sometimes let small fires burn. ⁸These fires clean up the forest floor. ⁹This periodic cleanup is part of the cycle of nature. ¹⁰Sometimes, officials go a step further. ¹¹They actually direct firefighters to set legal fires to get rid of dead trees and also to kill off aggressive trees. ¹²Aggressive trees are trees that grow quickly and block the sun from other trees and plants. ¹³When these trees burn, more sunlight gets through for smaller plants. ¹⁴The smaller plants prosper, and so do the animals that eat those smaller plants. ¹⁵In fact, research shows that an area has three times as many plants and animals after a fire as before a fire. ¹⁶The managers at Yosemite National Park in California burn more than 2,500 acres every single year.

_____ 1. In sentence 9, the word *periodic* means
    A. happening from time to time.
    B. happening every day.
    C. rare.
    D. terrible.

_____ 2. In sentence 14, the word *prosper* means
    A. die out.
    B. grow smaller.
    C. stay as they are.
    D. do very well.

_____ 3. The main idea of this passage is found in
    A. sentence 1.
    B. sentence 2.
    C. sentence 7.
    D. sentence 16.

_____ 4. According to the passage, an area of forest has
   A. three times fewer plants and animals after a fire as before a fire.
   B. twice the number of plants and animals after a fire as before a fire.
   C. about the same number of plants and animals after a fire as before a fire.
   D. three times as many plants and animals after a fire as before a fire.

_____ 5. One reason for letting small fires burn is that
   A. they quickly become big fires.
   B. they make it easier for aggressive trees to take over the forest.
   C. they clean up the forest floor.
   D. it is a waste of manpower to put them out.

_____ 6. The relationship of sentence 2 to sentence 1 is one of
   A. contrast.
   B. an example.
   C. cause and effect.
   D. addition.

_____ 7. The relationship of sentence 6 to sentence 5 is one of
   A. contrast.
   B. addition.
   C. cause and effect.
   D. time.

_____ 8. We can conclude from this passage that
   A. firefighters would rather put out small forest fires than large forest fires.
   B. there are more legal forest fires today than there were during the 1900s.
   C. during the 1900s, great forest fires occurred because there were many dead trees and plants on the forest floor.
   D. all of the above.

COMBINED SKILLS: Test 6

Read the passage below. Then, in the space provided, write the letter of the best answer to each question that follows.

[1]Two of America's most beloved presidents were assassinated—Abraham Lincoln and John F. Kennedy. [2]There are a number of striking coincidences in President Lincoln's and President Kennedy's lives. [3]Lincoln was elected president in 1860, one hundred years before Kennedy was elected president. [4]Both had a vice president named Johnson. [5]Andrew Johnson was Lincoln's vice president. [6]Lyndon Johnson was Kennedy's. [7]Both Johnsons were Southern Democrats who had served in the U.S. Senate. [8]Andrew Johnson was born in 1808, and Lyndon Johnson was born in 1908. [9]Furthermore, both Lincoln and Kennedy supported racial equality and were advocates of civil rights. [10]Both were shot in the head, both on a Friday and in the presence of their wives. [11]John Wilkes Booth, Lincoln's killer, was born in 1839, a hundred years before Kennedy's killer, Lee Harvey Oswald, was born. [12]Both assassins were themselves killed before they could be brought to justice.

_____ 1. In sentence 2, the word *striking* means
   A. hitting.
   B. dull.
   C. common.
   D. remarkable.

_____ 2. In sentence 9, the word *advocates* means
   A. victims.
   B. critics.
   C. supporters.
   D. historians.

_____ 3. The main idea of the paragraph is stated in
   A. sentence 1.
   B. sentence 2.
   C. sentence 3.
   D. sentence 10.

_____ 4. According to the paragraph, both Lincoln and Kennedy
    A. were born in Illinois.
    B. had the same birthday.
    C. had a vice president who had served in the Senate.
    D. were Southerners.

_____ 5. TRUE OR FALSE? Both Lincoln and Kennedy were killed by men who themselves were killed before they could be put on trial for murder.

_____ 6. The relationship of sentence 9 to the sentences before it is one of
    A. time.
    B. an example.
    C. contrast.
    D. addition.

_____ 7. We can conclude that
    A. both Lincoln and Kennedy were assassinated because of their support for civil rights.
    B. both Andrew Johnson and Lyndon Johnson were part of an assassination plot.
    C. Booth and Oswald did not share the feelings of love that most Americans had for these two presidents.
    D. few Southerners were glad when Lincoln and Kennedy were assassinated.

_____ 8. We can infer that
    A. the deaths of John Wilkes Booth and Lee Harvey Oswald left many unanswered questions.
    B. Booth and Oswald acted alone in carrying out their assassinations.
    C. neither Andrew Johnson nor Lyndon Johnson was a believer in civil rights.
    D. both Booth and Oswald were killed to protect others who were involved in the assassinations.

COMBINED SKILLS: Test 7

Read the passage below. Then, in the space provided, write the letter of the best answer to each question that follows.

[1]Everyone knows doctors wear white coats. [2]Medical students even take part in a White Coat Ceremony to celebrate their career choice. [3]But why exactly do doctors wear them? [4]The white coat has become a symbolic doctor's uniform for several reasons. [5]To begin with, the color white is associated with good health. [6]Doctors and nurses in the 1800s often wore black coats and uniforms. [7]Patients often died then, and people connected the color black with death and mourning. [8]Doctors didn't like that connection, so they began wearing white in the early 1900s. [9]Another reason for wearing white was that it was associated with science. [10]Around the same time, other doctors started wearing white coats because they looked like scientists' lab coats. [11]Doctors wanted to remind people that medicine was a science. [12]Finally, white coats set doctors apart from other people. [13]The white coat was a sign that the doctor was not your friend or neighbor or a member of your family. [14]Today, the white coat is a sign of a doctor's skill in dealing with health issues, just as a police uniform is a sign of an officer's authority to enforce the law.

_____ 1. In sentence 5, the word *associated* means
     A. connected.
     B. described.
     C. explained.
     D. organized.

_____ 2. In sentence 14, the word *authority* means
     A. lack of control.
     B. kindness.
     C. confusion.
     D. power.

_____ 3. The main idea of this passage is found in
     A. sentence 1.
     B. sentence 2.
     C. sentence 4.
     D. sentence 14.

_____ 4. According to the passage, people in the 1800s
   A. knew that chances were good that doctors would be able to cure them.
   B. connected doctors who wore black with death and mourning.
   C. preferred doctors who wore white to doctors who wore black.
   D. suggested to their doctors that they wear white clothing, not black.

_____ 5. Doctors started to wear white coats
   A. in the mid-1800s.
   B. in the late 1800s.
   C. within the past fifty years.
   D. in the early 1900s.

_____ 6. The signal words used for this passage are mainly
   A. time words.
   B. addition words.
   C. contrast words.
   D. example words.

_____ 7. The passage suggests that in the 1800s
   A. doctors weren't very successful at healing people.
   B. medical science was nearly as advanced as it is today.
   C. doctors didn't try very hard to heal their patients.
   D. doctors killed most of their patients.

_____ 8. Three of the items below are supporting details for an argument. Write the letter of the statement that represents the **point** of the argument.
   A. In the 1800s, scientists wore white lab coats.
   B. People connected black with death and mourning.
   C. Doctors had good reasons for switching from black to white coats.
   D. The color white was associated with health.

COMBINED SKILLS: Test 8

Read the passage below. Then, in the space provided, write the letter of the best answer to each question that follows.

¹When you think about a snowman, you probably don't think about fire. ²But in some places, towns hold an event called "Burning the Snowman" to celebrate the end of winter. ³Traditionally, the people of small German towns built a giant snowman each March. ⁴They used wood, paper, and other flammable items. ⁵They made the snowman larger than life, sometimes reaching 8 to 10 feet tall. ⁶Then the whole town gathered for the ceremony of burning the snowman. ⁷The mayor of the town set the snowman on fire, and the townspeople celebrated as it went up in flames. ⁸The snowman represented winter. ⁹Burning it let villagers act out the triumph of warm seasons over cold. ¹⁰Today, this tradition continues in several countries, including Germany, Switzerland, and even some northern parts of the United States. ¹¹In the Swiss city of Zurich, they fill the snowman's head with fireworks, so that the ceremony ends with a bang! ¹²In some European cities, "Burning the Snowman" is the grand finale of an entire spring festival filled with parades, costumes, music, and food.

_____ 1. In sentence 4, the word *flammable* means
   A. fireproof.
   B. able to be burned.
   C. unusual.
   D. disposable.

_____ 2. In sentence 12, the word *finale* means
   A. starting point.
   B. celebration.
   C. review.
   D. ending.

_____ 3. The sentence that best expresses the main idea of the passage is
   A. sentence 1.
   B. sentence 2.
   C. sentence 3.
   D. sentence 12.

_____ 4. The month that Europeans traditionally burn the snowman is
   A. January.
   B. February.
   C. March.
   D. April.

_____ 5. The relationship of sentence 2 to sentence 1 is one of
   A. addition.
   B. illustration.
   C. contrast.
   D. time.

_____ 6. We can conclude that
   A. in some European countries, winters were long and hard.
   B. most European countries have bitterly cold winters.
   C. "Burning the Snowman" is no longer practiced in Europe.
   D. winters in Europe were generally mild.

_____ 7. The passage suggests that
   A. "Burning the Snowman" is the most popular European celebration.
   B. European settlers brought the tradition of burning the snowman to America.
   C. only men are permitted to set the snowman on fire.
   D. European winters have gotten milder in recent years.

8. In the following group, one statement is the point, two statements are support for the point, and one statement is unrelated to the point. Identify the point with a **P**, each statement of support with an **S**, and the unrelated statement with an **X**.

   _____ A. In Zurich, Switzerland, people fill a snowman's head with fireworks and light it to celebrate the end of winter.

   _____ B. Fireworks were invented in China about 2,000 years ago.

   _____ C. Fireworks are used to celebrate special occasions in Europe and America.

   _____ D. In America, we set off fireworks on the 4th of July.

COMBINED SKILLS: Test 9

Read the passage below. Then, in the space provided, write the letter of the best answer to each question that follows.

> [1]During the 1800s, Western women often wore long bathing gowns when they planned to swim in an ocean or lake. [2]In order to ensure privacy, the gowns had high necklines, elbow-length sleeves, and knee-length skirts. [3]The outfits, often made of flannel, were so heavy when wet that they could weigh as much as the swimmer. [4]In addition, the women wore puffy shorts, stockings, and canvas shoes. [5]In the late 1800s, women took advantage of a new invention called the "bathing machine." [6]After a woman climbed into the machine, it was rolled into shallow water. [7]The woman, safely inside the hidden dressing chamber, changed into a full-length swimming gown. [8]Then she walked down the ramp and into the water. [9]She was protected from onlookers by curtains and female attendants who kept watch for stray male eyes.

_____ 1. Which statement best states the implied main idea of the selection?
  A. During the 1800s, Western women often wore long bathing gowns while swimming.
  B. In the late 1800s, Western women took advantage of a new invention called the "bathing machine."
  C. During the 1800s, few Western women went swimming.
  D. During the 1800s, Western women took great care to protect their modesty while swimming.

_____ 2. The passage describes the "bathing machine" as
  A. being similar to a washing machine.
  B. a dressing room which could be rolled into shallow water.
  C. a bedroom on wheels.
  D. a gym on wheels.

_____ 3. According to the passage, bathing women needed to be protected from
  A. drowning.
  B. stray male eyes.
  C. sunburn.
  D. sharks.

_____ 4. The relationship of sentence 4 to sentence 3 is one of
   A. illustration.
   B. time.
   C. addition.
   D. cause and effect.

_____ 5. The relationship of sentence 8 to sentence 7 is one of
   A. addition.
   B. cause and effect.
   C. illustration.
   D. time.

_____ 6. This passage suggests that in the 1800s,
   A. men were often arrested for staring at women as they bathed.
   B. women were encouraged to cover their bodies when in public.
   C. women often drowned because of the long bathing gowns they wore.
   D. many women protested the fact that they were forced to wear long bathing gowns.

_____ 7. We can infer that
   A. a woman from the 1800s would probably be shocked by today's bathing suits.
   B. in the 1800s, long bathing gowns were designed to protect women from the harmful effects of the sun.
   C. men in the 1800s were used to seeing respectable women wear skimpy clothing.
   D. very few women went swimming in the 1800s.

8. In the following group, one statement is the point, and the other three statements are support for the point. Identify the point with a **P** and each statement of support with an **S**.

   _____ A. The bathing gowns women wore could weigh as much as the swimmer when wet.

   _____ B. The bathing gowns were created with high necklines, elbow-length sleeves, and knee-length skirts.

   _____ C. In the 1800s, it was difficult for women to actually swim in their bathing outfits.

   _____ D. In the 1800s, women wore puffy shorts, stockings, and canvas shoes in addition to their bathing gowns.

COMBINED SKILLS: Test 10

Read the passage below. Then, in the space provided, write the letter of the best answer to each question that follows.

> [1]Doctors race against the clock in order to perform organ transplants. [2]They have to find a proper recipient and then fly the organ to wherever that person lives. [3]Doctors refrigerate the organs, but, for example, a refrigerated heart stays fresh for only 4 hours. [4]They can't freeze the organs because ice crystals form and damage the tissue. [5]That's why researchers are studying the common U.S. and Canadian wood frog. [6]The wood frog has "freeze tolerance." [7]In the winter, it becomes basically a frog-shaped ice cube. [8]About ⅔ of the water in its body freezes, and it looks dead. [9]But it's not. [10]The frog's liver makes glucose, a natural sugar that acts like antifreeze. [11]It makes some of the frog's body water remain liquid and limits the ice formation in the frog. [12]It also keeps the cells from shrinking, so that ice crystals don't tear the tissue. [13]When the temperature warms up, the frog simply thaws out and hops away. [14]Researchers would like to make that happen in donor organs. [15]If doctors could freeze organs, medical teams would have more time to transport them. [16]Many more lives would be saved. [17]Keeping organs fresh is a major obstacle to organ transplants, but wood frogs just might help researchers solve that problem.

_____ 1. In sentence 2, the word *recipient* means
   A. someone who learns something.
   B. someone who gives something.
   C. someone who receives something.
   D. a means of transportation.

_____ 2. In sentence 6, the word *tolerance* means
   A. interest.
   B. ability to put up with something.
   C. disability.
   D. dislike for something.

_____ 3. The sentence that best expresses the main idea of the passage is
   A. sentence 1.
   B. sentence 2.
   C. sentence 5.
   D. sentence 17.

_____ 4. Scientists can't freeze organs because
   A. ice crystals form and damage the tissue.
   B. the organs are needed right away for transplants.
   C. it is currently against the law to do so.
   D. no method has been found to safely thaw them out.

_____ 5. The relationship between sentence 9 and sentence 8 is one of
   A. contrast.
   B. time.
   C. cause and effect.
   D. addition.

_____ 6. We can infer from this passage that at present
   A. there is little need for transplanted organs.
   B. most transplanted organs are human hearts.
   C. some organs don't get to the people who need them in time.
   D. in the future, fewer people will need organ transplants.

_____ 7. We can conclude from this passage that
   A. in the future, it may be possible to freeze human organs.
   B. some organs can be frozen while others can't.
   C. wood frogs are only one of many animals which have "freeze tolerance."
   D. human beings can be trained to have "freeze tolerance."

8. In the following group, one statement is the point, two statements are support for the point, and one statement is unrelated to the point. Identify the point with a **P**, each statement of support with an **S**, and the unrelated statement with an **X**.

   _____ A. The glucose in a wood frog's body limits ice formation during freezing weather.

   _____ B. The glucose in a wood frog's body keeps the cells from shrinking during freezing weather.

   _____ C. Glucose is also produced by plants.

   _____ D. Glucose is a sugar which helps the wood frog survive freezing weather.

COMBINED SKILLS: Test 11

Read the passage below. Then, in the space provided, write the letter of the best answer to each question that follows.

[1]There are real differences between people with high self-esteem and those with low self-esteem. [2]Researchers have found that people with good self-concepts tend to be more accepting of others. [3]They are also more accepting of their own failures. [4]However, they fail less, since they tend to be better achievers than people with low self-esteem. [5]High self-esteem is also related to independence and open-mindedness. [6]People with positive self-images will be more willing to accept criticism and suggestions. [7]On the other hand, persons with low self-esteem are sensitive to criticism and blame themselves whenever things go wrong. [8]And because they lack confidence, they will give in to pressure and can often be easily influenced. [9]They also seek flattery and criticize others in order to improve their self-images.

_____ 1. The main idea of the passage is found in
   A. sentence 1.
   B. sentence 2.
   C. sentence 3.
   D. sentence 5.

_____ 2. According to the passage, people with high self-esteem
   A. blame themselves when things go wrong.
   B. often criticize others.
   C. are very sensitive to criticism.
   D. are more accepting of their own failures.

_____ 3. According to the passage, people with low self-esteem
   A. are usually independent and open-minded.
   B. easily give in to pressure.
   C. fail less than other people.
   D. like to flatter others.

_____ 4. The relationship of sentence 7 to sentence 6 is one of
   A. illustration.
   B. cause and effect.
   C. addition.
   D. contrast.

_____ 5. The relationship between the two parts of sentence 8 is one of
   A. contrast.
   B. cause and effect.
   C. time.
   D. example.

_____ 6. This passage suggests that people with high self-esteem
   A. never fail.
   B. are more likely to feel anger toward members of different ethnic groups and races.
   C. are harder to bully than people with low self-esteem.
   D. have a hard time recovering from setbacks.

_____ 7. This passage suggests that people with low self-esteem
   A. are more likely to follow leaders who express anger toward others.
   B. are more likely to succeed than people with high self-esteem.
   C. can never develop high self-esteem.
   D. are very accepting of different ethnic groups and races.

8. In the following group, one statement is the point, and the other three statements are support for the point. Identify the point with a **P** and each statement of support with an **S**.

   _____ A. People with high self-esteem tend to be better achievers than people with low self-esteem.

   _____ B. People with high self-esteem share several positive personality traits.

   _____ C. People with high self-esteem tend to be open-minded and independent.

   _____ D. People with high self-esteem are more willing to accept criticism and suggestions.

COMBINED SKILLS: Test 12

Read the passage below. Then, in the space provided, write the letter of the best answer to each question that follows.

[1]The United States has one of the highest divorce rates in the world, with more than one million divorces a year. [2]There are several reasons why divorce is more common today than it was in the past. [3]One reason is that women are less financially dependent on their husbands. [4]Even with children, they manage to go to school and train for positions in today's job market. [5]With their own income, they are not trapped at home as they were in the past. [6]Another reason for divorce is less opposition. [7]Legally, it is easier to obtain a divorce than was the case with earlier generations. [8]There is less religious opposition as well, and less of a social stigma. [9]Divorced people, who were once the subject of whispers and scandal, are now all around us. [10]A third reason for the increase in divorce is that people expect more from marriage now. [11]They want their mates to enrich their lives, help them develop their potential, and be loving companions and good sexual partners. [12]They are not as willing as their parents were to settle for less. [13]Finally, men and women today are more realistic. [14]If a marriage does not work out, they are more ready to simply accept that fact. [15]Perhaps the marriage is not meant to be, they may decide, and to try to continue it might only damage both of them as well as their children. [16]The talk shows and newspaper and magazine articles are full of stories about people who go on to make new beginnings in their lives. [17]Couples in unhappy marriages are prompted to react in a similar way: better to put a bad experience to an end, and to make a new start in life.

_____ 1. In sentence 8, the word *stigma* means
   A. approval.
   B. shame.
   C. reaction.
   D. interest.

_____ 2. The main idea of the selection is stated in
   A. sentence 1.
   B. sentence 2.
   C. sentence 9.
   D. sentence 17.

_____ 3. People now expect their marriages to provide them with
   A. loving companions and good sexual partners.
   B. a mate who will cook and clean for them, if they are men.
   C. a mate who will be the breadwinner, if they are women.
   D. all of the above.

_____ 4. According to the selection, some people are prompted to end unhappy marriages by
   A. greedy divorce lawyers.
   B. stories about people who go on to make new beginnings in their lives.
   C. church leaders who advise them that their marriage was not meant to be.
   D. pressures put upon them by their children.

_____ 5. The relationship of sentence 13 to sentence 12 is one of
   A. addition.
   B. cause and effect.
   C. illustration.
   D. time.

_____ 6. This selection suggests that in the past
   A. most people were happily married.
   B. married people were more realistic than they are today.
   C. the American divorce rate was about the same as it is today.
   D. a lot of people felt trapped in unhappy marriages.

_____ 7. We can conclude from this selection that
   A. the American divorce rate will continue to rise.
   B. many people who stay married now do so because they want to, not because they have to.
   C. the American divorce rate will begin to decline.
   D. divorced people should be treated with whispers and scandal.

_____ 8. The author's attitude toward divorce seems to be that it is
   A. too common in the United States.
   B. to be avoided at all costs.
   C. disgraceful.
   D. better than staying in an unhappy marriage.

Pronunciation Guide

Each word in Chapter 3, "Vocabulary in Context," is followed by information in parentheses that shows you how to pronounce the word. (There are also pronunciations for the vocabulary items that follow the readings in Parts II and III.) The guide below and on the next page explains how to use that information.

Long Vowel Sounds		Other Vowel Sounds		Consonant Sounds	
ā	pay	â	care	j	jump
ē	she	ä	card	k	kiss
ī	hi	îr	here	l	let
ō	go	ô	all	m	meet
ōō	cool	oi	oil	n	no
yōō	use	ou	out	p	put
		ûr	fur	r	red
Short Vowel Sounds		ə	ago, item, easily, gallop, circus	s	sell
				t	top
ă	hat			v	very
ĕ	ten			w	way
ĭ	sit	**Consonant Sounds**		y	yes
ŏ	lot	b	big	z	zero
ŏŏ	look	d	do	ch	church
ŭ	up	f	fall	sh	dish
yŏŏ	cure	g	get	*th*	then
		h	he	th	thick
				zh	usual

Note that each pronunciation symbol above is paired with a common word that shows the sound of the symbol. For example, the symbol ā has the sound of the *a* in the common word *pay*. The symbol ă has the sound of the *a* in the common word *hat*. The symbol ə, which looks like an upside-down *e* and is known as the schwa, has the unaccented sound in the common word *ago*. It sounds like the "uh" a speaker often says when hesitating.

Accent marks are small black marks that tell you which syllable to emphasize as you say a word. A bold accent mark (′) shows which syllable should be stressed. A lighter accent mark (′) in some words indicates a secondary stress. Syllables without an accent mark are unstressed.

Writing Assignments

A BRIEF GUIDE TO EFFECTIVE WRITING

Here in a nutshell is what you need to do to write effectively.

Step 1: Explore Your Topic through Informal Writing

To begin with, explore the topic that you want to write about or that you have been assigned to write about. You can examine your topic through **informal writing**, which usually means one of three things.

First, you can **freewrite** about your topic for at least ten minutes. In other words, for ten minutes write whatever comes into your head about your subject. Write without stopping and without worrying at all about spelling or grammar. Simply get down on paper all the information about the topic that occurs to you.

A second thing you can do is to **make a list of ideas and details** that could go into your paper. Simply pile these items up, one after another, like a shopping list, without worrying about putting them in any special order. Try to accumulate as many details as you can think of.

A third way to explore your topic is to **write down a series of questions and answers** about it. Your questions can start with words like *what, why, how, when*, and *where*.

Getting your thoughts and ideas down on paper will help you think more about your topic. With some raw material to look at, you are now in a better position to decide on just how to proceed.

Step 2: Plan Your Paper with an Informal Outline

After exploring your topic, plan your paper using an informal outline. Do two things:

- **Decide on and write out the point of your paper.** It is often a good idea to begin your paragraph with this point, which is known as the **topic sentence**. If you are writing an essay of several paragraphs, you will probably want to include your main point somewhere in your first paragraph. In a paper of several paragraphs, the main point is called the **central point**, or **thesis**.

- **List the supporting reasons, examples, or other details that back up your point.** In many cases, you should have at least two or three items of support.

Step 3: Use Transitions

Once your outline is worked out, you will have a clear "road map" for writing your paper. As you write the early drafts of your paper, use **transitions** to introduce each of the separate supporting items you present to back up your point. For instance, you might introduce your first supporting item with the transitional words *first of all*. You might begin your second supporting item with words such as *another reason* or *another example*. And you might indicate your final supporting detail with such words as *last of all* or *a final reason*.

Step 4: Edit and Proofread Your Paper

After you have a solid draft, edit and proofread the paper. Ask yourself several questions to evaluate your paper:

1 Is the paper **unified**? Does all the material in the paper truly support the opening point?

2 Is the paper **well supported**? Is there plenty of specific evidence to back the opening point?

3 Is the paper **clearly organized**? Does the material proceed in a way that makes sense? Do transitions help connect ideas?

4 Is the paper **well written**? When the paper is read aloud, do the sentences flow smoothly and clearly? Has the paper been checked carefully for grammar, punctuation, and spelling mistakes?

WRITING ASSIGNMENTS FOR THE NINETEEN READINGS

Note: Your instructor may also permit you to write a paper that is based upon one of the discussion questions that follow each reading.

The Struggle Continues

1. Juan says he believes in "success through education." Write a paragraph telling about a time in your life when your education was (or is) helpful to you.

   Begin with a sentence in which you state a specific time that your education has helped you (or helps you now), for example:

   My education was helpful to me when I applied for the job I have now.

   My education is helpful when I assist my daughter with her homework.

   In your paragraph, give details about exactly how your education helped you in the situation you are describing. In addition, you might wish to describe what the situation might have been like if you had *not* had your level of education.

2. Imagine not being able to read. Write a paragraph about how you would be affected by your inability to read. Organize your paragraph in one of two ways:

   • By time order. Describe what your day as a nonreader would be like from the time you get up through the time you go to bed.

   • By categories. Describe what your day as a nonreader would be like in three or four different settings (for instance, at home, at work, at school, and driving somewhere).

   Your main point might be similar to this:

   If I couldn't read, life would be much more difficult in many ways.

   Before you write your paragraph, spend some time exploring all the little ways that reading affects your life, such as the following:

   • Reading the directions on a food package

   • Reading street signs

   • Reading store signs

   • Reading the news or sports section of a newspaper

   Alternatively, write a paragraph about how your life would be affected by an inability to write. For this paragraph, consider the ways writing is useful in your life, such as for creating to-do lists, notes to friends, and e-mail.

A Lesson in Love

1. The little girl in the reading obviously trusted her mother very much. Write a paragraph about a person you have deeply trusted. In your paragraph, tell who this person was, what his or her relationship was to you, and what it was about the person that inspired such trust in you. Provide at least one example that shows why you feel as you do (or felt as you did) about the person.

     Begin with your main point, which might go something like this:

     My grandmother was a person I trusted with all my heart.

   A paragraph with the above point would continue by stating why the grandmother was so trustworthy ("I knew she would never lie to me, even if the truth wasn't what I wanted to hear"). It would also contain at least one detailed example of a time the grandmother told the writer the truth when it might have been easier not to.

2. "A Lesson in Love" tells of a frightening incident in which the people involved faced the possibility of death. Write a paper describing the most frightening incident you have ever experienced.

     In order to make your reader understand what you experienced, your paper should answer most (if not all) of the following questions:

     • Was the incident human-made (like a car accident) or an act of nature (like a tornado)?
     • How did you become involved?
     • Were you immediately very frightened, or did your fear grow?
     • How serious was the actual danger? Was your life threatened?
     • How did you get out of the situation?

   Begin your paper with a sentence that states your main point, including the nature of the incident. Here's an example of such a statement:

     The most terrifying experience I have ever had happened when my car stalled on railroad tracks.

Friendship and Living Longer

1. "Friendship and Living Longer" states that we especially need friends and relatives when we face major life changes. Think about a time when you experienced a difficult change—for example, when you began a new job, moved to a new town, changed schools, or lost a loved one. Now think about the person who, more than anyone else, helped you adjust to the situation. Write a paragraph about how this friend helped you through the difficult period.

Begin with your main point, which might be worded something like this one:

> The support of my best friend, Angela, really helped me deal with my parents' divorce.

Then describe why the situation was difficult for you and specific ways the friend or relative helped you. You might conclude with how you think the situation would have been different without that person's support.

2. The company of friends and family is essential to our well-being. Sometimes, however, privacy is just as important. Write a paper that begins with this point:

> There are times when it is important to me to be alone.

Describe one or two such times (for example, when you have to make a decision or when you're very tired), how you like to spend such private time, and what the benefits of privacy at those times are. Include at least one or two specific examples of private times you have experienced, to help your reader get a sense of how such quiet time plays a role in your life.

From Horror to Hope

1. At first, Phany's uncle's invitation to work in his doughnut shop seemed kind. Later, though, Phany felt that her uncle and aunt had only wanted to use her. Have you ever found that someone who seemed friendly or helpful really wished to take advantage of you? Write a paragraph about the incident. Begin with a topic sentence, like the one below, that tells in general how you were used.

> I was flattered when a popular girl at school started being nice to me, but soon I realized she only wanted to use me to meet my good-looking cousin.

Your paragraph should answer the following questions:

- Who was involved in the incident?
- What was your first impression of that person's behavior toward you?
- How did you realize you were being taken advantage of?
- How did you respond at that point?

2. If you had a chance to meet Phany, what would you like to say to her? Write her a letter in response to her story. In your letter, you might do some of the following:

- Tell her what parts of her story you think were most memorable, touching, or troubling.
- Share an experience of your own that you think she could relate to because it is in some way similar to something she has gone through.

- Tell her what you think of her plan to return to Cambodia to work on behalf of women's education there.

- Tell her what kind of person you think she must be, judging from her story.

Begin with a topic sentence that covers most or all of the details of your letter, such as either of these examples:

> I greatly admire your persistence and goals.

> Because of some of my own experiences, I believe I know how you feel about how your uncle and aunt treated you.

A Parent Gets a Reading Lesson

1. What attitude did your parents take towards reading? How did their attitude affect your own? Write a paragraph in which you explain how their attitudes and your own are alike or different. Here is a sample topic sentence:

   > Although reading was not important to my parents, I have always liked to read.

   In your paragraph, explain how you could tell what your parents' attitude about reading was, from their actions and comments. Then explain your own attitude about reading. Comment on whether the attitudes are the same or different, and in what ways.

2. What did you think of the mother in "A Parent Gets a Reading Lesson"? Did you have a good impression of her, a bad impression, or a mixed impression? Write a paragraph that explains what you thought of her and why. Use examples from the essay to back up the impression that you formed.

Discovering Words

1. Write a paragraph about one of your significant early memories of reading. Maybe it involves being read to by a parent or teacher. Maybe it's about reading the back of a cereal box at breakfast. Maybe it's about a favorite childhood book. Or maybe it's about the frustration of trying to read in school.

   Begin your paragraph with a sentence that summarizes the memory you are writing about. Here are some examples:

   > One of my best early memories of reading is of my Grandpa reading me stories.

   > When I was very young and realized I could read street signs, I felt wonderful.

Fear and confusion are what I felt when I tried to read in elementary school.

Follow your first sentence with a description of what happened and how you felt about it. Be sure to include details that will help your reader understand when and where this event occurred.

2. Malcolm X writes that reading made him feel free. What activity makes you feel especially free? Is it reading, as with Malcolm? Walking alone through the city? Driving your car? Running? Dancing? Painting? Making music?

Write a paragraph that explains what makes you feel free. Use descriptive words that help the reader experience what you experience. Everyone has a different understanding of what it means to feel free, so be sure to explain what it is about this experience that is so appealing to you.

One Less Sucker Lives

1. In "One Less Sucker Lives," the author describes how she was taken advantage of by a con man who told her a hard-luck story. When have you been taken advantage of by someone who, like the con man, appealed to your trust or generosity and then treated you unfairly? Write a paper about what happened. Begin with a topic statement that explains when you were taken advantage of and who did it, like this:

Last summer, my cousin Terrence took advantage of me.

Just last week, a young woman in the train station took advantage of me.

As you write your paper, explain how the person approached you and what he or she did to gain your trust. Describe what the person then did to take advantage of you. Explain why you feel that you were not treated fairly. Conclude by writing how you now feel about the person who took advantage of you.

2. Jeanne Smith says that the encounter with the con man taught her a lesson—to be less trusting and more cynical. Write a paragraph about an incident that taught you a lesson. Your topic sentence should briefly mention both the incident and the lesson. An example:

A scary incident last summer taught me to be more careful about locking my apartment door.

In the paragraph, tell the story of what happened in time order, from beginning to end. Conclude by explaining what lesson you learned from it, and how you have applied that lesson to your life.

Classroom Notetaking

1. Draw a line down the middle of a notebook page. On the top left-hand side, write, "Things I do." On the top right-hand side, write, "Things I don't do." In the first column, list the notetaking tips from the selection that you already use. In the second column, list those things you don't do now, but according to the article, might help you take better notes.

   Then write a paragraph that explains how the notetaking tips that you *do* use help you. For the tips you *don't* use, explain which ones you'd like to try, and why.

2. The author says that the best lecturers "combine knowledge with showmanship" and "can make any subject . . . leap vividly to life." Write a paragraph about a teacher you have had who is both well-informed and entertaining. Provide at least two detailed illustrations of how this teacher has kept your attention. Come to some conclusion about how the teacher's attitude affected your learning.

   Or, instead, write a paragraph describing a teacher who was unbelievably boring. Provide several detailed examples of how this teacher failed to be "informative and entertaining." In your conclusion, tell about how your learning in that class was affected.

Winning the Job Interview Game

1. "Winning the Job Interview Game" gives excellent advice on how to make a great impression at a job interview. But how do you go about "Losing the Job Interview Game"? Write a comical paragraph in which you advise job applicants on how to make the worst possible impression. Look at "Winning the Job Interview Game" for ideas: for instance, write about the worst way to dress, the worst way to answer questions, and so on.

2. Of all the people you know personally—that is, not celebrities that you've just read or heard about—whose job would you most like to have? Why? Write a paragraph on that topic. Your topic sentence might be something like this:

   Of all the people I know, my uncle Bernie has the best job.

   Develop your paragraph by explaining who the person is, how you know him or her, and what job he or she holds. Then explain what it is about the job that makes it desirable to you.

Learning Survival Skills

1. What career plans have you made so far? Write a paragraph about your plans and how your college classes relate to those plans. If you are not sure yet about your career choice, write about a likely possibility.

In your paragraph, describe your interests and how they have led to your plans for a career. Then explain how your program of study will contribute to your success. Here are some sample topic sentences for such a paragraph:

My interest in animals and science has led me to enroll in a program to become a veterinary assistant.

Because I have always loved art and design, I am earning a degree in graphic arts.

I intend to earn a double degree in horticulture and business because my dream is to have my own landscaping company.

2. Coleman writes, "To not be open to growth is to die a little each day." Whom do you know who seems to have chosen slow death over growth and positive change? Here are a few examples of behavior by people who refuse to take advantage of opportunities for growth:

- They skip class and miss assignments, even though they are in danger of flunking out of school.
- They refuse to take on added responsibilities at work, even though these could lead to a higher salary or a more interesting job.
- They hang onto self-destructive habits such as overeating, watching too much TV (or some other form of addiction), or spending time with the wrong people.

Write a paragraph about how the person you have chosen has decided not to grow. In the paragraph, introduce the person, and explain how you know him or her. Next, describe the harmful behavior. Be specific. For example, don't just say someone spends too much time with the wrong people—give a detailed example or two of people who are negative influences and why they are negative. You might conclude by suggesting some positive behavior changes that person could make and how they would help him or her.

Migrant Child to College Woman

1. Throughout her life, Maria Cardenas has forced herself to do things that were very difficult for her. For example, she made herself learn to read on her own. She forced herself to begin college, despite her fears. She did these things because she believed the long-term benefits would be more important than any short-term discomfort.

When have you made yourself do something difficult, even though it would have been easier not to? Maybe it's been one of these:

- Apologizing for something you did wrong
- Starting a new class or job
- Moving to a new town
- Speaking up for yourself to someone who was treating you badly

Write a paragraph about what you did and why. In it, answer these questions:

- What did I do that was difficult?
- Why did I find doing it so hard or frightening?
- Why did I think doing it would be worthwhile?
- How did I feel about myself after I'd done it?

2. Maria feels a strong drive to help migrant children. She wants to help them learn to speak English and to "stand on their own two feet."

If you were offered the chance to help a particular group of people, who would it be? What kind of help would you most like to offer them? Write a paragraph in which you explain what group you would help, why you'd like to help them, and, finally, what you would do to help the people in this group.

Or instead, if you are now a volunteer with a particular group, write a paragraph about your experiences with that group. Tell why you decided to volunteer, what you actually do, and what your rewards are from the experience. Remember to give specific examples from your experience to support your general points.

Life Over Death

1. Think of an animal that has played a role in your life. Perhaps it was a pet in your own home or in the home of someone you visited frequently. Perhaps it was a neighborhood animal that you often observed outdoors. Write a paragraph about one characteristic of that animal, such as any of the following:

- Cleverness
- Stupidity
- Laziness
- Playfulness
- Stubbornness
- Loyalty

Begin with a topic sentence that names the animal and the characteristic. For instance, that sentence might be similar to this one:

My sister's kitten, Muffin, is the most affectionate animal I've ever known.

Then, describe two or three specific events or behaviors that are good examples of the characteristic you have chosen.

2. The author of "Life Over Death" felt he "had no choice"—that he *had* to help the injured cat. For this assignment, write a letter to the author telling him about a time you also did something because you thought it was the only right thing to do. A topic sentence for this letter could be worded something like this:

When my sister lost her job, I had no choice—I had to invite her and her children to live with me for a while.

After your topic sentence, describe the situation that you faced, and then explain the decision you made. Conclude by telling what finally happened.

Dare to Think Big

1. Ben Carson mentions that when he was in high school, peer pressure "sidetracked me for a time." Have you found peer pressure to be a negative influence in your life? A positive influence? Or has it not been an influence at all? Write a paragraph describing your experience with peer pressure. Begin with a statement of your topic, like this:

   > For me, peer pressure has been a positive influence on my life.

   Develop your paragraph by describing who your peers were, how they influenced you, and how you responded to their influence. Give at least two specific examples of how the influence of other young people affected you. For instance, you might write: "Because my best friend signed up for a summer tutoring program, I decided to sign up as well."

2. Write a paragraph in which you contrast a "cool guy" and a "nerd" that you're acquainted with. Tell how they are different in three categories. For instance, you might talk about how they dress, how they walk, their attitude towards school, how they speak, their interests, how they spend their spare time, etc. In each category, be very specific about how the two individuals are different.

Why We Shop

1. What kind of shopper are you? Are you a sensible shopper, who goes shopping only when you need something specific? Are you a recreational shopper, who likes to shop just for fun? Or are you a binge shopper, whose shopping and spending are truly out of control? Write a paragraph in which you describe your own shopping style. Your topic sentence will identify you as one of the three types of shoppers. Here's an example:

   > I consider myself a recreational shopper.

   To develop your paragraph, describe your typical shopping experience. Fill your paragraph with concrete details, such as the name of your favorite mall and favorite stores and what sorts of items tempt you as you shop.

2. In the essay, the Cooper family feels competitive with the Ballard family, and so buys items in order to keep up with them. Who is someone that you feel competitive with? In what way are the two of you competitive? Perhaps you compete with a sibling for your parents' attention, or with a classmate for better grades, or with a teammate for a better athletic record. Write a paragraph explaining who it is you compete with and what you compete about. Here are a couple of possible topic sentences:

My friend Alex and I often compete for the same girlfriends.

My mom and I compete to see who is better-dressed.

As you develop your paragraph, give a couple of examples of times that you and the other person have demonstrated your competition.

Learning to Read: The Marvel Kretzmann Story

1. When Marvel realized her life was getting more difficult rather than easier, she returned to school—a decision that changed her life. Like Marvel, we all have made decisions that changed our lives, such as the decision to do any of the following:

   - Marry or divorce
   - Have a child
   - Get a new job
   - Move to another town
   - End a destructive relationship
   - Go back to school

   Write a paragraph about a life-changing decision you have made and its effects. In your paper, answer the following questions:

   - What decision did I make?
   - Why did I make it?
   - What happened to me as a result of my decision?
   - If I had it to do over again, would I make the same decision?

   Begin by choosing a decision you might wish to write about. Next, check to see if you have enough supporting details to write about that decision. To do so, you might write down the above questions and list as many answers to each as you can think of.

2. Marvel is surprised to find herself looked up to by fellow students who also have difficulty reading. However, she realizes that if *they* think she can help them, she probably *can* help them—and also help herself.

   Whom do you know (perhaps yourself?) who has struggled with an obstacle and was later able to help others with that same problem? Write a paragraph that includes the following:

   - The person's problem
   - How he or she learned to deal with it
   - How that person later helped someone else deal with the same problem

The Fist, the Clay, and the Rock

1. The author writes of Mr. Gery, "[He] worked us very hard, but he was not a mean person. We all knew he was a kind man who wanted us to become strong." Write a paragraph about an adult in your life who, like Mr. Gery, was tough but kind. In your paragraph, tell who the person was, what his or her relationship was to you, and why you considered him or her "tough but kind." Provide at least one example that shows the person's toughness and kindness.

    Start with your main point, which might be like this:

    Mr. D'Angelo, my boss at the supermarket, was a tough but kind man.

    The paragraph that began like this would go on to describe why Mr. D'Angelo impressed the writer as being both tough and kind. ("He expected me to work hard, but he always let me know that he appreciated me.") The paragraph would include at least one detailed example of a time Mr. D'Angelo showed the writer both his toughness and his kindness.

2. Mr. Gery warned his students that life would give them some "heavy hits." Write a paragraph about a heavy hit you've taken in life—something that happened that was very difficult to deal with.

    Begin by stating what the "hit" was. For example:

    Life gave me a heavy hit when my aunt died in a car accident.

    In your paragraph, give a detailed account of what happened. Be sure to explain why the incident was personally difficult for you. In the case of the topic sentence above, for instance, the writer might say, "My aunt took care of me whenever my mother was at work. She was like a second mom in my life."

Joe Davis

1. Like Joe Davis, many of us have learned painful lessons from life. And like him, we wish we could pass those lessons on to young people to save them from making the same mistakes. Write a letter to a young person in which you use your own experience as a lesson. Begin with a topic sentence stating the lesson you'd like to teach, as in these examples:

    My own experience is a lesson on why it's a bad idea to get involved with drugs and the people who take them.

    I hope you can learn from my experience that dropping out of high school is a big mistake.

    I know from firsthand experience that teenage girls should not let their boyfriends pressure them into a sexual relationship.

As you develop your letter, describe in detail the hard lesson you learned and how you learned it.

2. One of Joe's goals is to regain the trust of the friends and family members he abused during his earlier life. Have you ever given a second chance to someone who treated you poorly? Write a paragraph about what happened. In your paragraph, answer the following questions:

   - What did the person do to lose your trust? Was it an obviously hurtful action, like physically harming you or stealing from you, or something more subtle, like embarrassing you or hurting your feelings?

   - Why did you decide to give the person another chance? Did the person apologize? Did you decide the mistreatment was not as bad as you first thought?

   - What happened as a result of your giving the person a second chance? Did he or she treat you better this time? Or did the bad treatment start over again?

   Conclude your paragraph with one or more thoughts about what you learned from the experience.

Rosa: A Success Story

1. Edward Patrick writes, "Almost all of us came to America from somewhere else." What do you know about your family's arrival in this country? Write a paragraph that tells what you know about your first relatives in the United States. Answer as many of the following questions as you can:

   - Who were your first relatives in the United States?
   - Where did they come from?
   - When did they arrive?
   - Why did they come to the United States?
   - What was life in the U.S. like for them at first?

   If you don't know much about your first relatives in the United States, write instead about the earliest generation you do know about.

2. Rosa's college classes prepared her for a career in child care. If you want your education to lead to a specific career, write a paragraph about that career and why you've picked it. Give specific examples of the type of work you'd like to do and why. If you're not sure about the career you want, write about one or two that you're considering. Your topic sentence for this paragraph might be worded like either of these:

I'm aiming for a career in accounting for several reasons.

Although I haven't made a final decision, I'm considering the pros and cons of a career as a chef.

The Lady, or the Tiger?

1. Pretend the story ends with paragraph 15. The final sentence is, "Without pausing for a moment, he threw open the door on the right." Now, write your own ending to the story. What happened after the young man threw open the door? Use your imagination! In your version of the ending, write more than what happened immediately. Consider answering some of these questions: Why did what happened happen? How did the crowd react? How did the princess and king react?

2. "The Lady, or the Tiger?" is about a difficult decision that a princess had to make. Write a paragraph about a time you had to make a difficult decision. Begin with a sentence that describes the decision you faced, like this:

   > When my parents divorced, I had to decide whether to live with my mother or my dad.

   In the paragraph, explain why the decision was difficult for you. Describe the good and bad points that either choice would have. For instance, the writer of the above paragraph about living with her father or mother might write, "If I lived with my mother, I would stay in my familiar house in my own neighborhood. On the other hand, my mom and I argued a lot." After describing the alternatives, tell the reader what you decided and why. Conclude your paragraph by saying how you now feel about your decision.

Limited Answer Key

An important note: To strengthen your reading skills, you must do more than simply find out which of your answers are right and which are wrong. You also need to figure out (with the help of this book, the teacher, or other students) *why* you missed the questions you did. By using each of your wrong answers as a learning opportunity, you will strengthen your understanding of the skills. You will also prepare yourself for the review and mastery tests in Part II and the reading comprehension questions in Part III, for which answers are not given here.

ANSWERS TO THE PRACTICES IN PART I

1 Phonics I: Consonants

Practice 1: Sounds of c

3. soft	7. soft
4. hard	8. hard
5. soft	9. hard
6. hard	10. soft

Practice 2: Sounds of g

3. soft	7. soft
4. hard	8. soft
5. soft	9. hard
6. hard	10. hard

Practice 3: Blends That Begin with s

A. 1. slip   4. squeal
2. crisp   5. west
3. mask

B. 1. speaks   4. post
2. small   5. street
3. asked

Practice 4: Blends That End in l

A. 1. blank   4. imply
2. class   5. inflame
3. glass

B. 1. Florida   4. blame
2. play   5. glad
3. plenty

Practice 5: Blends That End in r

A. 1. across   4. jawbreaker
2. entrance   5. trade
3. frog

B. 1. driveway   4. transmission
2. brakes   5. problems
3. grab

Practice 6: Other Blends

A. 1. bumper   4. punt
2. handcuff   5. sank
3. mild

B. 1. difficult   4. children
2. camp   5. find
3. Rhode   6. start
Island

Practice 7: Consonant Digraphs

1. mouth	6. crashed
2. Chinese	7. cholesterol
3. starfish	8. phony
4. shop	9. Chicago
5. phrase	10. rough

Practice 8: Silent Consonants

1. **know**
2. **Cocoa Puffs**
3. lam**b**
4. **k**nead
5. **c**heck
6. crum**b**s
7. mu**g**gy
8. **w**holesale
9. messa**g**e
10. **w**rite

2   Phonics II: Vowels

Practice 1A: Short a Sound

3. ă	7. ă
4. ă	8. X
5. X	9. ă
6. X	10. X

Practice 1B: Short e Sound

3. X	7. X
4. ĕ	8. X
5. X	9. ĕ
6. ĕ	10. ĕ

Practice 1C: Short i Sound

3. ĭ	7. ĭ
4. X	8. X
5. ĭ	9. ĭ
6. X	10. X

Practice 1D: Short o Sound

3. X	7. X
4. X	8. ŏ
5. ŏ	9. X
6. ŏ	10. ŏ

Practice 1E: Short u Sound

3. ŭ	7. X
4. X	8. X
5. ŭ	9. ŭ
6. ŭ	10. X

Practice 2: Rule for Short Vowel Sounds

1. stop
2. back
3. hungry
4. fat
5. rubber
6. Nevada
7. butter
8. bad
9. think
10. body

Practice 3A: Long a Sound

3. X	7. X
4. ā	8. X
5. ā	9. X
6. ā	10. ā

Practice 3B: Long e Sound

3. ē	7. X
4. X	8. ē
5. X	9. X
6. ē	10. ē

Practice 3C: Long i Sound

3. ī	7. X
4. X	8. ī
5. ī	9. X
6. X	10. ī

Practice 3D: Long o Sound

3. ō	7. ō
4. ō	8. X
5. X	9. ō
6. X	10. X

Practice 3E: Long u Sound

3. X	7. ū
4. ū	8. X
5. ū	9. ū
6. X	10. X

Practice 4: Silent-e Rule

1. pine
2. like
3. notebook
4. unsafe
5. brave

Practice 5: Two-Vowels-Together Rule

1. train
2. Greece
3. day
4. soap
5. team

Practice 6: Final Single Vowel

1. also
2. spider
3. over
4. erase
5. famous

Practice 7: Sounds of y

4. ē	7. y
5. ī	8. ē
6. ĭ	9. y
	10. ĭ

Practice 8: Long and Short Vowels and Vowels Followed by r

4. ā	7. ē
5. r	8. ŭ
6. r	9. r
	10. ĭ

Practice 9: Long and Short oo

3. o͞o	7. o͝o
4. o͝o	8. o͞o
5. o͞o	9. o͞o
6. o͝o	10. o͝o

Practice 8: Dividing between the Words in a Compound Word

1. note-book   4. work-shop
2. rain-coat   5. sea-shell
3. pop-corn

3 Phonics III: Syllables

Practice 1: Numbers of Vowels, Vowel Sounds, and Syllables

1.	2	1	1	6.	2	1	1
2.	2	1	1	7.	3	3	3
3.	2	1	1	8.	2	1	1
4.	2	1	1	9.	3	2	2
5.	2	2	2	10.	3	2	2

Practice 2: Dividing between Two Consonants

1. can-dy   4. trum-pet
2. nap-kin   5. muf-fin
3. har-bor

Practice 3: Dividing between Three Consonants

1. cen-tral   4. at-tract
2. ad-dress   5. ob-scure
3. com-plete

Practice 4: Dividing before a Single Consonant

1. bo-nus   4. ma-jor
2. i-tem   5. u-nit
3. fi-nal

Practice 5: Dividing before a Consonant + le

1. i-dle   4. ti-tle
2. rip-ple   5. gar-gle
3. pur-ple

Practice 6: Dividing after Prefixes and before Suffixes

1. mis-sion   6. na-tion
2. ad-vice   7. mind-less
3. un-bend   8. con-sist
4. play-ful   9. re-act
5. ex-port   10. dis-ease

Practice 7: The Suffix -ed

1. separate   4. separate
2. not separate 5. separate
3. not separate

4 Phonics IV: Word Parts

Practice 1

1–2. B. include
      C. expired
      D. impersonal

3–4. A. precedes
      B. postscript
      C. postpone
      D. preface

5–6. A. subway
      B. supernatural
      C. subfloor
      D. supervisor

7–8. A. mistake
      B. monotone
      C. Monogamy
      D. misbehave

9–10. A. repeat
      B. unlikely
      C. unable
      D. return

Practice 2

11–12. A. manageable
       B. imitation
       C. comfortable
       D. reunion

13–14. A. visitor
       B. scientist
       C. waiter
       D. pianist

15–16. A. thankful
       B. grateful
       C. careless
       D. helpless

17–18. A. Catholicism
       B. imprisonment
       C. excitement
       D. vandalism

19–20. A. childish
       B. immediately
       C. boyish
       D. eagerly

Practice 3

21–22. A. portable
        B. beneficial
        C. benevolent
        D. porter

23–24. A. Biofeedback
        B. convention
        C. avenue
        D. biography

25–26. A. manipulate
        B. peddlers
        C. manicure
        D. pedestrians

27–28. A. television
        B. automobile
        C. autobiography
        D. telephone

29–30. A. audio-visual
        B. audition
        C. spectators
        D. spectacles

ANSWERS TO THE PRACTICES IN PART II

2   Dictionary Use

Practice 1

1. campus, canary, cancer
2. holdup, holiday, hog
3. letter, lettuce, level
4. railroad, raise, raincoat
5. sharp, shapely, shampoo

Practice 2

1. revise
2. kidnap
3. please
4. believe
5. really
6. schoolteacher
7. writing
8. library
9. definitely
10. across

Practice 3

1. frag•ment, 2
2. in•jec•tion, 3
3. com•pli•cate, 3
4. in•sen•si•tive, 4
5. com•mu•ni•ca•tion, 5

Practice 4

1. A
2. A
3. A
4. B
5. B
6. B
7. B
8. A
9. B
10. B

Practice 5

2. miracle, 2
3. offense, 1
4. intelligent, 2
5. reliable, 2

Practice 6

1. 2; first
2. 3; second
3. 3; first
4. 4; second
5. 4; second   ,

Practice 7

1. verb, noun
2. noun, verb
3. verb, noun
4. verb, noun
5. adjective, noun, verb

Practice 8

1. parties
2. wrote, written
3. lives
4. spoke, spoken
5. littler, littlest

Practice 9

1. Definition 1
2. Definition 1
3. Definition 2

3   Vocabulary in Context

Practice 1: Examples

1. *Examples:* the thumbs-up sign, hands on the hips, a shrug of the shoulders; A
2. *Examples:* quotations which were never said, events that never occurred; C
3. *Examples:* burping, loud talking, playing around; A
4. *Examples:* exercising daily, eating nutritious foods; C
5. *Examples:* coughing, sighing, scraping of chairs; B

Practice 2: Synonyms

1. admit
2. unwilling
3. ridiculous
4. fearful
5. false idea

Practice 3: Antonyms

1. *Antonym:* simple; C
2. *Antonym:* famous; A
3. *Antonym:* unrelated; B
4. *Antonym:* out of order; B
5. *Antonym:* criticized; C

Practice 4: General Sense of the Passage

1. B
2. A
3. C
4. B
5. B

4   Main Ideas

Practice 1

1. goldfish: S
   parakeet: S
   pet: G
   dog: S
   cat: S

2. square: S
   circle: S
   triangle: S
   shape: G
   diamond: S

3. up: S
   down: S
   direction: G
   sideways: S
   north: S

4. soda: S
   beer: S
   orange juice: S
   beverage: G
   water: S

5. high-risk job: G
   astronaut: S
   firefighter: S
   policeman: S
   miner: S

6. sleeping bag: S
   sheet: S
   pillow: S
   blanket: S
   bedding: G

7. "hello": S
   greeting: G
   a wave: S
   "hi": S
   open arms: S

8. screech: S
   noise: G
   crash: S
   off-key music: S
   sirens: S

9. jump: S
   command: G
   stop: S
   move: S
   sit down: S

10. jail: S
    hanging: S
    suspension: S
    fine: S
    punishment: G

Practice 2

Answers will vary. Here are some possibilities:

1. Jennifer Lopez, George Clooney
2. tiger, elephant
3. table, sofa
4. cake, pie
5. New York, Las Vegas
6. New Year's Day, Independence Day
7. basketball, football
8. canary, swan
9. broccoli, carrots
10. Mars, Venus

Practice 3

1. SD	3. T
SD	SD
T	MI
MI	SD

2. SD	4. MI
SD	T
MI	SD
T	SD

Practice 4

1. *Topic:* B
2. *Main idea:* Sentence 1

3. *Topic:* C
4. *Main idea:* Sentence 6

5. *Topic:* B
6. *Main idea:* Sentence 2

7. *Topic:* C
8. *Main idea:* Sentence 7

5   Supporting Details

Practice 1

1. SD	3. MI
MI	SD
SD	SD

2. SD	4. SD
SD	SD
MI	MI

Practice 2 (Wording of outlines may vary.)

Passage 1

1. Don't make a big deal of the mistake.
2. Use humor.
3. Ask for help.
   Ex.—Tell the waiter, "Sorry; I need some help cleaning up here."

Words that introduce a list: different ways

Words that introduce
   First major detail: One
   Second major detail: Another
   Last major detail: third

Passage 2

1. The delinquent group
2. The academic subculture
3. The fun subculture
   a. Interested in their social status
   b. Focus on material things like clothes and cars

Words that introduce a list: three subcultures

Words that introduce
   First major detail: first
   Second major detail: next
   Third major detail: Last of all

Practice 3 (Wording of map items may vary.)

Passage 1

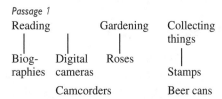

Words that introduce a list: four most popular hobbies

Words that introduce
   First major detail: one
   Second major detail: second
   Third major detail: next
   Fourth major detail: final

Passage 2

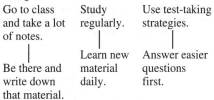

Words that introduce a list: several suggestions

Words that introduce
   First major detail: To begin with
   Second major detail: Another
   Third major detail: Finally

6 Finding Main Ideas

Practice 1

1. *Main idea:* Sentence 1
2. *Main idea:* Sentence 2
3. *Main idea:* Sentence 3
4. *Main idea:* Sentence 1

Practice 2

1. *Main idea:* Sentence 7
2. *Main idea:* Sentence 1
3. *Main idea:* Sentence 2
4. *Main idea:* Sentence 1

7 Signal Words I

Practice 1

1. C Finally
2. A also
3. B Another
4. D In addition
5. E second

Practice 2 *(Wording of outlines may vary.)*

A. Main idea: *There are several signs of stress in young people.*

1. Unusual tiredness (*Addition word:* one)
2. Temper tantrums
   (*Addition word:* Another)
3. Forgetting known facts
   (*Addition word:* third)

B. Main idea: *Pizza contains healthful ingredients.*

1. The crust is rich in B vitamins.
   (*Addition word:* First of all)
2. The tomato sauce is an excellent source of vitamin A. (*Addition word:* Also)
3. The mozzarella cheese contains protein and calcium. (*Addition word:* finally)

C. Main idea: *Walking can be a rewarding experience.*

1. Lets you chat with neighbors
   (*Addition word:* To begin with)
2. Excellent and inexpensive form of exercise (*Addition word:* In addition)
3. Natural anti-depressant
   (*Addition word:* Moreover)

Practice 3

1. A After
2. C Then
3. D until
4. B Before
5. E When

Practice 4 *(Wording of outlines may vary.)*

A.

1. Soon
2. Next
3. Finally

B. Main idea: *Use the following tips to find the right boyfriend or girlfriend.*

1. Trust your own instincts.
   (*Time word:* First)
2. Widen your social circle.
   (*Time word:* next)
3. Don't settle for just anyone who is willing to date you.
   (*Time word:* last)

C. Main idea: *A noticeable stain or burn in a carpet can be corrected.*

1. Cut out the damaged area with a sharp utility knife. (*Time word:* First)
2. Cut a patch the same size and shape from leftover carpet or from an unnoticeable spot. (*Time word:* Second)
3. Cut a piece of cardboard a little larger than the patch. (*Time word:* Next)
4. Place the cardboard where you cut out the damaged piece of carpet.
   (*Time word:* Then)
5. Glue the carpet patch to the cardboard.
   (*Time word:* Last)

8 Signal Words II

Practice 1

1. A. For example (*or* For instance)
2. E. such as
3. B. For instance (*or* For example)
4. C. including
5. D. Once

Practice 2 *(Wording of map answers may vary.)*

A. *phobia*; definition—sentence 1; example —sentence 2 (*or* 3)

B. *functional illiteracy*; definition—sentence 1; example—sentence 3 (*or* 4 *or* 5)

C. *Regeneration*: the ability to renew lost body parts

| An octopus can regrow lost tentacles. | One leg of a sea star that includes part of its center can regenerate a whole new body. |

Practice 3

1. A. Even though
2. C. in contrast
3. D. In spite of
4. E. Rather than
5. B. however

Practice 4 *(Wording of answers may vary.)*

A. Main idea: *There are two different views of the value of computers in the classroom.*

1. They will help children learn more efficiently.
2. They will get in the way of children's learning.
    (*Contrast words:* different, But)

B. Main idea: *Doctors and scientists do not agree about when a person is truly dead.*

1. Some think death occurs when blood circulation and breathing stop.
2. Others say death occurs when the entire brain stops functioning.
    (*Contrast words:* However, But)

C. Main idea: *There are two kinds of gamblers.*

1. Gamblers who have harmless fun
2. Gamblers who are addicted and who ruin their lives
    (*Contrast words:* Yet, Unlike)

Practice 5

1. C. result
2. E. Therefore
3. A. because
4. D. so
5. B. effect

Practice 6 *(Wording of answers may vary.)*

A. Main idea: *Laughing can be good for you.*

1. It relaxes the facial muscles.
2. It increases the oxygen in the brain.
3. It reduces stress.
    (*Cause and effect words:* causing, resulting, therefore)

B. Main idea: *Changes at the end of the 1800s created more work for women.*

1. A greater emphasis on being clean caused women to spend more time washing, dusting, and scrubbing.
2. The availability of a greater variety of foods resulted in women spending more time on food preparation.
    (*Cause and effect words:* As a result, consequently)

C. Main idea: Being unemployed *can have harmful health effects.*

| Increased alcohol and tranquilizer abuse | High blood pressure and rise in heart disease |

9   Inferences

Practice 1	Practice 2
A. 2, 4	1. C
B. 1, 4	2. D
C. 3, 4	3. D

10   The Basics of Argument

Practice 1

Group 1	Group 3
A. S	A. S
B. S	B. S
C. S	C. S
D. P	D. P

Group 2
A. S
B. S
C. P
D. S

Practice 2	Practice 3
1. B	1. B, C, D
2. A	2. A, B, C
3. C	3. A, B, E

Practice 4

Group 1. A
Group 2. B
Group 3. D

Acknowledgments

Angel, Juan. "The Struggle Continues." Reprinted by permission.

Cardenas, Maria. "Migrant Child to College Woman." Reprinted by permission.

Carson, Dr. Ben. "Dare to Think Big." Taken from *The Big Picture* by Dr. Benjamin Carson, with Gregg A. Lewis. Copyright © 1999 by Benjamin Carson. Used by permission of Zondervan.

Chan, Vicky. "Friendship and Living Longer." Reprinted by permission.

Coleman, Jean. "Learning Survival Skills." Reprinted by permission.

Glasbergen, Randy. Cartoons on pages 47, 143, 211, 214, 216, 218, 223, 243, 275, 405, 407, 417, 431, and 437. Copyright © by Randy Glasbergen and reprinted (at times with altered captions) with the permission of the artist.

Hawley, Casey. "A Lesson in Love." Reprinted by permission.

Herndon, Lucia. "A Parent Gets a Reading Lesson." Reprinted with the permission of the *Philadelphia Inquirer.*

Holland, Donald. "The Fist, the Clay, and the Rock." Reprinted by permission.

Johnson, Beth. "Joe Davis." Reprinted by permission of Joe Davis.

Malcolm X, with Alex Haley. "Discovering Words." From *The Autobiography of Malcolm X* by Malcolm X and Alex Haley, copyright © 1964 by Alex Haley and Malcolm X. Copyright © 1965 by Alex Haley and Betty Shabazz. Used by permission of Random House, Inc.

Patrick, Edward. "Rosa: A Success Story." Reprinted by permission.

Prentergast, Marcia. "Winning the Job Interview Game." Reprinted by permission.

Rab, Anita. "Why We Shop." Reprinted by permission.

Ryder, Phil. Cartoon on page 427. Reprinted by permission.

Sarann, Phany. "From Horror to Hope." Reprinted by permission.

Sherry, Mary. "Learning to Read: The Marvel Kretzmann Story." Reprinted by permission.

"Shoe" cartoon on page 429. Copyright © Tribune Media Services, Inc. All Rights Reserved. Reprinted with permission.

Smith, Jeanne R. "One Less Sucker Lives." Reprinted by permission.

White, Robin. "Classroom Notetaking." Reprinted by permission.

Index

Accent marks in dictionary entries, 182–183

Addition:

words that show, 281–284, 340–343

Angel, Juan, "The Struggle Continues," 29–34

Antonyms:

as context clues, 215–217

in dictionary, 175, 187

Argument, the basics of, 437–466

evaluating arguments, 438

making a logical point, 444–446

mastery tests for, 455–466

point and support, 438–440

practice in evaluating arguments, 438–442

review tests for, 448–454

Blends, consonant, 15–20

Broderick, Bill, "Life Over Death," 386–392

Cardenas, Maria, "Migrant Child to College Woman," 350–360

Carson, Dr. Ben, "Dare to Think Big," 419–424

Cause and effect, words that show, 380–383

Central point, 254

Chan, Vicky, "Friendship and Living Longer," 94–98

"Classroom Notetaking," Robin White, 258–262

Coleman, Jean, "Learning Survival Skills," 319–326

Combined–skills tests, 523–549

Consonants, 9–46

combinations:

blends, 15–20

digraphs, 20–22

silent, 23–24

listed, 10

mastery tests for, 35–46

review tests for, 27–34

with just one sound, 10–11

with more than one sound, 11–14

Consonant blends, 15–20

Consonant combinations, 15–24

Consonant digraphs, 20–22

Context, definition of, 210

Context clues, vocabulary:

antonyms, 215–217

examples, 211–213

general sense of the sentence or passage, 218–220

synonyms, 213–215

Contrast, words that show, 377–379

"Dare to Think Big," Dr. Ben Carson, 419–424

Definitions:

in dictionary, 185–186

in textbooks, 220, 375–376

Details, supporting, 275–308

definition of, 276

identifying, 276–278

major and minor, 279–288

in outlines, 279–284

in maps, 284–288

mastery tests for, 297–308

Details, supporting—*Cont.*
  review tests for, 289–296
  ways of locating:
    addition words, 281–284
    list words, 281–284
Dictionary, 173–208
  definitions (meanings), 185–186
  entry, 178–187
    sample, 173, 178
  finding words in, 176–178
    spelling hints for, 177–178
    using guidewords for, 176–178
  irregular word forms and spellings,
    184–185
  mastery tests for, 197–208
  online dictionary, 175
  parts of speech, 183–184
  pronunciation symbols and accent marks,
    179–183
  review tests for, 189–196
  spelling, 179
  syllables, 179, 182
  synonyms and antonyms, 187
Digraphs, consonant, 20–22
"Discovering Words," Malcolm X with Alex
    Haley, 191–196
Dividing words into syllables, rules for:
  before a consonant + **le**, 87
  after prefixes and before suffixes, 87–89
  before a single consonant, 86
  between three consonants, 85
  between two consonants, 84–85
  between words in a compound word, 90

Examples:
  as context clues, 211–213
  with definitions, 375–376
  words that introduce, 374

Final single vowel, rule for, 56–57
Finding words in dictionary, 176–178
"Fist, the Clay, and the Rock, The," Donald
    Holland, 483–490
"Friendship and Living Longer," Vicky
    Chan, 94–98

"From Horror to Hope," Phany Sarann,
    122–128

General sense of the sentence or passage as
    context clue, 218–220
General versus specific ideas, 246–248
Guidewords in dictionary, 176–178

Hawley, Casey, "A Lesson in Love," 64–68
Herndon, Lucia, "A Parent Gets a Reading
    Lesson," 155–158
Holland, Donald, "The Fist, the Clay, and
    the Rock," 483–490

Implied main ideas, 413–415
Inferences, 405–436
  about book cover, 408
  about cartoon, 405–407
  about photographs, 409
  about reading materials, 410–413
  about visual materials, 406–410
  inferring main ideas, 413–415
  mastery tests for, 425–436
  review tests for, 417–424
Irregular forms and spellings in dictionary
    entries, 184–185

"**J**oe Davis," Beth Johnson, 491–502
Johnson, Beth, "Joe Davis," 491–502

"**L**ady, or the Tiger? The," Frank R.
    Stockton, 513–521
"Learning Survival Skills," Jean Coleman,
    319–326
"Learning to Read: The Marvel Kretzmann
    Story," Mary Sherry, 469–481
"Lesson in Love, A" Casey Hawley, 64–68
"Life Over Death," Bill Broderick, 386–392
Limited answer key, 568–575
List words, 281–284
Locating main ideas, 243–274, 309–338
Long and short **oo**, 58–59
Long vowel sounds, 52–57
  rules for:
    final single vowel, 56–57

Long vowel sounds, rules for—*Cont.*
    silent **e**, 54–55
    two vowels together, 55–56

Main ideas, 243–274, 309–338
    definition of, 243–245
    finding, 309–338
    implied, or unstated, 413–415
    locations of, 309–338
    mastery tests for, 263–274, 327–338
    review tests for, 255–262, 317–326
    topics and, 249–254
Major and minor supporting details,
    279–288
Malcolm X with Alex Haley, "Discovering
    Words," 191–196
Maps, 284–288
"Migrant Child to College Woman," Maria
    Cardenas, 350–360

"One Less Sucker Lives," Jeanne R. Smith,
    225–230
Outlines, 279–284

"Parent Gets a Reading Lesson, A," Lucia
    Herndon, 155–158
Parts of speech in dictionary entries,
    183–184
Patrick, Edward, "Rosa: A Success Story,"
    503–511
Phonics, 7–140
    consonants, 10–46
        mastery tests for, 35–46
        review tests for, 27–34
    definition of, 9
    syllables, 81–110
        mastery tests for, 99–110
        review tests for, 92–98
    vowels, 47–80
        mastery tests for, 69–80
        review tests for, 61–68
Point and support, 438–440
Prefixes:
    as word parts, 111–114
    dividing after, 87–88

Prentergast, Marcia, "Winning the Job
    Interview Game," 291–296
Pronunciation guide, 551–552
Pronunciation symbols in dictionary entries,
    179–182

Rab, Anita, "Why We Shop," 450–454
Reading performance chart, *inside back cover*
Roots, as word parts, 116–119
"Rosa: A Success Story," Edward Patrick,
    503–511

Sarann, Phany, "From Horror to Hope,"
    122–128
Schwa, 180
Sense of the passage, as context clue,
    218–220
Sherry, Mary, "Learning to Read:
    The Marvel Kretzmann Story,"
    469–481
Short vowel sounds, 48–51
Signal words I, 339–372
    addition words, 340–343
    mastery tests for, 361–372
    review tests for, 347–360
    time words, 343–346
Signal words II, 373–404
    cause and effect words, 380–383
    contrast words, 377–379
    example words, 374–376
    mastery tests for, 393–404
    review tests for, 384–392
Silent consonants, 23–24
Silent–**e** rule, 54–55
Single consonants:
    with just one sound, 10–11
    with more than one sound, 11–14
Smith, Jeanne R., "One Less Sucker Lives,"
    225–230
Sounds of vowels followed by **r**, 58
Specific versus general ideas, 246–248
Spelling in dictionary entries, 177, 179,
    184–185
Stockton, Frank R., "The Lady, or the
    Tiger?" 513–521

"Struggle Continues, The," Juan Angel, 29–34
Suffixes:
    as word parts, 114–116
    dividing before, 87–89
Supporting details, 275–308
    definition of, 276
    identifying, 276–278
    major and minor, 279–288
    in maps, 284–288
    mastery tests for, 297–308
    in outlines, 279–284
    review tests for, 289–296
    ways of locating:
        addition words, 281–284
        list words, 281–284
Syllables, 81–110
    definition of, 81
    in dictionary entries, 179
    mastery tests for, 99–110
    pronouncing words, 81–82
        tips for, 84, 86
    review tests for, 92–98
    rules for dividing words into:
        before a consonant + **le**, 87
        with -**ed**, 89
        after prefixes and before suffixes, 87–89
        before a single consonant, 86
        between three consonants, 85
        between two consonants, 84–85
        between words in a compound word, 90
        in words with more than one vowel in a syllable, 82–83
Synonyms:
    as context clues, 213–215
    in dictionary, 187

Thesaurus, 187
Time, words that show, 343–346
Topic, 249–254
Transitions (*See also* Signal words I and II)
    addition words, 281–284, 340–343

Transitions—*Cont.*
    cause and effect words, 380–383
    contrast words, 377–379
    example words, 374–376
    time words, 343–346
Two-vowels-together rule, 55–56

Unstated main ideas, 413–415

Vocabulary in context, 209–242
    antonym clues, 215–217
    context, definition of, 210
    example clues, 211–213
    general sense of the sentence or passage clues, 218–220
    mastery tests for, 231–242
    review tests for, 222–230
    synonym clues, 213–215
Vowels, 47–80
    long and short **oo**, 58–59
    long sounds, 52–57
    mastery tests for, 69–80
    review tests for, 61–68
    rules for, 50–51, 54–59
    short sounds, 48–51
    sounds of followed by **r**, 58
    y as a vowel, 57

White, Robin, "Classroom Notetaking," 258–262
"Why We Shop," Anita Rab, 450–454
"Winning the Job Interview Game," Marcia Prentergast, 291–296
Word parts, 111–140
    mastery tests for, 129–140
    prefixes, 111–114
    review tests for, 120–128
    roots, 116–119
    suffixes, 114–116
Writing assignments, 553–567
    guidelines for, 553–554

Y as a vowel, 57